416 - 890-3304

@dmcy

SINGLE AND COMPOUND ANGLE MEMBERS

Structural Analysis and Design

SINGLE AND COMPOUND ANGLE MEMBERS

Structural Analysis and Design

MURTY K. S. MADUGULA

Ph.D., M.C.S.C.E., F.I.E. (India), P.Eng.

Professor of Civil Engineering, University of Windsor, Ontario, Canada

and

JOHN B. KENNEDY

D.Sc. (Wales), Ph.D., F.A.S.C.E., M.C.S.C.E., P.Eng.

Professor of Civil Engineering, University of Windsor, Ontario, Canada

ELSEVIER APPLIED SCIENCE PUBLISHERS

LONDON and NEW YORK

ELSEVIER APPLIED SCIENCE PUBLISHERS LTD
Crown House, Linton Road, Barking, Essex IG11 8JU, England

Sole Distributor in the USA and Canada
ELSEVIER SCIENCE PUBLISHING CO., INC.
52 Vanderbilt Avenue, New York, NY 10017, USA

British Library Cataloguing in Publication Data

Madugula, Murty K. S.
   Single and compound angle members: structural
   analysis and design.
   1. Steel, Structural   2. Steel—Analysis
   I. Title   II. Kennedy, John B.
   624.1'821   TA684

ISBN 0-85334-364-0

WITH 52 TABLES AND 127 ILLUSTRATIONS

© ELSEVIER APPLIED SCIENCE PUBLISHERS LTD 1985

The selection and presentation of material and the opinions expressed in this publication
are the sole responsibility of the authors concerned.

Filmset and printed in Northern Ireland by The Universities Press (Belfast) Ltd.

To

Indira, Suryakala and Rama

M.K.S.M.

My family

J.B.K.

PREFACE

Angles as structural members are used extensively and are designed to carry various kinds of loadings that can cause tension, compression, bending and twisting, or a combination thereof. Because of their awkward cross-sectional shape, angle members so loaded can become fairly complex to analyze and design properly.

The intention of this book is to give readers a thorough knowledge of the fundamentals of angle member behaviour, and to provide the practicing engineer with the necessary design aids in the form of graphs and tables for the proper selection of the member size. The reader, with only some knowledge of elementary mechanics and strength of materials, can follow the material in the book with relative ease. It should appeal to students, teachers and practicing members of the structural engineering profession.

Chapter 1 presents the cross-sectional properties of hot-rolled and cold-formed angles. The tables reproduced in this chapter give these properties for various sizes of angles in Imperial as well as the SI metric unit systems. Chapter 2 deals with angles as tension members subjected to concentric and eccentric loads. As a design aid, a graphical method of analysis is also given. The behaviour of angles as beams is discussed in Chapter 3, considering applied loads that cause not only bending but twisting of the angle member. Extensive tables are provided to aid in the design and to assess member deflections. Chapter 4 treats angles as compression members analyzed under elastic and inelastic conditions; a method for designing compression angle members in trusses is presented. The analysis and design of angles used in connections are given in Chapter 5; web-framing angles, stiffened and unstiffened seat angles are discussed. A critical review of the research done on angle members is presented in Chapter 6 with suggestions for further research work. Chapter 7 discusses the current design practices, recommendations and specifications adopted by various countries; the presentation deals with hot-rolled and cold-rolled steel angles as well as aluminium angles. Extensive design tables and graphs are included in this chapter. Finally, design aids in the form of tables and graphs are presented in the last chapter for angles subjected to axial and eccentric compression.

Wherever appropriate, solved examples have been provided at the end of the chapter to illustrate the analysis and design of angle members as well as the use of tables and graphs. Moreover, many references are given to the published literature so that the reader may ascertain whether his particular problem has been investigated, and if so, where to find it.

It is too much to expect that a book containing so much detail and so many illustrations will be entirely free from errors and the authors would be grateful to have their attention drawn to any that readers detect.

In writing a book of this type, the authors had to rely heavily on the published literature on the subject; and therefore, they wish to thank the many people and organizations who have contributed to the material in the book. The authors also wish to express their gratitude to their wives for their tolerance and encouragement, and to Miss Anne-Marie Bartlett for her care in typing many of the tables. Last, but certainly not least, the authors are indebted to Mrs Judy Assef for her patience and for her accurate and extraordinarily efficient typing of the manuscript.

M.K.S.M.
J.B.K.

ACKNOWLEDGEMENTS

The authors would like to acknowledge with thanks the following organizations and individuals for permission to use their copyright material:

1. American Institute of Steel Construction, Chicago, IL, USA:
   (a) Figure EE 7.2 (page 90) in *Stability of Metal Structures: A World View*.
   (b) The table 'Usual Gages for Angles, inches', page 4-135, and figures and equations on pages 4-88 and 4-89 in the *Manual of Steel Construction*, 8th Edition (1980).
   (c) Figures 3-2, 3-11, 4-12 and 4-14 in *Engineering for Steel Construction* (1984).
   (d) Equations (F1-18), (F1-19), (B5-1), (B5-2) and (Appendix B5.3) in *Load and Resistance Factor Design Specifications for Structural Steel Buildings* (1983).
2. American Iron and Steel Institute, Washington, DC, USA:
   (a) The equations in Clause 3.6.1.2 in *Specification for the Design of Cold-formed Steel Structural Members* (1980).
   (b) Figure 1.1 and equation in Sections 2.1.1.2.2 and 2.1.2.2.2.1, figure and formulas in Section 2.2.1.1, Part III (1971); Charts V.3.6.1.2 (A)i to (E)i and V.3.7.2 (A)i and (B)i, Part V (1977), of the AISI *Cold-formed Steel Design Manual*.
3. American Society of Civil Engineers, New York, NY, USA: Formulas (5) to (14) in the ASCE Manual No. 52 (1971).
4. Architectural Institute of Japan, Tokyo, Japan:
   (a) Tables 17, 18 and 19, Figures 17 and 18, and Equations 17 and 19 in AIJ *Standard for Structural Calculation of Steel Tower Structures* (1960).
   (b) Equation (8-1) and Clauses 8.1(1)(a), 11.4(2) and 12.3 in *Design Standard for Steel Structures* (1979).

5. Australian Institute of Steel Construction, Milsons Point, NSW, Australia: Figures 7 and 12 in 'The design of single angle struts', by S. T. Woolcock and S. Kitipornchai, *Journal of the Australian Institute of Steel Construction*, **14** (4) (1980).
6. Dr. R. Bez, Ecole Polytechnique Fédérale de Lausanne, Switzerland: Figures 2, 3, 4, 5, 6 and 7 in 'Dimensionnement plastique et phénomènes d'instabilité de cornières métalliques', by R. Bez and M. A. Hirt, *Construction Métallique*, No. 1 (1982).
7. British Standards Institution, London, UK:
   (a) Clauses 4.2.2, 4.3.2, F2, G2 and G3, Tables 5, 6 and 7, and Figures 1, 26 and 29 in BS CP 118 (1969).
   (b) Tables 17a, 17b and 17c and Subclauses 30c, 37, 45 and 49 in BS 449: Part 2 (1969).
   (c) Tables 5, 6, 9 and 10 in Addendum No. 1 (1975) to BS 449: Part 2 (1969).
   Complete copies can be obtained from the BSI at Linford Wood, Milton Keynes MK14 6LE, UK.
8. Broken Hill Proprietary Company Ltd, Melbourne, Australia: The figures and equations in Report No. MRL 22/2, *Laterally Unsupported Angles with Equal and Unequal Legs*, by J. M. Leigh and M. G. Lay (July 1970).
9. Canadian Institute of Steel Construction, Willowdale, Ontario, Canada: The table 'Usual Gauges for Angles, millimetres', page 6–125 of the *Handbook of Steel Construction* (1980).
10. Canadian Society for Civil Engineering, Montreal, Quebec, Canada: Equations 44 to 46 and Figures 6, 8, 9 and 11 of 'Interaction curves for steel sections under axial load and biaxial bending, by W. F. Chen and T. Atsuta, *Transactions of the CSCE* (73-CSCE-16, EIC-74-BR and STR3, EIC, Vol. 17, No. A-3) published in the *Engineering Journal* (March–April 1974).
11. Canadian Standards Association, Rexdale, Ontario, Canada:
   (a) Table 4 and Figures 4, 5 and 6, Clause 6.2.3 in CSA S37-1981, *Antenna Towers and Antenna Supporting Structures*.
   (b) Table 1.2 in CAN3-S157-M83, *Strength Design in Aluminum*.
   (c) Clauses 1.5.2, 1.5.3, 1.7.6, 1.7.10, 1.7.11, 6.3.3, 6.6.1, 6.6.3, 6.6.4, 6.6.7 and 6.7.4 in CAN3-S136-M84, *Cold-formed Steel Structural Members* (1984).
12. Collins Professional and Technical Books, London, UK: Table 'Spacing of Holes in Angles' (page 710) in *Steel Designers' Manual*

(May 1972), prepared for Constructional Steel Research and Development Organization.

13. Corona Publishing Company Ltd, Tokyo, Japan: Figures and formulae for (i) Condition 34 (pages 1–16 and 1–17), (ii) Figure 1 (page 1–147), (iii) Profiles 5 and 6 (page 1–151), (iv) Condition 9 (page 1–200), (v) Condition 8 (page 1–202) in *Handbook of Structural Stability*, Column Research Committee of Japan, Editor (1971).

14. DIN Deutsches Institut für Normung eV, Berlin, West Germany: Tables 1 and 2, Figures 5(d), 6, 7, 8, 12 and 13, and Clauses 8.211 to 8.214, 8.22, 8.224, 8.231 to 8.234, 10.02, 10.04 and 10.05 in DIN 4114: Vol. 1 (1952).

   The edition of this Standard with the latest date of issue, to be obtained from Beuth Verlag GmbH, Burggrafenstrasse 4–10, D-1000 Berlin 30, is the authoritative version for implementation of the Standard.

15. European Convention for Constructional Steelwork, Brussels, Belgium:
    (a) Equations 1 to 14, Figure 2 (page 264), Figure 6b (page 267), Figure 7 (page 270), Figure 8 (page 271), Figure 11 (page 272) and the tables on pages 269 and 272 of the *Stability Manual*.
    (b) Clause R.4.1.5.3, σ_K/σ_r values for column curves 'a_0' and 'b', and Tables B3-36, B3-43, B3-51, B4-36, B4-43 and B4-51 in *European Recommendations for Steel Construction* (1978).

16. Harper & Row, Publishers, Inc., New York, NY, USA: Figures 13.3.1, 13.3.2, 13.3.3, 13.4.1a and 13.4.4 in *Steel Structures: Design and Behavior*, 2nd Edition by Charles G. Salmon and John E. Johnson (Intext Publishers), Copyright © 1980 by Charles G. Salmon and John E. Johnson.

17. The James F. Lincoln Arc Welding Foundation, Cleveland, OH, USA: Table 3 and figure and formulas for thin-lipped angle (pages 2.2–10) in *Design of Welded Structures* by O. W. Blodgett (1966).

18. John Wiley & Sons, Inc., New York, NY, USA: Figure 5.36 in *Design of Steel Structures* by B. Bresler and T. Y. Lin (1960).

19. Prentice-Hall, Inc., Englewood Cliffs, NJ, USA:
    (a) William McGuire, *Steel Structures*, © 1968, pp. 343, 931.
    (b) Bogdan O. Kuzmanovic and Nicholas Willems, *Steel Design for Structural Engineers*, 2nd Edition, © 1983, pp. 355, 356, 370, 374.

20. Standards Association of Australia, North Sydney, NSW, Australia:
   (a) Table 4.8, 'Gauge Lines for Angles', and Figure 4.26A in *Steel Structures: Part 4—Connections* (1979) prepared by the Australian Institute of Steel Construction.
   (b) Table 6.1.1 in *SAA Steel Structures Code* (AS 1250-1981).
21. Mr Gene M. Wilhoite, Chattanooga, TN, USA: The equations and figures in the paper 'Design recommendations for cold-formed angles', presented at the 1984 ASCE Spring Convention, Atlanta, GA.

CONTENTS

Chapter 1

CROSS-SECTIONAL PROPERTIES OF ANGLES

1.1. INTRODUCTION

Angles are very common structural shapes found in almost any structure; they are quite often seen in latticed electrical transmission towers and antenna-supporting towers. They are used as chord and web members of trusses, web members of long-span open-web joists, and bracing members to provide lateral support to the primary load-carrying members of a structure. Angles are easy to fabricate and erect because of the basic simplicity of their cross-section. They are classified as equal or unequal angles, single or compound (i.e. built-up) angles, hot-rolled or cold-formed angles. They can be plain angles, lipped angles or bulb angles, of steel or aluminium. Angles are loaded concentrically or eccentrically, axially or transversely, inducing stresses either below or beyond the proportional limit of the material.

While an angle is a very simple section to fabricate and erect, its analysis is relatively difficult for the following reasons: (i) the principal axes of the cross-section do not coincide with the direction of the imposed external loading; this causes biaxial bending, and the resulting deflection of the angle will not be in the same plane as that of the applied loads; (ii) due to lack of symmetry in the cross-section, the shear centre† does not coincide with the centroid of the cross-section. This induces twisting moment on the cross-section, in addition to bending moments, since the lines of action of the most commonly applied loads do not pass through the shear centre.

---

† Shear centre, also called the centre of twist, is a point in the plane of the cross-section. The locus of the shear centres of the cross-sections along the member is called the 'axis of twist'. Bending without twisting occurs only when the plane of the applied load passes through the locus of the shear centres.

1

1.2. CROSS-SECTIONAL PROPERTIES

Whether angles are used in tension, compression, bending, combined tension and bending, or combined compression and bending, their structural analysis requires the calculation of their cross-sectional properties. Some of these geometric properties are available in standard specifications and handbooks (e.g. American Institute of Steel Construction, 1980; Canadian Institute of Steel Construction, 1980; Standards Association of Australia, 1979; British Standards Institution, 1972, etc.); while other properties are not so readily available. For completeness, formulae are now given for the calculation of the geometric properties of angles.

1.2.1. Hot-rolled Angles

The computations are based on the idealized rectangular section shown in Fig. 1.1 in which the toe and the fillet radii have been omitted as is customary; the shear centre (SC) is located at the intersection of the centrelines of the legs of the angle. Thus

$$\text{Area} = (b + a - t)t \qquad (1.1)$$

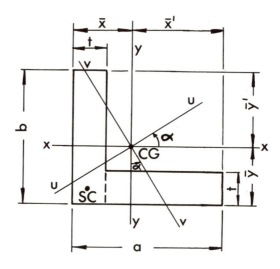

Fig. 1.1. Angle idealized by two rectangles $(b > a)$.

Location of Centroid

$$\bar{x} = \frac{bt\frac{t}{2} + (a-t)t\left(t + \frac{a-t}{2}\right)}{(b+a-t)t} = \frac{bt + a^2 - t^2}{2(b+a-t)} \tag{1.2}$$

$$\bar{y} = \frac{bt\frac{b}{2} + (a-t)t\frac{t}{2}}{(b+a-t)t} = \frac{b^2 + at - t^2}{2(b+a-t)} \tag{1.3}$$

Or, in terms of $\bar{x}'$ and $\bar{y}'$ (Fig. 1.1)

$$\bar{x}' = a - \bar{x} \tag{1.2a}$$

$$\bar{y}' = b - \bar{y} \tag{1.3a}$$

Moments of Inertia

Final expressions for the moments of inertia, I_x and I_y, and product of inertia I_{xy} are as follows:

$$I_x = \tfrac{1}{12}tb^3 + bt\left(\frac{b}{2} - \bar{y}\right)^2 + \tfrac{1}{12}(a-t)t^3 + (a-t)t\left(\bar{y} - \frac{t}{2}\right)^2 \tag{1.4}$$

$$I_y = \tfrac{1}{12}bt^3 + bt\left(\bar{x} - \frac{t}{2}\right)^2 + \tfrac{1}{12}t(a-t)^3 + (a-t)t\left(\frac{a+t}{2} - \bar{x}\right)^2 \tag{1.5}$$

$$I_{xy} = -bt\left(\frac{b}{2} - \bar{y}\right)\left(\bar{x} - \frac{t}{2}\right) - t(a-t)\left(\bar{y} - \frac{t}{2}\right)\left(\frac{a+t}{2} - \bar{x}\right) \tag{1.6}$$

I_x, I_y and I_{xy} for compound (i.e. built-up) angles can be readily computed using the parallel-axis theorem. Minimum and maximum moments of inertia, I_{min} and I_{max}, are computed from

$$I_{min} = \frac{I_x + I_y}{2} - \sqrt{\left(\frac{I_x - I_y}{2}\right)^2 + I_{xy}^2} \tag{1.7}$$

$$I_{max} = \frac{I_x + I_y}{2} + \sqrt{\left(\frac{I_x - I_y}{2}\right)^2 + I_{xy}^2} \tag{1.8}$$

It is to be noted that the sum of the moments of inertia about any pair of mutually perpendicular axes is constant; thus from eqns (1.7) and (1.8)

$$I_x + I_y = I_{max} + I_{min} \tag{1.9}$$

The inclination α between the horizontal axis (x–x axis) and the major principal axis (u–u axis) is calculated as follows

$$\tan 2\alpha = -\frac{2I_{xy}}{I_x - I_y} \qquad (1.10)$$

Positive inclinations are measured counterclockwise from the x–x axis.

The minimum radius of gyration of an angle cross-section is defined as

$$r_{min} = \sqrt{\frac{I_{min}}{\text{Area}}} \qquad (1.11)$$

St Venant's torsion constant, J, can be computed from

$$J = \tfrac{1}{3}t^3(b + a - t) \qquad (1.12)$$

A more accurate value for J can be obtained from the following expressions developed by El-Darwish and Johnston (1965). Referring to Fig. 1.2, for a single angle

$$J = \tfrac{1}{3}b_1 t^3 + \tfrac{1}{3}b_2 t^3 + \gamma D^4 - 0\cdot315 t^4 \qquad (1.13)$$

in which the juncture diameter parameter

$$D = 0\cdot343\rho + 1\cdot172t \qquad (1.14)$$

and the juncture coefficient

$$\gamma = 0\cdot0728 + 0\cdot0571\left(\frac{\rho}{t}\right) - 0\cdot0049\left(\frac{\rho}{t}\right)^2 \qquad (1.15)$$

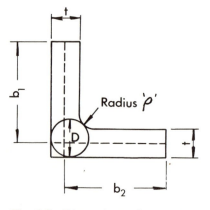

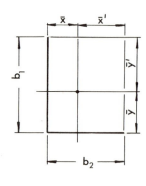

Fig. 1.2. Dimensions of an angle for calculating the torsion constant, J.

Fig. 1.3. Dimensions of an angle whose thickness, t, is small.

The torsion constant, J, of a compound angle is obtained by summing up the J values for the component angles.

The warping constant, C_w, of a single angle is given by

$$C_w = \frac{\left(b - \frac{t}{2}\right)^3 t^3}{36} + \frac{\left(a - \frac{t}{2}\right)^3 t^3}{36} \tag{1.16}$$

whereas the warping constant C_w of a compound angle is the numerical summation of the warping constants of component angles.

When the thickness, t, of an angle is small, Fig. 1.3, computations can be simplified by using the following approximate equations. With b_1 and b_2 being the centreline dimensions

$$\text{Area} = (b_1 + b_2)t \tag{1.17}$$

$$\bar{x} = \frac{b_2^2}{2(b_1 + b_2)} \tag{1.18}$$

$$\bar{y} = \frac{b_1^2}{2(b_1 + b_2)} \tag{1.19}$$

$$\bar{x}' = b_2 - \bar{x} \tag{1.20}$$

$$\bar{y}' = b_1 - \bar{y} \tag{1.21}$$

$$I_x = \frac{tb_1^3(4b_2 + b_1)}{12(b_1 + b_2)} \tag{1.22}$$

$$I_y = \frac{tb_2^3(b_2 + 4b_1)}{12(b_1 + b_2)} \tag{1.23}$$

$$I_{xy} = -\frac{tb_1^2 b_2^2}{4(b_1 + b_2)} \tag{1.24}$$

$$J = \frac{t^3}{3}(b_1 + b_2) \tag{1.25}$$

$$C_w = \frac{t^3(b_1^3 + b_2^3)}{36} \tag{1.26}$$

Tables 1.1(a) and (b) list all the cross-sectional properties required by the stress analyst for the analysis of hot-rolled angles listed in the *Handbook of steel construction* published by the Canadian Institute of Steel Construction (1980), while Tables 1.2(a) and (b) list the properties of angles in Imperial units given in the *Manual of steel construction*

Single and Compound Angle Members

Table 1.1(a)
Cross-sectional Properties of Hot-rolled Angles—Equal Angles

Size (long leg × short leg)	Thickness	Mass	Dead load	Area A	Axis x–x I_x	Axis x–x $\bar{y}$	Axis y–y I_y	Axis y–y $\bar{x}$	I_{xy}
(mm × mm)	(mm)	(kg/m)	(kN/m)	(mm²)	(10^6 mm⁴)	(mm)	(10^6 mm⁴)	(mm)	(10^6 mm⁴)
200 × 200	30	87·1	0·855	11 100	40·3	60·9	40·3	60·9	−23·7
	25	73·6	0·722	9 380	34·8	59·2	34·8	59·2	−20·6
	20	59·7	0·585	7 600	28·8	57·4	28·8	57·4	−17·1
	16	48·2	0·473	6 140	23·7	55·9	23·7	55.9	−14·2
	13	39·5	0·387	5 030	19·7	54·8	19·7	54·8	−11·8
	10	30·6	0·300	3 900	15·5	53·7	15.5	53·7	−9·27
150 × 150	20	44·0	0·431	5 600	11·6	44·8	11·6	44·8	−6·86
	16	35·7	0·350	4 540	9·63	43·4	9·63	43·4	−5·73
	13	29·3	0·287	3 730	8·05	42·3	8·05	42·3	−4·80
	10	22·8	0·223	2 900	6·37	41·2	6·37	41·2	−3·81
125 × 125	16	29·4	0·288	3 740	5·41	37·1	5·41	37·1	−3·20
	13	24·2	0·237	3 080	4·54	36·0	4·54	36·0	−2·70
	10	18·8	0·185	2 400	3·62	34·9	3·62	34·9	−2·16
	8	15·2	0·149	1 940	2·96	34·2	2·96	34·2	−1·77
100 × 100	16	23·1	0·227	2 940	2·65	30·8	2·65	30·8	−1·56
	13	19·1	0·187	2 430	2·24	29·8	2·24	29·8	−1·33
	10	14·9	0·146	1 900	1·80	28·7	1·80	28·7	−1·07
	8	12·1	0·118	1 540	1·48	28·0	1·48	28·0	−0·885
	6	9·14	0·090	1 160	1·14	27·2	1·14	27·2	−0·685
90 × 90	13	17·0	0·167	2 170	1·60	27·2	1·60	27·2	−0·946
	10	13·3	0·131	1 700	1·29	26·2	1·29	26·2	−0·768
	8	10·8	0·106	1 380	1·07	25·5	1·07	25·5	−0·636
	6	8·20	0·080	1 040	0·826	24·7	0·826	24·7	−0·494
75 × 75	13	14·0	0·137	1 780	0·892	23·5	0·892	23·5	−0·522
	10	11·0	0·108	1 400	0·725	22·4	0·725	22·4	−0·429
	8	8·92	0·087	1 140	0·602	21·7	0·602	21·7	−0·358
	6	6·78	0·066	864	0·469	21·0	0·469	21·0	−0·280
	5	5·69	0·056	725	0·398	20·6	0·398	20·6	−0·238
65 × 65	10	9·42	0·092	1 200	0·459	19·9	0·459	19·9	−0·270
	8	7·66	0·075	976	0·383	19·2	0·383	19·2	−0·227
	6	5·84	0·057	744	0·300	18·5	0·300	18·5	−0·179
	5	4·91	0·048	625	0·255	18·1	0·255	18·1	−0·153
55 × 55	10	7·85	0·077	1 000	0·268	17·4	0·268	17·4	−0·156
	8	6·41	0·063	816	0·225	16·7	0·225	16·7	−0·133
	6	4·90	0·048	624	0·177	16·0	0·177	16·0	−0·105
	5	4·12	0·040	525	0·152	15·6	0·152	15·6	−0·090
	4	3·33	0·033	424	0·125	15·2	0·125	15·2	−0·074
	3	2·52	0·025	321	0·096	14·9	0·096	14·9	−0·057

Table 1.1(a)—*contd.*

| Axis u–u | | Axis v–v | | | Location of shear centre | | | | | |
| I_u | α (degrees) | I_v | r_v | J | $x_s{}^a$ | $y_s{}^a$ | I_{ps} | C_w | β_1 | β_2 |
$(10^6\,mm^4)$		$(10^6\,mm^4)$	(mm)	$(10^3\,mm^4)$	(mm)	(mm)	$(10^6\,mm^4)$	$(10^6\,mm^6)$	(mm)	(mm)
63·7	45·0	16·9	39·0	3330	45·9	45·9	127	9500	0	256
55·3	45·0	14·3	39·1	1950	46·7	46·7	111	5720	0	261
45·9	45·0	11·7	39·3	1010	47·4	47·4	91·8	3050	0	266
37·8	45·0	9·58	39·5	524	47·9	47·9	75·6	1610	0	270
31·5	45·0	7·93	39·7	283	48·3	48·3	62·9	884	0	273
24·8	45·0	6·21	39·9	130	48·7	48·7	49·5	412	0	275
18·4	45·0	4·81	29·3	747	34·8	34·8	36·8	1220	0	194
15·3	45·0	3·92	29·4	388	35·4	35·4	30·6	652	0	199
12·8	45·0	3·27	29·6	210	35·8	35·8	25·7	361	0	201
10·2	45·0	2·58	29·8	96·7	36·2	36·2	20·3	169	0	204
8·59	45·0	2·23	24·4	319	29·1	29·1	17·2	365	0	163
7·23	45·0	1·85	24·5	174	29·5	29·5	14·4	203	0	166
5·78	45·0	1·46	24·7	80·0	29·9	29·9	11·5	96·0	0	169
4·73	45·0	1·19	24·8	41·3	30·2	30·2	9·46	50·4	0	171
4·18	45·0	1·12	19·5	251	22·8	22·8	8·36	177	0	127
3·56	45·0	0·924	19·5	137	23·3	23·3	7·12	99·8	0	130
2·86	45·0	0·737	19·7	63·3	23·7	23·7	5·73	47·6	0	133
2·36	45·0	0·604	19·8	32·8	24·0	24·0	4·73	25·2	0	134
1·82	45·0	0·459	19·9	14·0	24·2	24·2	3·64	11·0	0	137
2·53	45·0	0·672	17·6	122	20·7	20·7	5·06	71·1	0	116
2·05	45·0	0·527	17·6	56·7	21·2	21·2	4·11	34·1	0	119
1·71	45·0	0·432	17·7	29·4	21·5	21·5	3·42	18·1	0	120
1·32	45·0	0·333	17·9	12·5	21·7	21·7	2·63	7·90	0	123
1·41	45·0	0·379	14·6	100	17·0	17·0	2·81	39·2	0	93·7
1·15	45·0	0·298	14·6	46·7	17·4	17·4	2·30	19·1	0	97·6
0·958	45·0	0·246	14·7	24·2	17·7	17·7	1·92	10·2	0	99·2
0·749	45·0	0·189	14·8	10·4	18·0	18·0	1·50	4·48	0	101
0·635	45·0	0·161	14·9	6·04	18·1	18·1	1·27	2·65	0	102
0·725	45·0	0·194	12·7	40·0	14·9	14·9	1·45	12·0	0	82·5
0·609	45·0	0·157	12·7	20·8	15·2	15·2	1·22	6·46	0	84·9
0·478	45·0	0·122	12·8	8·93	15·5	15·5	0·958	2·86	0	86·7
0·406	45·0	0·104	12·9	5·21	15·6	15·6	0·814	1·70	0	87·6
0·422	45·0	0·115	10·7	33·3	12·4	12·4	0·844	6·94	0	68·1
0·357	45·0	0·093	10·7	17·4	12·7	12·7	0·713	3·77	0	70·5
0·281	45·0	0·073	10·8	7·49	13·0	13·0	0·565	1·69	0	72·3
0·243	45·0	0·061	10·8	4·38	13·1	13·1	0·484	1·01	0	73·9
0·200	45·0	0·050	10·9	2·26	13·2	13·2	0·398	0·529	0	74·7
0·153	45·0	0·039	11·0	0·963	13·4	13·4	0·307	0·230	0	74·9

Table 1.1(a)—contd.

Size (long leg × short leg)	Thickness	Mass	Dead load	Area A	Axis x–x		Axis y–y		
					I_x	$\bar{y}$	I_y	$\bar{x}$	I_{xy}
$(mm \times mm)$	(mm)	(kg/m)	(kN/m)	(mm^2)	$(10^6\ mm^4)$	(mm)	$(10^6\ mm^4)$	(mm)	$(10^6\ mm^4)$
45×45	8	5·15	0·050	656	0·118	14·2	0·118	14·2	−0·069
	6	3·96	0·039	504	0·094	13·4	0·094	13·4	−0·056
	5	3·34	0·033	425	0·081	13·1	0·081	13·1	−0·048
	4	2·70	0·026	344	0·067	12·7	0·067	12·7	−0·040
	3	2·05	0·020	261	0·052	12·4	0·052	12·4	−0·031
35×35	6	3·01	0·030	384	0·042	10·9	0·042	10·9	−0·025
	5	2·55	0·025	325	0·036	10·6	0·036	10·6	−0·021
	4	2·07	0·020	264	0·030	10·2	0·030	10·2	−0·018
	3	1·58	0·015	201	0·024	9·86	0·024	9·86	−0·014
25×25	5	1·77	0·017	225	0·012	8·06	0·012	8·06	−0·007
	4	1·44	0·014	184	0·010	7·71	0·010	7·71	−0·006
	3	1·11	0·011	141	0·008	7·35	0·008	7·35	−0·005

[a] All the values of x_s and y_s in Table 1.1(a) should be taken as negative in computing the parameters β_1 and β_2.

Table 1.1(b)
Cross-sectional Properties of Hot-rolled Angles—Unequal Angles

Size (long leg × short leg)	Thickness	Mass	Dead load	Area A	Axis x–x		Axis y–y		
					I_x	$\bar{y}$	I_y	$\bar{x}$	I_{xy}
$(mm \times mm)$	(mm)	(kg/m)	(kN/m)	(mm^2)	$(10^6\ mm^4)$	(mm)	$(10^6\ mm^4)$	(mm)	$(10^6\ mm^4)$
200×150	25	63·8	0·625	8120	31·6	66·3	15·1	41·3	−12·8
	20	51·8	0·508	6600	26·2	64·5	12·7	39·5	−10·7
	16	42·0	0·411	5340	21·6	63·1	10·5	38·1	−8·90
	13	34·4	0·337	4380	17·9	62·0	8·77	37·0	−7·44
200×100	20	44·0	0·431	5600	22·6	74·3	3·84	24·3	−5·22
	16	35·7	0·350	4540	18·7	72·8	3·22	22·8	−4·39
	13	29·3	0·287	3730	15·6	71·7	2·72	21·7	−3·71
	10	22·8	0·223	2900	12·3	70·5	2·18	20·5	−2·96
150×100	16	29·4	0·288	3740	8·40	50·9	3·00	25·9	−2·92
	13	24·2	0·237	3080	7·03	49·9	2·53	24·9	−2·47
	10	18·8	0·185	2400	5·58	48·8	2·03	23·8	−1·98
	8	15·2	0·149	1940	4·55	48·0	1·67	23·0	−1·62

Table 1.1(a)—contd.

Axis u–u		Axis v–v			Location of shear centre					
I_u	α (de-grees)	I_v	r_v	J	$x_s{}^a$	$y_s{}^a$	I_{ps}	C_w	β_1	β_2
$(10^6\,mm^4)$		$(10^6\,mm^4)$	(mm)	$(10^3\,mm^4)$	(mm)	(mm)	$(10^6\,mm^4)$	$(10^6\,mm^6)$	(mm)	(mm)
0·186	45·0	0·050	8·76	14·0	10·2	10·2	0·373	1·96	0	55·8
0·149	45·0	0·039	8·79	6·05	10·4	10·4	0·297	0·889	0	58·6
0·129	45·0	0·033	8·82	3·54	10·6	10·6	0·258	0·533	0	59·3
0·107	45·0	0·027	8·87	1·83	10·7	10·7	0·213	0·283	0	60·5
0·083	45·0	0·021	8·93	0·783	10·9	10·9	0·166	0·124	0	61·0
0·066	45·0	0·018	6·81	4·61	7·90	7·90	0·132	0·393	0	44·1
0·057	45·0	0·015	6·83	2·71	8·10	8·10	0·115	0·238	0	44·8
0·048	45·0	0·012	6·86	1·41	8·20	8·20	0·096	0·128	0	46·2
0·038	45·0	0·010	6·91	0·603	8·36	8·36	0·076	0·056	0	47·0
0·019	45·0	0·005	4·87	1·88	5·56	5·56	0·038	0·079	0	30·5
0·016	45·0	0·004	4·87	0·981	5·71	5·71	0·032	0·043	0	31·6
0·013	45·0	0·003	4·89	0·423	5·85	5·85	0·026	0·019	0	32·8

Table 1.1(b)—contd.

Axis u–u		Axis v–v			Location of shear centre					
I_u	α (de-grees)	I_v	r_v	J	$x_s{}^a$	$y_s{}^a$	I_{ps}	C_w	β_1	β_2
$(10^6\,mm^4)$		$(10^6\,mm^4)$	(mm)	$(10^3\,mm^4)$	(mm)	(mm)	$(10^6\,mm^4)$	$(10^6\,mm^6)$	(mm)	(mm)
38·4	28·5	8·32	32·0	1690	28·8	53·8	76·9	3990	82·7	215
32·1	28·8	6·80	32·1	880	29·5	54·5	64·3	2130	82·7	222
26·5	29·0	5·57	32·3	456	30·1	55·1	53·2	1130	82·7	226
22·0	29·1	4·63	32·5	247	30·5	55·5	44·2	623	82·8	228
23·9	14·4	2·54	21·3	747	14·3	64·3	50·7	1690	137	174
19·8	14·7	2·08	21·4	388	14·8	64·8	42·0	894	137	180
16·6	14·9	1·74	21·6	210	15·2	65·2	35·0	492	138	183
13·1	15·2	1·38	21·8	96·7	15·5	65·5	27·6	230	138	187
9·66	23·5	1·75	21·6	319	17·9	42·9	19·5	414	78·3	152
8·11	23·7	1·45	21·7	174	18·4	43·4	16·4	230	78·4	155
6·46	24·0	1·15	21·9	80·0	18·8	43·8	13·1	109	78·5	158
5·28	24·1	0·939	22·0	41·3	19·0	44·0	10·7	56·8	78·7	161

Single and Compound Angle Members

Table 1.1(b)—contd.

Size (long leg × short leg)	Thickness	Mass	Dead load	Area A	Axis x–x		Axis y–y		I_{xy}
					I_x	$\bar{y}$	I_y	$\bar{x}$	
(mm × mm)	(mm)	(kg/m)	(kN/m)	(mm²)	(10⁶ mm⁴)	(mm)	(10⁶ mm⁴)	(mm)	(10⁶mm⁴)
125×90	16	25·0	0·245	3180	4·84	42·2	2·09	24·7	−1·85
	13	20·6	0·202	2630	4·07	41·2	1·77	23·7	−1·58
	10	16·1	0·158	2050	3·25	40·1	1·42	22·6	−1·27
	8	13·0	0·127	1660	2·66	39·3	1·18	21·8	−1·05
125×75	13	19·1	0·187	2430	3·82	43·9	1·04	18·9	−1·15
	10	14·9	0·146	1900	3·05	42·8	0·841	17·8	−0·928
	8	12·1	0·118	1540	2·50	42·1	0·697	17·1	−0·769
	6	9·14	0·090	1160	1·92	41·3	0·542	16·3	−0·597
100×90	13	18·1	0·177	2300	2·17	31·1	0·166	26·1	−1·12
	10	14·1	0·139	1800	1·74	30·0	1·33	25·0	−0·906
	8	11·4	0·112	1460	1·43	29·3	1·10	24·3	−0·749
	6	8·67	0·085	1100	1·11	28·5	0·853	23·5	−0·581
100×75	13	16·5	0·162	2110	2·04	33·4	0·976	20·9	−0·823
	10	13·0	0·127	1650	1·64	32·3	0·791	19·8	−0·670
	8	10·5	0·103	1340	1·35	31·5	0·656	19·0	−0·556
	6	7·96	0·078	1010	1·04	30·8	0·511	18·3	−0·433
90×75	13	15·5	0·152	1980	1·51	29·3	0·946	21·8	−0·700
	10	12·2	0·119	1550	1·22	28·2	0·767	20·7	−0·571
	8	9·86	0·097	1260	1·01	27·5	0·636	20·0	−0·475
	6	7·49	0·073	954	0·779	26·8	0·495	19·3	−0·370
	5	6·28	0·062	800	0·660	26·4	0·421	18·9	−0·314
90×65	10	11·4	0·112	1450	1·16	29·8	0·507	17·3	−0·448
	8	9·23	0·090	1180	0·958	29·1	0·422	16·6	−0·374
	6	7·02	0·069	894	0·743	28·4	0·330	15·9	−0·293
	5	5·89	0·058	750	0·629	28·0	0·281	15·5	−0·249
80×60	10	10·2	0·100	1300	0·808	26·5	0·388	16·5	−0·327
	8	8·29	0·081	1060	0·670	25·8	0·324	15·8	−0·274
	6	6·31	0·062	804	0·522	25·1	0·254	15·1	−0·216
	5	5·30	0·052	675	0·443	24·7	0·217	14·7	−0·184
75×50	8	7·35	0·072	936	0·525	25·5	0·187	13·0	−0·182
	6	5·60	0·055	714	0·410	24·7	0·148	12·2	−0·144
	5	4·71	0·046	600	0·349	24·4	0·127	11·9	−0·124
65×50	8	6·72	0·066	856	0·351	21·3	0·180	13·8	−0·147
	6	5·13	0·050	654	0·275	20·6	0·142	13·1	−0·117
	5	4·32	0·042	550	0·235	20·2	0·122	12·7	−0·100
	4	3·49	0·034	444	0·192	19·9	0·100	12·4	−0·082
55×35	6	3·96	0·039	504	0·152	19·0	0·048	9·04	−0·049
	5	3·34	0·033	425	0·130	18·7	0·041	8·68	−0·043

Table 1.1(b)—*contd.*

Axis u–u		Axis v–v			Location of shear centre					
I_u	α	I_v	r_v	J	x_s^a	y_s^a	I_{ps}	C_w	β_1	β_2
	(de-grees)									
$(10^6\ mm^4)$	*grees)*	$(10^6\ mm^4)$	*(mm)*	$(10^3\ mm^4)$	*(mm)*	*(mm)*	$(10^6 mm^4)$	$(10^6\ mm^6)$	*(mm)*	*(mm)*
5·76	26·5	1·17	19·2	272	16·7	34·2	11·5	245	56·8	131
4·86	26·8	0·980	19·3	148	17·2	34·7	9·79	137	56·9	134
3·89	27·1	0·780	19·5	68·3	17·6	35·1	7·83	65·1	56·9	137
3·20	27·2	0·638	19·6	35·3	17·8	35·3	6·43	34·2	57·0	139
4·22	19·6	0·638	16·2	137	12·4	37·4	8·63	121	74·4	119
3·39	20·0	0·505	16·3	63·3	12·8	37·8	6·92	57·5	74·6	123
2·78	20·2	0·414	16·4	32·8	13·1	38·1	5·70	30·3	74·8	125
2·14	20·4	0·320	16·6	14·0	13·3	38·3	4·37	13·1	75·0	127
3·05	38·5	0·779	18·4	130	19·6	24·6	6·11	85·4	17·6	122
2·45	38·7	0·616	18·5	60·0	20·0	25·0	4·92	40·9	17·6	125
2·03	38·7	0·505	18·6	31·1	20·3	25·3	4·07	21·6	17·6	127
1·58	38·8	0·385	18·7	13·2	20·5	25·5	3·14	9·43	17·5	129
2·48	28·4	0·540	16·0	119	14·4	26·9	4·98	69·5	41·4	106
2·00	28·8	0·428	16·1	55·0	14·8	27·3	4·02	33·3	41·4	110
1·65	29·0	0·352	16·2	28·5	15·0	27·5	3·32	17·7	41·4	113
1·28	29·2	0·268	16·3	12·2	15·3	27·8	2·57	7·72	41·4	115
1·97	33·9	0·482	15·6	111	15·3	22·8	3·95	55·1	25·9	103
1·61	34·2	0·382	15·7	51·7	15·7	23·2	3·20	26·6	25·8	106
1·33	34·3	0·315	15·8	26·8	16·0	23·5	2·66	14·1	25·8	108
1·03	34·5	0·241	15·9	11·4	16·3	23·8	2·07	6·19	25·8	110
0·876	34·6	0·205	16·0	6·67	16·4	23·9	1·75	3·65	25·8	111
1·39	26·8	0·280	13·9	48·3	12·3	24·8	2·78	23·1	40·7	96·3
1·15	27·1	0·231	14·0	25·1	12·6	25·1	2·31	12·3	40·7	98·1
0·893	27·4	0·180	14·2	10·7	12·9	25·4	1·80	5·38	40·7	99·5
0·759	27·5	0·151	14·2	6·25	13·0	25·5	1·52	3·17	40·8	101
0·983	28·5	0·213	12·8	43·3	11·5	21·5	1·97	16·3	33·1	86·3
0·818	28·8	0·176	12·9	22·5	11·8	21·8	1·65	8·74	33·1	88·1
0·640	29·0	0·136	13·0	9·65	12·1	22·1	1·29	3·85	33·1	90·1
0·546	29·2	0·114	13·0	5·63	12·2	22·2	1·09	2·28	33·1	91·9
0·603	23·5	0·109	10·8	20·0	9·00	21·5	1·22	6·48	39·2	75·6
0·473	23·8	0·085	10·9	8·57	9·20	21·7	0·955	2·86	39·3	78·4
0·405	24·0	0·071	10·9	5·00	9·40	21·9	0·817	1·70	39·2	79·4
0·435	29·8	0·096	10·6	18·3	9·80	17·3	0·869	4·61	25·1	71·7
0·342	30·1	0·075	10·7	7·85	10·1	17·6	0·686	2·05	25·1	73·6
0·293	30·2	0·064	10·8	4·58	10·2	17·7	0·587	1·22	25·1	74·5
0·240	30·4	0·052	10·8	2·37	10·4	17·9	0·482	0·641	25·1	75·5
0·171	21·6	0·029	7·55	6·05	6·04	16·0	0·347	1·04	30·7	53·9
0·147	21·9	0·024	7·59	3·54	6·18	16·2	0·299	0·622	30·7	54·9

Single and Compound Angle Members

Table 1.1(b)—contd.

Size (long leg × short leg)	Thickness	Mass	Dead load	Area A	Axis x–x		Axis y–y		
					I_x	$\bar{y}$	I_y	$\bar{x}$	I_{xy}
$(mm \times mm)$	(mm)	(kg/m)	(kN/m)	(mm^2)	$(10^6\,mm^4)$	(mm)	$(10^6\,mm^4)$	(mm)	$(10^6 mm^4)$
	4	2·70	0·026	344	0·107	18·3	0·034	8·31	−0·036
	3	2·05	0·020	261	0·083	17·9	0·027	7·94	−0·028
45×30	6	3·25	0·032	414	0·082	15·7	0·029	8·22	−0·028
	5	2·75	0·027	350	0·070	15·4	0·025	7·86	−0·024
	4	2·23	0·022	284	0·058	15·0	0·021	7·49	−0·020
	3	1.70	0·017	216	0·045	14·6	0·016	7·12	−0·016

^{a} All the values of x_s and y_s in Table 1.1(b) should be taken as negative in computing the parameters β_1 and β_2.

Table 1.2(a)
Cross-sectional Properties of Hot-rolled Angles—Equal Angles (Imperial Units)

Size (long leg × short leg) $(in \times in)$	Thickness (in)	Weight per foot (lb)	Area A (in^2)	Axis x–x		Axis y–y		
				I_x (in^4)	$\bar{y}$ (in)	I_y (in^4)	$\bar{x}$ (in)	I_{xy} (in^4)
8×8	$1\frac{1}{8}$	56·9	16·7	98·0	2·41	98·0	2·41	−57·4
	1	51·0	15·0	89·0	2·37	89·0	2·37	−52·5
	$\frac{7}{8}$	45·0	13·2	79·6	2·32	79·6	2·32	−47·1
	$\frac{3}{4}$	38·9	11·4	69·7	2·28	69·7	2·28	−41·2
	$\frac{5}{8}$	32·7	9·61	59·4	2·23	59·4	2·23	−35·4
	$\frac{9}{16}$	29·6	8·68	54·1	2·21	54·1	2·21	−32·2
	$\frac{1}{2}$	26·4	7·75	48·6	2·19	48·6	2·19	−29·0
6×6	1	37·4	11·0	35·5	1·86	35·5	1·86	−20·4
	$\frac{7}{8}$	33·1	9·73	31·9	1·82	31·9	1·82	−18·6
	$\frac{3}{4}$	28·7	8·44	28·2	1·78	28·2	1·78	−16·7
	$\frac{5}{8}$	24·2	7·11	24·2	1·73	24·2	1·73	−14·3
	$\frac{9}{16}$	21·9	6·43	22·1	1·71	22·1	1·71	−13·2
	$\frac{1}{2}$	19·6	5·75	19·9	1·68	19·9	1·68	−11·9

Table 1.1(b)—*contd.*

Axis u–u		Axis v–v			Location of shear centre					
I_u	α	I_v	r_v	J	x_s^a	y_s^a	I_{ps}	C_w	β_1	β_2
$(10^6\,mm^4)$	(de-grees)	$(10^6\,mm^4)$	(mm)	$(10^3\,mm^4)$	(mm)	(mm)	$(10^6 mm^4)$	$(10^6\,mm^6)$	(mm)	(mm)
0·121	22·1	0·020	7·65	1·83	6·31	16·3	0·246	0·329	30·8	56·1
0·094	22·3	0·016	7·72	0·783	6·44	16·4	0·191	0·143	30·8	57·2
0·094	23·1	0·017	6·44	4·97	5·22	12·7	0·189	0·563	23·5	44·0
0·080	23·4	0·015	6·47	2·92	5·36	12·9	0·163	0·339	23·5	45·1
0·067	23·7	0·012	6·51	1·51	5·49	13·0	0·136	0·180	23·5	46·5
0·052	24·0	0·009	6·57	0·648	5·62	13·1	0·105	0·079	23·6	47·6

Table 1.2(a)—*contd.*

Axis u–u		Axis v–v			Location of shear centre					
I_u	α	I_v	r_v	J	x_s^a	y_s^a	I_{ps}	C_w	β_1	β_2
(in^4)	(degrees)	(in^4)	(in)	(in^4)	(in)	(in)	(in^4)	(in^6)	(in)	(in)
155·4	45	40·6	1·56	7·06	1·847	1·847	310·0	32·5	0	10·33
141·5	45	36·5	1·56	5·00	1·870	1·870	282·9	23·4	0	10·44
126·7	45	32·5	1·57	3·38	1·882	1·882	252·8	16·1	0	10·59
110·9	45	28·5	1·58	2·14	1·905	1·905	222·1	10·4	0	10·65
94·8	45	24·0	1·58	1·25	1·917	1·917	189·5	6·16	0	10·83
86·3	45	21·9	1·59	0·916	1·929	1·929	172·8	4·55	0	10·83
77·6	45	19·6	1·59	0·646	1·940	1·940	155·5	3·23	0	10·89
55·9	45	15·1	1·17	3·67	1·360	1·360	111·7	9·24	0	7·56
50·5	45	13·3	1·17	2·48	1·382	1·382	101·0	6·41	0	7·69
44·9	45	11·6	1·17	1·58	1·405	1·405	89·7	4·17	0	7·82
38·5	45	9·90	1·18	0·926	1·417	1·417	77·0	2·50	0	7·94
35·3	45	8·95	1·18	0·678	1·429	1·429	70·5	1·85	0	8·01
31·8	45	8·01	1·18	0·479	1·430	1·430	63·3	1·32	0	8·14

Table 1.2(a)—*contd.*

Size (long leg × short leg) (in × in)	Thickness (in)	Weight per foot (lb)	Area A (in²)	Axis x–x I_x (in⁴)	$\bar{y}$ (in)	Axis y–y I_y (in⁴)	$\bar{x}$ (in)	I_{xy} (in⁴)
	$\frac{7}{16}$	17·2	5·06	17·7	1·66	17·7	1·66	−10·5
	$\frac{3}{8}$	14·9	4·36	15·4	1·64	15·4	1·64	−9·23
	$\frac{5}{16}$	12·4	3·65	13·0	1·62	13·0	1·62	−7·74
5×5	$\frac{7}{8}$	27·2	7·98	17·8	1·57	17·8	1·57	−10·2
	$\frac{3}{4}$	23·6	6·94	15·7	1·52	15·7	1·52	−9·10
	$\frac{5}{8}$	20·0	5·86	13·6	1·48	13·6	1·48	−8·00
	$\frac{1}{2}$	16·2	4·75	11·3	1·43	11·3	1·43	−6·71
	$\frac{7}{16}$	14·3	4·18	10·0	1·41	10·0	1·41	−5·94
	$\frac{3}{8}$	12·3	3·61	8·74	1·39	8·74	1·39	−5·20
	$\frac{5}{16}$	10·3	3·03	7·42	1·37	7·42	1·37	−4·43
4×4	$\frac{3}{4}$	18·5	5·44	7·67	1·27	7·67	1·27	−4·38
	$\frac{5}{8}$	15·7	4·61	6·66	1·23	6·66	1·23	−3·36
	$\frac{1}{2}$	12·8	3·75	5·56	1·18	5·56	1·18	−3·27
	$\frac{7}{16}$	11·3	3·31	4·97	1·16	4·97	1·16	−2·93
	$\frac{3}{8}$	9·8	2·86	4·36	1·14	4·36	1·14	−2·58
	$\frac{5}{16}$	8·2	2·40	3·71	1·12	3·71	1·12	−2·21
	$\frac{1}{4}$	6·6	1·94	3·04	1·09	3·04	1·09	−1·81
3½×3½	$\frac{1}{2}$	11·1	3·25	3·64	1·06	3·64	1·06	−2·12
	$\frac{7}{16}$	9·8	2·87	3·26	1·04	3·26	1·04	−1·92
	$\frac{3}{8}$	8·5	2·48	2·87	1·01	2·87	1·01	−1·70
	$\frac{5}{16}$	7·2	2·09	2·45	0·990	2·45	0·990	−1·45
	$\frac{1}{4}$	5·8	1·69	2·01	0·968	2·01	0·968	−1·20
3×3	$\frac{1}{2}$	9·4	2·75	2·22	0·932	2·22	0·932	−1·28
	$\frac{7}{16}$	8·3	2·43	1·99	0·910	1·99	0·910	−1·16
	$\frac{3}{8}$	7·2	2·11	1·76	0·888	1·76	0·888	−1·03
	$\frac{5}{16}$	6·1	1·78	1·51	0·865	1·51	0·865	−0·892
	$\frac{1}{4}$	4·9	1·44	1·24	0·842	1·24	0·842	−0·735
	$\frac{3}{16}$	3·71	1·09	0·962	0·820	0·962	0·820	−0·575
2½×2½	$\frac{1}{2}$	7·7	2·25	1·23	0·806	1·23	0·806	−0·696
	$\frac{3}{8}$	5·9	1·73	0·984	0·762	0·984	0·762	−0·574
	$\frac{5}{16}$	5·0	1·46	0·849	0·740	0·849	0·740	−0·500
	$\frac{1}{4}$	4·1	1·19	0·703	0·717	0·703	0·717	−0·416
	$\frac{3}{16}$	3·07	0·902	0·547	0·694	0·547	0·694	−0·326
2×2	$\frac{3}{8}$	4·7	1·36	0·479	0·636	0·479	0·636	−0·273
	$\frac{5}{16}$	3·92	1·15	0·416	0·614	0·416	0·614	−0·241
	$\frac{1}{4}$	3·19	0·938	0·348	0·592	0·348	0·592	−0·205
	$\frac{3}{16}$	2·44	0·715	0·272	0·569	0·272	0·569	−0·161
	$\frac{1}{8}$	1·65	0·484	0·190	0·546	0·190	0·546	−0·113

[a] All the values of x_s and y_s should be taken as negative in computing the parameters β_1 and β_2.

Table 1.2(a)—*contd.*

Axis $u-u$		Axis $v-v$			Location of shear centre					
I_u (in^4)	α (degrees)	I_v (in^4)	r_v (in)	J (in^4)	$x_s{}^a$ (in)	$y_s{}^a$ (in)	I_{ps} (in^4)	C_w (in^6)	β_1 (in)	β_2 (in)
28·2	45	7·17	1·19	0·323	1·441	1·441	56·4	0·899	0	8·14
24·6	45	6·17	1·19	0·204	1·453	1·453	49·2	0·575	0	8·20
20·7	45	5·26	1·20	0·119	1·464	1·464	41·6	0·338	0	8·20
28·1	45	7·56	0·973	2·04	1·132	1·132	56·1	3·54	0	6·23
24·8	45	6·60	0·975	1·301	1·145	1·145	49·6	2·32	0	6·41
21·6	45	5·61	0·978	0·763	1·167	1·167	43·2	1·40	0	6·52
18·0	45	4·59	0·983	0·396	1·180	1·180	35·8	0·744	0	6·68
15·9	45	4·06	0·986	0·267	1·191	1·191	31·9	0·509	0	6·72
13·9	45	3·54	0·990	0·169	1·203	1·203	27·9	0·327	0	6·76
11·9	45	2·99	0·994	0·098 5	1·214	1·214	23·8	0·193	0	6·79
12·1	45	3·29	0·778	1·02	0·895	0·895	24·1	1·12	0	4·95
10·5	45	2·80	0·779	0·600	0·917	0·917	21·1	0·680	0	5·07
8·83	45	2·29	0·782	0·313	0·930	0·930	17·6	0·366	0	5·24
7·90	45	2·04	0·785	0·211	0·941	0·941	15·8	0·252	0	5·28
6·94	45	1·78	0·788	0·134	0·953	0·953	13·9	0·162	0	5·33
5·92	45	1·50	0·791	0·078 2	0·964	0·964	11·9	0·096 3	0	5·38
4·85	45	1·23	0·795	0·040 4	0·965	0·965	9·69	0·050 5	0	5·48
5·76	45	1·52	0·683	0·271	0·810	0·810	11·5	0·238	0	4·48
5·18	45	1·34	0·684	0·183	0·821	0·821	10·4	0·164	0	4·54
4·57	45	1·17	0·687	0·116	0·823	0·823	9·10	0·107	0	4·65
3·91	45	0·995	0·690	0·068 0	0·834	0·834	7·81	0·063 4	0	4·69
3·21	45	0·814	0·694	0·035 2	0·843	0·843	6·42	0·033 4	0	4·74
3·50	45	0·938	0·584	0·229	0·682	0·682	7·00	0·144	0	3·78
3·15	45	0·832	0·585	0·155	0·691	0·691	6·30	0·100	0	3·85
2·79	45	0·727	0·587	0·098 9	0·701	0·701	5·59	0·065 2	0	3·91
2·40	45	0·618	0·589	0·057 9	0·709	0·709	4·81	0·039 0	0	3·98
1·98	45	0·505	0·592	0·029 9	0·717	0·717	3·96	0·020 6	0	4·04
1·54	45	0·387	0·596	0·012 8	0·726	0·726	3·07	0·008 99	0	4·09
1·93	45	0·534	0·487	0·188	0·556	0·556	3·85	0·079 1	0	3·04
1·56	45	0·410	0·487	0·081 3	0·575	0·575	3·11	0·036 2	0	3·20
1·35	45	0·349	0·489	0·047 7	0·584	0·584	2·69	0·021 8	0	3·26
1·12	45	0·287	0·491	0·024 7	0·592	0·592	2·24	0·011 6	0	3·33
0·873	45	0·221	0·495	0·010 6	0·600	0·600	1·74	0·005 10	0	3·39
0·752	45	0·206	0·389	0·063 7	0·448	0·448	1·51	0·017 4	0	2·47
0·657	45	0·175	0·390	0·037 5	0·458	0·458	1·31	0·010 6	0	2·54
0·553	45	0·143	0·391	0·019 5	0·467	0·467	1·11	0·005 72	0	2·61
0·433	45	0·111	0·394	0·008 38	0·475	0·475	0·867	0·002 54	0	2·67
0·303	45	0·076 7	0·398	0·002 52	0·484	0·484	0·606	0·007 89	0	2·73

Table 1.2(b)
Cross-sectional Properties of Hot-rolled Angles—Unequal Angles (Imperial Units)

Size (long leg × short leg) (in × in)	Thickness (in)	Weight per foot (lb)	Area A (in²)	Axis x–x I_x (in⁴)	Axis x–x $\bar{y}$ (in)	Axis y–y I_y (in⁴)	Axis y–y $\bar{x}$ (in)	I_{xy} (in⁴)
9×4	$\frac{5}{8}$	26·3	7·73	64·9	3·36	8·32	0·858	−12·8
	$\frac{9}{16}$	23·8	7·00	59·1	3·33	7·63	0·834	−11·8
	$\frac{1}{2}$	21·3	6·25	53·2	3·31	6·92	0·810	−10·7
8×6	1	44·2	13·0	80·8	2·65	38·8	1·65	−32·3
	$\frac{7}{8}$	39·1	11·5	72·3	2·61	34·9	1·61	−29·2
	$\frac{3}{4}$	33·8	9·94	63·4	2·56	30·7	1·56	−25·9
	$\frac{5}{8}$	28·5	8·36	54·1	2·52	26·3	1·52	−22·2
	$\frac{9}{16}$	25·7	7·56	49·3	2·50	24·0	1·50	−20·4
	$\frac{1}{2}$	23·0	6·75	44·3	2·47	21·7	1·47	−18·3
	$\frac{7}{16}$	20·2	5·93	39·2	2·45	19·3	1·45	−16·2
8×4	1	37·4	11·0	69·6	3·05	11·6	1·05	−15·3
	$\frac{3}{4}$	28·7	8·44	54·9	2·95	9·36	0·953	−12·6
	$\frac{9}{16}$	21·9	6·43	42·8	2·88	7·43	0·882	−10·1
	$\frac{1}{2}$	19·6	5·75	38·5	2·86	6·74	0·859	−9·13
7×4	$\frac{3}{4}$	26·2	7·69	37·8	2·51	9·05	1·01	−10·4
	$\frac{5}{8}$	22·1	6·48	32·4	2·46	7·84	0·963	−9·06
	$\frac{1}{2}$	17·9	5·25	26·7	2·42	6·53	0·917	−7·61
	$\frac{3}{8}$	13·6	3·98	20·6	2·37	5·10	0·870	−5·96
6×4	$\frac{7}{8}$	27·2	7·98	27·7	2·12	9·75	1·12	−9·18
	$\frac{3}{4}$	23·6	6·94	24·5	2·08	8·68	1·08	−8·29
	$\frac{5}{8}$	20·0	5·86	21·1	2·03	7·52	1·03	−7·29
	$\frac{9}{16}$	18·1	5·31	19·3	2·01	6·91	1·01	−6·72
	$\frac{1}{2}$	16·2	4·75	17·4	1·99	6·27	0·987	−6·07
	$\frac{7}{16}$	14·3	4·18	15·5	1·96	5·60	0·964	−5·46
	$\frac{3}{8}$	12·3	3·61	13·5	1·94	4·90	0·941	−4·79
	$\frac{5}{16}$	10·3	3·03	11·4	1·92	4·18	0·918	−4·05
6×3½	$\frac{1}{2}$	15·3	4·50	16·6	2·08	4·25	0·833	−4·82
	$\frac{3}{8}$	11·7	3·42	12·9	2·04	3·34	0·787	−3·81
	$\frac{5}{16}$	9·8	2·87	10·9	2·01	2·85	0·763	−3·23
5×3½	$\frac{3}{4}$	19·8	5·81	13·9	1·75	5·55	0·996	−4·94
	$\frac{5}{8}$	16·8	4·92	12·0	1·70	4·83	0·951	−4·35
	$\frac{1}{2}$	13·6	4·00	9·99	1·66	4·05	0·906	−3·69
	$\frac{7}{16}$	12·0	3·53	8·90	1·63	3·63	0·883	−3·31
	$\frac{3}{8}$	10·4	3·05	7·78	1·61	3·18	0·861	−2·93
	$\frac{5}{16}$	8·7	2·56	6·60	1·59	2·72	0·838	−2·49
	$\frac{1}{4}$	7·0	2·06	5·39	1·56	2·23	0·814	−2·05
5×3	$\frac{5}{8}$	15·7	4·61	11·4	1·80	3·06	0·796	−3·31
	$\frac{1}{2}$	12·8	3·75	9·45	1·75	2·58	0·750	−2·81

Table 1.2(b)—*contd.*

Axis u–u		Axis v–v			Location of shear centre					
I_u (in⁴)	α (degrees)	I_v (in⁴)	r_v (in)	J (in⁴)	$x_s{}^a$ (in)	$y_s{}^a$ (in)	I_{ps} (in⁴)	C_w (in⁶)	β_1 (in)	β_2 (in)
67·7	12·2	5·55	0·847	1·01	0·545	3·047	147.3	4·79	6·56	7·97
61·7	12·3	5·06	0·850	0·738	0·553	3·049	133·9	3·53	6·58	8·06
55·6	12·4	4·56	0·854	0·521	0·560	3·060	120·6	2·51	6·58	8·13
98·3	28·5	21·3	1·28	4·33	1·150	2·150	196·9	16·3	3·31	8·63
88·4	28·7	18·8	1·28	2·93	1·172	2·172	177·3	11·3	3·31	8·76
77·6	28·9	16·5	1·29	1·86	1·185	2·185	155·5	7·28	3·31	8·91
66·5	29·0	13·9	1·29	1·09	1·207	2·207	133·3	4·33	3·31	9·04
60·5	29·1	12·8	1·30	0·797	1·219	2·219	121·7	3·20	3·31	9·04
54·6	29·2	11·4	1·30	0·563	1·220	2·220	109·3	2·28	3·31	9·19
48·3	29·2	10·2	1·31	0·379	1·231	2·231	97·0	1·55	3·31	9·18
73·3	13·9	7·87	0·846	3·67	0·550	2·550	156·1	12·9	5·45	6·62
58·1	14·5	6·13	0·852	1·58	0·578	2·575	123·0	5·75	5·48	7·06
45·5	14·8	4·77	0·861	0·678	0·601	2·599	96·0	2·53	5·51	7·31
40·9	14·9	4·30	0·865	0·479	0·609	2·610	86·5	1·80	5·51	7·37
41·2	18·0	5·69	0·860	1·44	0·635	2·135	85·0	3·97	4·36	6·42
35·4	18·2	4·85	0·865	0·844	0·650	2·147	72·9	2·37	4·38	6·60
29·2	18·5	3·99	0·872	0·438	0·667	2·170	60·3	1·25	4·38	6·73
22·6	18·8	3·08	0·880	0·187	0·683	2·182	46·5	0·544	4·39	6·89
31·6	22·8	5·86	0·857	2·04	0·682	1·682	63·8	4·04	3·13	5·79
28·1	23·2	5·13	0·860	1·30	0·705	1·705	56·8	2·64	3·13	5·91
24·3	23·5	4·37	0·864	0·763	0·717	1·717	48·9	1·59	3·13	6·11
22·2	23·7	3·98	0·866	0·560	0·729	1·729	44·9	1·18	3·13	6·16
20·1	23·7	3·60	0·870	0·396	0·737	1·740	40·6	0·843	3·14	6·22
17·9	23·9	3·19	0·873	0·267	0·745	1·741	36·1	0·575	3·14	6·31
15·6	24·0	2·78	0·877	0·169	0·753	1·752	31·5	0·369	3·14	6·37
13·2	24·1	2·36	0·882	0·098 5	0·762	1·764	26·8	0·217	3·15	6·41
18·3	19·0	2·59	0·759	0·375	0·583	1·830	37·5	0·779	3·68	5·78
14·2	19·3	2·01	0·767	0·160	0·600	1·852	29·2	0·341	3·69	5·89
12·0	19·4	1·71	0·772	0·093 5	0·607	1·854	24·7	0·201	3·70	5·97
16·2	24·9	3·25	0·748	1·09	0·621	1·375	32·7	1·52	2·40	4·95
14·1	25·3	2·78	0·751	0·641	0·638	1·387	28·3	0·918	2·41	5·12
11·8	25·6	2·28	0·755	0·333	0·656	1·410	23·7	0·491	2·40	5·26
10·5	25·7	2·03	0·758	0·225	0·664	1·411	21·1	0·336	2·41	5·35
9·19	25·9	1·77	0·762	0·143	0·674	1·422	18·5	0·217	2·41	5·40
7·82	26·1	1·50	0·766	0·083 3	0·682	1·434	15·8	0·128	2·41	5·45
6·40	26·2	1·22	0·770	0·043 0	0·689	1·435	12·8	0·067 0	2·42	5·55
12·6	19·2	1·91	0·644	0·600	0·483	1·487	25·7	0·830	2·96	4·59
10·5	19·6	1·58	0·648	0·313	0·500	1·500	21·4	0·444	2·98	4·77

Single and Compound Angle Members

Table 1.2(b)—contd.

Size (long leg × short leg) (in × in)	Thickness (in)	Weight per foot (lb)	Area A (in²)	Axis x–x I_x (in⁴)	$\bar{y}$ (in)	Axis y–y I_y (in⁴)	$\bar{x}$ (in)	I_{xy} (in⁴)
	$\frac{7}{16}$	11·3	3·31	8·43	1·73	2·32	0·727	−2·54
	$\frac{3}{8}$	9·8	2·86	7·37	1·70	2·04	0·704	−2·24
	$\frac{5}{16}$	8·2	2·40	6·26	1·68	1·75	0·681	−1·92
	$\frac{1}{4}$	6·6	1·94	5·11	1·66	1·44	0·657	−1·58
$4 \times 3\frac{1}{2}$	$\frac{5}{8}$	14·7	4·30	6·37	1·29	4·52	1·04	−3·10
	$\frac{1}{2}$	11·9	3·50	5·32	1·25	3·79	1·00	−2·62
	$\frac{7}{16}$	10·6	3·09	4·76	1·23	3·40	0·978	−2·37
	$\frac{3}{8}$	9·1	2·67	4·18	1·21	2·95	0·955	−2·16
	$\frac{5}{16}$	7·7	2·25	3·56	1·18	2·55	0·932	−1·79
	$\frac{1}{4}$	6·2	1·81	2·91	1·16	2·09	0·909	−1·47
4×3	$\frac{5}{8}$	13·6	3·98	6·03	1·37	2·87	0·871	−2·36
	$\frac{1}{2}$	11·1	3·25	5·05	1·33	2·42	0·827	−2·03
	$\frac{7}{16}$	9·8	2·87	4·52	1·30	2·18	0·804	−1·83
	$\frac{3}{8}$	8·5	2·48	3·96	1·28	1·92	0·782	−1·61
	$\frac{5}{16}$	7·2	2·09	3·38	1·26	1·65	0·759	−1·38
	$\frac{1}{4}$	5·8	1·69	2·77	1·24	1·36	0·736	−1·14
$3\frac{1}{2} \times 3$	$\frac{1}{2}$	10·2	3·00	3·45	1·13	2·33	0·875	−1·63
	$\frac{7}{16}$	9·1	2·65	3·10	1·10	2·09	0·853	−1·50
	$\frac{3}{8}$	7·9	2·30	2·72	1·08	1·85	0·830	−1·31
	$\frac{5}{16}$	6·6	1·93	2·33	1·06	1·58	0·808	−1·14
	$\frac{1}{4}$	5·4	1·56	1·91	1·04	1·30	0·785	−0·941
$3\frac{1}{2} \times 2\frac{1}{2}$	$\frac{1}{2}$	9·4	2·75	3·24	1·20	1·36	0·705	−1·20
	$\frac{7}{16}$	8·3	2·43	2·91	1·18	1·23	0·682	−1·09
	$\frac{3}{8}$	7·2	2·11	2·56	1·16	1·09	0·660	−0·967
	$\frac{5}{16}$	6·1	1·78	2·19	1·14	0·939	0·637	−0·837
	$\frac{1}{4}$	4·9	1·44	1·80	1·11	0·777	0·614	−0·696
$3 \times 2\frac{1}{2}$	$\frac{1}{2}$	8·5	2·50	2·08	1·00	1·30	0·750	−0·937
	$\frac{7}{16}$	7·6	2·21	1·88	0·978	1·18	0·728	−0·858
	$\frac{3}{8}$	6·6	1·92	1·66	0·956	1·04	0·706	−0·772
	$\frac{5}{16}$	5·6	1·62	1·42	0·933	0·898	0·683	−0·660
	$\frac{1}{4}$	4·5	1·31	1·17	0·911	0·743	0·661	−0·549
	$\frac{3}{16}$	3·39	0·996	0·907	0·888	0·577	0·638	−0·431
3×2	$\frac{1}{2}$	7·7	2·25	1·92	1·08	0·672	0·583	−0·624
	$\frac{7}{16}$	6·8	2·00	1·73	1·06	0·609	0·561	−0·574
	$\frac{3}{8}$	5·9	1·73	1·53	1·04	0·543	0·539	−0·517
	$\frac{5}{16}$	5·0	1·46	1·32	1·02	0·470	0·516	−0·456
	$\frac{1}{4}$	4·1	1·19	1·09	0·993	0·392	0·493	−0·381
	$\frac{3}{16}$	3·07	0·902	0·842	0·970	0·307	0·470	−0·298
$2\frac{1}{2} \times 2$	$\frac{3}{8}$	5·3	1·55	0·912	0·831	0·514	0·581	−0·392
	$\frac{5}{16}$	4·5	1·31	0·788	0·809	0·446	0·559	−0·344
	$\frac{1}{4}$	3·62	1·06	0·654	0·787	0·372	0·537	−0·290
	$\frac{3}{16}$	2·75	0·809	0·509	0·764	0·291	0·514	−0·229

[a] All the values of x_s and y_s in Table 1.2(b) should be taken as negative in computing the parameters β_1 and β_2.

Table 1.2(b)—contd.

| Axis u–u | | Axis v–v | | | Location of shear centre | | | | | |
I_u (in⁴)	α (degrees)	I_v (in⁴)	r_v (in)	J (in⁴)	$x_s{}^a$ (in)	$y_s{}^a$ (in)	I_{ps} (in⁴)	C_w (in⁶)	β_1 (in)	β_2 (in)
9·35	19·8	1·40	0·651	0·211	0·508	1·511	19·2	0·304	2·98	4·84
8·19	20·0	1·22	0·654	0·134	0·516	1·512	16·7	0·196	2·99	4·93
6·97	20·2	1·04	0·658	0·078 2	0·525	1·524	14·2	0·116	2·99	4·99
5·70	20·4	0·853	0·663	0·040 4	0·532	1·535	11·7	0·060 6	2·99	5·04
8·67	36·7	2·22	0·719	0·559	0·727	0·977	17·3	0·560	0·877	4·69
7·29	36·9	1·82	0·722	0·292	0·750	1·000	14·6	0·302	0·874	4·81
6·54	37·0	1·62	0·724	0·197	0·759	1·011	13·1	0·208	0·870	4·86
5·72	37·1	1·41	0·727	0·125	0·767	1·023	11·5	0·134	0·868	4·92
4·91	37·1	1·20	0·730	0·073 1	0·776	1·024	9·82	0·079 8	0·874	5·00
4·03	37·2	0·975	0·734	0·037 8	0·784	1·035	8·05	0·041 9	0·871	5·06
7·29	28·1	1·62	0·637	0·519	0·558	1·057	14·6	0·472	1·66	4·16
6·14	28·5	1·33	0·639	0·271	0·577	1·080	12·3	0·255	1·65	4·30
5·52	28·7	1·18	0·641	0·183	0·585	1·081	11·0	0·176	1·66	4·40
4·85	28·9	1·03	0·644	0·116	0·595	1·092	9·72	0·114	1·66	4·46
4·16	29·0	0·875	0·647	0·068 0	0·603	1·104	8·34	0·067 6	1·65	4·51
3·41	29·2	0·716	0·651	0·035 2	0·611	1·115	6·86	0·035 6	1·65	4·56
4·62	35·5	1·16	0·621	0·250	0·625	0·880	9·28	0·191	0·866	4·06
4·17	35·7	1·03	0·622	0·169	0·634	0·881	8·31	0·132	0·872	4·16
3·67	35·8	0·898	0·625	0·108	0·642	0·892	7·35	0·085 8	0·868	4·21
3·15	35·9	0·759	0·627	0·062 9	0·652	0·904	6·31	0·051 2	0·865	4·28
2·59	36·0	0·621	0·631	0·032 6	0·660	0·915	5·20	0·027 0	0·862	4·33
3·82	25·9	0·784	0·534	0·229	0·455	0·950	7·65	0·159	1·62	3·57
3·44	26·2	0·696	0·535	0·155	0·463	0·961	6·91	0·110	1·62	3·65
3·04	26·4	0·609	0·537	0·098 9	0·473	0·972	6·12	0·071 4	1·62	3·71
2·61	26·6	0·519	0·540	0·057 9	0·481	0·984	5·26	0·042 6	1·62	3·77
2·15	26·8	0·426	0·544	0·029 9	0·489	0·985	4·32	0·022 5	1·62	3·85
2·70	33·7	0·676	0·520	0·208	0·500	0·750	5·41	0·112	0·865	3·34
2·46	33·9	0·600	0·521	0·141	0·509	0·759	4·91	0·077 7	0·862	3·42
2·18	34·1	0·523	0·522	0·090 1	0·518	0·768	4·35	0·050 7	0·861	3·49
1·87	34·2	0·447	0·525	0·052 8	0·527	0·777	3·75	0·030 4	0·861	3·56
1·55	34·4	0·365	0·528	0·027 3	0·536	0·786	3·10	0·016 1	0·860	3·62
1·20	34·5	0·283	0·533	0·011 7	0·544	0·794	2·41	0·007 05	0·860	3·67
2·18	22·5	0·412	0·428	0·188	0·333	0·830	4·39	0·090 8	1·57	2·81
1·97	22·8	0·368	0·429	0·127	0·342	0·841	3·99	0·063 2	1·57	2·88
1·75	23·2	0·320	0·430	0·081 3	0·351	0·852	3·54	0·041 3	1·56	2·96
1·52	23·5	0·273	0·432	0·047 7	0·360	0·864	3·07	0·024 8	1·56	3·04
1·26	23·7	0·225	0·435	0·024 7	0·368	0·868	2·54	0·013 2	1·57	3·11
0·975	24·0	0·174	0·439	0·010 6	0·376	0·876	1·97	0·005 76	1·57	3·18
1·15	31·5	0·273	0·420	0·072 5	0·393	0·643	2·31	0·026 8	0·851	2·75
1·00	31·8	0·233	0·422	0·042 6	0·403	0·653	2·01	0·016 2	0·850	2·82
0·835	32·0	0·191	0·424	0·022 1	0·412	0·662	1·67	0·008 68	0·849	2·89
0·653	32·3	0·148	0·427	0·009 48	0·420	0·670	1·31	0·003 82	0·849	2·96

published by the American Institute of Steel Construction (1980). It should be noted that the information in Tables 1.1(a) and (b) given in SI units will also be useful to designers in other countries such as Australia and the United Kingdom since the sizes of their angle sections are quite close to those milled in Canada.

1.2.2. Cold-formed Angles

A typical cold-formed angle section is shown in Fig. 1.4. Its geometric properties depend on the inside bend radius, r. Defining c_1 as the length of the straight portion of horizontal (short) leg (or $c_1 = a - (r+t)$); c_2 as the length of the straight portion of the vertical (long) leg (or $c_2 = b - (r+t)$); r as the inside bend radius; and t as the thickness of leg, then

$$\text{Area} = A = (c_1 + c_2)t + \frac{\pi}{4}[(r+t)^2 - r^2] \tag{1.27}$$

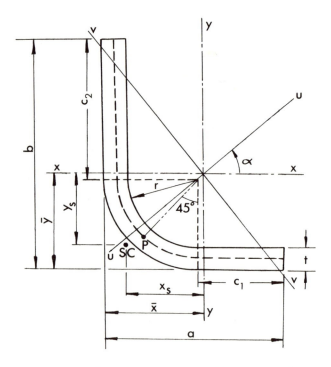

Fig. 1.4. Typical section for a cold-formed angle.

Location of Centroid

$$\bar{x} = \frac{A_1 x_1 + A_2 x_2 + A_3 x_3 - A_4 x_4}{A} \tag{1.28}$$

$$\bar{y} = \frac{A_1 y_1 + A_2 y_2 + A_3 y_3 - A_4 y_4}{A} \tag{1.29}$$

where $A_1 = c_1 t$; $A_2 = c_2 t$; $A_3 = (\pi/4)(r+t)^2$; $A_4 = \pi r^2/4$; $x_1 = a - c_1/2$; $x_2 = t/2$; $x_3 = (r+t) - 4(r+t)/(3\pi)$; $x_4 = (r+t) - 4r/(3\pi)$; $y_1 = t/2$; $y_2 = b - c_2/2$; $y_3 = x_3 = (r+t) - 4(r+t)/(3\pi)$; and $y_4 = x_4 = (r+t) - 4r/(3\pi)$.

Moments of Inertia

Final expressions for I_x, I_y and I_{xy} are as follows:

$$
\begin{aligned}
I_x &= \frac{c_1 t^3}{12} + c_1 t \left(\bar{y} - \frac{t}{2} \right)^2 + \frac{c_2^3 t}{12} + c_2 t \left(b - \bar{y} - \frac{c_2}{2} \right)^2 + \left\{ \tfrac{1}{16} \pi (r+t)^4 - \frac{\pi(r+t)^2}{4} \right. \\
&\quad \left. \times \left[\frac{4(r+t)}{3\pi} \right]^2 + \frac{\pi(r+t)^2}{4} \left[y - (r+t) + \frac{4(r+t)}{3\pi} \right]^2 \right\} \\
&\quad - \left\{ \tfrac{1}{16} \pi r^4 - \frac{\pi r^2}{4} \left(\frac{4r}{3\pi} \right)^2 + \frac{\pi r^2}{4} \left[\bar{y} - (r+t) + \frac{4r}{3\pi} \right]^2 \right\}
\end{aligned} \tag{1.30}
$$

$$
\begin{aligned}
I_y &= \frac{c_1^3 t}{12} + c_1 t \left(a - \bar{x} - \frac{c_1}{2} \right)^2 + \frac{c_2 t^3}{12} + c_2 t \left(\bar{x} - \frac{t}{2} \right)^2 + \left\{ \tfrac{1}{16} \pi (r+t)^4 - \frac{\pi(r+t)^2}{4} \right. \\
&\quad \left. \times \left[\frac{4(r+t)}{3\pi} \right]^2 + \frac{\pi(r+t)^2}{4} \left[\bar{x} - (r+t) + \frac{4(r+t)}{3\pi} \right]^2 \right\} \\
&\quad - \left\{ \tfrac{1}{16} \pi r^4 - \frac{\pi r^2}{4} \left(\frac{4r}{3\pi} \right)^2 + \frac{\pi r^2}{4} \left[\bar{x} - (r+t) + \frac{4r}{3\pi} \right]^2 \right\}
\end{aligned} \tag{1.31}
$$

$$
\begin{aligned}
I_{xy} &= c_1 t \left[-\left(\bar{y} - \frac{t}{2} \right) \right] \left(a - \bar{x} - \frac{c_1}{2} \right) + c_2 t \left[-\left(\bar{x} - \frac{t}{2} \right) \right] \left(b - \bar{y} - \frac{c_2}{2} \right) \\
&\quad + \frac{\pi(r+t)^2}{4} \left\{ \left[\bar{x} - (r+t) + \frac{4(r+t)}{3\pi} \right] \left[\bar{y} - (r+t) + \frac{4(r+t)}{3\pi} \right] \right\} \\
&\quad - \frac{\pi r^2}{4} \left[\bar{x} - (r+t) + \frac{4r}{3\pi} \right] \left[\bar{y} - (r+t) + \frac{4r}{3\pi} \right] + \frac{(r+t)^4}{8} - \frac{r^4}{8} \\
&\quad - \frac{\pi(r+t)^2}{4} \left[\frac{4(r+t)}{3\pi} \right]^2 + \frac{\pi r^2}{4} \left(\frac{4r}{3\pi} \right)^2
\end{aligned} \tag{1.32}
$$

I_{min}, I_{max}, α, r_{min} are calculated as for hot-rolled angles.

The St Venant's torsion constant is given by

$$J = \tfrac{1}{3}t^3\left[c_1 + c_2 + \frac{\pi}{2}\left(r + \frac{t}{2}\right)\right]$$ (1.33)

The shear centre for cold-formed angles is assumed to be at point P as shown in Fig. 1.4. More accurate location of the shear centre and the magnitude of the warping constant can only be obtained by detailed computations.

Tables 1.3(a) and (b), generated by a computer program (Madugula and Ray, 1984b), present the geometric data for various sizes of cold-formed angles; in these tables the inside bend radius is taken as '$2t$' for $t \le 4$ mm, and '$3t$' for $t > 4$ mm, where 't' is the thickness of the leg of the angle. These bend radii are satisfactory for steels having guaranteed yield stress of 300 MPa (Algoma Steel Co. Ltd, 1978). For higher strength steels, larger bend radii are required, and in this case the computer program referred to above, available from the authors, can be used to calculate the cross-sectional properties of angles with any leg size, thickness and bend radius. Tables 1.1(a) and (b), 1.2(a) and (b) and 1.3(a) and (b) also include two parameters β_1 and β_2 as well as the polar moment of inertia about the shear centre I_{ps}

$$\beta_1 = \frac{1}{I_u}\left(\int_A v^3 \, \mathrm{d}A + \int_A u^2 v \, \mathrm{d}A\right) - 2v_s$$ (1.34)

$$\beta_2 = \frac{1}{I_v}\left(\int_A u^3 \, \mathrm{d}A + \int_A uv^2 \, \mathrm{d}A\right) - 2u_s$$ (1.35)

$$I_{ps} = I_x + I_y + (A)(x_s^2 + y_s^2) = I_u + I_v + (A)(u_s^2 + v_s^2)$$ (1.36)

where (x_s, y_s) are the coordinates of the shear centre as shown in Fig. 1.4. Axes u–u and v–v are the centroidal principal axes of inertia and (u_s, v_s) are the coordinates of the shear centre with reference to those axes. These quantities are required for calculating the buckling loads of eccentrically loaded angle columns.

1.2.3. Lipped Angles

(i) Equal-leg Angle with Equal Lips
Referring to Fig. 1.5, and in accordance with the *Cold-formed steel design manual* of the American Iron and Steel Institute (1971), page III-14, if A' is the outer dimension of the leg; c' is the outer dimension of the lip; R is the radius of the centreline of the bend; t is the

thickness; a' is the straight portion of the leg $= A' - (2R + t)$; $\bar{a}$ is the centreline dimension $= A' - t$; c is the straight portion of the lip $= c' - (R + t/2)$; $\bar{c} = c' - t/2$; $u =$ curved length of each $90°$ bend $= \pi R/2$; then

$$\text{cross-sectional area} = A = t[2a' + 2c + 3u] \qquad (1.37)$$

Moment of inertia about the x–x axis (axis of symmetry)

$$I_x = 2t\left\{a'\left[\frac{1}{2}\left(\frac{a'}{2} + R\right)^2 + 0 \cdot 0417a'^2\right]\right.$$

$$+ 0 \cdot 143R^3 + c\left[\frac{1}{2}\left(R + a' - \frac{c}{2}\right)^2 + 0 \cdot 0417c^2\right] \qquad (1.38)$$

$$\left. + u(0 \cdot 707a' + 0 \cdot 898R)^2 + 0 \cdot 014R^3\right\}$$

Distance between the centroid and the centreline of corner

$$\bar{x} = \frac{2t}{A}\left\{a'(0 \cdot 353a' + 0 \cdot 293R) + \frac{u}{2}(0 \cdot 102R)\right.$$

$$\left. + c(0 \cdot 707a' + 0 \cdot 353c + 1 \cdot 707R) + u(0 \cdot 707a' + R)\right\} \qquad (1.39)$$

Moment of inertia about the y–y axis:

$$I_y = 2t\{a'(0 \cdot 353a' + 0 \cdot 293R)^2 + 0 \cdot 0417a'^3 + 0 \cdot 015R^3$$

$$+ u(0 \cdot 707a' + R)^2 + c(0 \cdot 707a' + 0 \cdot 353c + 1 \cdot 707R)^2 \qquad (1.40)$$

$$+ 0 \cdot 0417c^3 + 0 \cdot 285R^3\} - A(\bar{x})^2$$

Distance between the shear centre and the centreline of corner (Fig. 1.5)

$$m = \frac{t\bar{a}(\bar{c})^2}{3\sqrt{2}I_x}(3\bar{a} - 2\bar{c}) \qquad (1.41)$$

The St Venant torsion constant

$$J = \frac{t^3}{3}[2a' + 2c + 3u] \qquad (1.42)$$

The warping constant

$$C_w = \frac{t^2(\bar{a})^4(\bar{c})^3}{18I_x}(4\bar{a} + 3\bar{c}) \qquad (1.43)$$

Table 1.3(a)
Cross-sectional Properties (Full Section) of Cold-formed Angles—Equal Angles

Size (long leg × short leg) (mm × mm)	Thickness (mm)	Inside bend radius (mm)	Mass (kg/m)	Dead load (kN/m)	Area A (mm²)	Axis x–x I_x (10⁶ mm⁴)	$\bar{y}$ (mm)	Axis y–y I_y (10⁶ mm⁴)	$\bar{x}$ (mm)	I_{xy} (10⁶ mm⁴)
200×200	25	75	66·2	0·649	8440	31·3	66·0	31·3	66·0	−23·1
	20	60	54·9	0·539	7000	26·7	62·5	26·7	62·5	−18·8
	16	48	45·2	0·443	5760	22·4	59·8	22·4	59·8	−15·2
	13	39	37·5	0·368	4780	18·9	57·8	18·9	57·8	−12·5
	10	30	29·4	0·289	3750	15·0	55·9	15·0	55·9	−9·69
150×150	20	60	39·2	0·385	5000	10·3	50·5	10·3	50·5	−7·72
	16	48	32·7	0·320	4160	8·86	47·6	8·86	47·6	−6·32
	13	39	27·3	0·268	3480	7·57	45·5	7·57	45·5	−5·21
	10	30	21·6	0·212	2750	6·10	43·5	6·10	43·5	−4·05
125×125	16	48	26·4	0·259	3360	4·85	41·6	4·85	41·6	−3·59
	13	39	22·2	0·218	2830	4·20	39·4	4·20	39·4	−2·98
	10	30	17·7	0·173	2250	3·42	37·4	3·42	37·4	−2·33
	8	24	14·4	0·142	1840	2·84	36·1	2·84	36·1	−1·88
100×100	16	48	20·1	0·197	2560	2·27	35·7	2·27	35·7	−1·78
	13	39	17·1	0·168	2180	2·01	33·4	2·01	33·4	−1·49
	10	30	13·7	0·135	1750	1·67	31·2	1·67	31·2	−1·18
	8	24	11·3	0·111	1440	1·40	29·9	1·40	29·9	−0·953
	6	18	8·71	0·085	1110	1·10	28·6	1·10	28·6	−0·723
90×90	13	39	15·0	0·148	1920	1·41	31·0	1·41	31·0	−1·07
	10	30	12·2	0·119	1550	1·18	28·8	1·18	28·8	−0·850
	8	24	10·0	0·099	1280	1·00	27·4	1·00	27·4	−0·691
	6	18	7·77	0·076	990	0·791	26·1	0·791	26·1	−0·525
75×75	13	39	12·0	0·118	1530	0·748	27·6	0·748	27·6	−0·597
	10	30	9·81	0·096	1250	0·646	25·2	0·646	25·2	−0·483
	8	24	8·16	0·080	1040	0·554	23·8	0·554	23·8	−0·395
	6	18	6·36	0·062	810	0·444	22·4	0·444	22·4	−0·301
	5	15	5·40	0·053	687	0·381	21·8	0·381	21·8	−0·253
65×65	10	30	8·24	0·081	1050	0·397	22·9	0·397	22·9	−0·307
	8	24	6·91	0·068	880	0·346	21·4	0·346	21·4	−0·254
	6	18	5·42	0·053	690	0·280	20·0	0·280	20·0	−0·195
	5	15	4·61	0·045	587	0·242	19·3	0·242	19·3	−0·164
55×55	10	30	6·67	0·065	850	0·221	20·6	0·221	20·6	−0·179
	8	24	5·65	0·055	720	0·197	19·0	0·197	19·0	−0·150
	6	18	4·47	0·044	570	0·163	17·5	0·163	17·5	−0·117
	5	15	3·83	0·038	487	0·142	16·8	0·142	16·8	−0·098
	4	8	3·19	0·031	407	0·121	15·9	0·121	15·9	−0·078
	3	6	2·44	0·024	311	0·094	15·3	0·094	15·3	−0·059
45×45	8	24	4·39	0·043	560	0·098	16·7	0·098	16·7	−0·079
	6	18	3·53	0·035	450	0·084	15·1	0·084	15·1	−0·063
	5	15	3·04	0·030	387	0·074	14·4	0·074	14·4	−0·053
	4	8	2·57	0·025	327	0·064	13·4	0·064	13·4	−0·042
	3	6	1·97	0·019	251	0·050	12·8	0·050	12·8	−0·032

^a All the values of x_s and y_s in Table 1.3(a) should be taken as negative in computing the parameters β_1 and β_2.

Table 1.3(a)—*contd.*

Axis u–u		Axis v–v			Location of shear centre					
I_u (10^6 mm^4)	α (degrees)	I_v (10^6 mm^4)	r_v (mm)	J (10^3 mm^4)	x_s^a (mm)	y_s^a (mm)	I_{ps} (10^6 mm^4)	C_w (10^6 mm^6)	β_1 (mm)	β_2 (mm)
54·4	45·0	8·24	31·3	1760	41·3	41·3	90·9	1520	0·00	292
45·5	45·0	7·90	33·6	933	44·5	44·5	81·0	721	0·00	290
37·7	45·0	7·19	35·3	491	46·6	46·6	69·8	308	0·00	288
31·4	45·0	6·39	36·6	269	47·9	47·9	59·7	131	0·00	287
24·7	45·0	5·33	37·7	125	48·9	48·9	48·0	41·9	0·00	286
18·1	45·0	2·61	22·8	667	30·0	30·0	29·5	326	0·00	220
15·2	45·0	2·55	24·7	355	32·8	32·8	26·6	161	0·00	218
12·8	45·0	2·36	26·1	196	34·5	34·5	23·4	75·1	0·00	217
10·2	45·0	2·05	27·3	91·7	35·8	35·8	19·3	25·9	0·00	216
8·44	45·0	1·26	19·4	287	25·5	25·5	14·0	97·2	0·00	183
7·17	45·0	1·22	20·8	159	27·5	27·5	12·6	49·5	0·00	181
5·75	45·0	1·10	22·1	75·0	29·2	29·2	10·7	18·4	0·00	180
4·72	45·0	0·965	22·9	39·3	30·0	30·0	8·99	7·31	0·00	180
4·05	45·0	0·495	13·9	218	17·9	17·9	6·12	44·1	0·00	149
3·50	45·0	0·515	15·4	123	20·3	20·3	5·78	26·7	0·00	146
2·84	45·0	0·494	16·8	58·3	22·3	22·3	5·06	11·3	0·00	145
2·35	45·0	0·450	17·7	30·7	23·3	23·3	4·37	4·81	0·00	144
1·82	45·0	0·379	18·5	13·3	24·1	24·1	3·49	1·45	0·00	144
2·48	45·0	0·335	13·2	108	17·2	17·2	3·93	18·8	0·00	133
2·03	45·0	0·333	14·7	51·7	19·4	19·4	3·52	8·66	0·00	131
1·69	45·0	0·310	15·6	27·3	20·6	20·6	3·08	3·86	0·00	130
1·32	45·0	0·266	16·4	11·9	21·5	21·5	2·50	1·21	0·00	129
1·35	45·0	0·151	9·94	86·0	12·3	12·3	1·94	9·12	0·00	112
1·13	45·0	0·163	11·4	41·7	15·0	15·0	1·85	5·10	0·00	110
0·949	45·0	0·159	12·4	22·2	16·4	16·4	1·66	2·52	0·00	109
0·745	45·0	0·142	13·3	9·72	17·5	17·5	1·38	0·857	0·00	108
0·635	45·0	0·128	13·7	5·73	17·9	17·9	1·20	0·405	0·00	108
0·704	45·0	0·090	9·24	35·0	12·0	12·0	1·09	3·07	0·00	96·4
0·599	45·0	0·092	10·2	18·8	13·5	13·5	1·01	1·71	0·00	94·9
0·475	45·0	0·086	11·1	8·28	14·8	14·8	0·859	0·633	0·00	94·0
0·406	45·0	0·079	11·6	4·90	15·3	15·3	0·757	0·310	0·00	93·7
0·400	45·0	0·042	7·06	28·3	8·52	8·52	0·558	1·52	0·00	83·1
0·347	45·0	0·047	8·05	15·4	10·5	10·5	0·549	0·994	0·00	81·1
0·279	45·0	0·046	9·01	6·84	11·9	11·9	0·487	0·424	0·00	79·9
0·240	45·0	0·044	9·46	4·06	12·5	12·5	0·436	0·219	0·00	79·5
0·199	45·0	0·043	10·2	2·17	13·3	13·3	0·384	0·030	0·00	77·9
0·153	45·0	0·034	10·5	0·934	13·5	13·5	0·301	0·008	0·00	77·9
0·177	45·0	0·019	5·86	11·9	7·16	7·16	0·251	0·443	0·00	67·7
0·146	45·0	0·021	6·85	5·40	9·01	9·01	0·239	0·238	0·00	66·0
0·127	45·0	0·021	7·33	3·23	9·71	9·71	0·220	0·135	0·00	65·4
0·106	45·0	0·022	8·17	1·74	10·7	10·7	0·202	0·021	0·00	63·7
0·082	45·0	0·018	8·45	0·754	10·9	10·9	0·160	0·006	0·00	63·7

Single and Compound Angle Members

Table 1.3(b)
Cross-sectional Properties (Full Section) of Cold-formed Angles—Unequal Angles

Size (long leg × short leg (mm × mm)	Thickness (mm)	Inside bend radius (mm)	Mass (kg/m)	Dead load (kN/m)	Area A (mm²)	Axis x–x I_x (10^6 mm⁴)	Axis x–x $\bar{y}$ (mm)	Axis y–y I_y (10^6 mm⁴)	Axis y–y $\bar{x}$ (mm)	I_{xy} (10^6 mm⁴)
200×150	25	75	56·4	0·553	7190	27·0	75·4	13·6	47·1	−14·5
	20	60	47·1	0·462	6000	23·5	71·2	11·7	43·7	−11·9
	16	48	38·9	0·382	4960	19·9	68·1	9·93	41·2	−9·70
	13	39	32·4	0·318	4130	16·9	65·9	8·41	39·4	−7·97
200×100	20	60	39·2	0·385	5000	18·9	83·5	3·59	27·5	−5·95
	16	48	32·7	0·320	4160	16·5	79·7	3·06	25·1	−4·89
	13	39	27·3	0·268	3480	14·2	77·0	2·61	23·3	−4·04
	10	30	21·6	0·212	2750	11·5	74·4	2·12	21·7	−3·16
150×100	16	48	26·4	0·259	3360	7·30	57·0	2·76	29·1	−3·28
	13	39	22·2	0·218	2830	6·34	54·5	2·38	27·2	−2·73
	10	30	17·7	0·173	2250	5·19	52·1	1·94	25·4	−2·13
	8	24	14·4	0·142	1840	4·32	50·6	1·61	24·3	−1·72
125×90	16	48	22·0	0·216	2800	4·08	48·3	1·87	28·4	−2·11
	13	39	18·6	0·183	2370	3·60	45·7	1·63	26·3	−1·76
	10	30	14·9	0·146	1900	2·99	43·3	1·35	24·4	−1·39
	8	24	12·2	0·120	1560	2·50	41·8	1·13	23·2	−1·12
125×75	13	39	17·1	0·168	2180	3·27	49·2	0·960	21·3	−1·29
	10	30	13·7	0·135	1750	2·75	46·6	0·796	19·5	−1·02
	8	24	11·3	0·111	1440	2·32	45·0	0·669	18·3	−0·830
	6	18	8·71	0·085	1110	1·82	43·4	0·527	17·2	−0·631
100×90	13	39	16·1	0·158	2050	1·91	35·1	1·48	29·5	−1·26
	10	30	13·0	0·127	1650	1·60	32·8	1·24	27·4	−0·998
	8	24	10·7	0·105	1360	1·34	31·4	1·04	26·1	−0·810
	6	18	8·24	0·081	1050	1·06	30·1	0·821	24·8	−0·615
100×75	13	39	14·5	0·143	1850	1·73	38·1	0·872	23·9	−0·936
	10	30	11·8	0·115	1500	1·47	35·6	0·733	21·9	−0·745
	8	24	9·73	0·095	1240	1·25	34·1	0·621	20·6	−0·606
	6	18	7·54	0·074	960	0·988	32·6	0·492	19·4	−0·461
90×75	13	39	13·5	0·133	1720	1·27	33·8	0·828	25·2	−0·798
	10	30	11·0	0·108	1400	1·09	31·4	0·702	23·1	−0·638
	8	24	9·10	0·089	1160	0·927	29·9	0·597	21·7	−0·520
	6	18	7·06	0·069	900	0·738	28·4	0·474	20·5	−0·396
	5	15	5·99	0·059	762	0·632	27·7	0·407	19·9	−0·332
90×65	10	30	10·2	0·100	1300	1·01	33·4	0·464	19·5	−0·504
	8	24	8·48	0·083	1080	0·869	31·8	0·396	18·2	−0·413
	6	18	6·59	0·065	840	0·696	30·2	0·316	16·9	−0·315
	5	15	5·59	0·055	712	0·598	29·5	0·272	16·3	−0·265
80×60	10	30	9·03	0·089	1150	0·692	30.1	0·349	18·8	−0·371
	8	24	7·53	0·074	960	0·601	28·5	0·300	17·5	−0·305

Table 1.3(b)—*contd.*

Axis u–u		Axis v–v			Location of shear centre					
I_u (10^6 mm^4)	α (degrees)	I_v (10^6 mm^4)	r_v (mm)	J (10^3 mm^4)	$x_s{}^a$ (mm)	$y_s{}^a$ (mm)	I_{ps} (10^6 mm^4)	C_w (10^6 mm^6)	β_1 (mm)	β_2 (mm)
36·3	32·6	4·35	24·6	1500	22·5	39·0	54·8	1680	65·7	215
30·9	31·9	4·31	26·8	800	25·9	46·3	51·9	690	69·2	231
25·8	31·4	4·02	28·5	423	28·1	50·7	46·5	281	73·2	237
21·7	31·0	3·62	29·6	232	29·9	53·5	40·8	103	76·2	240
21·0	18·9	1·55	17·6	667	18·8	47·8	35·6	464	123	−12·2
18·1	18·1	1·46	18·8	355	17·6	55·4	33·5	214	128	85·8
15·4	17·5	1·34	19·6	196	17·1	59·9	30·2	96·2	132	127
12·4	17·0	1·15	20·5	91·7	16·9	63·3	25·4	37·1	136	152
9·02	27·7	1·03	17·6	287	15·1	33·5	14·5	132	65·8	139
7·73	27·0	0·991	18·7	159	17·4	38·4	13·7	45·7	69·1	156
6·25	26·3	0·885	19·8	75·0	19·2	41·9	11·9	18·6	72·8	165
5·16	25·9	0·776	20·5	39·3	19·4	43·3	10·1	7·39	75·1	166
5·36	31·2	0·599	14·6	239	12·8	23·6	7·91	100	45·5	120
4·64	30·4	0·600	15·9	134	14·6	28·3	7·62	47·1	47·4	136
3·78	29·7	0·558	17·1	63·3	16·6	32·2	6·81	14·4	50·5	143
3·13	29·3	0·500	17·9	33·3	17·9	34·2	5·95	5·23	52·7	146
3·85	24·1	0·381	13·2	123	11·5	28·8	6·29	22·7	64·2	85·1
3·18	23·2	0·358	14·3	58·3	13·6	34·1	5·89	11·6	67·8	114
2·66	22·6	0·323	15·0	30·7	13·8	36·3	5·15	5·39	70·6	122
2·08	22·1	0·271	15·6	13·3	13·8	37·8	4·15	1·59	73·0	126
2·97	40·2	0·413	14·2	115	16·4	19·8	4·71	25·6	13·5	136
2·43	39·9	0·402	15·6	55·0	18·2	22·5	4·20	11·5	14·6	135
2·02	39·7	0·370	16·5	29·0	19·3	23·9	3·66	5·14	15·4	135
1·57	39·5	0·314	17·3	12·6	20·1	25·0	2·96	1·63	16·2	135
2·33	32·7	0·270	12·1	104	11·0	18·7	3·44	29·3	32·7	105
1·93	31·9	0·269	13·4	50·0	12·9	23·1	3·24	10·8	34·6	116
1·62	31·4	0·251	14·2	26·5	14·1	25·4	2·90	4·40	36·6	119
1·26	30·9	0·216	15·0	11·5	15·3	27·2	2·41	1·10	38·6	121
1·88	37·2	0·222	11·4	97·0	11·5	15·5	2·72	20·8	19·7	110
1·56	36·6	0·228	12·8	46·7	13·6	19·4	2·57	8·88	20·8	114
1·31	36·2	0·216	13·7	24·7	14·7	21·4	2·30	4·21	22·1	115
1·02	35·8	0·189	14·5	10·8	15·7	22·9	1·90	1·34	23·5	116
0·870	35·6	0·169	14·9	6·35	16·1	23·5	1·66	0·579	24·1	116
1·31	30·7	0·164	11·2	43·3	10·1	19·4	2·09	8·82	33·3	95·6
1·11	30·1	0·157	12·1	23·0	11·5	22·2	1·94	3·27	35·3	102
0·874	29·5	0·138	12·8	10·1	12·7	24·4	1·65	0·858	37·5	105
0·746	29·2	0·124	13·2	5·94	13·2	25·1	1·44	0·422	38·5	106
0·929	32·6	0·111	9·84	38·3	8·98	15·6	1·40	6·86	26·3	86·0
0·791	31·9	0·110	10·7	20·5	10·4	18·5	1·33	2·83	27·7	92·5

Table 1.3(b)—*contd.*

Size (long leg × short leg) (mm × mm)	Thickness (mm)	Inside bend radius (mm)	Mass (kg/m)	Dead load (kN/m)	Area A (mm²)	I_x (10^6 mm⁴)	$\bar{y}$ (mm)	I_y (10^6 mm⁴)	$\bar{x}$ (mm)	I_{xy} (10^6 mm⁴)
	6	18	5·89	0·058	750	0·485	26·9	0·242	16·2	−0·234
	5	15	5·00	0·049	637	0·419	26·2	0·208	15·6	−0·196
75×50	8	24	6·59	0·065	840	0·456	28·5	0·172	14·6	−0·205
	6	18	5·18	0·051	660	0·374	26·8	0·140	13·3	−0·158
	5	15	4·42	0·043	562	0·325	26·0	0·121	12·7	−0·133
65×50	8	24	5·96	0·058	760	0·303	24·1	0·162	15·7	−0·167
	6	18	4·71	0·046	600	0·250	22·5	0·133	14·3	−0·129
	5	15	4·02	0·039	512	0·218	21·8	0·116	13·7	−0·109
	4	8	3·35	0·033	427	0·185	20·7	0·098	12·9	−0·086
55×35	6	18	3·53	0·035	460	0·130	21·4	0·044	10·2	−0·056
	5	15	3·04	0·030	387	0·116	20·5	0·039	9·57	−0·048
	4	8	2·57	0·025	327	0·101	19·3	0·033	8·73	−0·038
	3	6	1·97	0·019	251	0·080	18·6	0·026	8·24	−0·029
45×30	6	18	2·83	0·028	360	0·067	18·2	0·026	9·55	−0·032
	5	15	2·45	0·024	312	0·061	17·3	0·023	8·86	−0·028
	4	8	2·09	0·021	267	0·054	16·0	0·020	7·96	−0·022
	3	6	1·62	0·016	206	0·043	15·3	0·016	7·45	−0·017

ˢ All the values of x_s and y_s in Table 1.3(b) should be taken as negative in computing the parameters β_1 and β_2.

Distance from centroid to shear centre

$$x_s = -(\bar{x} + m) \tag{1.44}$$

the negative sign indicates that the distance is measured in the negative x-direction.

$$\beta_1 = 0 \tag{1.45}$$

$$\beta_2 = \frac{\sqrt{2}t}{24I_y}[(\bar{a})^4 + 4(\bar{a})^3(\bar{c}) - 6(\bar{a})^2(\bar{c})^2 + (\bar{c})^4] - 2x_s \tag{1.46}$$

(ii) Unequal-leg Angle with Unequal Lips

Assuming that the thickness is small and that the rounding of corners is ignored (Fig. 1.6) then according to Blodgett (1966)

$$\text{Area} = (a + b + c + d)t \tag{1.47}$$

$$\bar{y} = \frac{a^2 + 2cd + d^2}{2(a + b + c + d)} \tag{1.48}$$

Table 1.3(b)—*contd.*

Axis u–u		Axis v–v			Location of shear centre					
I_u ($10^6\,mm^4$)	α (*Degrees*)	I_v ($10^6\,mm^4$)	r_v (*mm*)	J ($10^3\,mm^4$)	$x_s{}^a$ (*mm*)	$y_s{}^a$ (*mm*)	I_{ps} ($10^6\,mm^4$)	C_w ($10^6\,mm^6$)	β_1 (*mm*)	β_2 (*mm*)
0·627	31·2	0·100	11·5	9·00	11·5	20·7	1·14	0·855	29·7	95·4
0·536	30·9	0·091	11·9	5·31	12·1	21·6	1·02	0·348	30·7	96·3
0·564	27·7	0·065	8·77	17·9	7·57	16·8	0·909	2·06	32·9	69·7
0·454	26·8	0·060	9·55	7·92	9·05	19·9	0·826	0·509	35·2	79·9
0·390	26·3	0·055	9·92	4·69	9·60	21·0	0·744	0·291	36·4	82·3
0·413	33·5	0·052	8·25	16·2	7·77	12·9	0·634	1·90	19·9	73·5
0·333	32·7	0·050	9·13	7·20	9·06	15·5	0·576	0·637	21·4	77·9
0·287	32·4	0·047	9·54	4·27	9·61	16·5	0·520	0·301	22·3	78·8
0·238	31·5	0·045	10·2	2·28	10·5	17·9	0·466	0·031	24·0	78·8
0·158	26·2	0·017	6·08	5·40	5·16	12·1	0·251	0·282	25·9	43·7
0·139	25·5	0·016	6·46	3·23	5·81	13·8	0·241	0·122	26·9	52·0
0·118	24·0	0·017	7·13	1·74	6·54	15·9	0·232	0·022	29·3	57·2
0·092	23·7	0·014	7·37	0·754	6·62	16·4	0·184	0·006	30·2	58·0
0·084	28·7	0·008	4·78	4·32	4·07	7·92	0·120	0·176	19·3	29·3
0·075	27·8	0·008	5·18	2·60	4·43	9·72	0·119	0·113	19·6	40·3
0·065	26·0	0·009	5·93	1·42	5·68	12·4	0·124	0·015	21·7	48·3
0·051	25·6	0·008	6·18	0·619	5·78	13·0	0·101	0·005	22·6	49·0

$$I_x = \frac{t(a^3 + 3cd^2 + d^3)}{3} - \frac{t(a^2 + 2cd + d^2)^2}{4(a + b + c + d)} \tag{1.49}$$

It can also be shown that

$$\bar{x} = \frac{b^2 + 2ab + c^2}{2(a + b + c + d)} \tag{1.50}$$

$$I_y = \frac{t}{3}(b^3 + c^3 + 3ab^2) - \frac{t(b^2 + 2ab + c^2)^2}{4(a + b + c + d)} \tag{1.51}$$

1.2.4. Bulb Angles

For such angles (Fig. 1.7) the torsion constant, J, according to the Column Research Committee of Japan (1971) is

$$J = \tfrac{1}{3}st^3\left\{1 + \frac{4\cdot14 + 4\cdot71(r/t)^4}{s/t}\right\} \tag{1.52}$$

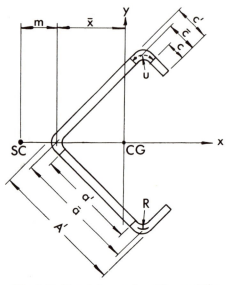

Fig. 1.5. Equal-leg angle with equal lips.

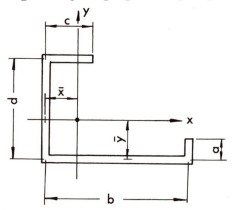

Fig. 1.6. Unequal-leg angle with unequal lips.

where r is the radius of the bulb and s is the length of the middle line of wall terminated by the centre of the bulb as shown in Fig. 1.7.

The warping constant of an angle with a bulb is (Fig. 1.8)

$$C_\mathrm{w} = \frac{t_1^3 h^3}{18} \left\{ \frac{1}{2} \left[1 + \left(\frac{t_2 b}{t_1 h} \right)^3 \right] + 4 \cdot 5 \pi \frac{(r/t_1)^4}{(h/t_1)} \right\} \tag{1.53}$$

where t_1, t_2, h, b and r are defined in Fig. 1.8.

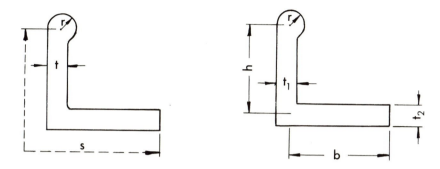

Fig. 1.7. Dimensions of a bulb angle for calculating its torsion constant, *J*.

Fig. 1.8. Dimensions of a bulb angle for calculating its warping constant, C_w.

Several examples will now be worked out using the aforementioned formulae.

1.3. SOLVED EXAMPLES

Example 1.1

For the hot-rolled angle shown in Fig. 1.9, compute the principal moments of inertia and determine the principal axes of inertia.

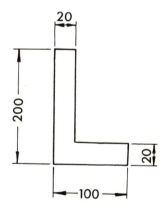

Fig. 1.9. Hot-rolled angle for Example 1.1 (dimensions in mm).

Solution

Substituting $b = 200$ mm, $a = 100$ mm, $t = 20$ mm in eqns (1.2) to (1.8) and eqn (1.10), yields:

From eqn (1.2)

$$\bar{x} = \frac{(200)(20) + (100)^2 - (20)^2}{2(200 + 100 - 20)} = 24\cdot29 \text{ mm}$$

From eqn (1.3)

$$\bar{y} = \frac{(200)^2 + (100)(20) - (20)^2}{2(200 + 100 - 20)} = 74\cdot29 \text{ mm}$$

From eqn (1.4)

$$I_x = (\tfrac{1}{12})(20)(200)^3 + (200)(20)\left(\frac{200}{2} - 74\cdot29\right)^2$$

$$+ \tfrac{1}{12}(100 - 20)(20)^3 + (100 - 20)(20)\left(74\cdot29 - \frac{20}{2}\right)^2$$

$$= 22\cdot64 \times 10^6 \text{ mm}^4$$

From eqn (1.5)

$$I_y = \tfrac{1}{12}(200)(20)^3 + (200)(20)\left(24\cdot29 - \frac{20}{2}\right)^2$$

$$+ (\tfrac{1}{12})(20)(100 - 20)^3 + (100 - 20)(20)\left(\frac{100 + 20}{2} - 24\cdot29\right)^2$$

$$= 3\cdot84 \times 10^6 \text{ mm}^4$$

From eqn (1.6)

$$I_{xy} = -(200)(20)\left(\frac{200}{2} - 74\cdot29\right)\left(24\cdot29 - \frac{20}{2}\right)$$

$$- (20)(100 - 20)\left(74\cdot29 - \frac{20}{2}\right)\left(\frac{100 + 20}{2} - 24\cdot29\right)$$

$$= -5\cdot14 \times 10^6 \text{ mm}^4$$

From eqn (1.7)

$$I_{min} = \frac{22\cdot64 \times 10^6 + 3\cdot84 \times 10^6}{2} -$$

$$- \sqrt{\left(\frac{22\cdot64 \times 10^6 - 3\cdot84 \times 10^6}{2}\right)^2 + (-5\cdot14 \times 10^6)^2}$$

$$= 13\cdot24 \times 10^6 - 10\cdot71 \times 10^6$$

$$= 2\cdot53 \times 10^6 \text{ mm}^4$$

From eqn (1.8)

$$I_{max} = 13 \cdot 24 \times 10^6 + 10 \cdot 71 \times 10^6$$
$$= 23 \cdot 95 \times 10^6 \text{ mm}^4$$

From eqn (1.10)

$$\tan 2\alpha = -\frac{(2)(-5 \cdot 14 \times 10^6)}{22 \cdot 64 \times 10^6 - 3 \cdot 84 \times 10^6}$$
$$= +0 \cdot 5468$$

Therefore

$$2\alpha = +28 \cdot 67°; \quad \text{or} \quad \alpha = +14 \cdot 34° \text{ (see Fig. 1.1)}.$$

Example 1.2

For the hot-rolled angle shown in Fig. 1.9, calculate the St Venant's torsion constant J using the approximate equation (1.12) and the more exact equation (1.13) assuming a fillet radius of 12 mm. Also calculate the warping constant using eqn (1.16).

Solution

From eqn (1.12), with $b = 200$ mm, $a = 100$ mm, $t = 20$ mm

$$J = \tfrac{1}{3}(20)^3(200 + 100 - 20)$$
$$= 747 \times 10^3 \text{ mm}^4$$

Referring to Fig. 1.2, $b_1 = b - t/2 = 200 - 10 = 190$ mm, and $b_2 = a - t/2 = 100 - 10 = 90$ mm.

From eqn (1.14)

$$D = (0 \cdot 343)(12) + (1 \cdot 172)(20)$$
$$= 27 \cdot 556 \text{ mm}$$

From eqn (1.15)

$$\gamma = 0 \cdot 0728 + 0 \cdot 0571(\tfrac{12}{20}) - 0 \cdot 0049(\tfrac{12}{20})^2$$
$$= 0 \cdot 1053$$

From eqn (1.13),

$$J = \tfrac{1}{3}(190)(20)^3 + \tfrac{1}{3}(90)(20)^3 + (0 \cdot 1053)(27 \cdot 556)^4 - (0 \cdot 315)(20)^4$$
$$= 757 \times 10^3 \text{ mm}^4$$

From eqn (1.16)

$$C_w = \frac{(200 - 10)^3(20)^3}{36} + \frac{(100 - 10)^3(20)^3}{36}$$
$$= 1686 \times 10^6 \text{ mm}^6$$

Example 1.3

For a $55 \times 35 \times 3$ mm angle, compute the properties using the approximate equations (1.17) to (1.26).

Solution

Substituting $b_1 = 55 - 3/2 = 53 \cdot 5$ mm, and $b_2 = 35 - 3/2 = 33 \cdot 5$ mm, then from eqn (1.17), area $= (53 \cdot 5 + 33 \cdot 5)(3) = 261$ mm².

From eqn (1.18)

$$\bar{x} = \frac{(33 \cdot 5)^2}{2(53 \cdot 5 + 33 \cdot 5)} = 6 \cdot 45 \text{ mm, from the centreline of the long leg}$$

From eqn (1.19)

$$\bar{y} = \frac{(53 \cdot 5)^2}{2(53 \cdot 5 + 33 \cdot 5)} = 16 \cdot 45 \text{ mm, from the centreline of the short leg}$$

From eqn (1.22)

$$I_x = \frac{(3)(53 \cdot 5)^3 (4 \times 33 \cdot 5 + 53 \cdot 5)}{12(53 \cdot 5 + 33 \cdot 5)}$$
$$= 82 \cdot 5 \times 10^3 \text{ mm}^4$$

From eqn (1.23)

$$I_y = \frac{(3)(33 \cdot 5)^3 (33 \cdot 5 + 4 \times 53 \cdot 5)}{12(53 \cdot 5 + 33 \cdot 5)}$$
$$= 26 \cdot 7 \times 10^3 \text{ mm}^4$$

From eqn (1.24)

$$I_{xy} = -\frac{(3)(53 \cdot 5)^2 (33 \cdot 5)^2}{4(53 \cdot 5 + 33 \cdot 5)}$$
$$= -27 \cdot 7 \times 10^3 \text{ mm}^4$$

From eqn (1.25)

$$J = \frac{(3)^3}{3} (53 \cdot 5 + 33 \cdot 5) = 783 \text{ mm}^4$$

From eqn (1.26)

$$C_w = \frac{(3)^3 (53 \cdot 5^3 + 33 \cdot 5^3)}{36}$$
$$= 143 \times 10^3 \text{ mm}^6$$

Example 1.4

Using eqns (1.27) to (1.33), compute the properties of a $125 \times 75 \times 13$ mm cold-formed angle, with an inside bend radius, $r = 3t = 39$ mm.

Solution

Referring to Fig. 1.4, width of long leg 'b' $= 125$ mm; width of short leg 'a' $= 75$ mm; thus

$$c_1 = a - (r + t) = 75 - (39 + 13) = 23 \text{ mm}$$
$$c_2 = b - (r + t) = 125 - (39 + 13) = 73 \text{ mm}$$

From eqn (1.27)

$$\text{Area } A = (23 + 73)(13) + \frac{\pi}{4}[(39 + 13)^2 - 39^2]$$
$$= 2177 \text{ mm}^2$$

With $A_1 = (23)(13) = 299$ mm^2; $A_2 = (73)(13) = 949$ mm^2;
$A_3 = (\pi/4)(39 + 13)^2 = 2123 \cdot 7$ mm^2; $A_4 = (\pi/4)(39)^2 = 1194 \cdot 6$ mm^2;
$x_1 = 75 - 23/2 = 63 \cdot 5$ mm; $x_2 = 13/2 = 6 \cdot 5$ mm;
$x_3 = (39 + 13) - [4/(3\pi)](39 + 13) = 29 \cdot 93$ mm;
$x_4 = (39 + 13) - [4/(3\pi)](39) = 35 \cdot 45$ mm; $y_1 = 13/2 = 6 \cdot 5$ mm;
$y_2 = 125 - 73/2 = 88 \cdot 5$ mm;
$y_3 = (39 + 13) - [4/(3\pi)](39 + 13) = 29 \cdot 93$ mm;
$y_4 = (39 + 13) - [4/(3\pi)](39) = 35 \cdot 45$ mm; then from eqn (1.28)

$$\bar{x} = \frac{(299)(63 \cdot 5) + (949)(6 \cdot 5) + (2123 \cdot 7)(29 \cdot 93) - (1194 \cdot 6)(35 \cdot 45)}{2177}$$
$$= 21 \cdot 30 \text{ mm}$$

From eqn (1.29)

$$\bar{y} = \frac{(299)(6 \cdot 5) + (949)(88 \cdot 5) + (2123 \cdot 7)(29 \cdot 93) - (1194 \cdot 6)(35 \cdot 45)}{2177}$$
$$= 49 \cdot 22 \text{ mm}$$

From eqn (1.30)
$$I_x = 3 \cdot 27 \times 10^6 \text{ mm}^4$$

From eqn (1.31)
$$I_y = 0 \cdot 96 \times 10^6 \text{ mm}^4$$

From eqn (1.32)
$$I_{xy} = -1 \cdot 29 \times 10^6 \text{ mm}^4$$

and from eqn (1.33)
$$J = \tfrac{1}{3}(13)^3\left[23 + 73 + \frac{\pi}{2}(39 + \tfrac{13}{2})\right]$$
$$= 122 \cdot 6 \times 10^3 \text{ mm}^4$$

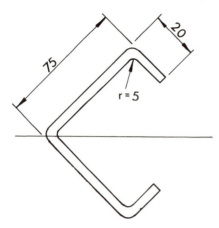

Fig. 1.10. Cold-formed equal-leg angle with equal lips for Example 1.5 (dimensions in mm).

Example 1.5

For the cold-formed equal-leg angle with equal lips shown in Fig. 1.10, calculate the cross-sectional properties.

Solution

Using the notation shown in Fig. 1.5, $A' = 75\cdot0$ mm; $c' = 20$ mm; $R = r + t/2 = 5 + 2\cdot5/2 = 6\cdot25$ mm; $a' = 75 - (2 \times 6\cdot25 + 2\cdot5) = 60$ mm; $\bar{a} = 75 - 2\cdot5 = 72\cdot5$ mm; $c = 20 - (6\cdot25 + 2\cdot5/2) = 12\cdot5$ mm; $\bar{c} = 20 - 2\cdot5/2 = 18\cdot75$ mm; and $u = (1\cdot57)(6\cdot25) = 9\cdot81$ mm. Thus, from eqn (1.37)

$$A = (2\cdot5)[(2)(60) + (2)(12\cdot5) + (3)(9\cdot81)] = 436 \text{ mm}^2$$

From eqn (1.38)

$$I_x = (2)(2\cdot5)\bigg\{(60)[\tfrac{1}{2}(\tfrac{60}{2} + 6\cdot25)^2 + (0\cdot0417)(60)^2]$$

$$+ (0\cdot143)(6\cdot25)^3 + (12\cdot5)\bigg[\tfrac{1}{2}\bigg(6\cdot25 + 60 - \frac{12\cdot5}{2}\bigg)^2$$

$$+ (0\cdot0417)(12\cdot5)^2\bigg] + (9\cdot81)[(0\cdot707)(60) + (0\cdot898)(6\cdot25)]^2$$

$$+ (0\cdot014)(6\cdot25)^3\bigg\}$$

$$= 468\ 400 \text{ mm}^4$$

From eqn (1.39)

$$\bar{x} = \frac{(2)(2\cdot5)}{436}\left\{ 60[(0\cdot353)(60) + (0\cdot293)(6\cdot25)]\right.$$

$$+ \left(\frac{9\cdot81}{2}\right)(0\cdot102)(6\cdot25) + (12\cdot5)[(0\cdot707)(60)$$

$$\left. + (0\cdot353)(12\cdot5) + (1\cdot707)(6\cdot25)] + (9\cdot81)[(0\cdot707)(60) + 6\cdot25]\right\}$$

$$= 29\cdot6 \text{ mm}$$

From eqn (1.40)

$$I_y = (2)(2\cdot5)\{(60)[(0\cdot353)(60) + (0\cdot293)(6\cdot25)]^2$$
$$+ (0\cdot0417)(60)^3 + (0\cdot015)(6\cdot25)^3 + (9\cdot81)[(0\cdot707)(60)$$
$$+ 6\cdot25]^2 + (12\cdot5)[(0\cdot707)(60) + (0\cdot353)(12\cdot5)$$
$$+ (1\cdot707)(6\cdot25)]^2 + (0\cdot0417)(12\cdot5)^3 + (0\cdot285)(6\cdot25)^3\}$$
$$- (436)(29\cdot6)^2$$
$$= 145\,500 \text{ mm}^4$$

From eqn (1.41)

$$m = \frac{(2\cdot5)(72\cdot5)(18\cdot75)^2}{(3\sqrt{2})(468\,400)}[(3)(72\cdot5) - (2)(18\cdot75)]$$

$$= 5\cdot77 \text{ mm}$$

From eqn (1·42)

$$J = \frac{(2\cdot5)^3}{3}[(2)(60) + (2)(12\cdot5) + (3)(9\cdot81)]$$

$$= 908 \text{ mm}^4$$

From eqn (1·43)

$$C_w = \frac{(2\cdot5)^2(72\cdot5)^4(18\cdot75)^3}{(18)(468\,400)}[(4)(72\cdot5) + (3)(18\cdot75)]$$

$$= 46\cdot7 \times 10^6 \text{ mm}^6$$

From eqn (1.44)

$$x_s = -(29\cdot6 + 5\cdot77) = -35\cdot37 \text{ mm}$$

From eqn (1.45)

$$\beta_1 = 0$$

From eqn (1·46)

$$\beta_2 = \frac{(\sqrt{2})(2 \cdot 5)}{(24)(145\ 500)} [(72 \cdot 5)^4 + (4)(72 \cdot 5)^3 (18 \cdot 75)$$

$$- (6)(72 \cdot 5)^2 (18 \cdot 75)^2 + (18 \cdot 75)^4] - (2)(-35 \cdot 37)$$

$$= 116 \cdot 5 \text{ mm}$$

Chapter 2

ANGLES AS TENSION MEMBERS

2.1. INTRODUCTION

Angle members carry tension in different arrangements such as: single angles (Fig. 2.1(a)); two angles connected to the same side of a gusset plate (Fig. 2.1(b)); two angles connected back to back on the opposite sides of a gusset plate (Fig. 2.1(c)); two angles in a star-shaped arrangement (Fig. 2.1(d)); or two angles connected to two gusset plates and joined together by stay plates (Fig. 2.1(e)). Several other arrangements are also possible. The load carrying capacity of such members is obtained by multiplying the permissible tensile stress by the effective net area. The effective net area is based on the net area and the arrangement of the end connections. For example, when the connections are by means of welds and there are no holes either drilled or punched, the net area is equal to the gross area of the section; however, when holes are either punched or drilled for riveted and bolted connections, deductions must be made for such holes. The holes are generally made slightly larger than the nominal diameter of the bolt or rivet to make the joining of the parts easier. Some specifications take into account also the damage caused by the punching and drilling operations and consider the effective hole diameter (d'_{eff}) larger than the actual hole diameter (d').

2.2. NET AREA OF ANGLES WITH HOLES

The net area of an angle with holes is computed as the net width (measured through the centre of the thickness) times the thickness. Figure 2.2(a) shows an angle section with holes in both legs with uniform pitch. The gauge distances, g, depend on the leg size. The

39

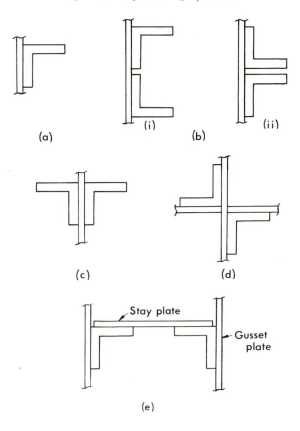

Fig. 2.1. Angles as tension members.

usual values of 'g' according to North American practice in SI metric units for different leg sizes are given in Table 2.1(a) and those in Imperial units are presented in Table 2.1(b). Tables 2.1(c) and (d) give the usual values of gauges according to Australian and British practices, respectively.

The angle section is first developed into a plate section with all holes in one plane as shown in Fig. 2.2(b); with $w_g =$ (gross width ABCD measured through the centre-of-thickness) $= (b + a - t)$ the deduction for the two holes on the line ABCD $= 2d'_{eff}$. Then the

$$\text{Net width} = w_n = (b + a - t) - 2d'_{eff} \qquad (2.1)$$

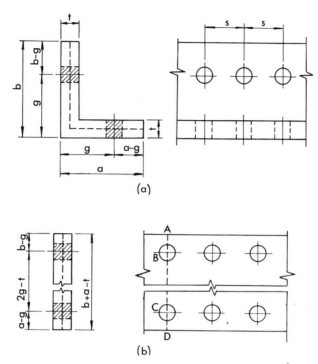

Fig. 2.2. Calculation of net area of angle with fastener holes—no stagger.

Therefore, net area = (net width)(thickness); or

$$A_n = (w_n)(t) \qquad (2.2)$$

When the holes in the two legs of the angle are staggered, as shown in Fig. 2.3, failure of the angle in tension can take place either along path ABC or along path ABDE. The net width along path ABC can be readily determined by subtracting the magnitude of one effective bolt hole diameter (d'_{eff}) (to take into account the presence of hole at B) from the gross width (w_g) along ABC. Now for staggered holes it is possible that the net width along the zigzag line ABDE is less than the net width along ABC. The net width along any zigzag line is calculated as follows:

Net width (w_n) = gross width $(w_g) - \sum d'_{\text{eff}}$ of all holes on the zigzag line $+ \sum \dfrac{s^2}{4g}$ for all the gauge spaces along the zigzag line $\qquad (2.3)$

Table 2.1(a)
Usual Gauges for Angles—SI Metric Units

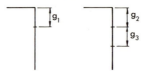

Nominal leg length (mm)	Maximum diameter of bolt (mm) for one gauge	Gauge distance g_1 (mm)	Maximum diameter of bolt (mm) for two gauges	Gauge distance g_2 (mm)	Gauge distance g_3 (mm) $g_3 \not< (2\frac{2}{3}) \times$ (bolt diameter)
200	36	115	30	80	80
150	36	90	24	55	65
125	30	80	20	45	54
100	27	65	—	—	—
90	24	60	—	—	—
80	24	50	—	—	—
75	24	45	—	—	—
65	24	35	—	—	—
60	24	30	—	—	—
55	22	27	—	—	—
50	16	30	—	—	—
45	16	23	—	—	—
35	12	17	—	—	—

Ref.: Canadian Institute of Steel Construction (1980).

Table 2.1(b)
Usual Gauges for Angles—Imperial Units

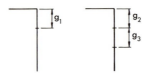

Nominal leg length (in)	8	7	6	5	4	$3\frac{1}{2}$	3	$2\frac{1}{2}$	2	$1\frac{3}{4}$	$1\frac{1}{2}$	$1\frac{3}{8}$	$1\frac{1}{4}$	1
g_1 (in)	$4\frac{1}{2}$	4	$3\frac{1}{2}$	3	$2\frac{1}{2}$	2	$1\frac{3}{4}$	$1\frac{3}{8}$	$1\frac{1}{8}$	1	$\frac{7}{8}$	$\frac{7}{8}$	$\frac{3}{4}$	$\frac{5}{8}$
g_2 (in)	3	$2\frac{1}{2}$	$2\frac{1}{4}$	2	—	—	—	—	—	—	—	—	—	—
g_3 (in)	3	3	$2\frac{1}{2}$	$1\frac{3}{4}$	—	—	—	—	—	—	—	—	—	—

Ref.: American Institute of Steel Construction (1980).

Table 2.1(c)
Gauge Distances for Angles According to Australian Practice

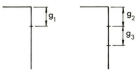

Nominal leg length (mm)	Maximum diameter of bolt (mm)	Gauge distances		
		g_1 (mm)	g_2 (mm)	g_3 (mm)
200	24	120	75	75
150	20	90	55	55
130	20	75	45	50
100	20	55	—	—
90	20	55	—	—
75	20	45	—	—
65	16	35	—	—
60	16	35	—	—

Ref.: Australian Institute of Steel Construction (1979).

where s is the centre-to-centre spacing of two consecutive holes along the zigzag line, measured along the length of angle (staggered pitch); and g is the centre-to-centre spacing of the same two holes measured perpendicular to the length of the angle (gauge). The gauge for holes in opposite legs should be measured along the centre of the thickness of the section.

2.3. EFFECTIVE NET AREA

Average tensile stress of an angle at failure, calculated as (failure load)/(net area), is generally less than the coupon tensile strength, unless both legs of the angle are connected in such a manner as to provide a uniform stress distribution. This discrepancy is due to the concentration of shear stress in the vicinity of the connection, creating shear lag action. Most specifications account for this by reducing the effective net area of angles in tension connected by one leg only, as shown below.

Table 2.1(d)
Usual Gauges for Angles—British Practice

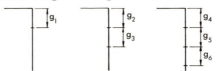

	Gauge distances					
Nominal leg length (mm)	g_1 (mm)	g_2 (mm)	g_3 (mm)	g_4 (mm)	g_5 (mm)	g_6 (mm)
229	—	75	100	65	65	65
203	—	75	75	55	55	55
178	—	55	75	—	—	—
152	90	55	55	—	—	—
137	75	45	50	—	—	—
127	75	45	50	—	—	—
102	55	—	—	—	—	—
89	55	—	—	—	—	—
76	45	—	—	—	—	—
63	35	—	—	—	—	—
57	32	—	—	—	—	—
51	30	—	—	—	—	—
44	25	—	—	—	—	—
38	22	—	—	—	—	—
32	20	—	—	—	—	—
25	15	—	—	—	—	—

Ref.: Constructional Steel Research and Development Organization (1972).

(a) *American Institute of Steel Construction (1978) (sections 1.14.2.2 and 1.14.2.3)*
If the connection has three or more rivets or bolts per line in the direction of stress, then the

Effective net area = (0·85)(net area)

If the connection has two fasteners per line in the direction of stress, the

Effective net area = (0·75)(net area)

For angle splices, effective net area is equal to actual net area but not greater than 85% of gross area.

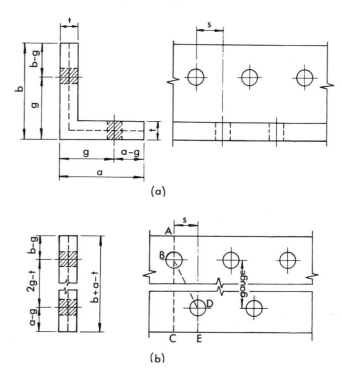

Fig. 2.3. Calculation of net area of angle with fastener holes—with stagger.

(b) *British Standards Institution (1969) (subclause 42a), Indian Standards Institution (1984) (clauses 4.2.1.1 and 4.2.1.2) and Standards Association of Australia (1981) (clause 7.3.2(a))*

(i) For single angle connected through one leg, the effective net area of the angle $= A_1[1 + (3A_2)/(3A_1 + A_2)]$ where A_1 is the net cross-sectional area of connected leg, and A_2 is the gross cross-sectional area of the unconnected leg. Referring to Fig. 2.4, $A_2 = (a - t/2)t$.

(ii) For two angles, back-to-back and connected to one side of a gusset plate as shown in Fig. 2.1(b), the effective cross-sectional area of each angle $= A_1[1 + (5A_2)/(5A_1 + A_2)]$.

(c) *American Association of State Highway and Transportation Officials (1983) (Article 10.9)*

For angles arranged as in Figs 2.1(a) and (b) the effective net area = net area of the connected leg + (1/2)(area of the outstanding leg). For

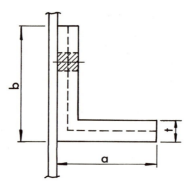

Fig. 2.4. Definition of area of unconnected leg of a single angle.

angles arranged as shown in Figs 2.1(c) and (e), the effective net area = actual net area.

(d) *Canadian Standards Association* (*1978*) (*clause 12.3.4*)
CAN3-S16.1-M78 specifications do not consider the effect of eccentricity of load when this is applied through a gusset plate connected to one leg of the angle; the effective net area is taken as the actual net area. However, the net area is limited to the following maximum values depending on the ratio of the yield stress σ_y to the ultimate stress σ_u of the material:

If $\dfrac{\sigma_y}{\sigma_u} \leqslant 0 \cdot 75$, $A_n \not> (0 \cdot 85)(\text{gross area } A_g)$

If $0 \cdot 75 < \dfrac{\sigma_y}{\sigma_u} \leqslant 0 \cdot 85$, $A_n \not> 0 \cdot 90 A_g$

If $0 \cdot 85 < \dfrac{\sigma_y}{\sigma_u}$, $A_n \not> 0 \cdot 95 A_g$

Such restrictions are not present in the Australian (AS 1250-1981), British (BS 449: 1969) or Indian (IS: 800-1984) Standards. The American Institute of Steel Construction (1978) specification limits the maximum net area to 85% of the gross area only for angle splices.

In actual practice, these various specifications lead to practically the same design, as far as the effective net area is concerned.

(e) *British Standard CP 118-1969 for Aluminium* (*British Standards Institution, 1969*)

For eccentrically loaded single-bay tension members of single and double angles, the effective net area is obtained by deducting part of the area of the outstanding leg from the gross area as shown in Table 7.15.

For end bays of multiple-bay aluminium angles, the effective net area must be calculated in the same manner as for single-bay angles. For intermediate bays of multiple-bay angles, the effective area is the gross area minus the deductions for holes.

2.4. DOUBLE ANGLES IN TENSION

Figures 2.1(b), (c) and (e) show three of the several possible ways in which double angle tension members can be connected to gusset plates. When two angles are connected back to back to the same side of the gusset plate as in Fig. 2.1(b), their behaviour is practically the same as that of two single angles each connected by one leg. As already seen, most specifications treat these as if they were two single angles. If the two angles are connected back to back on the opposite sides of a gusset plate, Fig. 2.1(c), the symmetry causes a more favourable condition to develop as shown in Fig. 2.5(a); here, the two angles tend to press against the gusset plate. The force, *P*, acts close to the centroidal axis of the angle, and the behaviour is similar to that of two concentrically loaded angles.

For the double angles shown in Fig. 2.1(e), the stay plates create again a favourable condition as shown in Fig. 2.5(b). In such a case, the full net area can be considered as effective. Without the stay plates, the favourable distribution of stresses is no longer present and their behaviour is similar to two single angles. For the stay plates to be effective they should be located as near to the gusset plates as practicable.

2.5. EFFECTIVE DIAMETER OF HOLES

The rivet or bolt holes are usually fabricated 1·5 to 2 mm larger than the nominal diameter of the rivet or bolt. In addition, punching or drilling operation causes damage to an additional 1·5 to 2 mm material

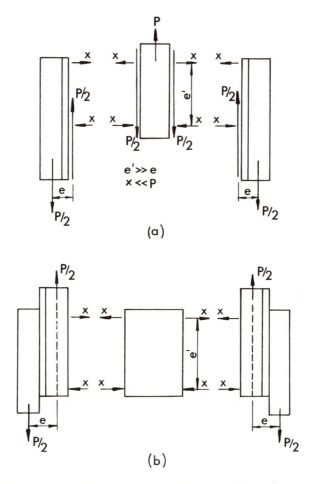

Fig. 2.5. Load distribution in double angles in tension.

surrounding the holes. Therefore, according to specifications of the Canadian Standards Association (1978), clause 12.3.2, in calculating the net area of angles with rivet or bolt holes, the effective diameter of the bolt hole, d'_{eff}, is taken as 2 mm greater than the nominal diameter of the rivet or bolt hole d', while the specifications of the American Institute of Steel Construction (1978), section 1.14.4, using Imperial units, require the effective diameter of the bolt hole to be $\frac{1}{16}$ in greater than the nominal diameter of the rivet or bolt hole. According to SAA

Steel Structures Code AS 1250-1981 (Standards Association of Australia, 1981), clause 4.4.1, the effective diameter of a hole is the same as the actual diameter of the hole (i.e., no allowance is given for the damage caused by the punching or drilling of the holes). Subclause 17a of British Standard 449: Part 2: 1969 (British Standards Institution, 1969a) states that the hole can be assumed to be 2 mm larger than the nominal diameter of the rivet or bolt, unless otherwise specified. Also, according to Indian Standard 800–1984 (Indian Standards Institution, 1984), clause 3.6.1, for rivet diameters equal to or less than 25 mm, the diameter of the hole is taken as 1·5 mm larger than the diameter of the rivet. For rivet diameters greater than 25 mm, the diameter of the hole is 2·0 mm larger than the diameter of the rivet. For all sizes of bolts, the bolt hole is assumed to be 1·5 mm larger than the nominal diameter of the bolt. As is the case with Australian specifications, British and Indian specifications also give no allowance for damage due to punching and drilling operations.

The damage to the surrounding material is considerable when holes are punched; however, no significant damage occurs if holes are drilled. Therefore, it is good practice to take the effective diameter of punched holes slightly larger than their actual diameters, whether required by the Codes of Practice or not.

2.6. PLACEMENT OF WELDS IN END CONNECTIONS

When angle members are subjected to static loads only, the fillet welds between the angles and the gusset plates can be placed in any manner, as long as the total length of weld is sufficient to carry the load; see Fig. 2.6(a). However, when a member is subjected to repeated loads (e.g. fatigue), fasteners or welds in the end connections should be placed such that their centre of gravity lies on the centroidal axis of the member, as shown in Fig. 2.6(b). Otherwise, provision must be made in the design for the effect of the resulting eccentricity.

2.7. ANGLES SUBJECTED TO ECCENTRIC TENSILE FORCE

The stress σ at any point (x, y) on the cross-section of an angle subjected to a tensile force, P, acting at point (x_p, y_p), Fig. 2.7, is given

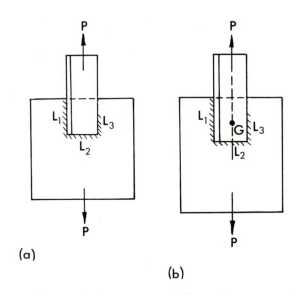

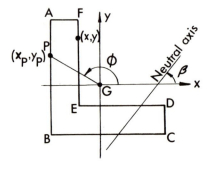

Fig. 2.6. Placement of fillet welds.

Fig. 2.7. An angle subjected to eccentric tensile force.

by (Batho, 1915)

$$\sigma = P\left[\frac{1}{A} + \frac{I_x y_p}{I_x^2 - I_{xy}^2}\left(y - \frac{I_{xy}x}{I_y}\right) + \frac{I_y x_p}{I_y^2 - I_{xy}^2}\left(x - \frac{I_{xy}y}{I_x}\right)\right] \qquad (2.4)$$

The angle of inclination of the neutral axis with the x-axis is given by

$$\tan \beta = \frac{I_x - I_{xy}\tan \phi}{I_{xy} - I_y \tan \phi} \qquad (2.5)$$

where ϕ is the angle made by the radius vector GP with the x-axis, Fig. 2.7.

The stress σ can also be calculated in terms of β as

$$\sigma = P\left[\frac{1}{A} + \frac{y - x \tan \beta}{I_{xy} - I_y \tan \beta}x_p\right] \qquad (2.6)$$

or

$$\sigma = P\left[\frac{1}{A} + \frac{y - x \tan \beta}{I_x - I_{xy}\tan \beta}y_p\right] \qquad (2.7)$$

The above formulae take into account the axial tensile stress and the stresses due to bending about the two principal axes of the cross-section.

2.8. THE S-POLYGON

A graphical method is used to study the effect of the variation of the point of application of the tensile force on the bending stress. This graphical method, sometimes referred to as the S-polygon, was first introduced by Johnson (1906); it gives at a glance the location and magnitude of the maximum bending stress in the angle for any position of load. From eqn (2.6), the stress due to bending is

$$\sigma_{\text{bending}} = P\left(\frac{y - x \tan \beta}{I_{xy} - I_y \tan \beta}\right)x_p \qquad (2.8)$$

Substituting for $\tan \beta$ from eqn (2.5) in eqn (2.8) and rearranging

$$\sigma_{\text{bending}} = Pr\left[\frac{(yI_y - xI_{xy})\sin \phi + (xI_x - yI_{xy})\cos \phi}{I_xI_y - I_{xy}^2}\right] \qquad (2.9)$$

where

$$r = \sqrt{x_p^2 + y_p^2} \qquad (2.10)$$

Eqn (2.9) can be written as

$$\sigma_{\text{bending}} = \frac{M}{S} = \frac{Pr}{S} \qquad (2.11)$$

where M is the bending moment $= Pr$, and S is the modified section modulus, given by

$$S = \frac{I_x I_y - I_{xy}^2}{(yI_y - xI_{xy})\sin\phi + (xI_x - yI_{xy})\cos\phi} \qquad (2.12)$$

For any given point of load application, ϕ is known and therefore $\sin\phi$ and $\cos\phi$ can be calculated. If the stress at a point (x, y) is required for different values of ϕ then eqn (2.12) becomes useful, since it is a polar equation of a straight line with a radius vector S and angle ϕ. This line is termed the S-line for the point (x, y). Figure 2.8 shows the S-line for point B. Similar S-lines can be drawn for all critical points to obtain an S-polygon. Referring to Fig. 2.7, the critical points for maximum bending stress are: A, B, C, D and F. The S-polygon will thus have five sides corresponding to the five critical points ('E' is not considered to be a critical point). Even if an S-line is drawn for point E, it will be outside the polygon bounded by the S-lines for points A, B, C, D and F, thus indicating that the bending stress at E will not be critical, no matter where the load point is.

Instead of drawing the S-lines for each critical point, the S-polygon can be readily drawn by computing the coordinates for the apexes of the polygon. If it is desired to compute the coordinates of the point of

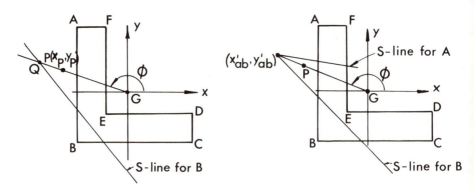

Fig. 2.8. S-line for point B in angle subjected to eccentric tensile force.

Fig. 2.9. Intersection of the two S-lines for points A and B.

intersection of the S-lines for any two points, say A and B (point (x'_{ab}, y'_{ab}) in Fig. 2.9), the following procedure can be adopted.

Rewriting eqn (2.12) for point A, using $S \sin \phi = y'_{ab}$, and $S \cos \phi = x'_{ab}$, we find

$$y'_{ab}(yI_y - xI_{xy}) + x'_{ab}(xI_x - yI_{xy}) = I_x I_y - I_{xy}^2 \qquad (2.13)$$

Since point (x'_{ab}, y'_{ab}) lies on the S-line for point A, we can substitute x_a and y_a for x and y in eqn (2.13) to yield

$$y'_{ab}(y_a I_y - x_a I_{xy}) + x'_{ab}(x_a I_x - y_a I_{xy}) = I_x I_y - I_{xy}^2 \qquad (2.14)$$

Similarly for point B (x_b, y_b)

$$y'_{ab}(y_b I_y - x_b I_{xy}) + x'_{ab}(x_b I_x - y_b I_{xy}) = I_x I_y - I_{xy}^2 \qquad (2.15)$$

Solving eqns (2.14) and (2.15) for x'_{ab} and y'_{ab}, yields

$$x'_{ab} = \frac{(x_a - x_b)I_{xy} - (y_a - y_b)I_y}{x_a y_b - x_b y_a} \qquad (2.16a)$$

$$y'_{ab} = \frac{(x_a - x_b)I_x - (y_a - y_b)I_{xy}}{x_a y_b - x_b y_a} \qquad (2.16b)$$

Equations (2.16a) and (2.16b) can be considerably simplified since any two consecutive corner points of an angle section have either the x or the y coordinates equal. For example, referring to Fig. 2.8

$$x_a = x_b, \qquad x_e = x_f, \qquad x_c = x_d$$

and

$$y_a = y_f, \qquad y_b = y_c, \qquad y_d = y_e$$

For two points on an angle cross-section lying on a line parallel to the y-axis, the x-coordinates are the same. Thus, eqns (2.16a) and (2.16b) reduce to

$$x'_{ab} = \frac{I_y}{x_a} = \frac{I_y}{x_b}; \qquad y'_{ab} = \frac{I_{xy}}{x_a} = \frac{I_{xy}}{x_b} \qquad (2.17)$$

For two points on an angle cross-section lying on a line parallel to the x-axis, the coordinates of the point of intersection of the corresponding S-lines are

$$x'_{ab} = \frac{I_{xy}}{y_a} = \frac{I_{xy}}{y_b}; \qquad y'_{ab} = \frac{I_x}{y_a} = \frac{I_x}{y_b} \qquad (2.18)$$

Since I_x, I_y, I_{xy} and the coordinates of all corners of the angle with

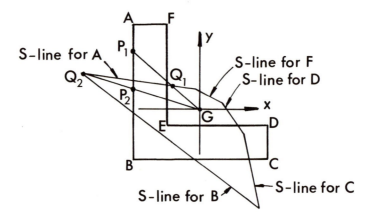

Fig. 2.10. A typical S-polygon.

respect to the centroidal axes Gx and Gy are known, the coordinates of the apexes of the S-polygon are very easily computed and the S-polygon can be readily drawn. A typical S-polygon is shown in Fig. 2.10.

To determine the point of maximum stress, simply join the centroid, G, with the load point, P. Line GP, extended if necessary, intersects one side of the S-polygon and the point corresponding to the S-line intersected is the most highly stressed point. If the line GP intersects an apex, the points corresponding to the two adjoining sides of the apex of the S-polygon are both critical and have the same maximum stress. For example, in Fig. 2.10 if:

(i) Load acts at P_1: GP_1 intersects the S-line for A.
Point A is the most highly stressed point

$$\sigma_{\text{bending}} = \frac{(\text{Load})(GP_1)}{(GQ_1)}$$

(ii) Load acts at P_2: GP_2 intersects one of the apexes of the S-polygon. The adjoining sides are the S-lines for A and B. Points A and B are the most highly stressed points, thus

$$\sigma_{\text{bending}} = \frac{(\text{Load})(GP_2)}{(GQ_2)}$$

2.9. EFFECT OF RESIDUAL STRESSES

Residual stresses present within an angle tension member will cause some portion of the cross-section to yield before other portions. However, as the tensile load is increased, the stress on the yielded portion remains sensibly at the yield strength of the material. Eventually, the stress on the remaining portions also reaches the yield strength. Thus, residual stresses do not cause any reduction in the ultimate load-carrying capacity of angle members in tension.

2.10. MAXIMUM PERMISSIBLE SLENDERNESS RATIOS

The maximum slenderness ratios of tension members should be limited for serviceability conditions created by vibrations, rattling, etc. The maximum values permitted vary among the various specifications, depending on the type of structure in which the angle members are used.

2.11. SOLVED EXAMPLES

Example 2.1
For the angle shown in Fig. 2.11(a), calculate the net area. Effective bolt hole diameter = 24 mm.

Solution
The angle section is developed as shown in Fig. 2.11(b) using the dimensions measured along the centre of the thickness.
Net width of path 1–2–4–5 (Fig. 2.11(b)) is

$$240 - (2)(24) = 240 - 48 = 192 \text{ mm}$$

Net width of path 1–2–3–4–5 (*zig-zag line*) from eqn (2.3) is

$$240 - (3)(24) + \left[\frac{75^2}{(4)(65)} + \frac{75^2}{(4)(110)} \right] = 202 \cdot 4 \text{ mm}$$

Path 1–2–4–5 gives the least net width. Therefore

$$\text{Net area} = (\text{net width})(\text{thickness})$$
$$= (192)(10) = 1920 \text{ mm}^2$$

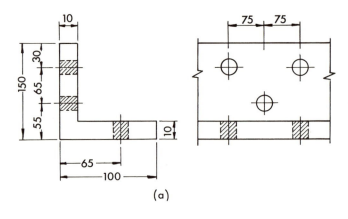

(a)

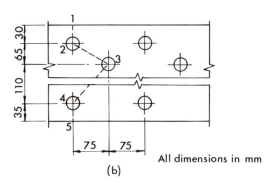

All dimensions in mm

(b)

Fig. 2.11. Angle in Example 2.1.

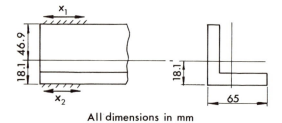

All dimensions in mm

Fig. 2.12. Angle in Example 2.2.

Example 2.2
A $65 \times 65 \times 5$ mm angle is to be connected to a gusset plate by means of 6 mm size fillet welds. If the total length of weld required is 200 mm and is to be placed as shown in Fig. 2.12, proportion the weld such that the moments of the weld capacities about the gravity axis of the member are balanced.

Solution
From Table 1.1(a) the centroid of a $65 \times 65 \times 5$ mm angle, shown in Fig. 2.12, is $18 \cdot 1$ mm above the heel.
    Total length of weld $= x_1 + x_2 = 200$ mm. Taking moments about the gravity axis

$$(x_2)(18 \cdot 1) = (x_1)(46 \cdot 9)$$

Solving the two equations

$$x_1 = 55 \cdot 7 \text{ mm}, \qquad x_2 = 144 \cdot 3 \text{ mm}$$

The values will be rounded off in practice to 56 mm and 144 mm, respectively.

Example 2.3
A $125 \times 75 \times 10$ mm angle is subjected to repeated stress variations making any connection eccentricity undesirable. If a total of 330 mm length of weld is required, proportion the placement of the welds along the sides and end of the angle.

Solution
From Table 1.1(b) the centroid of the angle, shown in Fig. 2.13, is $42 \cdot 8$ mm above the heel.

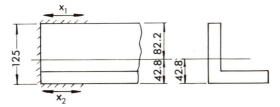

All dimensions in mm

Fig. 2.13. Angle in Example 2.3.

Total length of weld: $x_1 + x_2 + 125 = 330$ mm. Taking moments about the gravity axis

$$(x_1)(82 \cdot 2) + (125)\left(82 \cdot 2 - \frac{125}{2}\right) = (x_2)(42 \cdot 8)$$

Solving for x_1 and x_2

$$x_1 = 50 \cdot 5 \text{ mm}, \qquad x_2 = 154 \cdot 5 \text{ mm}$$

Use $x_1 = 50$ mm and $x_2 = 155$ mm

Example 2.4

Locate the neutral axis of a $65 \times 65 \times 5$ mm hot-rolled angle shown in Fig. 2.14, when a 10 kN tension load acts at a point $(-23 \cdot 1, 46 \cdot 9)$ mm.

Solution

From Table 1.1(a): $A = 625 \text{ mm}^2$; $I_x = I_y = (0 \cdot 255)(10^6) \text{ mm}^4$; $I_{xy} = (-0 \cdot 153)(10^6) \text{ mm}^4$; $\bar{x} = \bar{y} = 18 \cdot 1$ mm. Referring to Fig. 2.7

$$\tan \phi = \frac{46 \cdot 9}{-23 \cdot 1} = -2 \cdot 0303$$

From eqn (2.5)

$$\tan \beta = \frac{[(0 \cdot 255)(10^6)] - [(-0 \cdot 153)(10^6)](-2 \cdot 0303)}{[(-0 \cdot 153)(10^6)] - [(0 \cdot 255)(10^6)](-2 \cdot 0303)} = -0 \cdot 1524$$

Hence $180° - \beta = 8 \cdot 67°$, or $\beta = 171 \cdot 33°$. To locate the neutral axis we

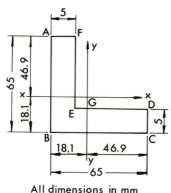

All dimensions in mm

Fig. 2.14. Angle in Example 2.4.

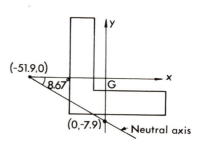

All dimensions in mm

Fig. 2.15. Location of neutral axis for angle in Example 2.4.

use eqn (2.6) and equate the stress σ to zero. Thus

$$\sigma = P\left[\frac{1}{A} + \frac{y - x \tan \beta}{I_{xy} - I_y \tan \beta} x_p\right] = 0$$

i.e., $\dfrac{1}{625} + \dfrac{y - x(-0\cdot1524)}{[(-0\cdot153)(10^6)] - [(0\cdot255)(10^6)](-0\cdot1524)}(-23\cdot1) = 0$

Or,

$$x + 6\cdot56y + 51\cdot87 = 0$$

To obtain the point of intersection of the neutral axis with the x-axis we put $y = 0$; hence, $x = -51\cdot9$ mm. Similarly, to obtain the point of intersection of the neutral axis with the y-axis we substitute $x = 0$, giving $y = -7\cdot9$. The neutral axis is shown in Fig. 2.15.

Example 2.5
Compute the stress at point A for the $65 \times 65 \times 5$ mm angle shown in Fig. 2.14, when a 10 kN tensile force acts at a point whose coordinates with respect to centroidal x and y axes are $-23\cdot1$ and $46\cdot9$ mm.

Solution
From Table 1.1(a): $A = 625$ mm^2; $I_x = I_y = (0\cdot255)(10^6)$ mm^4; $I_{xy} = (-0\cdot153)(10^6)$ mm^4; $\bar{x} = \bar{y} = 18\cdot1$ mm. Referring to Fig. 2.14, the coordinates of point A are $-18\cdot1$, $46\cdot9$ mm. Using eqn (2.4), with $x = -18\cdot1$, $y = 46\cdot9$, $x_p = -23\cdot1$, $y_p = 46\cdot9$, the stress σ at A is

$$\sigma = 10\,000\left[\frac{1}{625} + \frac{(0\cdot255)(10^6)(46\cdot9)}{[(0\cdot255)(10^6)]^2 - [(-0\cdot153)(10^6)]^2}\right.$$
$$\times\left(46\cdot9 - \frac{(-0\cdot153)(10^6)(-18\cdot1)}{(0\cdot255)(10^6)}\right)$$
$$+ \frac{(0\cdot255)(10^6)(-23\cdot1)}{[(0\cdot255)(10^6)]^2 - [(-0\cdot153)(10^6)]^2}$$
$$\left.\times\left(-18\cdot1 - \frac{(-0\cdot153)(10^6)(46\cdot9)}{(0\cdot255)(10^6)}\right)\right]$$
$$= 105 \text{ MPa}$$

Example 2.6
Construct the S-polygon for a $65 \times 65 \times 5$ mm angle.

Solution

Referring to Fig. 2.14 and Table 1.1(a): $I_x = I_y = (0 \cdot 255)(10^6)$ mm^4; $I_{xy} = (-0 \cdot 153)(10^6)$ mm^4; $\bar{x} = \bar{y} = 18 \cdot 1$ mm. Coordinates of the corners with reference to the centroidal x and y axes are: A $(-18 \cdot 1, 46 \cdot 9)$ mm; B $(-18 \cdot 1, -18 \cdot 1)$ mm; C $(46 \cdot 9, -18 \cdot 1)$ mm; D $(46 \cdot 9, -13 \cdot 1)$ mm; E $(-13 \cdot 1, -13 \cdot 1)$ mm; F $(-13 \cdot 1, 46 \cdot 9)$ mm. Sides AB, EF, CD are parallel to the y-axis. Therefore, using eqn (2.17)

$$x'_{ab} = \frac{I_y}{x_a} = \frac{I_y}{x_b} = \frac{(0 \cdot 255)(10^6)}{-18 \cdot 1} = -14\,088 \text{ mm}^3$$

$$y'_{ab} = \frac{I_{xy}}{x_a} = \frac{I_{xy}}{x_b} = \frac{(-0 \cdot 153)(10^6)}{-18 \cdot 1} = 8453 \text{ mm}^3$$

Similarly

$$x'_{ef} = \frac{(0 \cdot 255)(10^6)}{-13 \cdot 1} = -19\,466 \text{ mm}^3; \qquad y'_{ef} = \frac{(-0 \cdot 153)(10^6)}{-13 \cdot 1}$$
$$= 11\,679 \text{ mm}^3$$

$$x'_{cd} = \frac{(0 \cdot 255)(10^6)}{46 \cdot 9} = 5437 \text{ mm}^3; \qquad y'_{cd} = \frac{(-0 \cdot 153)(10^6)}{46 \cdot 9} = -3262 \text{ mm}^3$$

Sides AF, DE and BC are parallel to the x-axis. Therefore, using eqn (2.18)

$$x'_{af} = \frac{(-0 \cdot 153)(10^6)}{46 \cdot 9} = -3262 \text{ mm}^3; \qquad y'_{af} = \frac{(0 \cdot 255)(10^6)}{46 \cdot 9}$$
$$= 5437 \text{ mm}^3$$

$$x'_{de} = \frac{(-0 \cdot 153)(10^6)}{-13 \cdot 1} = 11\,679 \text{ mm}^3; \qquad y'_{de} = \frac{(0 \cdot 255)(10^6)}{-13 \cdot 1} = -19\,466 \text{ mm}^3$$

$$x'_{bc} = \frac{(-0 \cdot 153)(10^6)}{-18 \cdot 1} = 8453 \text{ mm}^3; \qquad y'_{bc} = \frac{(0 \cdot 255)(10^6)}{-18 \cdot 1} = -14\,088 \text{ mm}^3$$

The required S-polygon is drawn to a convenient scale as shown in Fig. 2.16.

Example 2.7

For a $65 \times 65 \times 5$ mm angle, a tensile load of 10 kN can act anywhere along the path 1–2–3–4 in Fig. 2.16. Using the S-polygon constructed

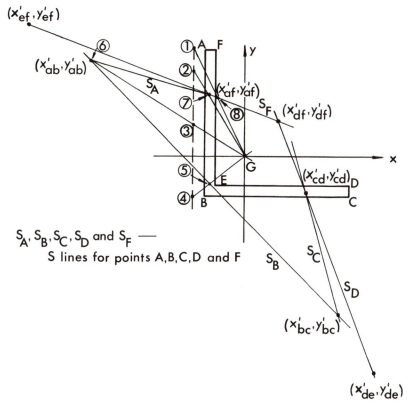

Fig. 2.16. S-polygon for a $65 \times 65 \times 5$ mm angle in Example 2.6.

in Example 2.6, determine the most critical point for bending. Compute the bending stress and the total stress.

Solution
If the load acts anywhere between 1 and 2 in Fig. 2.16, the radius vector cuts the S-line for point F and therefore point F has the maximum bending stress.

Load at 1: Draw the radius vector r joining G to load point 1. Length G to $1 = 53$ mm. This intersects the S-polygon at point 8 in Fig. 2.16. The value of S is obtained by measuring the length of the line from point G to point 8. Therefore

$S = $ (length G–8)(scale for S-polygon) $= 5800 \text{ m}^3$

$M = (10\ 000\ \text{N})(\text{length G–1}) = 530\ 000\ \text{N.mm}$

$$\sigma_{\text{bending}} \text{ at } F = \frac{M}{S} = \frac{530\ 000}{5800} = 91\ \text{MPa}$$

$$\text{Axial stress} = \frac{P}{A} = \frac{10\ 000}{625} = 16\ \text{MPa}$$

Total stress at $F = 16 + 91 = 107\ \text{MPa}$

Load at 2: Draw the radius vector r joining G to load point 2. This intersects the S-polygon at point 7, the apex joining the S-lines for A and F $(x'_{\text{af}}, y'_{\text{af}})$.

Maximum stress occurs at A and F, both stresses being equal. Value of S is obtained by measuring the length from point G to point 7. Therefore

$S = $ (length G–7)(scale for S-polygon) $= 6400\ \text{mm}^3$

$M = (10\ 000)(\text{length G–2}) = 450\ 000\ \text{N.mm}$

$$\sigma_{\text{bending}} \text{ at A or } F = \frac{450\ 000}{6400} = 70\ \text{MPa}$$

σ_{total} at A or $F = 16 + 70 = 86\ \text{MPa}$

When the load acts between 2 and 3, point A will have the maximum stress.

Load at 3: Length G to $3 = $ radius vector r. When extended, the radius vector intersects the S-polygon at point 6, the apex joining the S-lines for A and B $(x'_{\text{ab}}, y'_{\text{ab}})$. The maximum stress occurs at A and B, both stresses being equal. Therefore

$S = $ (length G–6)(scale for S-polygon) $= 16\ 400\ \text{m}^3$

$M = (10\ 000)(\text{length G–3}) = 270\ 000\ \text{N.mm}$

Hence

$$\sigma_{\text{bending}} \text{ (at A or B)} = \frac{M}{S} = \frac{270\ 000}{16\ 400} = 16\ \text{MPa}$$

Thus

σ_{total} (at A or B) $= 16 + 16 = 32\ \text{MPa}$

When the load acts between 3 and 4, point B will have the maximum stress.

Load at 4: Radius vector, r = length from point G to 4. This radius vector intersects the S-line for B at point 5. Therefore

S = (length G–5)(scale for S-polygon) = 4 000 mm^3

M = (10 000)(length G–4) = 300 000 N.mm

Hence

$$\sigma_{bending} \text{ at B} = \frac{300\,000}{4\,000} = 75 \text{ MPa}$$

Thus

σ_{total} at B = 16 + 75 = 91 MPa

Chapter 3

ANGLES AS BEAMS

3.1. INTRODUCTION

When an angle section is acted upon by a couple M, the neutral axis of the cross-section will coincide with the axis of the couple M if and only if the couple vector M is along one of the principal centroidal axes of inertia of the section. Figure 3.1(a) shows an unequal angle section with principal axes 'u–u' and 'v–v', and acted upon by a moment M whose vector is along the 'u–u' axis; in this case the neutral axis coincides with the axis of the couple vector ('u–u' axis). Similarly, in Fig. 3.1(b) the moment is directed along the minor principal axis of inertia 'v–v' and therefore the neutral axis coincides with 'v–v'. The usual equations for simple bending are applicable in such cases. Thus, the bending stress in the angle in Fig. 3.1(a) at any point is

$$\sigma = \frac{(M)(v)}{I_u} \qquad (3.1a)$$

and, in Fig. 3.1(b) the stress is

$$\sigma = \frac{(M)(u)}{I_v} \qquad (3.1b)$$

where I_u and I_v are the principal centroidal moments of inertia of the section and u and v are the coordinates of the point with respect to the axes u–u and v–v.

3.2. ANGLE SECTION ACTED UPON BY A COUPLE M IN ANY ARBITRARY DIRECTION

If the couple vector M is not directed along one of the principal centroidal axes, the neutral axis does not coincide with the axis of the

64

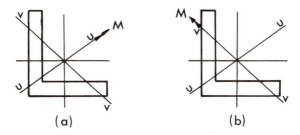

Fig. 3.1. Angle section subjected to a couple *M* along a principal axis.

couple. The principle of superposition may be used in such cases to determine the stresses at any point and to locate the neutral axis.

Consider the case of an angle section subjected to a couple *M*, whose axis is inclined at an arbitrary angle θ with the major principal axis, as shown in Fig. 3.2(a). The couple *M* can be resolved into components M_u and M_v along the principal centroidal axes *u–u* and *v–v* as shown in Fig. 3.2(b). From the theory of simple bending, the stress due to M_u is

$$\sigma_u = \frac{M_u v}{I_u} \qquad (3.2a)$$

and is tensile for all fibres above the *u–u* axis (i.e. in all fibres having positive '*v*' coordinates).

Similarly, the stress due to M_v is

$$\sigma_v = -\frac{M_v u}{I_v} \qquad (3.2b)$$

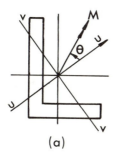
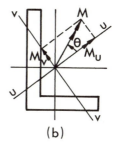

Fig. 3.2. Angle section subjected to a couple *M* at an arbitrary angle to a principal axis.

The negative sign is required because the stresses are compressive at points to the right of the v–v axis, i.e. at those points having positive 'u' coordinates.

By the principle of superposition, the total stress at any point (u, v) due to an arbitrary couple M, is

$$\sigma = \sigma_u + \sigma_v = \frac{M_u v}{I_u} - \frac{M_v u}{I_v} \qquad (3.2c)$$

It should be noted that eqn (3.2c) is valid only when the principle of superposition is valid.

The neutral axis of the cross-section is readily located by equating the total stress given by eqn (3.2c) to zero. Thus

$$\frac{M_u v}{I_u} - \frac{M_v u}{I_v} = 0 \qquad (3.3a)$$

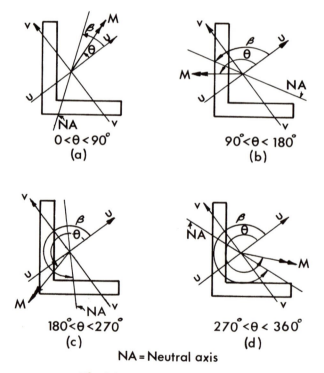

$0 < \theta < 90°$
(a)

$90° < \theta < 180°$
(b)

$180° < \theta < 270°$
(c)

$270° < \theta < 360°$
(d)

NA = Neutral axis

Fig. 3.3. Location of neutral axis.

Rearranging

$$v = \left(\frac{I_u}{I_v}\frac{M_v}{M_u}\right)u \tag{3.3b}$$

Substituting $M_u = M \cos \theta$ and $M_v = M \sin \theta$ in eqn (3.3b) yields

$$v = \left(\frac{I_u}{I_v}\tan \theta\right)u \tag{3.3c}$$

This is the equation of a straight line with a slope given by

$$\tan \beta = \frac{I_u}{I_v}\tan \theta \tag{3.4}$$

where β is the inclination of the neutral axis with the u–u axis. Since I_u and I_v are both positive, β has the same sign as θ. Also, since I_u is greater than I_v, 'tan β' is always greater than 'tan θ'. This leads to the important conclusion that the neutral axis is located invariably between the axis of the couple vector M and the minor principal axis of inertia v–v (see Figs. 3.3(a) to (d)).

3.3. ANGLE BEAMS UNDER TRANSVERSE LOADING

Transverse loads on angle members can cause either bending or bending as well as twisting. When a transverse load, P, passes through the shear centre SC of the beam cross-section, Fig. 3.4(a), the beam bends without twisting; the load P is resolved into components P_u and P_v (Fig. 3.4(b)) and the problem can be readily solved by superposition as shown in Fig. 3.4(c). On the other hand, if the transverse load acts at any point other than the shear centre, (Fig. 3.5(a)), the beam bends as well as twists. If the principle of superposition is valid, the problem can be separated as bending and twisting problems as shown in Figs. 3.5(b), (c) and (d), and then analyzed.

In Fig. 3.4(c) and Fig. 3.5(d)(i) and (ii), the transverse loads produce shearing stresses in addition to bending stresses. The bending shear stresses can be computed from

$$\tau = \frac{VQ}{It} \tag{3.5}$$

where τ is the bending shear stress at any point, V is the shear force at

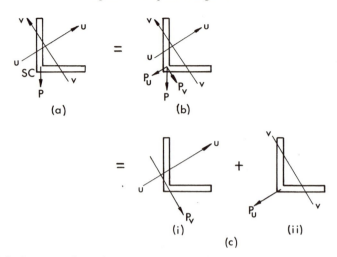

Fig. 3.4. Cross-section of angle member subjected to a load passing through shear centre (SC).

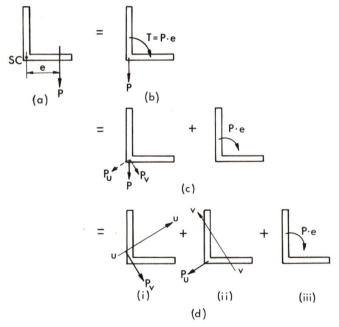

Fig. 3.5. Cross-section of angle member subjected to a load not passing through shear centre (SC).

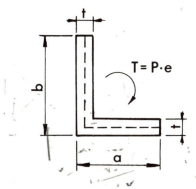

Fig. 3.6. Angle geometry for calculating torsional shear stress.

the section, and Q is the statical moment of area of that portion of the cross-section lying between the point at which the shear stress is computed and the extreme fibre; this moment is taken about the axis of bending, i.e. about the u–u axis in Fig. 3.5(d)(i) and about the v–v axis in Fig. 3.5(d)(ii). The torsional shear stress can be adequately estimated as

$$\tau_{\text{torsion}} = \frac{T}{\frac{1}{3}(b + a - t)t^2} \tag{3.6}$$

where b, a and t are as shown in Fig. 3.6. The total shear stress at any point is obtained by algebraically adding the shear stresses due to (i) bending about the u–u axis, (ii) bending about the v–v axis, and (iii) twisting.

3.4. DESIGN OF LINTELS

A lintel is a beam used to support a masonry wall above a door or a window opening. In the design of angles used as lintels, the problem is simplified because of construction constraints. The wall ties used in construction resist the twisting tendency of the angle; as a result, the angle is forced to bend about an axis parallel to the horizontal leg, i.e. the x–x axis shown in Fig. 3.7. Therefore, it is customary to compute the bending stresses in lintels from the formula

$$\sigma = \frac{My}{I_x} \tag{3.7}$$

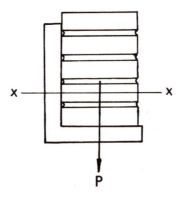

Fig. 3.7. Cross-section of angle member used as a lintel.

If the construction constraints are not present, the angle would be designed to resist the stresses due to combined bending and twisting.

3.5. ANALYSIS OF LATERALLY UNSUPPORTED ANGLES WHEN THE PRINCIPLE OF SUPERPOSITION IS NOT VALID

So far, it is assumed that the principle of superposition is valid, i.e. the deformations caused by any force or couple has no significant effect on the distribution of stresses due to other forces or couples acting on the member. If this assumption is not valid, the problem of analyzing angles becomes quite complicated as shown by the theoretical and experimental investigations of Leigh, Thomas and Lay (Leigh and Lay, 1969, 1970a, 1970b; Leigh *et al.*, 1984; Thomas and Leigh, 1970; Thomas *et al.*, 1973). To make the analysis mathematically less intractable, the angle sections were idealized by the aforementioned investigators as dual rectangles shown in Fig. 3.8. This idealization ignores fillets and toe radii. The following are the section properties of the idealized angle section shown in Fig. 3.8

$$I_x = \frac{Q^3 t(4B + Q)}{12(B + Q)} \tag{3.8}$$

$$S_x \text{ (Section modulus about the } x\text{–}x \text{ axis)} = \frac{Q^2 t(4B + Q)}{6(2B + Q)} \tag{3.9}$$

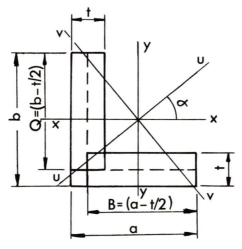

Fig. 3.8. Dual-rectangle idealization of an angle section.

$$I_y = \frac{B^3 t(B+4Q)}{12(B+Q)} \tag{3.10}$$

S_y (Section modulus about the y–y axis) $= \dfrac{B^2 t(B+4Q)}{6(B+2Q)}$ (3.11)

$$I_{xy} = -\frac{B^2 Q^2 t}{4(B+Q)} \tag{3.12}$$

$$I_u, I_v = \frac{t}{4(B+Q)}\left[\frac{Q^3(4B+Q)+B^3(B+4Q)}{6}\right.$$

$$\left.\pm\sqrt{\left\{\frac{Q^3(4B+Q)-B^3(B+4Q)}{6}\right\}^2 + B^4 Q^4}\right] \tag{3.13}$$

$$\tan 2\alpha = -\frac{2I_{xy}}{I_x - I_y} \tag{3.14}$$

S_u (Section modulus about the $u-u$ axis)

$$= \frac{2I_u(B+Q)}{(2BQ\cos\alpha + Q^2\cos\alpha + B^2\sin\alpha)} \tag{3.15}$$

S_v (Section modulus about the $v-v$ axis) $= \dfrac{2I_v(B+Q)}{(B^2\cos\alpha + Q^2\sin\alpha)}$ (3.16)

$$J = \frac{(B+Q)t^3}{3} \tag{3.17}$$

For equal angle, $Q = B$; thus eqns (3.8) to (3.17) reduce to the following

$$I_x = \frac{5B^3t}{24} \tag{3.8a}$$

$$S_x = \frac{5B^2t}{18} \tag{3.9a}$$

$$I_y = \frac{5B^3t}{24} \tag{3.10a}$$

$$S_y = \frac{5B^2t}{18} \tag{3.11a}$$

$$I_{xy} = -\frac{B^3t}{8} \tag{3.12a}$$

$$I_u = \frac{B^3t}{3} \tag{3.13a}$$

$$I_v = \frac{B^3t}{12} \tag{3.13b}$$

$$\alpha = 45° \tag{3.14a}$$

$$S_u = \frac{\sqrt{2}}{3} B^2t \tag{3.15a}$$

$$S_v = \frac{\sqrt{2}}{6} B^2t \tag{3.16a}$$

$$J = \frac{2}{3} Bt^3 \tag{3.17a}$$

Six loading cases, shown in Fig. 3.9, were considered by Leigh, Lay and Thomas:

Case I: Applied moment vector M_a parallel to the long leg;
Case II: Applied moment vector M_a parallel to the short leg;
Case III: Applied moment vector M_a parallel to the major principal axis ($u-u$ axis);
Case IV: Applied moment vector M_a parallel to the minor principal axis ($v-v$ axis);
Case V: Applied moment vector parallel to an axis between the $u-u$ and $y-y$ axes;
Case VI: Applied moment vector parallel to an axis between the $v-v$ and $x-x$ axes.

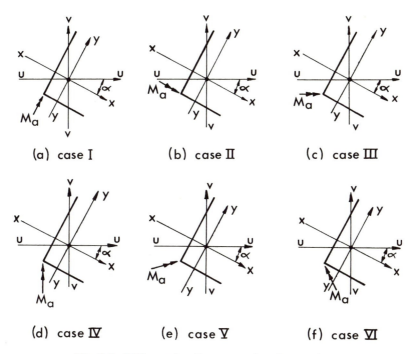

(a) case I   (b) case II   (c) case III

(d) case IV   (e) case V   (f) case VI

Fig. 3.9. Different loading cases of angle members.

The moment is assumed to be uniform along the entire laterally unsupported span. This is the most critical situation and the results obtained are therefore conservative for cases where there is a moment gradient.

The following criteria for the design of laterally unsupported angles were presented by Leigh and Lay (1970a):

Loading Case I (Fig. 3.9(a))

The bending stress σ_a is calculated as

$$\sigma_a \text{ (ksi)} = \frac{M_a \text{ (in-kips)}}{S_y \text{ (in}^3)} \tag{3.18}$$

If $\sigma_a < 300[(B + Q)/L]$, where L is the unsupported length (in) and B and Q are in inches, the maximum bending stress can be calculated, without considering either twist or deflections, from

$$\sigma_{\max} = 1 \cdot 25 \sigma_a \tag{3.19}$$

Otherwise

$$\sigma_{max} = M_a[\gamma_1 + \gamma_2 \phi_{max}] \tag{3.20}$$

v_{max} (displacement of shear centre along the v–v axis)

$$= \frac{M_a L^2}{EI_u} \left[\frac{\phi_{max} \cos \alpha}{\omega^2 L^2} + \gamma_3 \right] \tag{3.21}$$

u_{max} (displacement of shear centre along the u–u axis)

$$= \frac{M_a L^2}{EI_v} \left[\frac{\phi_{max} \sin \alpha}{\omega^2 L^2} - \gamma_4 \right] \tag{3.22}$$

x_{max} (displacement of shear centre in the loading plane)

$$= \sqrt{u_{max}^2 + v_{max}^2} \cos \left[\alpha + \tan^{-1} \left(\frac{v_{max}}{u_{max}} \right) \right] \tag{3.23}$$

where the constants γ_1, γ_2, γ_3 and γ_4 are determined from the relation-ships shown in Fig. 3.10 and Table 3.1; and

$$\omega^2 = \frac{\sigma_a^2 S_y^2 (I_u \sin^2 \alpha + I_v \cos^2 \alpha)}{EI_u I_v [GJ + \sigma_a S_y (\beta_1 \sin \alpha - \beta_2 \cos \alpha)]} \tag{3.24}$$

$$\beta_1 = \frac{t}{I_u} \left[\frac{1}{\sin^3 \alpha} \left\{ \frac{(v_2^4 - v_3^4)}{4} + \frac{Q^2 \cos \alpha (v_2^3 - v_3^3)}{3(B + Q)} + \frac{Q^4 (v_2^2 - v_3^2)}{8(B + Q)^2} \right\} \right. \tag{3.25}$$

$$+ \frac{1}{\cos^3 \alpha} \left\{ \frac{(v_1^4 - v_2^4)}{4} - \frac{B^2 \sin \alpha (v_1^3 - v_2^3)}{3(B + Q)} + \frac{B^4 (v_1^2 - v_2^2)}{8(B + Q)^2} \right\} \left. \right] - 2v_2$$

$$\beta_2 = \frac{t}{I_v} \left[\frac{1}{\sin^4 \alpha} \left\{ \frac{(v_3^4 - v_2^4) \cos \alpha}{4} + \frac{(v_3^3 - v_2^3)(2 \cos^2 \alpha + 1)Q^2}{6(B + Q)} \right. \right.$$

$$+ \frac{3Q^4 (v_3^2 - v_2^2) \cos \alpha}{8(B + Q)^2} + \frac{(v_3 - v_2)Q^6}{8(B + Q)^3} \left. \right\}$$

$$+ \frac{1}{\cos^4 \alpha} \left\{ \frac{(v_1^4 - v_2^4) \sin \alpha}{4} - \frac{(v_1^3 - v_2^3)(2 \sin^2 \alpha + 1)B^2}{6(B + Q)} \right. \tag{3.26}$$

$$+ \frac{3B^4 (v_1^2 - v_2^2) \sin \alpha}{8(B + Q)^2} - \frac{(v_1 - v_2)B^6}{8(B + Q)^3} \left. \right\} \left. \right] - 2u_2$$

$$\phi_{max} = - \frac{(\tan \alpha)(I_u - I_v)}{(I_u \tan^2 \alpha + I_v)} \left[\frac{1}{\cos \dfrac{\omega L}{2}} - 1 \right] \tag{3.27}$$

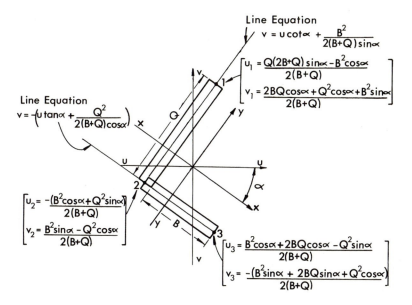

Line Equation

$$v = u\cot\alpha + \frac{B^2}{2(B+Q)\sin\alpha}$$

$$\begin{bmatrix} u_1 = \dfrac{Q(2B+Q)\sin\alpha - B^2\cos\alpha}{2(B+Q)} \\[2mm] v_1 = \dfrac{2BQ\cos\alpha + Q^2\cos\alpha + B^2\sin\alpha}{2(B+Q)} \end{bmatrix}$$

Line Equation

$$v = -\left(u\tan\alpha + \frac{Q^2}{2(B+Q)\cos\alpha}\right)$$

$$\begin{bmatrix} u_2 = \dfrac{-(B^2\cos\alpha + Q^2\sin\alpha)}{2(B+Q)} \\[2mm] v_2 = \dfrac{B^2\sin\alpha - Q^2\cos\alpha}{2(B+Q)} \end{bmatrix}$$

$$\begin{bmatrix} u_3 = \dfrac{B^2\cos\alpha + 2BQ\cos\alpha - Q^2\sin\alpha}{2(B+Q)} \\[2mm] v_3 = \dfrac{-(B^2\sin\alpha + 2BQ\sin\alpha + Q^2\cos\alpha)}{2(B+Q)} \end{bmatrix}$$

Fig. 3.10. Coordinates of some points on the idealized section.

Table 3.1
Constants for Angle Beams for Loading Case I

Constant	Equal angles	Unequal angles
δ_2	$\dfrac{7\cdot5}{B^3 t}$	$\dfrac{\sin^2\alpha}{I_v} + \dfrac{\cos^2\alpha}{I_u}$
δ_3	$-\dfrac{4\cdot5}{B^3 t}$	$\dfrac{\sin 2\alpha}{2I_u} - \dfrac{\sin 2\alpha}{2I_v}$
γ_1	$-\dfrac{4\cdot5}{B^2 t}$	$\dfrac{v_3\sin\alpha}{I_u} - \dfrac{u_3\cos\alpha}{I_v}$
γ_2	$\dfrac{1\cdot5}{B^2 t}$	$\dfrac{v_3\cos\alpha}{I_u} + \dfrac{u_3\sin\alpha}{I_v}$
γ_3	$\dfrac{\sqrt{2}}{10}$	$\dfrac{\sin\alpha}{8} - \dfrac{\delta_3\cos\alpha}{\delta_2\ 8}$
γ_4	$\dfrac{\sqrt{2}}{40}$	$\dfrac{\delta_3\sin\alpha}{\delta_2\ 8} + \dfrac{\cos\alpha}{8}$

For equal angles

$$\beta_1 = 0 \tag{3.25a}$$

$$\beta_2 = B\sqrt{2} \tag{3.26a}$$

$$\phi_{max} = -\frac{3}{5}\left(\frac{1}{\cos\dfrac{\omega L}{2}} - 1\right) \tag{3.27a}$$

Loading Case II (Fig. 3.9(b))

The bending stress σ_a is

$$\sigma_a\,(\text{ksi}) = \frac{M_a\,(\text{in-kips})}{S_x\,(\text{in}^3)} \tag{3.28}$$

If $\sigma_a < 340(B + Q)/L$, the stresses can be calculated, without considering either twist or deflection, as

$$\sigma_{max} = 1.25\sigma_a \tag{3.29}$$

Otherwise

$$\sigma_{max} = M_a[\gamma_5 + \gamma_6\phi_{max}] \tag{3.30}$$

$$v_{max} = \frac{M_a L^2}{EI_u}\left[-\frac{\phi_{max}\sin\alpha}{\omega^2 L^2} + \gamma_7\right] \tag{3.31}$$

$$u_{max} = \frac{M_a L^2}{EI_v}\left[\frac{\phi_{max}\cos\alpha}{\omega^2 L^2} - \gamma_8\right] \tag{3.32}$$

y_{max} (displacement of shear centre in the loading plane)

$$= \sqrt{u_{max}^2 + v_{max}^2}\,\sin\left[\alpha + \tan^{-1}\left(\frac{v_{max}}{u_{max}}\right)\right] \tag{3.33}$$

where the constants γ_5, γ_6, γ_7 and γ_8 are determined from the relationships shown in Fig. 3.10 and Table 3.2.

$$\omega^2 = \frac{\sigma_a^2 S_x^2(I_u\cos^2\alpha + I_v\sin^2\alpha)}{EI_u I_v[GJ + \sigma_a S_x(\beta_1\cos\alpha + \beta_2\sin\alpha)]} \tag{3.34}$$

and

$$\phi_{max} = \frac{(\cot\alpha)(I_u - I_v)}{I_u\cot^2\alpha + I_v}\left[\frac{1}{\cos\dfrac{\omega L}{2}} - 1\right] \tag{3.35}$$

Table 3.2
Constants for Angle Beams for Loading
Case II

Constant	Unequal angles
δ_5	$\dfrac{\cos^2\alpha}{I_v}+\dfrac{\sin^2\alpha}{I_u}$
δ_6	$\dfrac{\sin 2\alpha}{2I_v}-\dfrac{\sin 2\alpha}{2I_u}$
γ_5	$\dfrac{u_1\sin\alpha}{I_v}+\dfrac{v_1\cos\alpha}{I_u}$
γ_6	$\dfrac{u_1\cos\alpha}{I_v}-\dfrac{v_1\sin\alpha}{I_u}$
γ_7	$\dfrac{\cos\alpha}{8}+\dfrac{\delta_6}{\delta_5}\dfrac{\sin\alpha}{8}$
γ_8	$\dfrac{\delta_6}{\delta_5}\dfrac{\cos\alpha}{8}-\dfrac{\sin\alpha}{8}$

Loading Case III (Fig. 3.9(c))—Strong Axis (*u–u*) Loading

If point 1 in Fig. 3.10 is in tension, and if

$$\frac{L}{t}\leqslant\frac{14\,500}{\sigma_y\text{ (ksi)}}-\frac{3620}{\sigma_y\text{ (ksi)}}\frac{Q}{B}+\frac{I_v\pi^2v_1\beta_1}{2I_ut^2} \tag{3.36}$$

then

$$\sigma_{\max}=\frac{M_a}{S_u}=\frac{M_u}{S_u} \tag{3.37}$$

If point 1 in Fig. 3.10 is in compresion due to M_a being opposite to the direction shown in Fig. 3.9(c), and if

$$\frac{L}{t}\leqslant\frac{15\,900}{\sigma_y\text{ (ksi)}}-\frac{4350}{\sigma_y\text{ (ksi)}}\frac{Q}{B}-\frac{1\cdot5I_v\pi^2v_1\beta_1}{2I_ut^2} \tag{3.38}$$

then

$$\sigma_{\max}=\frac{M_a}{S_u}=\frac{M_u}{S_u} \tag{3.37}$$

Otherwise, the maximum permissible bending stress is calculated as follows. First, calculate the elastic buckling stress σ_{cr}:

$$\sigma_{cr}=\frac{EI_v\pi^2v_1\beta_1}{2I_ut^2}\left(\frac{t}{L}\right)^2\left[1\pm\sqrt{1+\left(\frac{L}{t}\right)^2\frac{(B+Q)t^5}{1\cdot95I_v\beta_1^2\pi^2}}\right] \tag{3.39}$$

If $\sigma_{cr} \leqslant \sigma_y$, the maximum permissible bending stress

$$\sigma_{max} = \left[0 \cdot 55 - 0 \cdot 1 \frac{\sigma_{cr}}{\sigma_y} \right] \sigma_{cr} \qquad (3.40)$$

If $\sigma_{cr} \geqslant \sigma_y$, the maximum permissible bending stress

$$\sigma_{max} = \left[0 \cdot 95 - 0 \cdot 5 \sqrt{\frac{\sigma_y}{\sigma_{cr}}} \right] \sigma_y \qquad (3.41)$$

The maximum loading plane deflection is

$$v_{max} = \frac{M_u L^2}{8 E I_u} \qquad (3.42)$$

For equal angles: When $L/t \leqslant 270$ for material with $\sigma_y = 36$ ksi and when $L/t \leqslant 190$ for material having a yield stress of 52 ksi, one can use

$$\sigma_{max} = \frac{M_u}{S_u} \qquad (3.37)$$

Otherwise, calculate the critical stress as

$$\sigma_{cr} = \frac{\pi E t}{2\sqrt{2 \cdot 6} L} \qquad (3.43)$$

Depending on the magnitude of σ_{cr}, use either eqn (3.40) or (3.41) to compute the maximum permissible bending stress. Maximum loading plane deflection v_{max} is calculated from eqn (3.42).

Loading Case IV (Fig. 3.9(d))
Since the moment is applied about the weakest axis (v–v axis), the beam will continue to bend about this axis only and the conventional beam formulae are applicable, namely

$$\sigma_{max} = \frac{M_v}{S_v} \qquad (3.44)$$

$$u_{max} = \frac{M_v L^2}{8 E I_v} \qquad (3.45)$$

Loading Cases V and VI (Figs 3.9(e) and (f))
The applied moment, M_a, is resolved into component moments about the principal axes closest to that of the applied moment and the formulae given earlier are then applied to each component moment.

3.6. SAFE LOAD TABLES FOR ANGLE BEAMS

The safe loads for laterally unsupported angle beams based on the theory presented by Leigh and Lay (1970*a*) were given by Leigh and Lay (1970*b*) and Leigh *et al.* (1984) for angles rolled in Australia. The associated maximum deflections in the loading plane due to self weight plus the superimposed load were also given.

Based on the same theory, safe loads in the SI system and Imperial system of units for angles used in North America were deduced and are presented in Tables 3.3 to 3.8; the maximum permissible bending stress of $0 \cdot 6\sigma_y$ (instead of $0 \cdot 66\sigma_y$ used by Leigh and Lay (1970*b*) and Leigh *et al.* (1984)) and the maximum permissible shear stress of $0 \cdot 40\sigma_y$ (instead of $0 \cdot 45\sigma_y$) were adopted. The yield stress used for the tables in the SI system (Tables 3.3 to 3.5) is 300 MPa (the most common value in Canada) and that used for the tables in the Imperial units (Tables 3.6 to 3.8) is 36 ksi (the most common value in the United States). The safe transverse load shown in the load tables is the uniformly distributed load causing a maximum bending moment equal to the safe uniform moment corresponding to either Case I or Case II loading and, therefore, is conservative.

3.7. PROCEDURE FOR THE CALCULATION OF SAFE TRANSVERSE LOADS

The procedure followed for the calculation of safe transverse load on an angle beam is identical to that given by Leigh and Lay (1970*b*) and is explained in the following.

3.7.1. Non-principal Axes Loading
Iterative methods were used to calculate the equivalent uniformly distributed load which produces a maximum bending stress of $0 \cdot 6\sigma_y$, starting with an initial approximation of $M_a = \sigma_a S_a$, where σ_a is the nominal applied stress and S_a is the section modulus referred to the axis of the applied load. For small angles of twist, σ_a and the maximum stress, σ_{max}, have the following relationship

$$\sigma_a = 0 \cdot 8\sigma_{max} = (0 \cdot 8)(0 \cdot 6\sigma_y) = 0 \cdot 48\sigma_y \tag{3.46}$$

Table 3.3

Safe Distributed Loads for Equal Angle Beams (Yield Stress = 300 MPa; Permissible Bending Stress = 180 MPa; Permissible Shear Stress = 120 MPa)

Safe distributed load (kN)/maximum loading plane deflection due to self-weight only (mm)/maximum loading plane deflection due to total load (mm)

Nominal leg size (mm)	Thickness (mm)	Self-weight (kN/m)	Span (m) 1	2	3	4	5	6
200×200	30	0·855	217 0·00 0·67	162 0·04 4·07	106 0·21 9·17	78·2 0·68 16·31	61·0 1·65 25·51	49·2 3·43 36·77
	25	0·722	157 0·00 0·56	138 0·04 4·03	90·8 0·21 9·06	66·8 0·66 16·13	52·1 1·61 25·23	42·0 3·34 36·37
	20	0·585	105 0·00 0·45	105 0·04 3·62	74·2 0·20 8·98	54·6 0·64 15·98	42·6 1·57 25·00	34·4 3·25 36·07
	16	0·473	69·7 0·00 0·36	69·3 0·04 2·91	60·2 0·20 8·93	44·3 0·63 15·90	34·5 1·54 24·89	27·8 3·19 35·92
	13	0·387	47·3 0·00 0·30	46·9 0·04 2·38	46·5 0·20 8·07	36·2 0·62 15·87	28·2 1·51 24·87	22·7 3·14 35·91
	10	0·300	28·7 0·00 0·23	28·4 0·04 1·84	28·1 0·19 6·24	27·6 0·61 15·89	21·5 1·49 24·90	17·3 3·09 35·95

150×150	20	0·431	99·1 / 0·00 / 1·06	61·4 / 0·07 / 5·39	40·2 / 0·37 / 12·14	29·4 / 1·18 / 21·60	22·7 / 2·88 / 33·81	18·1 / 5·99 / 48·79
	16	0·350	66·5 / 0·00 / 0·86	50·3 / 0·07 / 5·33	32·9 / 0·36 / 12·01	24·1 / 1·15 / 21·38	18·6 / 2·81 / 33·49	14·8 / 5·83 / 48·36
	13	0·287	45·5 / 0·00 / 0·70	41·5 / 0·07 / 5·29	27·2 / 0·36 / 11·94	19·8 / 1·12 / 21·27	15·3 / 2·75 / 33·34	12·2 / 5·70 / 48·18
	10	0·223	27·9 / 0·00 / 0·54	27·7 / 0·07 / 4·34	21·1 / 0·35 / 11·90	15·4 / 1·10 / 21·23	11·9 / 2·69 / 33·32	9·43 / 5·59 / 48·19
125×125	16	0·288	64·0 / 0·01 / 1·47	34·2 / 0·11 / 6·45	22·3 / 0·53 / 14·54	16·2 / 1·69 / 25·90	12·4 / 4·13 / 40·56	9·80 / 8·57 / 58·57
	13	0·237	44·1 / 0·01 / 1·20	28·4 / 0·10 / 6·39	18·5 / 0·52 / 14·41	13·4 / 1·65 / 25·68	10·3 / 4·03 / 40·26	8·13 / 8·36 / 58·19
	10	0·185	27·2 / 0·01 / 0·93	22·2 / 0·10 / 6·35	14·5 / 0·51 / 14·32	10·5 / 1·61 / 25·56	8·03 / 3·94 / 40·12	6·33 / 8·18 / 58·07
	8	0·149	17·9 / 0·01 / 0·75	17·8 / 0·10 / 6·03	11·6 / 0·50 / 14·31	8·42 / 1·58 / 25·57	6·43 / 3·87 / 40·17	5·05 / 8·05 / 58·16
100×100	16	0·227	42·9 / 0·01 / 2·05	21·1 / 0·17 / 8·19	13·7 / 0·87 / 18·46	9·84 / 2·74 / 32·87	7·46 / 6·69 / 51·49	5·78 / 13·89 / 74·36

Table 3.3—contd.

Nominal leg size (mm)	Thickness (mm)	Self-weight (kN/m)	Safe distributed load (kN)/maximum loading plane deflection due to self-weight only (mm)/maximum loading plane deflection due to total load (mm)					
			Span (m)					
			1	2	3	4	5	6
	13	0·187	35·9 / 0·01 / 2·02	17·7 / 0·17 / 8·08	11·4 / 0·84 / 18·21	8·25 / 2·65 / 32·47	6·24 / 6·47 / 50·90	4·85 / 13·43 / 73·58
	10	0·146	26·3 / 0·01 / 1·81	14·0 / 0·16 / 7·98	9·04 / 0·81 / 18·02	6·51 / 2·56 / 32·17	4·92 / 6·26 / 50·52	3·82 / 13·01 / 73·16
	8	0·118	17·4 / 0·01 / 1·46	11·3 / 0·16 / 7·94	7·33 / 0·79 / 17·95	5·26 / 2·51 / 32·10	3·98 / 6·14 / 50·47	3·07 / 12·76 / 73·17
	6	0·090	10·2 / 0·01 / 1·10	8·53 / 0·15 / 7·94	5·50 / 0·78 / 17·96	3·94 / 2·48 / 32·15	2·96 / 6·06 / 50·55	2·27 / 12·63 / 73·11
90 × 90	13	0·167	28·7 / 0·01 / 2·26	14·1 / 0·21 / 9·04	9·09 / 1·05 / 20·37	6·51 / 3·32 / 36·32	4·90 / 8·11 / 56·95	3·77 / 16·84 / 82·32
	10	0·131	22·8 / 0·01 / 2·22	11·2 / 0·20 / 8·91	7·21 / 1·01 / 20·11	5·17 / 3·21 / 35·91	3·88 / 7·84 / 56·39	2·98 / 16·30 / 81·68

Size	Thickness							
75×75	8	0·106	17·2 / 0·01 / 1·99	9·09 / 0·20 / 8·85	5·87 / 0·99 / 20·00	4·20 / 3·14 / 35·77	3·15 / 7·67 / 56·26	2·41 / 15·94 / 81·60
	6	0·080	10·0 / 0·01 / 1·50	6·89 / 0·19 / 8·82	4·43 / 0·96 / 19·98	3·16 / 3·05 / 35·80	2·36 / 7·47 / 56·36	1·79 / 15·56 / 81·62
	13	0·137	19·3 / 0·02 / 2·75	9·44 / 0·31 / 11·00	6·06 / 1·56 / 24·81	4·29 / 4·93 / 44·22	3·18 / 12·05 / 69·33	2·39 / 25·03 / 100·25
	10	0·108	15·5 / 0·02 / 2·69	7·56 / 0·30 / 10·80	4·85 / 1·50 / 24·38	3·44 / 4·74 / 43·52	2·55 / 11·58 / 68·37	1·91 / 24·07 / 99·04
	8	0·087	12·7 / 0·02 / 2·66	6·20 / 0·29 / 10·69	3·97 / 1·45 / 24·16	2·82 / 4·57 / 43·22	2·08 / 11·18 / 68·02	1·56 / 23·27 / 98·69
	6	0·066	9·70 / 0·02 / 2·64	4·73 / 0·28 / 10·62	3·03 / 1·40 / 24·07	2·14 / 4·44 / 43·16	1·58 / 10·87 / 68·04	1·18 / 22·66 / 98·72
	5	0·056	6·97 / 0·02 / 2·17	3·96 / 0·28 / 10·61	2·53 / 1·40 / 24·09	1·78 / 4·43 / 43·22	1·30 / 10·86 / 68·03	0·960 / 22·69 / 98·22
65×65	10	0·092	11·4 / 0·02 / 3·14	5·54 / 0·40 / 12·58	3·53 / 2·03 / 28·40	2·48 / 6·41 / 50·72	1·81 / 15·67 / 79·68	1·33 / 32·57 / 115·44
	8	0·075	9·37 / 0·02 / 3·09	4·57 / 0·39 / 12·42	2·91 / 1·96 / 28·08	2·04 / 6·22 / 50·23	1·49 / 15·21 / 79·07	1·09 / 31·66 / 114·76

Table 3.3—contd.

Safe distributed load (kN)/maximum loading plane deflection due to self-weight only (mm)/maximum loading plane deflection due to total load (mm)

Nominal leg size (mm)	Thickness (mm)	Self-weight (kN/m)	Span (m) 1	2	3	4	5	6
	6	0·057	7·21	3·51	2·23	1·56	1·14	0·830
			0·02	0·37	1·90	6·00	14·71	30·69
			3·06	12·30	27·89	50·03	78·95	114·66
	5	0·048	6·07	2·95	1·87	1·31	0·943	0·683
			0·02	0·37	1·87	5·93	14·54	30·42
			3·05	12·27	27·88	50·09	78·97	114·27
55×55	10	0·077	7·89	3·83	2·42	1·67	1·19	0·850
			0·04	0·58	2·93	9·27	22·66	47·16
			3·76	15·08	34·05	60·81	95·52	138·41
	8	0·063	6·56	3·18	2·01	1·39	0·992	0·705
			0·03	0·56	2·82	8·93	21·87	45·57
			3·70	14·83	33·53	60·01	94·47	137·16
	6	0·048	5·09	2·46	1·55	1·07	0·764	0·540
			0·03	0·53	2·71	8·57	21·01	43·92
			3·64	14·63	33·18	59·56	94·04	136·70
	5	0·040	4·30	2·08	1·31	0·903	0·640	0·450
			0·03	0·52	2·63	8·34	20·46	42·90
			3·62	14·57	33·12	59·56	94·05	136·31

Size									
45×45	4	0·033	3·48 0·03 3·60	1·68 0·52 14·55	1·05 2·64 33·15	0·717 8·37 59·59	0·501 20·60 93·52	0·343 43·48 133·68
	3	0·025	2·56 0·03 3·35	1·25 0·51 14·58	0·774 2·60 33·10	0·518 8·25 58·53	0·350 20·42 88·86	0·228 43·64 120·85
	8	0·050	4·24 0·05 4·59	2·04 0·85 18·42	1·27 4·31 41·66	0·863 13·65 74·55	0·596 33·43 117·39	0·401 69·81 170·48
	6	0·039	3·32 0·05 4·49	1·60 0·82 18·07	0·995 4·17 41·00	0·673 13·22 73·64	0·462 32·44 116·32	0·308 68·07 169·21
	5	0·033	2·83 0·05 4·45	1·36 0·81 17·95	0·844 4·09 40·82	0·569 12·97 73·48	0·389 31·89 116·16	0·256 67·22 168·61
	4	0·026	2·30 0·05 4·42	1·10 0·77 17·88	0·685 3·89 40·79	0·460 12·35 73·49	0·312 30·46 115·66	0·203 64·67 165·84
	3	0·020	1·74 0·05 4·41	0·831 0·76 17·90	0·510 3·86 40·83	0·335 12·29 72·70	0·220 30·53 111·19	0·135 65·89 152·64
35×35	6	0·030	1·93 0·09 5·89	0·916 1·43 23·68	0·557 7·26 53·73	0·362 23·01 96·52	0·233 56·63 152·55	0·136 119·74 222·04
	5	0·025	1·65 0·09 5·81	0·786 1·37 23·41	0·479 6·93 53·27	0·311 21·99 95·96	0·200 54·27 151·84	0·117 115·47 220·70

Table 3.3—*contd.*

Safe distributed load (kN)/maximum loading plane deflection due to self-weight only (mm)/maximum loading plane deflection due to total load (mm)

Nominal leg size (mm)	Thickness (mm)	Self-weight (kN/m)	Span (m) 1	2	3	4	5	6
	4	0·020	1·36 0·08 5·74	0·645 1·31 23·22	0·392 6·63 53·04	0·254 21·06 95·74	0·162 52·20 151·04	0·093 112·29 217·16
	3	0·015	1·04 0·08 5·70	0·492 1·25 23·17	0·297 6·34 53·07	0·189 20·22 95·00	0·117 50·63 146·21	0·063 111·07 201·95
25×25	5	0·017	0·790 0·17 8·37	0·368 2·80 33·75	0·215 14·21 76·83	0·130 45·21 138·47	0·071 112·57 219·28	0·026 244·61 319·00
	4	0·014	0·659 0·17 8·21	0·306 2·70 33·23	0·179 13·71 75·97	0·107 43·74 137·31	0·058 109·95 217·03	0·020 243·10 312·69
	3	0·011	0·513 0·17 8·08	0·237 2·65 32·91	0·137 13·49 75·62	0·080 43·36 135·97	0·041 111·19 210·24	0·010 249·96 291·63

Table 3.4

Safe Distributed Loads for Unequal Angle Beams: Load Parallel to Short Leg (Yield Stress = 300 MPa; Permissible Bending Stress = 180 MPa; Permissible Shear Stress = 120 MPa)

Nominal leg size (mm)	Thickness (mm)	Self-weight (kN/m)	Safe distributed load (kN)/maximum loading plane deflection due to self-weight only (mm)/maximum loading plane deflection due to total load (mm)					
			Span (m)					
			1	2	3	4	5	6
200 × 150	25	0·625	131	78·2	51·1	37·2	28·6	22·7
			0·01	0·08	0·41	1·31	3·20	6·65
			1·08	5·23	11·78	20·96	32·76	47·21
	20	0·508	88·6	64·7	42·3	30·8	23·7	18·8
			0·00	0·08	0·40	1·26	3·09	6·41
			0·86	5·15	11·60	20·64	32·27	46·50
	16	0·411	59·2	53·0	34·7	25·3	19·4	15·4
			0·00	0·08	0·39	1·23	3·00	6·22
			0·69	5·10	11·47	20·41	31·92	46·02
	13	0·337	40·3	40·0	28·6	20·9	16·1	12·7
			0·00	0·07	0·38	1·20	2·94	6·09
			0·57	4·53	11·39	20·27	31·71	45·73
200 × 100	20	0·431	58·3	28·5	18·3	13·0	9·59	7·20
			0·01	0·22	1·10	3·49	8·52	17·67
			1·86	7·44	16·75	29·79	46·56	67·06
	16	0·350	47·8	23·8	15·3	10·8	8·04	6·05
			0·01	0·21	1·05	3·33	8·13	16·86
			1·79	7·30	16·43	29·22	45·68	65·80

Table 3.4—*contd.*

Safe distributed load (kN)/maximum loading plane
deflection due to self-weight only (mm)/maximum
loading plane deflection due to total load (mm)

Nominal leg size (mm)	Thickness (mm)	Self-weight (kN/m)	Span (m)					
			1	2	3	4	5	6
	13	0·287	33·0	19·9	12·8	9·09	6·75	5·10
			0·01	0·20	1·01	3·21	7·84	16·26
			1·45	7·20	16·21	28·83	45·07	64·93
	10	0·223	20·4	15·8	10·1	7·20	5·36	4·05
			0·01	0·19	0·98	3·10	7·57	15·72
			1·12	7·11	16·01	28·47	44·50	64·11
150×100	16	0·288	46·2	22·7	14·6	10·5	7·85	6·01
			0·01	0·19	0·96	3·03	7·40	15·35
			1·92	7·68	17·28	30·74	48·06	69·27
	13	0·237	36·1	19·0	12·3	8·77	6·58	5·05
			0·01	0·18	0·93	2·93	7·15	14·84
			1·75	7·57	17·05	30·33	47·43	68·39
	10	0·185	22·4	15·0	9·69	6·93	5·21	3·99
			0·01	0·18	0·90	2·84	6·94	14·40
			1·35	7·48	16·84	29·97	46·89	67·62
	8	0·149	14·8	12·2	7·87	5·63	4·23	3·24
			0·01	0·17	0·88	2·77	6·78	14·08
			1·08	7·43	16·73	29·77	46·59	67·17

Size									
125×90	16	0·245	36·2 / 0·01 / 2·18	17·7 / 0·23 / 8·72	11·4 / 1·18 / 19·62	8·12 / 3·73 / 34·91	6·05 / 9·12 / 54·60	4·59 / 18·92 / 78·70
	13	0·202	30·4 / 0·01 / 2·14	14·9 / 0·22 / 8·58	9·60 / 1·14 / 19·31	6·84 / 3·59 / 34·38	5·10 / 8·78 / 53·78	3·88 / 18·22 / 77·55
	10	0·158	22·6 / 0·01 / 1·95	11·8 / 0·22 / 8·46	7·62 / 1·10 / 19·05	5·44 / 3·47 / 33·91	4·06 / 8·48 / 53·08	3·09 / 17·61 / 76·59
	8	0·127	15·0 / 0·01 / 1·56	9·65 / 0·21 / 8·39	6·21 / 1·07 / 18·90	4·43 / 3·37 / 33·66	3·31 / 8·25 / 52·71	2·52 / 17·13 / 76·06
125×75	13	0·187	21·2 / 0·02 / 2·53	10·3 / 0·35 / 10·12	6·56 / 1·79 / 22·78	4·59 / 5·64 / 40·51	3·33 / 13·79 / 63·35	2·43 / 28·61 / 91·31
	10	0·146	17·0 / 0·02 / 2·48	8·26 / 0·34 / 9·93	5·26 / 1·70 / 22·36	3·69 / 5·39 / 39·79	2·68 / 13·16 / 62·23	1·97 / 27·32 / 89·72
	8	0·118	13·7 / 0·02 / 2·38	6·78 / 0·33 / 9·82	4·32 / 1·65 / 22·12	3·03 / 5·23 / 39·36	2·21 / 12·78 / 61·58	1·62 / 26·53 / 88·79
	6	0·090	8·00 / 0·02 / 1·79	5·19 / 0·32 / 9·72	3·31 / 1·62 / 21·90	2·32 / 5·11 / 38·98	1·69 / 12·50 / 60·96	1·24 / 25·99 / 87·85
100×90	13	0·177	29·2 / 0·01 / 2·22	14·3 / 0·21 / 8·89	9·25 / 1·07 / 20·04	6·62 / 3·40 / 35·69	4·97 / 8·30 / 55·91	3·81 / 17·23 / 80·74

Table 3.4—*contd.*

Nominal leg size (mm)	Thickness (mm)	Self-weight (kN/m)	Safe distributed load (kN)/maximum loading plane deflection due to self-weight only (mm)/maximum loading plane deflection due to total load (mm)					
			Span (m)					
			1	2	3	4	5	6
	10	0·139	23·2	11·4	7·35	5·25	3·94	3·02
			0·01	0·21	1·04	3·29	8·04	16·71
			2·19	8·77	19·77	35·26	55·29	79·95
	8	0·112	16·4	9·27	5·98	4·27	3·20	2·45
			0·01	0·20	1·01	3·20	7·83	16·28
			1·84	8·70	19·64	35·06	55·05	79·67
	6	0·085	9·58	7·03	4·53	3·23	2·41	1·83
			0·01	0·20	0·99	3·14	7·67	15·97
			1·39	8·67	19·59	35·00	54·95	79·43
100×75	13	0·162	20·3	9·93	6·34	4·47	3·28	2·43
			0·02	0·33	1·67	5·29	12·92	26·81
			2·63	10·51	23·67	42·12	65·91	95·07
	10	0·127	16·3	7·95	5·09	3·59	2·64	1·96
			0·02	0·32	1·60	5·06	12·37	25·68
			2·58	10·31	23·24	41·39	64·81	93·54
	8	0·103	13·4	6·52	4·17	2·94	2·16	1·61
			0·02	0·31	1·56	4·92	12·04	25·01
			2·55	10·20	23·00	40·99	64·22	92·74

90×75	6	0·078	8·69 / 0·02 / 2·09	4·99 / 0·30 / 10·11	3·19 / 1·51 / 22·82	2·25 / 4·78 / 40·68	1·65 / 11·69 / 63·76	1·22 / 24·32 / 92·04
	13	0·152	20·0 / 0·02 / 2·67	9·75 / 0·32 / 10·69	6·24 / 1·63 / 24·08	4·41 / 5·14 / 42·89	3·25 / 12·57 / 67·15	2·42 / 26·09 / 96·91
	10	0·119	16·0 / 0·02 / 2·62	7·81 / 0·31 / 10·49	5·00 / 1·55 / 23·65	3·54 / 4·91 / 42·15	2·61 / 12·01 / 66·06	1·95 / 24·95 / 95·45
	8	0·097	13·1 / 0·02 / 2·59	6·40 / 0·30 / 10·38	4·10 / 1·52 / 23·42	2·90 / 4·80 / 41·78	2·13 / 11·75 / 65·54	1·59 / 24·42 / 94·77
	6	0·073	9·06 / 0·02 / 2·26	4·90 / 0·29 / 10·30	3·13 / 1·46 / 23·26	2·21 / 4·63 / 41·54	1·63 / 11·33 / 65·21	1·21 / 23·59 / 94·26
	5	0·062	6·43 / 0·02 / 1·89	4·10 / 0·29 / 10·27	2·62 / 1·46 / 23·21	1·84 / 4·63 / 41·45	1·35 / 11·34 / 64·98	0·999 / 23·64 / 93·67
90×65	10	0·112	12·1 / 0·03 / 2·98	5·86 / 0·44 / 11·94	3·72 / 2·21 / 26·90	2·59 / 6·99 / 47·90	1·87 / 17·08 / 74·99	1·35 / 35·46 / 108·21
	8	0·090	9·95 / 0·03 / 2·94	4·83 / 0·42 / 11·78	3·07 / 2·12 / 26·55	2·14 / 6·69 / 47·30	1·55 / 16·36 / 74·10	1·12 / 34·00 / 107·00
	6	0·069	7·66 / 0·03 / 2·91	3·72 / 0·41 / 11·64	2·36 / 2·06 / 26·26	1·65 / 6·53 / 46·83	1·19 / 15·98 / 73·40	0·857 / 33·25 / 105·97

Table 3.4—*contd.*

Safe distributed load (kN)/maximum loading plane deflection due to self-weight only (mm)/maximum loading plane deflection due to total load (mm)

Nominal leg size (mm)	Thickness (mm)	Self-weight (kN/m)	Span (m)					
			1	2	3	4	5	6
80×60	5	0·058	5·97	3·13	1·99	1·38	0·995	0·716
			0·03	0·40	2·03	6·44	15·77	32·87
			2·61	11·59	26·15	46·63	73·04	105·28
	10	0·100	10·1	4·88	3·08	2·14	1·53	1·09
			0·03	0·51	2·59	8·20	20·04	41·63
			3·27	13·10	29·51	52·56	82·31	118·82
	8	0·081	8·33	4·04	2·55	1·77	1·27	0·904
			0·03	0·49	2·49	7·88	19·27	40·06
			3·22	12·90	29·08	51·84	81·24	117·37
	6	0·062	6·44	3·12	1·97	1·37	0·977	0·696
			0·03	0·48	2·42	7·65	18·71	38·96
			3·18	12·73	28·73	51·27	80·41	116·18
	5	0·052	5·43	2·63	1·66	1·15	0·822	0·583
			0·03	0·47	2·37	7·51	18·39	38·35
			3·16	12·67	28·60	51·05	80·04	115·48
75×50	8	0·072	5·74	2·76	1·72	1·16	0·798	0·531
			0·05	0·76	3·83	12·12	29·62	61·59
			3·84	15·37	34·62	61·66	96·55	139·35

Size			C1	C2	C3	C4	C5	C6
	6	0·055	4·48 / 0·05 / 3·77	2·15 / 0·72 / 15·10	1·34 / 3·67 / 34·04	0·908 / 11·61 / 60·68	0·625 / 28·40 / 95·07	0·418 / 59·14 / 137·26
	5	0·046	3·80 / 0·04 / 3·74	1·83 / 0·70 / 14·98	1·14 / 3·57 / 33·80	0·771 / 11·31 / 60·26	0·531 / 27·69 / 94·41	0·356 / 57·75 / 136·21
65×50	8	0·066	5·59 / 0·05 / 3·93	2·70 / 0·73 / 15·74	1·68 / 3·69 / 35·50	1·15 / 11·67 / 63·29	0·795 / 28·55 / 99·23	0·539 / 59·40 / 143·41
	6	0·050	4·36 / 0·04 / 3·86	2·10 / 0·69 / 15·47	1·32 / 3·50 / 34·94	0·896 / 11·08 / 62·37	0·624 / 27·13 / 97·90	0·425 / 56·57 / 141·59
	5	0·042	3·70 / 0·04 / 3·83	1·78 / 0·68 / 15·36	1·12 / 3·42 / 34·72	0·759 / 10·84 / 62·03	0·528 / 26·56 / 97·37	0·359 / 55·50 / 140·69
	4	0·034	3·00 / 0·04 / 3·80	1·45 / 0·66 / 15·28	0·903 / 3·36 / 34·55	0·613 / 10·65 / 61·71	0·424 / 26·15 / 96·65	0·285 / 54·85 / 138·94
55×35	6	0·039	2·09 / 0·10 / 5·47	0·986 / 1·60 / 21·91	0·591 / 8·08 / 49·39	0·374 / 25·58 / 88·03	0·229 / 62·63 / 137·92	0·118 / 130·70 / 199·12
	5	0·033	1·79 / 0·10 / 5·40	0·846 / 1·55 / 21·63	0·508 / 7·85 / 48·79	0·322 / 24·86 / 87·00	0·197 / 60·93 / 136·34	0·103 / 127·46 / 196·84
	4	0·026	1·47 / 0·09 / 5·33	0·697 / 1·46 / 21·38	0·420 / 7·40 / 48·25	0·268 / 23·46 / 86·07	0·166 / 57·60 / 134·82	0·090 / 120·85 / 194·26

Table 3.4—*contd.*

Safe distributed load (kN)/maximum loading plane deflection due to self-weight only (mm)/maximum loading plane deflection due to total load (mm)

Nominal leg size (mm)	Thickness (mm)	Self-weight (kN/m)	Span (m) 1	2	3	4	5	6
45×30	3	0·020	1·13 0·09 5·27	0·535 1·44 21·16	0·321 7·28 47·77	0·204 23·11 85·03	0·125 56·95 132·53	0·066 120·17 189·54
	6	0·032	1·47 0·14 6·53	0·688 2·21 26·14	0·405 11·20 58·95	0·247 35·46 105·11	0·139 86·92 164·76	0·057 181·91 238·00
	5	0·027	1·27 0·13 6·42	0·595 2·12 25·73	0·351 10·76 58·07	0·215 34·08 103·63	0·122 83·67 162·53	0·052 175·63 234·77
	4	0·022	1·05 0·13 6·32	0·492 2·05 25·36	0·290 10·41 57·31	0·178 33·00 102·32	0·102 81·24 160·42	0·043 171·35 231·32
	3	0·017	0·813 0·13 6·24	0·380 2·01 25·06	0·223 10·20 56·65	0·136 32·42 100·99	0·077 80·24 157·59	0·031 170·31 225·39

Table 3.5

Safe Distributed Loads for Unequal Angle Beams: Load Parallel to Long Leg (Yield Stress = 300 MPa; Permissible Bending Stress = 180 MPa; Permissible Shear Stress = 120 MPa)

Safe distributed load (kN)/maximum loading plane deflection due to self-weight only (mm)/maximum loading plane deflection due to total load (mm)

Nominal leg size (mm)	Thickness (mm)	Self-weight (kN/m)	Span (m)					
			1	2	3	4	5	6
200×150	25	0·625	179	131	86·3	63·6	49·6	40·2
			0·00	0·04	0·20	0·62	1·52	3·16
			0·70	4·19	9·44	16·81	26·32	38·00
	20	0·508	120	107	70·6	52·0	40·6	32·8
			0·00	0·04	0·19	0·61	1·49	3·08
			0·56	4·15	9·35	16·66	26·11	37·73
	16	0·411	80·1	79·7	57·2	42·1	32·8	26·5
			0·00	0·04	0·19	0·60	1·46	3·02
			0·45	3·65	9·30	16·59	26·03	37·67
	13	0·337	54·5	54·2	46·7	34·3	26·7	21·6
			0·00	0·04	0·19	0·59	1·43	2·98
			0·37	2·99	9·30	16·60	26·07	37·76
200×100	20	0·431	150	100	65·9	48·5	37·8	30·5
			0·00	0·04	0·18	0·58	1·41	2·92
			0·78	4·35	9·84	17·62	27·79	40·45
	16	0·350	100	81·2	53·3	39·1	30·4	24·5
			0·00	0·04	0·18	0·56	1·38	2·87
			0·63	4·33	9·82	17·63	27·88	40·73

Table 3.5—*contd.*

Nominal leg size (mm)	Thickness (mm)	Self-weight (kN/m)	Safe distributed load (kN)/maximum loading plane deflection due to self-weight only (mm)/maximum loading plane deflection due to total load (mm) Span (m)					
			1	2	3	4	5	6
150×100	13	0·287	68·5 / 0·00 / 0·52	66·1 / 0·03 / 4·34	43·4 / 0·18 / 9·84	31·8 / 0·56 / 17·72	24·6 / 1·36 / 28·13	19·7 / 2·82 / 41·25
	10	0·223	42·0 / 0·00 / 0·40	41·8 / 0·03 / 3·27	32·9 / 0·17 / 9·94	24·1 / 0·55 / 17·95	18·6 / 1·34 / 28·60	14·8 / 2·79 / 42·11
	16	0·288	80·7 / 0·00 / 1·17	46·9 / 0·07 / 5·63	30·7 / 0·34 / 12·72	22·4 / 1·07 / 22·73	17·4 / 2·61 / 35·75	13·9 / 5·42 / 51·88
	13	0·237	55·5 / 0·00 / 0·96	38·6 / 0·07 / 5·60	25·3 / 0·33 / 12·66	18·5 / 1·05 / 22·67	14·3 / 2·56 / 35·73	11·4 / 5·32 / 51·97
	10	0·185	34·2 / 0·00 / 0·75	29·9 / 0·06 / 5·59	19·6 / 0·33 / 12·67	14·3 / 1·03 / 22·74	11·0 / 2·52 / 35·95	8·72 / 5·23 / 52·45
	8	0·149	22·5 / 0·00 / 0·60	22·4 / 0·06 / 4·87	15·5 / 0·32 / 12·74	11·3 / 1·01 / 22·90	8·68 / 2·48 / 36·27	6·86 / 5·16 / 53·01

	t							
125×90	16	0·245	65·4 0·01 1·69	32·3 0·10 6·75	21·1 0·50 15·25	15·3 1·59 27·23	11·8 3·89 42·78	9·32 8·08 62·02
	13	0·202	51·5 0·01 1·55	26·8 0·10 6·69	17·5 0·49 15·13	12·7 1·55 27·05	9·75 3·79 42·59	7·70 7·88 61·88
	10	0·158	32·0 0·01 1·20	20·9 0·09 6·65	13·6 0·48 15·07	9·89 1·52 27·02	7·57 3·71 42·67	5·96 7·72 62·19
	8	0·127	21·1 0·01 0·97	16·8 0·09 6·66	10·9 0·47 15·10	7·91 1·49 27·14	6·04 3·64 42·95	4·73 7·57 62·74
125×75	13	0·187	52·6 0·01 1·70	26·0 0·09 6·85	16·9 0·48 15·53	12·3 1·51 27·90	9·41 3·70 44·13	7·42 7·68 64·48
	10	0·146	35·3 0·01 1·40	20·3 0·09 6·82	13·2 0·47 15·51	9·54 1·47 27·98	7·28 3·61 44·49	5·71 7·50 65·35
	8	0·118	23·4 0·01 1·13	16·2 0·09 6·83	10·5 0·46 15·59	7·60 1·45 28·23	5·77 3·55 45·08	4·48 7·40 66·41
	6	0·090	13·6 0·01 0·85	12·0 0·09 6·89	7·77 0·45 15·78	5·56 1·44 28·68	4·18 3·53 45·89	3·20 7·37 67·43
100×90	13	0·177	35·2 0·01 2·05	17·3 0·16 8·20	11·2 0·82 18·50	8·11 2·59 33·01	6·15 6·33 51·80	4·78 13·15 74·98

Table 3.5—*contd.*

Safe distributed load (kN)/maximum loading plane deflection due to self-weight only (mm)/maximum loading plane deflection due to total load (mm)

Nominal leg size (mm)	Thickness (mm)	Self-weight (kN/m)	Span (m)					
			1	2	3	4	5	6
	10	0·139	27·6 0·01 1·96	13·7 0·16 8·11	8·88 0·80 18·31	6·39 2·52 32·73	4·84 6·16 51·45	3·76 12·81 74·61
	8	0·112	18·3 0·01 1·58	11·1 0·15 8·07	7·19 0·78 18·25	5·17 2·46 32·56	3·91 6·02 51·43	3·03 12·52 74·69
	6	0·085	10·7 0·01 1·19	8·36 0·15 8·06	5·41 0·76 18·26	3·88 2·42 32·72	2·92 5·92 51·58	2·25 12·32 74·90
100×75	13	0·162	34·1 0·01 2·10	16·8 0·16 8·42	10·9 0·79 19·02	7·86 2·51 34·01	5·97 6·13 53·53	4·65 12·73 77·73
	10	0·127	27·0 0·01 2·07	13·3 0·15 8·32	8·59 0·77 18·85	6·19 2·43 33·80	4·69 5·95 53·37	3·64 12·37 77·78
	8	0·103	20·0 0·01 1·82	10·7 0·15 8·29	6·95 0·75 18·82	4·99 2·39 33·84	3·77 5·85 53·60	2·91 12·17 78·32

Size	t																		
90×75	6	0·078	11·7	0·01	1·38	8·07	0·15	8·30	5·21	0·74	18·90	3·73	2·34	34·10	2·79	5·73	54·13	2·14	11·95	79·11
	13	0·152	27·7	0·01	2·31	13·6	0·20	9·28	8·81	1·01	20·95	6·33	3·20	37·41	4·77	7·82	58·77	3·68	16·25	85·18
	10	0·119	22·0	0·01	2·28	10·8	0·19	9·15	6·99	0·98	20·70	5·01	3·09	37·04	3·77	7·55	58·34	2·91	15·69	84·78
	8	0·097	17·9	0·01	2·26	8·80	0·19	9·09	5·68	0·96	20·60	4·06	3·04	36·95	3·05	7·43	58·35	2·34	15·45	85·00
	6	0·073	11·0	0·01	1·74	6·66	0·18	9·08	4·29	0·93	20·62	3·06	2·94	37·08	2·29	7·21	58·68	1·74	15·03	85·53
	5	0·062	7·78	0·01	1·45	5·53	0·18	9·09	3·55	0·93	20·67	2·53	2·95	37·22	1·88	7·23	58·86	1·42	15·12	85·50
90×65	10	0·112	21·5	0·01	2·32	10·5	0·19	9·34	6·81	0·96	21·18	4·88	3·03	38·02	3·67	7·41	60·14	2·82	15·42	87·80
	8	0·090	17·5	0·01	2·31	8·57	0·18	9·29	5·53	0·93	21·12	3·95	2·94	38·05	2·96	7·19	60·41	2·27	14·97	88·49
	6	0·069	11·8	0·01	1·95	6·48	0·18	9·29	4·16	0·92	21·20	2·96	2·90	38·38	2·20	7·11	61·14	1·66	14·84	89·61

Table 3.5—*contd.*

Safe distributed load (kN)/maximum loading plane deflection due to self-weight only (mm)/maximum loading plane deflection due to total load (mm)

Nominal leg size (mm)	Thickness (mm)	Self-weight (kN/m)	Span (m)					
			1	2	3	4	5	6
80×60	5	0·058	8·38 / 0·01 / 1·63	5·37 / 0·18 / 9·32	3·44 / 0·91 / 21·32	2·44 / 2·88 / 38·66	1·80 / 7·06 / 61·54	1·34 / 14·78 / 89·67
	10	0·100	16·9 / 0·02 / 2·62	8·26 / 0·24 / 10·52	5·32 / 1·23 / 23·83	3·79 / 3·90 / 42·76	2·83 / 9·54 / 67·59	2·15 / 19·85 / 98·57
	8	0·081	13·8 / 0·01 / 2·59	6·75 / 0·24 / 10·43	4·34 / 1·20 / 23·71	3·08 / 3·79 / 42·69	2·29 / 9·28 / 67·71	1·74 / 19·33 / 99·10
	6	0·062	10·5 / 0·01 / 2·58	5·13 / 0·23 / 10·41	3·28 / 1·17 / 23·74	2·32 / 3·72 / 42·96	1·71 / 9·12 / 68·41	1·28 / 19·05 / 100·22
	5	0·052	8·10 / 0·01 / 2·25	4·27 / 0·23 / 10·43	2·73 / 1·16 / 23·85	1·92 / 3·67 / 43·24	1·41 / 9·01 / 68·86	1·04 / 18·89 / 100·34
75×50	8	0·072	11·8 / 0·02 / 2·81	5·76 / 0·27 / 11·36	3·69 / 1·35 / 25·91	2·61 / 4·28 / 46·92	1·92 / 10·48 / 74·90	1·44 / 21·87 / 110·32

Size	t																				
65×50	6	0·055	9·01	0·02	2·80	4·39	0·26	11·33	2·80	1·32	26·03	1·96	4·17	47·47	1·43	10·24	76·17	1·05	21·47	112·11
	5	0·046	7·53	0·02	2·80	3·66	0·26	11·37	2·32	1·29	26·21	1·62	4·10	47·98	1·17	10·09	76·89	0·839	21·22	112·02
	8	0·066	8·94	0·02	3·21	4·36	0·37	12·92	2·78	1·88	29·36	1·95	5·94	52·87	1·43	14·54	83·87	1·05	30·34	122·75
	6	0·050	6·88	0·02	3·18	3·35	0·36	12·83	2·13	1·80	29·28	1·49	5·71	53·03	1·08	14·00	84·52	0·784	29·34	123·88
	5	0·042	5·78	0·02	3·17	2·81	0·35	12·82	1·78	1·77	29·37	1·24	5·62	53·36	0·889	13·81	85·07	0·639	29·03	124·05
	4	0·034	4·64	0·02	3·17	2·25	0·35	12·86	1·42	1·75	29·57	0·975	5·56	53·74	0·690	13·70	85·09	0·483	29·00	121·73
55×35	6	0·039	4·69	0·03	3·87	2·27	0·50	15·77	1·42	2·52	36·45	0·971	7·98	66·98	0·679	19·67	108·15	0·467	41·68	159·50
	5	0·033	3·96	0·03	3·86	1·91	0·49	15·78	1·19	2·48	36·73	0·803	7·88	67·84	0·551	19·47	109·18	0·368	41·60	158·20
	4	0·026	3·20	0·03	3·85	1·53	0·47	15·88	0·944	2·37	37·27	0·627	7·55	68·75	0·419	18·74	108·18	0·251	40·54	142·62

Table 3.5—*contd.*

Safe distributed load (kN)/maximum loading plane
deflection due to self-weight only (mm)/maximum
loading plane deflection due to total load (mm)

Nominal leg size (mm)	Thickness (mm)	Self-weight (kN/m)	Span (m)					
			1	2	3	4	5	6
45×30	3	0·020	2·39 0·03 3·87	1·13 0·47 16·11	0·683 2·37 37·88	0·436 7·56 67·86	0·253 19·00 92·95	0·136 42·32 117·55
	6	0·032	3·09 0·05 4·76	1·48 0·76 19·35	0·921 3·88 44·66	0·619 12·13 81·90	0·421 30·40 132·02	0·275 64·93 194·64
	5	0·027	2·63 0·05 4·72	1·26 0·75 19·30	0·776 3·78 44·86	0·516 12·03 82·70	0·345 29·83 133·05	0·218 64·41 193·16
	4	0·022	2·14 0·05 4·70	1·02 0·73 19·36	0·620 3·72 45·40	0·404 11·85 83·71	0·261 29·61 131·90	0·150 65·22 179·07
	3	0·017	1·61 0·05 4·70	0·758 0·73 19·60	0·452 3·70 46·16	0·282 11·86 82·69	0·160 30·14 116·00	0·075 69·24 146·19

Table 3.6
Safe Distributed Loads for Equal Angle Beams (Yield Stress = 36 ksi; Permissible Bending Stress = 21·6 ksi; Permissible Shear Stress = 14·4 ksi)

Nominal leg size (in)	Thickness (in)	Self-weight (lb/ft)	Safe distributed load (kips)/maximum loading plane deflection due to self-weight only (in)/maximum loading plane deflection due to total load (in)					
			Span (ft)					
			3	6	9	12	15	18
8×8	$1\tfrac{1}{8}$	56·9	37·1	32·7	21·5	15·8	12·3	9·96
			0·00	0·00	0·01	0·02	0·04	0·09
			0·02	0·11	0·24	0·43	0·68	0·98
	1	51·0	30·2	29·5	19·4	14·3	11·1	8·99
			0·00	0·00	0·01	0·02	0·04	0·09
			0·01	0·11	0·24	0·43	0·68	0·97
	$\tfrac{7}{8}$	45·0	23·7	23·6	17·2	12·7	9·89	7·99
			0·00	0·00	0·01	0·02	0·04	0·09
			0·01	0·10	0·24	0·43	0·67	0·97
	$\tfrac{3}{4}$	38·9	17·9	17·8	15·0	11·0	8·59	6·94
			0·00	0·00	0·01	0·02	0·04	0·09
			0·01	0·08	0·24	0·43	0·67	0·96
	$\tfrac{5}{8}$	32·7	12·8	12·7	12·6	9·28	7·24	5·84
			0·00	0·00	0·01	0·02	0·04	0·08
			0·01	0·07	0·23	0·42	0·66	0·96
	$\tfrac{9}{16}$	29·6	10·5	10·4	10·3	8·38	6·54	5·28
			0·00	0·00	0·01	0·02	0·04	0·08
			0·01	0·06	0·21	0·42	0·66	0·96

Table 3.6—contd.

Safe distributed load (kips)/maximum loading plane deflection due to self-weight only (in)/maximum loading plane deflection due to total load (in)

Nominal leg size (in)	Thickness (in)	Self-weight (lb/ft)	Span (ft)					
			3	6	9	12	15	18
6×6	$\frac{1}{2}$	26·4	8·42 0·00 0·01	8·34 0·00 0·06	8·27 0·01 0·19	7·47 0·02 0·42	5·82 0·04 0·66	4·70 0·08 0·96
	1	37·4	28·0 0·00 0·03	15·8 0·00 0·15	10·4 0·01 0·33	7·58 0·03 0·59	5·86 0·08 0·92	4·67 0·17 1·32
	$\frac{7}{8}$	33·1	22·3 0·00 0·03	14·2 0·00 0·15	9·28 0·01 0·33	6·78 0·03 0·58	5·24 0·08 0·91	4·18 0·16 1·31
	$\frac{3}{4}$	28·7	17·0 0·00 0·02	12·4 0·00 0·14	8·12 0·01 0·32	5·93 0·03 0·58	4·59 0·08 0·90	3·66 0·16 1·30
	$\frac{5}{8}$	24·2	12·2 0·00 0·02	10·5 0·00 0·14	6·90 0·01 0·32	5·04 0·03 0·57	3·90 0·07 0·89	3·11 0·15 1·29
	$\frac{9}{16}$	21·9	10·1 0·00 0·02	9·56 0·00 0·14	6·26 0·01 0·32	4·58 0·03 0·57	3·54 0·07 0·89	2·82 0·15 1·29

5×5

1/2	19·6	8·12 / 0·00 / 0·02	8·06 / 0·00 / 0·13	5·61 / 0·01 / 0·32	4·10 / 0·03 / 0·57	3·17 / 0·07 / 0·89	2·53 / 0·15 / 1·28
7/16	17·2	6·33 / 0·00 / 0·01	6·28 / 0·00 / 0·11	4·94 / 0·01 / 0·32	3·61 / 0·03 / 0·57	2·79 / 0·07 / 0·89	2·22 / 0·15 / 1·28
3/8	14·9	4·74 / 0·00 / 0·01	4·69 / 0·00 / 0·10	4·25 / 0·01 / 0·32	3·10 / 0·03 / 0·57	2·39 / 0·07 / 0·89	1·91 / 0·15 / 1·28
5/16	12·4	3·35 / 0·00 / 0·01	3·31 / 0·00 / 0·08	3·28 / 0·01 / 0·28	2·58 / 0·03 / 0·57	1·99 / 0·07 / 0·89	1·58 / 0·15 / 1·28
7/8	27·2	19·3 / 0·00 / 0·04	9·52 / 0·00 / 0·18	6·20 / 0·02 / 0·40	4·51 / 0·05 / 0·71	3·46 / 0·12 / 1·11	2·73 / 0·24 / 1·60
3/4	23·6	16·2 / 0·00 / 0·04	8·37 / 0·00 / 0·17	5·46 / 0·01 / 0·39	3·97 / 0·05 / 0·70	3·05 / 0·11 / 1·09	2·41 / 0·23 / 1·58
5/8	20·0	11·8 / 0·00 / 0·03	7·15 / 0·00 / 0·17	4·67 / 0·01 / 0·39	3·39 / 0·05 / 0·69	2·60 / 0·11 / 1·08	2·06 / 0·23 / 1·56
1/2	16·2	7·88 / 0·00 / 0·03	5·86 / 0·00 / 0·17	3·82 / 0·01 / 0·38	2·78 / 0·04 / 0·69	2·13 / 0·11 / 1·07	1·68 / 0·22 / 1·55
7/16	14·3	6·17 / 0·00 / 0·02	5·17 / 0·00 / 0·17	3·37 / 0·01 / 0·38	2·45 / 0·04 / 0·68	1·88 / 0·11 / 1·07	1·49 / 0·22 / 1·54

Single and Compound Angle Members

Table 3.6—*contd.*

Safe distributed load (kips)/maximum loading plane deflection due to self-weight only (in)/maximum loading plane deflection due to total load (in)

Nominal leg size (in)	Thickness (in)	Self-weight (lb/ft)	Span (ft)					
			3	6	9	12	15	18
4 × 4	$\frac{3}{8}$	12·3	4·64	4·47	2·92	2·12	1·62	1·28
			0·00	0·00	0·01	0·04	0·10	0·22
			0·02	0·17	0·38	0·68	1·07	1·54
	$\frac{5}{16}$	10·3	3·29	3·26	2·44	1·77	1·36	1·07
			0·00	0·00	0·01	0·04	0·10	0·21
			0·02	0·14	0·38	0·68	1·07	1·54
	$\frac{3}{4}$	18·5	10·4	5·13	3·32	2·39	1·81	1·41
			0·00	0·00	0·02	0·08	0·18	0·38
			0·06	0·22	0·50	0·89	1·39	2·01
	$\frac{5}{8}$	15·7	8·98	4·42	2·86	2·06	1·56	1·22
			0·00	0·00	0·02	0·07	0·18	0·37
			0·05	0·22	0·49	0·88	1·37	1·98
	$\frac{1}{2}$	12·8	7·41	3·65	2·37	1·70	1·29	1·00
			0·00	0·00	0·02	0·07	0·17	0·36
			0·05	0·22	0·49	0·87	1·36	1·96
	$\frac{7}{16}$	11·3	5·93	3·24	2·10	1·51	1·15	0·892
			0·00	0·00	0·02	0·07	0·17	0·35
			0·05	0·21	0·48	0·86	1·35	1·95

3½×3½	3/8	9·8	4·48 / 0·00 / 0·04	2·81 / 0·00 / 0·21	1·82 / 0·02 / 0·48	1·31 / 0·07 / 0·86	0·995 / 0·17 / 1·34	0·773 / 0·35 / 1·94
	5/16	8·2	3·20 / 0·00 / 0·03	2·37 / 0·00 / 0·21	1·54 / 0·02 / 0·48	1·11 / 0·07 / 0·85	0·837 / 0·16 / 1·34	0·650 / 0·34 / 1·94
	1/4	6·6	2·11 / 0·00 / 0·03	1·91 / 0·00 / 0·21	1·24 / 0·02 / 0·48	0·888 / 0·07 / 0·85	0·671 / 0·16 / 1·34	0·519 / 0·34 / 1·94
	1/2	11·1	5·57 / 0·00 / 0·06	2·73 / 0·01 / 0·25	1·77 / 0·03 / 0·56	1·26 / 0·09 / 1·00	0·950 / 0·23 / 1·56	0·729 / 0·48 / 2·26
	7/16	9·8	4·96 / 0·00 / 0·06	2·44 / 0·01 / 0·25	1·57 / 0·03 / 0·56	1·13 / 0·09 / 0·99	0·847 / 0·22 / 1·55	0·650 / 0·47 / 2·24
	3/8	8·5	4·33 / 0·00 / 0·06	2·12 / 0·01 / 0·24	1·37 / 0·03 / 0·55	0·981 / 0·09 / 0·98	0·737 / 0·22 / 1·54	0·566 / 0·46 / 2·23
	5/16	7·2	3·14 / 0·00 / 0·05	1·79 / 0·01 / 0·24	1·16 / 0·03 / 0·55	0·829 / 0·09 / 0·98	0·622 / 0·22 / 1·54	0·476 / 0·45 / 2·23
	1/4	5·8	2·07 / 0·00 / 0·04	1·45 / 0·01 / 0·24	0·936 / 0·03 / 0·55	0·669 / 0·09 / 0·98	0·501 / 0·21 / 1·54	0·383 / 0·45 / 2·23
3×3	1/2	9·4	3·99 / 0·00 / 0·07	1·95 / 0·01 / 0·29	1·25 / 0·04 / 0·66	0·889 / 0·13 / 1·18	0·660 / 0·32 / 1·85	0·497 / 0·67 / 2·66

Table 3.6—*contd.*

Safe distributed load (kips)/maximum loading plane deflection due to self-weight only (in)/maximum loading plane deflection due to total load (in)

Nominal leg size (in)	Thickness (in)	Self-weight (lb/ft)	Span (ft)					
			3	6	9	12	15	18
	$\frac{7}{16}$	8·3	3·57 / 0·00 / 0·07	1·75 / 0·01 / 0·29	1·12 / 0·04 / 0·66	0·796 / 0·13 / 1·17	0·591 / 0·31 / 1·83	0·445 / 0·65 / 2·64
	$\frac{3}{8}$	7·2	3·12 / 0·00 / 0·07	1·53 / 0·01 / 0·29	0·981 / 0·04 / 0·65	0·696 / 0·13 / 1·16	0·517 / 0·31 / 1·82	0·390 / 0·64 / 2·62
	$\frac{5}{16}$	6·1	2·65 / 0·00 / 0·07	1·30 / 0·01 / 0·29	0·833 / 0·04 / 0·64	0·591 / 0·12 / 1·15	0·438 / 0·30 / 1·81	0·330 / 0·63 / 2·61
	$\frac{1}{4}$	4·9	2·03 / 0·00 / 0·06	1·05 / 0·01 / 0·28	0·677 / 0·04 / 0·64	0·480 / 0·12 / 1·15	0·355 / 0·29 / 1·80	0·267 / 0·61 / 2·61
	$\frac{3}{16}$	3·71	1·18 / 0·00 / 0·05	0·798 / 0·01 / 0·28	0·511 / 0·04 / 0·64	0·361 / 0·12 / 1·15	0·266 / 0·29 / 1·81	0·199 / 0·60 / 2·62
$2\frac{1}{2} \times 2\frac{1}{2}$	$\frac{1}{2}$	7·7	2·67 / 0·00 / 0·09	1·30 / 0·01 / 0·36	0·827 / 0·06 / 0·81	0·579 / 0·20 / 1·44	0·421 / 0·48 / 2·25	0·308 / 1·00 / 3·25

2 × 2

		(1)	(2)	(3)	(4)	(5)	(6)
$\frac{3}{8}$	5·9	0·246 / 0·94 / 3·19	0·335 / 0·45 / 2·20	0·459 / 0·18 / 1·41	0·655 / 0·06 / 0·79	1·03 / 0·01 / 0·35	2·11 / 0·00 / 0·09
$\frac{5}{16}$	5·0	0·210 / 0·92 / 3·17	0·286 / 0·44 / 2·19	0·392 / 0·18 / 1·39	0·560 / 0·06 / 0·78	0·878 / 0·01 / 0·35	1·80 / 0·00 / 0·09
$\frac{1}{4}$	4·1	0·170 / 0·91 / 3·16	0·233 / 0·44 / 2·18	0·320 / 0·18 / 1·38	0·457 / 0·06 / 0·77	0·719 / 0·01 / 0·34	1·48 / 0·00 / 0·09
$\frac{3}{16}$	3·07	0·128 / 0·87 / 3·16	0·176 / 0·42 / 2·18	0·244 / 0·17 / 1·38	0·349 / 0·05 / 0·77	0·548 / 0·01 / 0·34	1·13 / 0·00 / 0·08
$\frac{3}{8}$	4·7	0·132 / 1·55 / 4·06	0·190 / 0·75 / 2·81	0·270 / 0·31 / 1·79	0·393 / 0·10 / 1·00	0·626 / 0·02 / 0·45	1·30 / 0·00 / 0·11
$\frac{5}{16}$	3·92	0·115 / 1·48 / 4·02	0·165 / 0·71 / 2·78	0·234 / 0·29 / 1·77	0·340 / 0·09 / 0·99	0·540 / 0·02 / 0·44	1·12 / 0·00 / 0·11
$\frac{1}{4}$	3·19	0·095 / 1·44 / 3·99	0·136 / 0·69 / 2·75	0·193 / 0·28 / 1·75	0·280 / 0·09 / 0·98	0·446 / 0·02 / 0·43	0·922 / 0·00 / 0·11
$\frac{3}{16}$	2·44	0·072 / 1·40 / 3·99	0·104 / 0·67 / 2·75	0·148 / 0·27 / 1·74	0·216 / 0·09 / 0·97	0·343 / 0·02 / 0·43	0·711 / 0·00 / 0·11
$\frac{1}{8}$	1·65	0·046 / 1·38 / 3·92	0·068 / 0·65 / 2·74	0·098 / 0·26 / 1·75	0·145 / 0·08 / 0·97	0·232 / 0·02 / 0·43	0·482 / 0·00 / 0·11

Table 3.7

Safe Distributed Loads for Unequal Angle Beams: Load Parallel to Short Leg (Yield Stress = 36 ksi; Permissible Bending Stress = 21·6 ksi; Permissible Shear Stress = 14·4 ksi)

Safe distributed load (kips)/maximum loading plane deflection due to self-weight only (in)/maximum loading plane deflection due to total load (in)

Nominal leg size (in)	Thickness (in)	Self-weight (lb/ft)	Span (ft)					
			3	6	9	12	15	18
9×4	$\frac{5}{8}$	26·3	8·53 / 0·00 / 0·04	5·07 / 0·01 / 0·19	3·25 / 0·03 / 0·43	2·30 / 0·09 / 0·77	1·70 / 0·23 / 1·20	1·27 / 0·47 / 1·72
	$\frac{9}{16}$	23·8	7·06 / 0·00 / 0·04	4·64 / 0·01 / 0·19	2·97 / 0·03 / 0·43	2·10 / 0·09 / 0·76	1·55 / 0·22 / 1·19	1·16 / 0·46 / 1·71
	$\frac{1}{2}$	21·3	5·70 / 0·00 / 0·03	4·19 / 0·01 / 0·19	2·68 / 0·03 / 0·42	1·90 / 0·09 / 0·75	1·40 / 0·22 / 1·18	1·05 / 0·45 / 1·70
8×6	1	44·2	25·2 / 0·00 / 0·03	16·7 / 0·00 / 0·14	10·9 / 0·01 / 0·32	7·94 / 0·03 / 0·56	6·11 / 0·09 / 0·88	4·85 / 0·18 / 1·26
	$\frac{7}{8}$	39·1	19·9 / 0·00 / 0·02	14·9 / 0·00 / 0·14	9·75 / 0·01 / 0·31	7·10 / 0·03 / 0·56	5·47 / 0·08 / 0·87	4·34 / 0·17 / 1·25
	$\frac{3}{4}$	33·8	15·1 / 0·00 / 0·02	13·1 / 0·00 / 0·14	8·53 / 0·01 / 0·31	6·22 / 0·03 / 0·55	4·79 / 0·08 / 0·86	3·80 / 0·17 / 1·24

Size	t																		
8×4	5/8	28·5	10·9	0·00	0·02	10·8	0·00	0·13	7·25	0·01	0·31	5·28	0·03	0·55	4·07	0·08	0·85	3·23	0·17	1·23
	9/16	25·7	8·95	0·00	0·01	8·88	0·00	0·12	6·58	0·01	0·31	4·80	0·03	0·54	3·70	0·08	0·85	2·94	0·16	1·23
	1/2	23·0	7·19	0·00	0·01	7·12	0·00	0·11	5·90	0·01	0·30	4·30	0·03	0·54	3·31	0·08	0·85	2·63	0·16	1·22
	7/16	20·2	5·60	0·00	0·01	5·54	0·00	0·09	5·20	0·01	0·30	3·79	0·03	0·54	2·92	0·08	0·84	2·32	0·16	1·22
7×4	1	37·4	14·7	0·00	0·05	7·20	0·01	0·20	4·61	0·03	0·46	3·26	0·10	0·82	2·41	0·24	1·28	1·80	0·50	1·84
	3/4	28·7	11·8	0·00	0·05	5·78	0·01	0·20	3·71	0·03	0·45	2·63	0·09	0·79	1·95	0·22	1·24	1·47	0·46	1·79
	9/16	21·9	7·29	0·00	0·04	4·55	0·01	0·19	2·92	0·03	0·44	2·08	0·09	0·78	1·54	0·21	1·21	1·17	0·44	1·75
	1/2	19·6	5·89	0·00	0·03	4·11	0·01	0·19	2·64	0·03	0·43	1·88	0·09	0·77	1·40	0·21	1·20	1·05	0·43	1·74
	3/4	26·2	11·6	0·00	0·05	5·66	0·01	0·20	3·64	0·03	0·46	2·59	0·09	0·81	1·93	0·21	1·27	1·46	0·44	1·83

Table 3.7—contd.

Safe distributed load (kips)/maximum loading plane deflection due to self-weight only (in)/maximum loading plane deflection due to total load (in)

Nominal leg size (in)	Thickness (in)	Self-weight (lb/ft)	Span (ft)					
			3	6	9	12	15	18
	$\frac{5}{8}$	22·1	9·15 / 0·00 / 0·05	4·87 / 0·01 / 0·20	3·14 / 0·03 / 0·45	2·24 / 0·08 / 0·80	1·67 / 0·21 / 1·25	1·27 / 0·43 / 1·80
	$\frac{1}{2}$	17·9	6·13 / 0·00 / 0·04	4·02 / 0·01 / 0·20	2·59 / 0·03 / 0·44	1·85 / 0·08 / 0·79	1·38 / 0·20 / 1·23	1·05 / 0·41 / 1·78
	$\frac{3}{8}$	13·6	3·61 / 0·00 / 0·03	3·10 / 0·00 / 0·19	2·00 / 0·02 / 0·44	1·43 / 0·08 / 0·78	1·07 / 0·19 / 1·22	0·814 / 0·40 / 1·75
6 × 4	$\frac{7}{8}$	27·2	12·7 / 0·00 / 0·05	6·22 / 0·01 / 0·21	4·01 / 0·03 / 0·48	2·86 / 0·09 / 0·85	2·14 / 0·21 / 1·33	1·63 / 0·44 / 1·91
	$\frac{3}{4}$	23·6	11·2 / 0·00 / 0·05	5·51 / 0·01 / 0·21	3·55 / 0·03 / 0·47	2·54 / 0·08 / 0·83	1·91 / 0·20 / 1·30	1·46 / 0·42 / 1·88
	$\frac{5}{8}$	20·0	9·60 / 0·00 / 0·05	4·74 / 0·01 / 0·21	3·06 / 0·03 / 0·46	2·19 / 0·08 / 0·82	1·64 / 0·20 / 1·28	1·26 / 0·41 / 1·85

Size	t							
	9/16	18·1	7·97 / 0·00 / 0·05	4·34 / 0·00 / 0·20	2·80 / 0·03 / 0·46	2·00 / 0·08 / 0·82	1·51 / 0·19 / 1·28	1·15 / 0·40 / 1·84
	1/2	16·2	6·45 / 0·00 / 0·04	3·92 / 0·00 / 0·20	2·53 / 0·02 / 0·46	1·81 / 0·08 / 0·81	1·36 / 0·19 / 1·27	1·04 / 0·39 / 1·83
	7/16	14·3	5·06 / 0·00 / 0·04	3·48 / 0·00 / 0·20	2·25 / 0·02 / 0·45	1·61 / 0·08 / 0·81	1·21 / 0·19 / 1·26	0·928 / 0·39 / 1·81
	3/8	12·3	3·81 / 0·00 / 0·03	3·02 / 0·00 / 0·20	1·95 / 0·02 / 0·45	1·40 / 0·08 / 0·80	1·05 / 0·18 / 1·25	0·808 / 0·38 / 1·80
	5/16	10·3	2·71 / 0·00 / 0·03	2·55 / 0·00 / 0·20	1·65 / 0·02 / 0·45	1·18 / 0·07 / 0·80	0·887 / 0·18 / 1·25	0·681 / 0·37 / 1·80
6 × 3½	1/2	15·3	6·01 / 0·00 / 0·06	3·00 / 0·01 / 0·23	1·92 / 0·03 / 0·51	1·36 / 0·11 / 0·91	1·01 / 0·26 / 1·43	0·754 / 0·55 / 2·06
	3/8	11·7	3·56 / 0·00 / 0·04	2·33 / 0·01 / 0·22	1·49 / 0·03 / 0·51	1·06 / 0·10 / 0·90	0·783 / 0·25 / 1·40	0·588 / 0·53 / 2·02
	5/16	9·8	2·54 / 0·00 / 0·03	1·97 / 0·01 / 0·22	1·27 / 0·03 / 0·50	0·897 / 0·10 / 0·89	0·664 / 0·25 / 1·40	0·499 / 0·52 / 2·01
5 × 3½	3/4	19·8	8·28 / 0·00 / 0·06	4·05 / 0·01 / 0·24	2·60 / 0·04 / 0·55	1·85 / 0·11 / 0·98	1·37 / 0·27 / 1·52	1·03 / 0·56 / 2·20

Table 3.7—*contd.*

Safe distributed load (kips)/maximum loading plane deflection due to self-weight only (in)/maximum loading plane deflection due to total load (in)

Nominal leg size (in)	Thickness (in)	Self-weight (lb/ft)	Span (ft)					
			3	6	9	12	15	18
	$\frac{5}{8}$	16·8	7·17 / 0·00 / 0·06	3·51 / 0·01 / 0·24	2·25 / 0·03 / 0·54	1·60 / 0·11 / 0·96	1·19 / 0·26 / 1·50	0·898 / 0·54 / 2·16
	$\frac{1}{2}$	13·6	5·95 / 0·00 / 0·06	2·91 / 0·01 / 0·24	1·87 / 0·03 / 0·53	1·33 / 0·10 / 0·94	0·991 / 0·25 / 1·47	0·751 / 0·52 / 2·12
	$\frac{7}{16}$	12·0	5·02 / 0·00 / 0·05	2·59 / 0·01 / 0·23	1·67 / 0·03 / 0·53	1·19 / 0·10 / 0·93	0·884 / 0·24 / 1·46	0·670 / 0·51 / 2·11
	$\frac{3}{8}$	10·4	3·80 / 0·00 / 0·05	2·26 / 0·01 / 0·23	1·45 / 0·03 / 0·52	1·03 / 0·10 / 0·93	0·771 / 0·24 / 1·45	0·584 / 0·50 / 2·09
	$\frac{5}{16}$	8·7	2·71 / 0·00 / 0·04	1·91 / 0·01 / 0·23	1·23 / 0·03 / 0·52	0·876 / 0·10 / 0·92	0·653 / 0·24 / 1·44	0·495 / 0·49 / 2·08
	$\frac{1}{4}$	7·0	1·78 / 0·00 / 0·03	1·55 / 0·01 / 0·23	0·997 / 0·03 / 0·51	0·710 / 0·09 / 0·92	0·529 / 0·23 / 1·43	0·401 / 0·48 / 2·07

Size	Thick.	Wt																		
5 × 3	5/8	15·7	5·24	0·00	0·07	2·55	0·01	0·28	1·62	0·05	0·62	1·13	0·16	1·10	0·821	0·38	1·73	0·597	0·80	2·49
	1/2	12·8	4·38	0·00	0·07	2·13	0·01	0·27	1·36	0·05	0·61	0·950	0·15	1·08	0·690	0·37	1·69	0·505	0·76	2·44
	7/16	11·3	3·91	0·00	0·07	1·91	0·01	0·27	1·21	0·05	0·60	0·850	0·15	1·07	0·619	0·36	1·68	0·453	0·74	2·41
	3/8	9·8	3·42	0·00	0·07	1·67	0·01	0·27	1·06	0·05	0·60	0·745	0·14	1·06	0·542	0·35	1·66	0·398	0·73	2·39
	5/16	8·2	2·51	0·00	0·06	1·42	0·01	0·26	0·903	0·04	0·59	0·634	0·14	1·05	0·462	0·34	1·65	0·340	0·71	2·37
	1/4	6·6	1·66	0·00	0·04	1·15	0·01	0·26	0·736	0·04	0·59	0·517	0·14	1·04	0·377	0·33	1·63	0·277	0·69	2·36
4 × 3½	5/8	14·7	6·88	0·00	0·06	3·37	0·01	0·25	2·17	0·03	0·56	1·55	0·10	0·99	1·16	0·25	1·55	0·886	0·51	2·24
	1/2	11·9	5·71	0·00	0·06	2·80	0·01	0·24	1·81	0·03	0·55	1·29	0·10	0·98	0·967	0·24	1·53	0·740	0·49	2·21
	7/16	10·6	5·08	0·00	0·06	2·49	0·01	0·24	1·61	0·03	0·54	1·15	0·10	0·97	0·861	0·23	1·52	0·658	0·48	2·19

Table 3.7—*contd.*

Safe distributed load (kips)/maximum loading plane
deflection due to self-weight only (in)/maximum
loading plane deflection due to total load (in)

Nominal leg size (in)	Thickness (in)	Self-weight (lb/ft)	Span (ft)					
			3	6	9	12	15	18
	$\frac{3}{8}$	9·1	4·14	2·17	1·40	1·00	0·751	0·575
			0·00	0·01	0·03	0·09	0·23	0·47
			0·06	0·24	0·54	0·96	1·51	2·18
	$\frac{5}{16}$	7·7	2·96	1·84	1·19	0·847	0·634	0·485
			0·00	0·01	0·03	0·09	0·22	0·47
			0·05	0·24	0·54	0·96	1·50	2·17
	$\frac{1}{4}$	6·2	1·95	1·49	0·959	0·685	0·512	0·391
			0·00	0·01	0·03	0·09	0·22	0·46
			0·04	0·24	0·54	0·95	1·50	2·16
4×3	$\frac{5}{8}$	13·6	5·03	2·45	1·57	1·10	0·809	0·599
			0·00	0·01	0·05	0·15	0·36	0·75
			0·07	0·29	0·65	1·15	1·79	2·59
	$\frac{1}{2}$	11·1	4·21	2·05	1·31	0·925	0·680	0·505
			0·00	0·01	0·04	0·14	0·34	0·71
			0·07	0·28	0·63	1·12	1·76	2·53
	$\frac{7}{16}$	9·8	3·76	1·83	1·17	0·828	0·609	0·453
			0·00	0·01	0·04	0·14	0·34	0·70
			0·07	0·28	0·63	1·11	1·74	2·51

Size	Thickness	Weight																		
3½ × 3	3/8	8·5	3·29	0·00	0·07	1·61	0·01	0·28	1·03	0·04	0·62	0·725	0·13	1·10	0·534	0·33	1·73	0·397	0·68	2·49
	5/16	7·2	2·72	0·00	0·07	1·36	0·01	0·27	0·873	0·04	0·61	0·616	0·13	1·09	0·453	0·32	1·71	0·337	0·67	2·47
	1/4	5·8	1·80	0·00	0·05	1·11	0·01	0·27	0·710	0·04	0·61	0·501	0·13	1·09	0·369	0·32	1·70	0·274	0·66	2·46
	1/2	10·2	4·10	0·00	0·07	2·01	0·01	0·29	1·29	0·04	0·65	0·910	0·14	1·15	0·672	0·33	1·80	0·503	0·69	2·59
	7/16	9·1	3·67	0·00	0·07	1·79	0·01	0·28	1·15	0·04	0·64	0·813	0·13	1·14	0·600	0·33	1·78	0·449	0·68	2·57
	3/8	7·9	3·21	0·00	0·07	1·57	0·01	0·28	1·01	0·04	0·63	0·712	0·13	1·13	0·526	0·32	1·77	0·394	0·66	2·55
	5/16	6·6	2·73	0·00	0·07	1·33	0·01	0·28	0·855	0·04	0·63	0·605	0·13	1·12	0·447	0·31	1·76	0·335	0·64	2·54
	1/4	5·4	1·90	0·00	0·06	1·08	0·01	0·28	0·694	0·04	0·62	0·491	0·13	1·11	0·362	0·31	1·75	0·271	0·64	2·53
3½ × 2½	1/2	9·4	2·84	0·00	0·08	1·38	0·01	0·34	0·871	0·07	0·76	0·604	0·21	1·36	0·432	0·52	2·13	0·308	1·08	3·07

Table 3.7—*contd.*

			Safe distributed load (kips)/maximum loading plane deflection due to self-weight only (in)/maximum loading plane deflection due to total load (in)					
Nominal leg size (in)	*Thickness (in)*	*Self-weight (lb/ft)*			*Span (ft)*			
			3	*6*	*9*	*12*	*15*	*18*
$3 \times 2\frac{1}{2}$	$\frac{7}{16}$	8·3	2·55 0·00 0·08	1·24 0·01 0·34	0·784 0·07 0·76	0·544 0·21 1·34	0·390 0·51 2·10	0·279 1·05 3·03
	$\frac{3}{8}$	7·2	2·24 0·00 0·08	1·09 0·01 0·33	0·690 0·06 0·75	0·479 0·20 1·33	0·344 0·49 2·08	0·247 1·02 3·00
	$\frac{5}{16}$	6·1	1·92 0·00 0·08	0·931 0·01 0·33	0·589 0·06 0·74	0·410 0·20 1·31	0·294 0·48 2·06	0·211 1·00 2·97
	$\frac{1}{4}$	4·9	1·570 0·00 0·08	0·762 0·01 0·32	0·483 0·06 0·73	0·336 0·19 1·30	0·242 0·47 2·04	0·174 0·97 2·94
	$\frac{1}{2}$	8·5	2·76 0·00 0·09	1·34 0·01 0·35	0·852 0·06 0·78	0·594 0·20 1·40	0·429 0·50 2·19	0·310 1·03 3·15
	$\frac{7}{16}$	7·6	2·48 0·00 0·09	1·21 0·01 0·34	0·765 0·06 0·77	0·534 0·20 1·38	0·385 0·49 2·16	0·279 1·01 3·12

3 × 2

Thickness	Wt.						
3/8	6·6	2·18 / 0·00 / 0·08	1·06 / 0·01 / 0·34	0·674 / 0·06 / 0·77	0·470 / 0·19 / 1·36	0·340 / 0·48 / 2·14	0·246 / 0·99 / 3·08
5/16	5·6	1·86 / 0·00 / 0·08	0·906 / 0·01 / 0·34	0·576 / 0·06 / 0·76	0·402 / 0·19 / 1·35	0·290 / 0·47 / 2·11	0·210 / 0·97 / 3·05
1/4	4·5	1·53 / 0·00 / 0·08	0·742 / 0·01 / 0·33	0·471 / 0·06 / 0·75	0·329 / 0·18 / 1·34	0·238 / 0·45 / 2·10	0·173 / 0·94 / 3·04
3/16	3·39	1·07 / 0·00 / 0·07	0·567 / 0·01 / 0·33	0·360 / 0·06 / 0·75	0·251 / 0·18 / 1·33	0·181 / 0·44 / 2·09	0·131 / 0·91 / 3·02
1/2	7·7	1·74 / 0·00 / 0·11	0·835 / 0·02 / 0·43	0·518 / 0·11 / 0·97	0·348 / 0·36 / 1·72	0·236 / 0·88 / 2·70	0·155 / 1·83 / 3·89
7/16	6·8	1·57 / 0·00 / 0·11	0·756 / 0·02 / 0·42	0·470 / 0·11 / 0·95	0·317 / 0·35 / 1·70	0·216 / 0·85 / 2·65	0·143 / 1·76 / 3·83
3/8	5·9	1·40 / 0·00 / 0·10	0·671 / 0·02 / 0·42	0·418 / 0·11 / 0·94	0·282 / 0·33 / 1·67	0·194 / 0·81 / 2·61	0·129 / 1·69 / 3·77
5/16	5·0	1·20 / 0·00 / 0·10	0·578 / 0·02 / 0·41	0·360 / 0·10 / 0·93	0·244 / 0·32 / 1·65	0·168 / 0·79 / 2·58	0·112 / 1·64 / 3·72
1/4	4·1	0·991 / 0·00 / 0·10	0·477 / 0·02 / 0·41	0·297 / 0·10 / 0·91	0·201 / 0·32 / 1·63	0·138 / 0·77 / 2·54	0·092 / 1·60 / 3·67

Table 3.7—*contd.*

Nominal leg size (in)	Thickness (in)	Self-weight (lb/ft)	Safe distributed load (kips)/maximum loading plane deflection due to self-weight only (in)/maximum loading plane deflection due to total load (in) Span (ft)					
			3	6	9	12	15	18
$2\frac{1}{2} \times 2$	$\frac{3}{16}$	3·07	0·765 0·00 0·10	0·368 0·02 0·40	0·230 0·09 0·90	0·156 0·30 1·61	0·108 0·74 2·52	0·073 1·53 3·63
	$\frac{3}{8}$	5·3	1·35 0·00 0·11	0·651 0·02 0·43	0·407 0·10 0·97	0·277 0·32 1·73	0·193 0·78 2·70	0·131 1·62 3·90
	$\frac{5}{16}$	4·5	1·16 0·00 0·11	0·561 0·02 0·42	0·351 0·10 0·95	0·239 0·31 1·70	0·167 0·76 2·66	0·114 1·57 3·85
	$\frac{1}{4}$	3·62	0·960 0·00 0·10	0·463 0·02 0·42	0·290 0·09 0·94	0·198 0·30 1·68	0·139 0·72 2·63	0·095 1·51 3·81
	$\frac{3}{16}$	2·75	0·740 0·00 0·10	0·357 0·02 0·41	0·224 0·09 0·93	0·153 0·29 1·66	0·107 0·70 2·61	0·073 1·46 3·78

Table 3.8

Safe Distributed Loads for Unequal Angle Beams: Load Parallel to Long Leg (Yield Stress = 36 ksi; Permissible Bending Stress = 21·6 ksi; Permissible Shear Stress = 14·4 ksi)

| Nominal leg size (in) | Thickness (in) | Self-weight (lb/ft) | Safe distributed load (kips)/maximum loading plane deflection due to self-weight only (in)/maximum loading plane deflection due to total load (in) | | | | | |
| | | | Span (ft) | | | | | |
			3	6	9	12	15	18
9×4	$\frac{5}{8}$	26·3	20·2	20·1	14·0	10·3	8·06	6·52
			0·00	0·00	0·00	0·01	0·03	0·06
			0·01	0·09	0·23	0·42	0·66	0·97
	$\frac{9}{16}$	23·8	16·6	16·6	12·6	9·27	7·24	5·85
			0·00	0·00	0·00	0·01	0·03	0·06
			0·01	0·08	0·24	0·42	0·67	0·97
	$\frac{1}{2}$	21·3	13·4	13·3	11·2	8·21	6·40	5·16
			0·00	0·00	0·00	0·01	0·03	0·06
			0·01	0·08	0·24	0·42	0·67	0·98
8×6	1	44·2	34·4	28·0	18·5	13·6	10·6	8·60
			0·00	0·00	0·01	0·02	0·04	0·08
			0·02	0·11	0·25	0·45	0·70	1·01
	$\frac{7}{8}$	39·1	27·1	24·9	16·4	12·1	9·44	7·64
			0·00	0·00	0·01	0·02	0·04	0·08
			0·01	0·11	0·25	0·45	0·70	1·01
	$\frac{3}{4}$	33·8	20·6	20·5	14·2	10·5	8·19	6·63
			0·00	0·00	0·01	0·02	0·04	0·08
			0·01	0·10	0·25	0·44	0·70	1·00

Table 3.8—*contd.*

Safe distributed load (kips)/maximum loading plane deflection due to self-weight only (in)/maximum loading plane deflection due to total load (in)

Nominal leg size (in)	Thickness (in)	Self-weight (lb/ft)	Span (ft)					
			3	6	9	12	15	18
	$\frac{5}{8}$	28·5	14·7 0·00 0·01	14·6 0·00 0·09	12·0 0·01 0·25	8·83 0·02 0·44	6·90 0·04 0·69	5·58 0·08 1·00
	$\frac{9}{16}$	25·7	12·1 0·00 0·01	12·0 0·00 0·08	10·8 0·00 0·25	7·97 0·02 0·44	6·23 0·04 0·69	5·03 0·08 1·00
	$\frac{1}{2}$	23·0	9·72 0·00 0·01	9·65 0·00 0·07	9·58 0·00 0·23	7·10 0·02 0·44	5·54 0·04 0·69	4·48 0·08 1·00
	$\frac{7}{16}$	20·2	7·56 0·00 0·01	7·50 0·00 0·06	7·43 0·00 0·21	6·20 0·02 0·44	4·84 0·04 0·69	3·90 0·08 1·00
8×4	1	37·4	42·4 0·00 0·02	26·2 0·00 0·12	17·3 0·00 0·26	12·7 0·02 0·47	9·96 0·04 0·74	8·07 0·08 1·07
	$\frac{3}{4}$	28·7	25·6 0·00 0·02	20·2 0·00 0·12	13·3 0·00 0·26	9·81 0·02 0·47	7·66 0·04 0·74	6·20 0·08 1·07

	Thickness							
7×4	9/16	21.9	15.2 0.00 0.01	15.1 0.00 0.11	10.1 0.00 0.26	7.43 0.01 0.47	5.80 0.04 0.74	4.68 0.08 1.07
	1/2	19.6	12.2 0.00 0.01	12.2 0.00 0.10	8.99 0.00 0.26	6.60 0.01 0.47	5.14 0.04 0.74	4.14 0.08 1.08
	3/4	26.2	23.1 0.00 0.02	15.6 0.00 0.13	10.3 0.01 0.30	7.54 0.02 0.53	5.88 0.05 0.83	4.74 0.10 1.20
	5/8	22.1	16.6 0.00 0.02	13.2 0.00 0.13	8.68 0.01 0.29	6.37 0.02 0.53	4.96 0.05 0.83	3.99 0.10 1.20
	1/2	17.9	11.1 0.00 0.02	10.7 0.00 0.13	7.00 0.01 0.29	5.14 0.02 0.53	3.99 0.05 0.83	3.21 0.10 1.20
	3/8	13.6	6.48 0.00 0.01	6.44 0.00 0.10	5.24 0.01 0.30	3.84 0.02 0.53	2.97 0.05 0.84	2.38 0.10 1.22
6×4	7/8	27.2	26.7 0.00 0.04	13.2 0.00 0.15	8.65 0.01 0.35	6.34 0.03 0.62	4.92 0.07 0.96	3.94 0.15 1.39
	3/4	23.6	20.5 0.00 0.03	11.6 0.00 0.15	7.58 0.01 0.34	5.55 0.03 0.61	4.30 0.07 0.96	3.45 0.15 1.38
	5/8	20.0	14.8 0.00 0.03	9.82 0.00 0.15	6.43 0.01 0.34	4.71 0.03 0.61	3.65 0.07 0.95	2.92 0.14 1.37

Table 3.8—*contd.*

Nominal leg size (in)	Thickness (in)	Self-weight (lb/ft)	Safe distributed load (kips)/maximum loading plane deflection due to self-weight only (in)/maximum loading plane deflection due to total load (in)					
			Span (ft)					
			3	6	9	12	15	18
	$\frac{9}{16}$	18·1	12·3	8·91	5·84	4·27	3·31	2·65
			0·00	0·00	0·01	0·03	0·07	0·14
			0·02	0·15	0·34	0·60	0·95	1·37
	$\frac{1}{2}$	16·2	9·92	7·98	5·23	3·82	2·96	2·37
			0·00	0·00	0·01	0·03	0·07	0·14
			0·02	0·15	0·34	0·60	0·95	1·37
	$\frac{7}{16}$	·14·3	7·76	7·02	4·60	3·36	2·60	2·08
			0·00	0·00	0·01	0·03	0·07	0·14
			0·02	0·15	0·34	0·60	0·95	1·37
	$\frac{3}{8}$	12·3	5·82	5·79	3·95	2·88	2·23	1·78
			0·00	0·00	0·01	0·03	0·07	0·14
			0·02	0·14	0·34	0·60	0·95	1·38
	$\frac{5}{16}$	10·3	4·13	4·10	3·28	2·39	1·84	1·47
			0·00	0·00	0·01	0·03	0·07	0·14
			0·01	0·11	0·34	0·61	0·96	1·39
$6 \times 3\frac{1}{2}$	$\frac{1}{2}$	15·3	10·7	7·80	5·11	3·74	2·89	2·31
			0·00	0·00	0·01	0·03	0·07	0·14
			0·02	0·15	0·34	0·61	0·97	1·41

5 × 3½	3/8	11·7	6·28 / 0·00 / 0·02	5·89 / 0·00 / 0·15	3·85 / 0·01 / 0·34	2·81 / 0·03 / 0·62	2·17 / 0·07 / 0·97	1·73 / 0·14 / 1·42
	5/16	9·8	4·46 / 0·00 / 0·02	4·43 / 0·00 / 0·13	3·20 / 0·01 / 0·35	2·33 / 0·03 / 0·62	1·79 / 0·07 / 0·98	1·42 / 0·14 / 1·44
	3/4	19·8	15·9 / 0·00 / 0·05	7·87 / 0·00 / 0·18	5·14 / 0·01 / 0·41	3·74 / 0·04 / 0·74	2·88 / 0·11 / 1·15	2·29 / 0·22 / 1·67
	5/8	16·8	13·6 / 0·00 / 0·05	6·72 / 0·00 / 0·18	4·39 / 0·01 / 0·41	3·20 / 0·04 / 0·73	2·46 / 0·10 / 1·14	1·95 / 0·21 / 1·65
	1/2	13·6	9·34 / 0·00 / 0·04	5·50 / 0·00 / 0·18	3·59 / 0·01 / 0·40	2·62 / 0·04 / 0·72	2·01 / 0·10 / 1·13	1·60 / 0·21 / 1·64
	7/16	12·0	7·34 / 0·00 / 0·03	4·86 / 0·00 / 0·18	3·17 / 0·01 / 0·40	2·31 / 0·04 / 0·72	1·78 / 0·10 / 1·13	1·41 / 0·21 / 1·64
	3/8	10·4	5·53 / 0·00 / 0·03	4·20 / 0·00 / 0·18	2·74 / 0·01 / 0·40	1·99 / 0·04 / 0·72	1·53 / 0·10 / 1·13	1·21 / 0·20 / 1·65
	5/16	8·7	3·94 / 0·00 / 0·02	3·51 / 0·00 / 0·18	2·29 / 0·01 / 0·40	1·66 / 0·04 / 0·72	1·27 / 0·10 / 1·14	1·00 / 0·20 / 1·66
	1/4	7·0	2·59 / 0·00 / 0·02	2·56 / 0·00 / 0·15	1·82 / 0·01 / 0·40	1·32 / 0·04 / 0·73	1·01 / 0·10 / 1·15	0·791 / 0·20 / 1·67

Table 3.8—contd.

Safe distributed load (kips)/maximum loading plane deflection due to self-weight only (in)/maximum loading plane deflection due to total load (in)

Nominal leg size (in)	Thickness (in)	Self-weight (lb/ft)	Span (ft)					
			3	6	9	12	15	18
5 × 3	$\frac{5}{8}$	15·7	13·3	6·55	4·28	3·12	2·40	1·91
			0·00	0·00	0·01	0·04	0·10	0·21
			0·05	0·18	0·42	0·74	1·17	1·70
	$\frac{1}{2}$	12·8	10·1	5·36	3·50	2·55	1·96	1·55
			0·00	0·00	0·01	0·04	0·10	0·20
			0·04	0·18	0·41	0·74	1·16	1·69
	$\frac{7}{16}$	11·3	7·97	4·74	3·09	2·25	1·73	1·37
			0·00	0·00	0·01	0·04	0·10	0·20
			0·04	0·18	0·41	0·74	1·16	1·70
	$\frac{3}{8}$	9·8	6·01	4·09	2·66	1·94	1·48	1·17
			0·00	0·00	0·01	0·04	0·10	0·20
			0·03	0·18	0·41	0·74	1·17	1·71
	$\frac{5}{16}$	8·2	4·29	3·42	2·22	1·61	1·23	0·969
			0·00	0·00	0·01	0·04	0·10	0·20
			0·03	0·18	0·41	0·74	1·18	1·72
	$\frac{1}{4}$	6·6	2·82	2·72	1·77	1·28	0·971	0·759
			0·00	0·00	0·01	0·04	0·09	0·20
			0·02	0·18	0·42	0·75	1·19	1·75

Section																				
4×3½	5/8	14·7	8·77	0·00	0·06	4·31	0·00	0·22	2·80	0·02	0·50	2·02	0·07	0·90	1·53	0·17	1·40	1·20	0·36	2·02
	1/2	11·9	7·24	0·00	0·05	3·56	0·00	0·22	2·31	0·02	0·50	1·67	0·07	0·88	1·27	0·17	1·38	0·989	0·35	2·00
	7/16	10·6	6·30	0·00	0·05	3·16	0·00	0·22	2·05	0·02	0·49	1·48	0·07	0·88	1·12	0·17	1·38	0·876	0·34	1·99
	3/8	9·1	4·77	0·00	0·05	2·75	0·00	0·22	1·78	0·02	0·49	1·29	0·07	0·87	0·977	0·16	1·37	0·761	0·34	1·99
	5/16	7·7	3·41	0·00	0·04	2·31	0·00	0·22	1·50	0·02	0·49	1·08	0·07	0·87	0·820	0·16	1·37	0·638	0·33	1·99
	1/4	6·2	2·25	0·00	0·03	1·86	0·00	0·22	1·21	0·02	0·49	0·869	0·06	0·87	0·657	0·16	1·37	0·510	0·33	1·99
4×3	5/8	13·6	8·53	0·00	0·06	4·20	0·00	0·23	2·73	0·02	0·51	1·97	0·07	0·92	1·50	0·17	1·44	1·17	0·35	2·08
	1/2	11·1	7·04	0·00	0·06	3·47	0·00	0·22	2·25	0·02	0·51	1·63	0·07	0·90	1·24	0·16	1·42	0·967	0·34	2·06
	7/16	9·8	6·26	0·00	0·06	3·08	0·00	0·22	2·00	0·02	0·50	1·44	0·07	0·90	1·10	0·16	1·41	0·857	0·33	2·05

Single and Compound Angle Members

Table 3.8—contd.

Safe distributed load (kips)/maximum loading plane deflection due to self-weight only (in)/maximum loading plane deflection due to total load (in)

Nominal leg size (in)	Thickness (in)	Self-weight (lb/ft)	Span (ft) 3	6	9	12	15	18
$3\frac{1}{2} \times 3$	$\frac{3}{8}$	8·5	5·14 / 0·00 / 0·05	2·67 / 0·00 / 0·22	1·74 / 0·02 / 0·50	1·25 / 0·06 / 0·90	0·952 / 0·16 / 1·41	0·742 / 0·33 / 2·05
	$\frac{5}{16}$	7·2	3·68 / 0·00 / 0·04	2·25 / 0·00 / 0·22	1·46 / 0·02 / 0·50	1·05 / 0·06 / 0·90	0·798 / 0·16 / 1·41	0·620 / 0·33 / 2·05
	$\frac{1}{4}$	5·8	2·43 / 0·00 / 0·03	1·81 / 0·00 / 0·22	1·17 / 0·02 / 0·50	0·843 / 0·06 / 0·90	0·637 / 0·15 / 1·42	0·493 / 0·32 / 2·07
	$\frac{1}{2}$	10·2	5·42 / 0·00 / 0·06	2·66 / 0·01 / 0·25	1·72 / 0·03 / 0·57	1·24 / 0·09 / 1·02	0·931 / 0·22 / 1·60	0·718 / 0·46 / 2·32
	$\frac{7}{16}$	9·1	4·83 / 0·00 / 0·06	2·37 / 0·01 / 0·25	1·53 / 0·03 / 0·57	1·10 / 0·09 / 1·01	0·828 / 0·22 / 1·59	0·638 / 0·46 / 2·30
	$\frac{3}{8}$	7·9	4·21 / 0·00 / 0·06	2·07 / 0·01 / 0·25	1·33 / 0·03 / 0·56	0·957 / 0·09 / 1·01	0·721 / 0·22 / 1·58	0·554 / 0·45 / 2·29

Size	t							
$3\frac{1}{2} \times 2\frac{1}{2}$	$\frac{5}{16}$	6·6	3·37 / 0·00 / 0·06	1·75 / 0·01 / 0·25	1·13 / 0·03 / 0·56	0·809 / 0·09 / 1·00	0·609 / 0·21 / 1·58	0·468 / 0·44 / 2·29
	$\frac{1}{4}$	5·4	2·23 / 0·00 / 0·05	1·41 / 0·01 / 0·25	0·911 / 0·03 / 0·56	0·652 / 0·09 / 1·00	0·489 / 0·21 / 1·58	0·374 / 0·44 / 2·30
	$\frac{1}{2}$	9·4	5·25 / 0·00 / 0·07	2·58 / 0·01 / 0·26	1·67 / 0·03 / 0·59	1·20 / 0·09 / 1·05	0·905 / 0·22 / 1·65	0·699 / 0·45 / 2·39
	$\frac{7}{16}$	8·3	4·68 / 0·00 / 0·06	2·30 / 0·01 / 0·26	1·49 / 0·03 / 0·58	1·07 / 0·09 / 1·04	0·806 / 0·21 / 1·64	0·622 / 0·44 / 2·38
	$\frac{3}{8}$	7·2	4·08 / 0·00 / 0·06	2·00 / 0·01 / 0·26	1·29 / 0·03 / 0·58	0·929 / 0·08 / 1·04	0·700 / 0·21 / 1·64	0·540 / 0·43 / 2·38
	$\frac{5}{16}$	6·1	3·45 / 0·00 / 0·06	1·69 / 0·01 / 0·26	1·09 / 0·03 / 0·58	0·783 / 0·08 / 1·04	0·589 / 0·21 / 1·64	0·453 / 0·43 / 2·39
	$\frac{1}{4}$	4·9	2·45 / 0·00 / 0·05	1·37 / 0·01 / 0·25	0·881 / 0·03 / 0·58	0·630 / 0·08 / 1·04	0·472 / 0·20 / 1·65	0·361 / 0·42 / 2·41
$3 \times 2\frac{1}{2}$	$\frac{1}{2}$	8·5	3·86 / 0·00 / 0·08	1·89 / 0·01 / 0·30	1·22 / 0·04 / 0·68	0·866 / 0·13 / 1·21	0·645 / 0·31 / 1·90	0·489 / 0·64 / 2·75
	$\frac{7}{16}$	7·6	3·45 / 0·00 / 0·07	1·69 / 0·01 / 0·30	1·09 / 0·04 / 0·67	0·774 / 0·12 / 1·20	0·576 / 0·30 / 1·89	0·436 / 0·63 / 2·73

Table 3.8—*contd.*

Safe distributed load (kips)/maximum loading plane deflection due to self-weight only (in)/maximum loading plane deflection due to total load (in)

Nominal leg size (in)	Thickness (in)	Self-weight (lb/ft)	Span (ft)					
			3	6	9	12	15	18
	$\frac{3}{8}$	6·6	3·02 / 0·00 / 0·07	1·48 / 0·01 / 0·30	0·951 / 0·04 / 0·67	0·677 / 0·12 / 1·19	0·504 / 0·30 / 1·87	0·381 / 0·62 / 2·72
	$\frac{5}{16}$	5·6	2·57 / 0·00 / 0·07	1·26 / 0·01 / 0·29	0·807 / 0·04 / 0·66	0·574 / 0·12 / 1·19	0·426 / 0·29 / 1·87	0·322 / 0·61 / 2·71
	$\frac{1}{4}$	4·5	2·09 / 0·00 / 0·07	1·02 / 0·01 / 0·29	0·656 / 0·04 / 0·66	0·465 / 0·12 / 1·18	0·345 / 0·28 / 1·87	0·260 / 0·59 / 2·72
	$\frac{3}{16}$	3·39	1·29 / 0·00 / 0·06	0·772 / 0·01 / 0·29	0·495 / 0·04 / 0·66	0·350 / 0·11 / 1·19	0·258 / 0·28 / 1·88	0·193 / 0·58 / 2·74
3×2	$\frac{1}{2}$	7·7	3·71 / 0·00 / 0·08	1·82 / 0·01 / 0·31	1·17 / 0·04 / 0·70	0·835 / 0·12 / 1·25	0·624 / 0·30 / 1·97	0·474 / 0·62 / 2·87
	$\frac{7}{16}$	6·8	3·32 / 0·00 / 0·08	1·63 / 0·01 / 0·31	1·05 / 0·04 / 0·70	0·747 / 0·12 / 1·24	0·558 / 0·29 / 1·96	0·424 / 0·60 / 2·85

Size	Thickness								
2½ × 2	3/8	5·9	2·91 / 0·00 / 0·08	1·42 / 0·01 / 0·30	0·916 / 0·04 / 0·69	0·653 / 0·12 / 1·24	0·487 / 0·28 / 1·95	0·369 / 0·59 / 2·85
	5/16	5·0	2·47 / 0·00 / 0·08	1·21 / 0·01 / 0·30	0·777 / 0·04 / 0·69	0·552 / 0·11 / 1·23	0·411 / 0·28 / 1·96	0·311 / 0·58 / 2·86
	1/4	4·1	2·01 / 0·00 / 0·07	0·981 / 0·01 / 0·30	0·629 / 0·04 / 0·69	0·445 / 0·11 / 1·24	0·329 / 0·28 / 1·97	0·247 / 0·58 / 2·89
	3/16	3·07	1·46 / 0·00 / 0·07	0·740 / 0·01 / 0·30	0·473 / 0·03 / 0·69	0·333 / 0·11 / 1·25	0·244 / 0·27 / 2·00	0·180 / 0·56 / 2·95
	3/8	5·3	2·03 / 0·00 / 0·09	0·989 / 0·01 / 0·36	0·631 / 0·06 / 0·82	0·444 / 0·18 / 1·46	0·325 / 0·44 / 2·29	0·240 / 0·91 / 3·33
	5/16	4·5	1·73 / 0·00 / 0·09	0·845 / 0·01 / 0·36	0·539 / 0·06 / 0·81	0·379 / 0·17 / 1·45	0·277 / 0·43 / 2·28	0·204 / 0·89 / 3·32
	1/4	3·62	1·42 / 0·00 / 0·09	0·691 / 0·01 / 0·35	0·441 / 0·05 / 0·80	0·309 / 0·17 / 1·44	0·226 / 0·41 / 2·28	0·166 / 0·86 / 3·33
	3/16	2·75	1·08 / 0·00 / 0·09	0·527 / 0·01 / 0·35	0·335 / 0·05 / 0·80	0·234 / 0·16 / 1·45	0·170 / 0·40 / 2·30	0·124 / 0·84 / 3·36

Thus the initial approximations using the expression for S_a are

For unequal angles
   Case I: Moment parallel to the long leg (load is parallel to the short leg)

$$M_a = 0 \cdot 48 \sigma_y \frac{B^2 t(B+4Q)}{6(B+2Q)} \qquad (3.47)$$

   Case II: Moment parallel to the short leg (load is parallel to the long leg)

$$M_a = 0 \cdot 48 \sigma_y \frac{Q^2 t(Q+4B)}{6(Q+2B)} \qquad (3.48)$$

For equal angles
   Case I only

$$M_a = 0 \cdot 48 \sigma_y \frac{B^2 t}{3 \cdot 6} \qquad (3.49)$$

For small angles of twist, these expressions give the actual value of the safe load directly. However, large angles of twist modify the value of maximum stress in the section thus changing its load carrying capacity.

3.7.2 Non-shear Centre Loads

In order to include the effect of non-shear centre loads, the torque on the beam is estimated as follows. The uniform applied bending moment is M_a. A concentrated load P at midspan produces a maximum bending moment of $PL/4$. Equating the two moments will yield

$$P = \frac{4M_a}{L} \qquad (3.50)$$

The amount of twist produced by this load, P, depends on the position of its centre of gravity relative to the shear centre. Three such load positions have been considered as shown in Fig. 3.11. These are:

(i) Load at a distance $e = (0 \cdot 5)$(width of horizontal leg) to the left of the shear centre (Fig. 3.11(a)),
(ii) Load through the shear centre (Fig. 3.11(b)),
(iii) Load at a distance $e = (0 \cdot 5)$(width of horizontal leg) to the right of the shear centre (Fig. 3.11(c)).

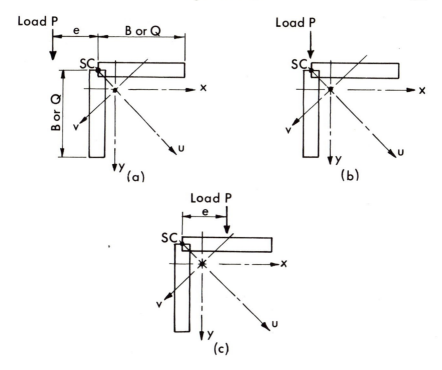

Fig. 3.11. Position of load with respect to shear centre (SC).

The twist produced by this effect is given by

$$\phi_t = \frac{\left(\dfrac{Pe}{2}\right)\left(\dfrac{L}{2}\right)}{GJ} = \frac{PeL}{4GJ} \qquad (3.51)$$

3.7.3. Total Twist ϕ_T of the Cross-section

The following are the other factors affecting the total twist, ϕ_T, of the cross-section:

(i) *Non-principal axis loading*

Here ϕ_{max} is given by eqns (3.27), (3.27a) and (3.35).

(ii) *Self-weight of the beam*

$$\phi_D = \frac{TL^2}{8GJ} \qquad (3.52)$$

where

$$T = \frac{mQ^2}{2(B+Q)} \tag{3.53a}$$

for Case I loading;

$$T = \frac{mB^2}{2(B+Q)} \tag{3.53b}$$

for Case II loading; and

$$T = \frac{mB}{4} \tag{3.53c}$$

for equal angles, where m is the weight per unit length of beam. Therefore,

$$\phi_T = \phi_t + \phi_D + \phi_{max} + \phi \tag{3.54}$$

where ϕ is due to initial imperfections estimated by Massey (1964).

3.7.4. Maximum Stress in the Cross-section

The maximum stress in the section can be found from

$$\sigma_{max} = M_a\{\gamma_1 + \gamma_2\phi_T\} \tag{3.55a}$$

for Case I loading and

$$\sigma_{max} = M_a\{\gamma_5 + \gamma_6\phi_T\} \tag{3.55b}$$

for Case II loading; whereas

$$\sigma_{max} = \frac{1 \cdot 5 M_a(3 - \phi_T)}{B^2 t} \tag{3.55c}$$

for equal angles.

3.8. LOADING PLANE DEFLECTION OF LATERALLY UNSUPPORTED ANGLE BEAMS

A simplified analysis based on an extension of first order theory (ignoring the effect of twist and deflection) has been used by Leigh and Lay (1970*b*) to find the maximum loading plane deflection. The same theory was followed in the computation of deflections in Tables 3.3 to

3.8. The computational procedure is as follows:

(a) Compute the total angle of twist ϕ_T from eqn (3.54).

(b) Allow the section to rotate through ϕ_T, keeping the applied moment M_a in its original direction. The moment M_a is that at mid-span due to a concentrated load P at mid-span and the self-weight per unit length of the beam, m.

(c) Resolve the applied moment M_a into components about the closest axes (Fig. 3.12).

Loading case I: load parallel to short leg
For ϕ_T positive

$$M_{u'} = \frac{M_a \sin \phi_T}{\cos \alpha}$$

$$M_{y'} = M_a(\cos \phi_T - \sin \phi_T \tan \alpha)$$

For ϕ_T negative

$$M_{v'} = \frac{M_a \sin \phi_T}{\sin \alpha}$$

$$M_{y'} = M_a(\cos \phi_T - \sin \phi_T \cot \alpha)$$

Loading case II: load parallel to long leg
For ϕ_T positive

$$M_{v'} = \frac{-M_a \sin \phi_T}{\cos \alpha}$$

$$M_{x'} = M_a(\cos \phi_T - \sin \phi_T \tan \alpha)$$

For ϕ_T negative

$$M_{u'} = \frac{M_a \sin \phi_T}{\sin \alpha}$$

$$M_{x'} = M_a(\cos \phi_T - \sin \phi_T \cot \alpha)$$

(d) Determine the principal axes deflections due to each component using eqns (3.21) and (3.22) for loading case I, and eqns (3.31) and (3.32) for loading case II and then algebraically add them to obtain u_{max} and v_{max}.

(e) Then loading plane deflection for case I becomes

$$x_{max} = \sqrt{u_{max}^2 + v_{max}^2} \cos \left[\alpha + \tan^{-1} \left(\frac{v_{max}}{u_{max}} \right) \right] \qquad (3.56)$$

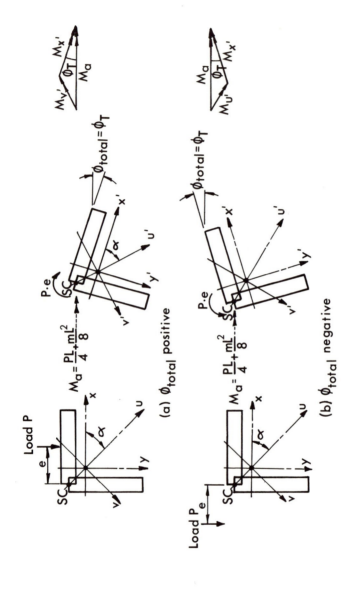

Fig. 3.12. Resolution of load along the principal axes for calculating deflection when load is parallel to long leg.

and, loading plane deflection for case II

$$y_{max} = \sqrt{u_{max}^2 + v_{max}^2} \sin\left[\alpha + \tan^{-1}\left(\frac{v_{max}}{u_{max}}\right)\right] \tag{3.57}$$

3.9. STANDARD SPECIFICATIONS FOR ANGLES IN BENDING

According to clause 5.4.2 of SAA Steel Structures Code (Standards Association of Australia, 1981), the maximum bending stress σ_b of a laterally unsupported angle section could be calculated from the following formulae based on an elastic flexural–torsional analysis.

If the maximum stress in the beam at elastic buckling, σ_{cr}, is equal to or less than σ_y, the permissible bending stress σ_b is given by

$$\sigma_b = \left[0\cdot55 - 0\cdot10\frac{\sigma_{cr}}{\sigma_y}\right]\sigma_{cr} \tag{3.58}$$

If the maximum stress in the beam at elastic buckling, σ_{cr}, is equal to or greater than σ_y,

$$\sigma_b = \left[0\cdot95 - 0\cdot50\sqrt{\frac{\sigma_y}{\sigma_{cr}}}\right]\sigma_y \tag{3.59}$$

Alternatively, it is permissible to use either the approximate solutions or the tabulated load capacities for laterally unsupported angles (Leigh *et al.*, 1984).

Subclause 19c of British Standard Specification BS 449: Part 2: 1969 (British Standards Institution, 1969a) specifies that the maximum permissible stress in the leg when loaded with the flange in compression shall not exceed the values given in Table 3.9. When loaded with the leg in compression, the permissible compressive stress is given in Table 8 of BS 449, depending on the value of the critical stress σ_{cr}. Similar provisions are also present in the Code of Practice for General Steel Construction IS: 800-1984 (Indian Standards Institution, 1984).

Of the various codes of practice, the SAA Steel Structures Code is the only code which considers the special characteristics of an angle section. Unlike the other codes, its provisions are based on extensive experimental and analytical research. In fact, other codes of practice either combine angles with tees or altogether ignore them. The safe load tables for angles (Tables 3.3 to 3.8) based on the Australian

Table 3.9
Maximum Permissible Stress in the Angle Leg when Loaded with
Flange in Compression, According to Subclause 19C of
BS 449: Part 2: 1969[a]

Ultimate tensile strength (MPa)	Max permissible stress (MPa)
430	165
500	230
550	280

[a] British Standards Institution (1969a).

research are therefore preferable to others. To compute the safe loads
for angle beams of any size and span in SI or Imperial units, a
computer program was developed in the Fortran language and is
available from the authors.

3.10. SOLVED EXAMPLES

Example 3.1
A $100 \times 100 \times 10$ mm angle, shown in Fig. 3.13(a), is subjected to a
pure bending moment, M, in the vertical plane. If the maximum stress
at any point in the cross-section cannot exceed 70 MPa, determine the
value of M. Assume that the angle is laterally supported.

Solution
From Table 1.1(a): $I_x = I_y = (1 \cdot 80)(10^6)$ mm^4; $I_u = (2 \cdot 86)(10^6)$ mm^4;
$I_v = (0 \cdot 737)(10^6)$ mm^4; $\alpha = 45°$; $A = 1900$ mm^2.

From eqn (3.4) the neutral axis NA must be between the x–x and
v–v axes (Fig. 3.13b). By inspection of Fig. 3.13(b), point A is the
farthest point from NA and therefore is the most heavily stressed.

Coordinates of point A with respect to the u–u and v–v axes are

$$u_A = \frac{90}{\sqrt{2}} - 18 \cdot 7\sqrt{2} = 37 \cdot 2 \text{ mm}; \qquad v_A = \frac{90}{\sqrt{2}} = 63 \cdot 6 \text{ mm}$$

Resolving the applied moment M acting along the x–x axis into its u–u
and v–v components:

$$M_u = M \cos 315° = \frac{M}{\sqrt{2}}; \qquad M_v = M \sin 315° = -\frac{M}{\sqrt{2}}$$

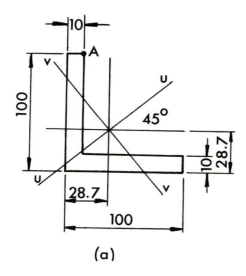

(a)

All dimensions in mm

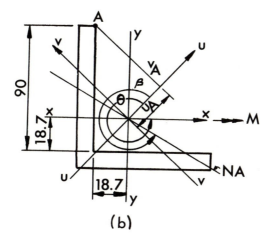

(b)

Fig. 3.13. Angle in Example 3.1.

From eqn (3.2a), the bending stress at A due to M_u

$$= \frac{M_u v_A}{I_u} = \frac{M}{\sqrt{2}} \left(\frac{63 \cdot 6}{(2 \cdot 86)(10^6)} \right)$$

From eqn (3.2b), the bending stress at A due to M_v

$$= -\frac{M_v u_A}{I_v} = -\left(\frac{-M}{\sqrt{2}} \right) \left(\frac{37 \cdot 2}{(0 \cdot 737)(10^6)} \right)$$

Equating the total bending stress to the permissible value of 70 MPa

$$70 = \frac{M}{\sqrt{2}} \left(\frac{63 \cdot 6}{(2 \cdot 86)(10^6)} \right) + \frac{M}{\sqrt{2}} \left(\frac{37 \cdot 2}{(0 \cdot 737)(10^6)} \right)$$

Solving, $M = (1 \cdot 36)(10^6)$ N . mm $= 1 \cdot 36$ kN . m.

Example 3.2
For the angle shown in Fig. 3.13(a) and (b) acted upon by a couple M in the vertical plane (the moment vector M is directed along the x–x axis), determine the location of the neutral axis.

Solution
From eqn (3.4)

$$\tan \beta = \frac{I_u}{I_v} \tan \theta$$

where the angle θ is measured counterclockwise from the u–u axis to the applied moment vector. Substituting $I_u = (2 \cdot 86)(10^6)$ mm^4, $I_v = (0 \cdot 737)(10^6)$ mm^4 and $\theta = 315°$

$$\tan \beta = \frac{(2 \cdot 86)(10^6)}{(0 \cdot 737)(10^6)} \tan 315° = -3 \cdot 88$$

Or

$$\tan (360° - \beta) = 3 \cdot 88; \qquad 360° - \beta = 75 \cdot 5°$$

Hence

$$\beta = 284 \cdot 5°$$

The neutral axis passes through the centroid and is inclined at an angle of $284 \cdot 5°$ (measured counterclockwise from the u–u axis) as shown in Fig. 3.13(b).

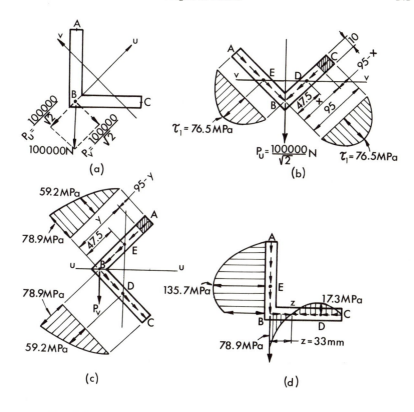

Fig. 3.14. Shear stress distribution for angle in Example 3.3.

Example 3.3

For the angle shown in Fig. 3.13(a), sketch the distribution of shearing stresses due to bending if it is acted upon by a vertical load of 100 kN passing through the shear centre (i.e. no twisting of the cross-section; see Fig. 3.4).

Solution

Resolve the 100 000 N vertical load along the principal axes as shown in Fig. 3.14(a).

Shear stress due to P_u (Fig. 3.14(b)). The section bends about the v–v axis. The shear stress τ_1 at any point x is computed as follows:

From eqn (3.5)

$$\tau_1 = \frac{VQ}{It} = \frac{P_u Q_v}{I_v t}$$

$$V = P_u = \frac{100\,000}{\sqrt{2}}\,\text{N}; \qquad I_v = (0 \cdot 737)(10^6)\,\text{mm}^4; \qquad t = 10\,\text{mm}$$

and

$$Q_v = (95 - x)(10)\left[(x - 47 \cdot 5) + \left(\frac{95 - x}{2}\right)\right]\sin 45°$$

$$= (5x)(95 - x)\sin 45°\,\text{mm}^3$$

Substituting for V, Q, I and t and various values for x in eqn (3.5) yields:

When $x = 95$ mm, i.e. at point C, $Q = 0$ and $\tau_1 = 0$.

When $x = 47 \cdot 5$ mm, i.e. at point D on the neutral axis, $Q = 7977$ mm^3 and $\tau_1 = 76 \cdot 5$ MPa.

When $x = 0$, at point B (i.e. at the shear centre), $Q = 0$ and $\tau_1 = 0$.

Since Q_v varies as the second power of x, the distribution of shear stress is as shown in Fig. 3.14(b).

Shear stress due to P_v (Fig. 3.14(c)). The section bends about the u–u axis. The shear stress τ_2 at any point y is computed as follows: Again from eqn (3.5)

$$\tau_2 = \frac{VQ}{It} = \frac{P_v Q_u}{I_u t}$$

$$V = P_v = \frac{100\,000}{\sqrt{2}}\,\text{N}; \qquad I_u = (2 \cdot 86)(10^6)\,\text{mm}^4; \qquad t = 10\,\text{mm}$$

and

$$Q_u = (95 - y)(10)\left[y + \frac{(95 - y)}{2}\right]\cos 45° = 5(9025 - y^2)\cos 45°\,\text{mm}^3$$

Substituting V, Q, I, t and various values of y in eqn (3.5) results in:

When $y = 95$ mm, i.e. point A, $Q = 0$ and $\tau_2 = 0$.

When $y = 47 \cdot 5$ mm, i.e. point E on axis v–v, $Q = 23\,931$ mm^3 and $\tau_2 = 59 \cdot 2$ MPa.

When $y = 0$, i.e. at point B, the shear centre, $Q = 31\,908$ mm^3 and $\tau_2 = 78 \cdot 9$ MPa.

Since Q_u varies as the second power of y, the distribution of shear stress is as shown in Fig. 3.14(c).

Total shear stress. Total shear stress, τ, at any point is obtained by algebraically adding τ_1 and τ_2. For the leg AB, the shear stresses τ_1 and τ_2 are in the same direction (from A to B in Figs 3.14(b) and (c)) and are therefore additive. On the other hand, for the leg BC, shear stress τ_2 acts from B to C. (Fig. 3.14(c)) while shear stress τ_1 acts from C to B (Fig. 3.14(b)). The net shear stress for leg BC is obtained by subtracting one from the other. There is a point of zero shear stress τ somewhere along leg BC at an unknown distance z from B; this distance can be evaluated by equating τ to zero.

For BC: $\tau_2 - \tau_1 = 0$ at a distance z from B; thus

$$\frac{P_v Q_u}{I_u t} - \frac{P_u Q_v}{I_v t} = 0$$

Since $P_v = P_u$

$$\frac{Q_u}{I_u} = \frac{Q_v}{I_v}$$

Or

$$\frac{5(9025 - z^2)\cos 45°}{(2 \cdot 86)(10^6)} = \frac{5z(95 - z)\sin 45°}{(0 \cdot 737)(10^6)}$$

Hence $z = 33$ mm.

Total stress at E = $76 \cdot 5 + 59 \cdot 2 = 135 \cdot 7$ MPa.
Total stress at D = $76 \cdot 5 - 59 \cdot 2 = 17 \cdot 3$ MPa.

The resultant shear stress distribution is as shown in Fig. 3.14(d).

Example 3.4
Calculate the additional shear stress due to twisting of the cross-section for the angle in Example 3.3, if the 100 kN load acts at a distance 10 mm from the shear centre, as shown in Fig. 3.15(a).

Solution
Referring to Fig. 3.15(a), the twisting moment $T = (100\,000)(10) = (1 \cdot 0)(10^6)$ N . mm. From eqn (3.6)

$$\tau_{\text{torsion}} = \frac{T}{\frac{1}{3}(b + a - t)t^2}$$

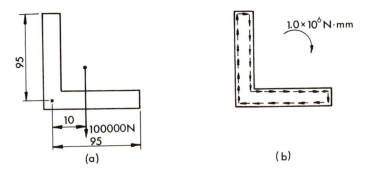

Fig. 3.15. Angle in Example 3.4. (All dimensions in mm.)

where $b + a - t = $ centreline   length $= 95 + 95 = 190$ mm; $t = 10$ mm. Therefore

$$\tau_{\text{torsion}} = \frac{(1)(10^6)}{(\frac{1}{3})(190)(10^2)} = 157 \cdot 9 \text{ MPa}$$

This torsional shear stress is maximum along the edges of the cross-section and its direction is as shown in Fig. 3.15(b).

Example 3.5
Compute the properties of a $100 \times 100 \times 10$ mm angle section using dual-rectangle idealization and compare the results with the values given in Table 1.1(a).

Solution

$$Q = 100 - \tfrac{10}{2} = 95 \text{ mm}; \qquad B = 95 \text{ mm}; \qquad t = 10 \text{ mm}; \qquad \alpha = 45^\circ$$

From eqn (3.8a)

$$I_x = \tfrac{5}{24}(95)^3(10) = (1 \cdot 79)(10^6) \text{ mm}^4 \text{ (tabulated value is } (1 \cdot 80)(10^6) \text{ mm}^4)$$

From eqn (3.12a)

$$I_{xy} = -\frac{(95)^3(10)}{8} = (-1 \cdot 07)(10^6) \text{ mm}^4 \text{ (same as the tabulated value)}$$

From eqn (3.13a)

$$I_u = \tfrac{1}{3}(95)^3(10) = (2 \cdot 86)(10^6) \text{ mm}^4 \text{ (same as the tabulated value)}$$

From eqn (3.13b)

$I_v = \frac{1}{12}(95)^3(10) = (0\cdot714)(10^6)$ mm^4 (tabulated value is
$$(0\cdot737)(10^6) \text{ mm}^4)$$

From eqn (3.26a)

$$\beta_2 = 95\sqrt{2} = 134 \text{ mm (tabulated value} = 133 \text{ mm)}$$

Example 3.6
Calculate the maximum stress in a $100 \times 100 \times 10$ mm angle section acted upon by a constant moment of $4\cdot0$ kN . m parallel to one of the legs over an unsupported length of 3 m. Use the theory of Leigh and Lay. Yield stress of steel $= 300$ MPa, $E = 200$ GPa, $G = 76\cdot9$ GPa.

Solution

$Q = B = 100 - \frac{10}{2} = 95$ mm; $t = 10$ mm; applied moment
$$M_a = 4\cdot0 \text{ kN . m}$$

From eqn (3.11a) the section modulus $S_y = (5/18)(95)^2(10) = 25\,069$ mm^3. From eqn (3.18)

$$\sigma_a = \frac{M_a}{S_y} = \frac{(4)(10^6) \text{ N . mm}}{25\,069 \text{ mm}^3} = 159\cdot6 \text{ MPa} = 23\cdot1 \text{ ksi}$$

$$300\left(\frac{B+Q}{L}\right) = 300\left(\frac{95+95}{3000}\right) = 19 \text{ ksi}$$

$$\sigma_a > 300\left(\frac{B+Q}{L}\right) \text{ ksi}$$

Therefore, use eqn (3.20) to compute maximum stress; thus

$$\sigma_{max} = M_a[\gamma_1 + \gamma_2\phi_{max}]$$

From Table 3.1

$$\gamma_1 = \frac{-4\cdot5}{B^2t} = \frac{-4\cdot5}{(95)^2(10)} = (-49\cdot86)(10^{-6}) \text{ mm}^{-3}$$

and

$$\gamma_2 = \frac{1\cdot5}{B^2t} = (16\cdot62)(10^{-6}) \text{ mm}^{-3}$$

From eqn (3.27a)

$$\phi_{max} = \frac{-3}{5} \left(\frac{1}{\cos \frac{\omega L}{2}} - 1 \right)$$

where ω is computed from eqn (3.24).

From Table 1.1(a), $I_u = (2\cdot86)(10^6)\,\text{mm}^4$; $I_v = (0\cdot737)(10^6)\,\text{mm}^4$; $\beta_1 = 0$; $\beta_2 = 133\,\text{mm}$; $\alpha = 45°$; $J = (63\cdot3)(10^3)\,\text{mm}^4$; thus

$$\omega^2 = \frac{(159\cdot6)^2(25\,069)^2[(2\cdot86)(10^6)(\tfrac{1}{2}) + (0\cdot737)(10^6)(\tfrac{1}{2})]}{(200\,000)(2\cdot86)(10^6)(0\cdot737)(10^6)}$$

$$\times \frac{1}{\left\{ (76\,900)(63\,300) + (159\cdot6)(25\,069)\left[0 - (133)\frac{1}{\sqrt{2}} \right] \right\}}$$

$$\omega^2 = (1\cdot52)(10^{-8})\,\text{mm}^{-2}; \quad \text{or} \quad \omega = (1\cdot233)(10^{-4})\,\text{mm}^{-1}$$

From eqn (3.27a)

$$\phi_{max} = \frac{-3}{5} \left\{ \frac{1}{\cos \left[\frac{(1\cdot233)(10^{-4})(3000)}{2} \right]} - 1 \right\} = -0\cdot01041 \text{ radians}$$

Substituting γ_1, γ_2 and ϕ_{max} in eqn (3.20)

$$\sigma_{max} = (4)(10^6)[(-49\cdot86)(10^{-6}) + (16\cdot62)(10^{-6})(-0\cdot01041)]$$

$$= -200\cdot1\,\text{MPa};$$

$$\text{i.e. } 200\cdot1\,\text{MPa compressive}$$

It is to be noted that this value is very close to the approximate value of σ_{max} given by eqn (3.19)

$$\sigma_{max} = 1\cdot25\sigma_a = (1\cdot25)(159\cdot6) = 199\cdot5\,\text{MPa}$$

since the effects of twist and deflections are negligible.

Example 3.7

For the angle in Example 3.6 calculate the maximum loading plane deflection of the shear centre.

Solution

1. Calculate v_{max} from eqn (3.21). From Table 3.1, $\gamma_3 = \sqrt{2}/10$; from Example 3.6, $\phi_{max} = -0\cdot01041$ radian and $\omega^2 = (1\cdot52)(10^{-8})\,\text{mm}^{-2}$.

Therefore

$$v_{max} = \frac{(4)(10^6)(3000)^2}{(200\,000)(2 \cdot 86)(10^6)} \left[\frac{-0 \cdot 01041 \cos 45°}{(1 \cdot 52)(10^{-8})(3000)^2} + \frac{\sqrt{2}}{10} \right]$$

$$= 5 \cdot 51 \text{ mm}$$

2. Calculate u_{max} from eqn (3.22). From Table 3.1, $\gamma_4 = \sqrt{2}/40 = 0 \cdot 035355$. Thus

$$u_{max} = \frac{(4)(10^6)(3000)^2}{(200\,000)(0 \cdot 737)(10^6)} \left[\frac{-0 \cdot 01041 \sin 45°}{(1 \cdot 52)(10^{-8})(3000)^2} - 0 \cdot 035355 \right]$$

$$= -21 \cdot 78 \text{ mm}$$

From eqn (3.23),

$$x_{max} = \sqrt{5 \cdot 51^2 + 21 \cdot 78^2} \cos \left[45° + \tan^{-1} \left(\frac{5 \cdot 51}{-21 \cdot 78} \right) \right]$$

$$= 22 \cdot 47 \cos [45° - 14 \cdot 2°] = 19 \cdot 3 \text{ mm}$$

Chapter 4

ANGLES AS COMPRESSION MEMBERS

4.1. INTRODUCTION

In this chapter the analysis of single and compound angles under concentric and eccentric axial compressive loading is presented. The classical theoretical analysis as well as plastic analysis are reviewed; some of the interaction curves at elastic and plastic limit states are presented. Design procedure is presented for single angle web compression members in trusses based on the behaviour of three-dimensional computer models.

4.2. CLASSICAL THEORETICAL ANALYSIS

4.2.1. Elastic Buckling: Concentric Loading

Concentrically loaded columns of angle construction can buckle in one of the following three modes:

(i) flexural buckling—by bending about the weaker principal axis;
(ii) torsional buckling—by twisting about the shear centre; or
(iii) torsional–flexural buckling—by simultaneous bending and twisting.

Concentrically loaded single *equal-leg* angles fail either by flexural buckling about the asymmetric minor principal axis of inertia or by simultaneous bending and twisting about the symmetric major principal axis of inertia, depending upon the length, cross-sectional dimensions and end-conditions of the member; whereas concentrically loaded single *unequal-leg* angles always fail by torsional–flexural buckling. Concentrically loaded compound angles which have one axis of

148

symmetry (Fig. 4.1(a)) fail either by flexural buckling about the asymmetric axis or by torsional–flexural buckling about the symmetric axis (similar to equal-leg single angles). Concentrically loaded compound angles which have two axes of symmetry (Fig. 4.1(b)) fail either by flexural buckling about the weak axis or by torsional buckling about the shear centre, which in this case coincides with the centroid of the cross-section.

The theory of elastic buckling of concentrically loaded columns was formulated by Euler (1759). Wagner (1929) was the first to investigate torsional buckling of open thin-walled sections. However, in his theory Wagner assumed arbitrarily that the centre of rotation coincides with the shear centre, which, in general, is not the case. In fact, Ostenfeld (1931) was the first to present the exact solutions for the torsional–flexural buckling of angle sections. Among the early investigators who studied the problem of torsional–flexural buckling were Bleich and Bleich (1936), Kappus (1937), Lundquist and Fligg (1937), Vlasov (1940), Goodier (1941, 1942) and Timoshenko (1945). Since the theories of flexural buckling and torsional–flexural buckling are well known (see Bleich, 1952, and Timeshenko and Gere, 1961), only the final results of the theoretical analysis are given herein.

4.2.1.1. *Critical Load for Columns with Doubly-Symmetric Sections (Fig. 4.1(b))*

The buckling load in this case is the least of the following three critical loads:

P_x = Euler load for flexural buckling about the centroidal principal x–x axis

$$= \frac{\pi^2 E I_x}{(K_x L)^2} \tag{4.1}$$

P_y = Euler load for flexural buckling about the centroidal principal y–y axis

$$= \frac{\pi^2 E I_y}{(K_y L)^2} \tag{4·2}$$

P_t = critical load for torsional buckling about the shear centre

$$= \frac{A}{I_{ps}} \left[GJ + \frac{\pi^2 E C_w}{(K_t L)^2} \right] \tag{4.3}$$

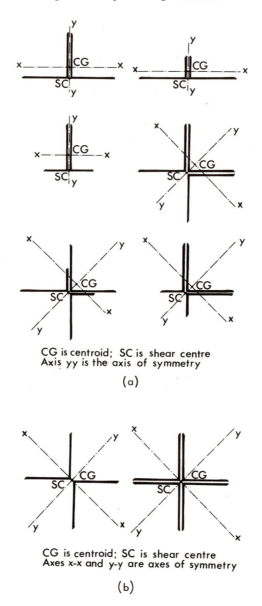

CG is centroid; SC is shear centre
Axis yy is the axis of symmetry

(a)

CG is centroid; SC is shear centre
Axes x-x and y-y are axes of symmetry

(b)

Fig. 4.1. Compound angles: (a) singly symmetric; (b) doubly symmetric.

in which A = cross-sectional area; K_t, K_x, K_y = effective length factors for torsional buckling, flexural buckling about the x–x axis and flexural buckling about the y–y axis, respectively; L = length of column between supports; and

$$G = \frac{E}{2(1+\nu)} \tag{4.4}$$

where ν is Poisson's ratio.

Quite often the concept of an equivalent radius of gyration r_t is useful in the analysis of torsional buckling; thus eqn (4.3) can be written as

$$P_t = \frac{\pi^2 E(Ar_t^2)}{(K_t L)^2} \tag{4.5}$$

in which

$$r_t = \sqrt{\frac{1}{I_{ps}}\left[\frac{J(K_t L)^2}{2\pi^2(1+\nu)} + C_w\right]} \tag{4.6}$$

It can be readily observed that the two flexural modes (eqns (4.1) and (4.2)) and the torsional mode (eqn (4.3)) are independent and therefore there is no coupling between flexural and torsional buckling for such columns.

4.2.1.2. Critical Load for Columns with Singly-Symmetric Sections

For singly-symmetric compound angles (Fig. 4.1(a)), the centroid and shear centre do not coincide and therefore, as stated earlier, failure will be either by

(i) Euler flexural buckling about the asymmetric $x - x$ axis; or by
(ii) flexural buckling about the symmetric $y - y$ axis and simultaneous twisting about the centre of rotation, which lies on the symmetric axis close to the shear centre.

The Euler flexural buckling load can be calculated from eqn (4.1). For the same end conditions for flexure and torsion, the critical torsional–flexural buckling load, P_{cr}, can be deduced from the following equation (Timoshenko and Gere, 1961, eqn 5.39):

$$\frac{I_{pc}}{I_{ps}} P_{cr}^2 - (P_y + P_t)P_{cr} + P_y P_t = 0 \tag{4.7}$$

in which I_{pc} = polar moment of inertia of the cross-section about the centroid.

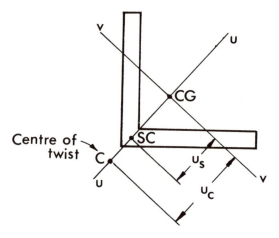

Fig. 4.2. Equal-leg single angle.

The quadratic eqn (4.7) provides two values for P_{cr}, one of which is smaller and the other larger than P_y and P_t; the smaller root is the torsional–flexural buckling load P_{ty}. A study of eqn (4.7) shows that when the ratio P_t/P_y is small, the critical load P_{ty} is very close to P_t and buckling is essentially in a torsional mode. For larger values of P_t/P_y, the critical load P_{ty} is close to P_y pertaining to flexural buckling. For an equal-leg single angle, the ratio $I_{pc}/I_{ps} = 0.625$ and the $u-u$ axis is the axis of symmetry as shown in Fig. 4.2. Substituting this value in eqn (4.7), the critical load P_{tu} for equal-leg single angles is

$$P_{tu} = 0.8[(P_u + P_t) - \sqrt{(P_u + P_t)^2 - 2.5 P_u P_t}] \tag{4.8}$$

where

$$P_u = \frac{\pi^2 E I_u}{(K_u L)^2} \tag{4.9}$$

P_{tu} can also be expressed as

$$P_{tu} = \frac{\pi^2 E (A r_{tu}^2)}{(K_t L)^2} \tag{4.10}$$

in which r_{tu} is computed from

$$\left(1 - \frac{r_u^2}{r_{tu}^2}\right)\left(1 - \frac{r_t^2}{r_{tu}^2}\right) - \frac{A u_s^2}{I_{ps}} = 0 \tag{4.11}$$

and $u_s =$ distance between the centroid and the shear centre as shown in Fig. 4.2.

It is found that each cross-section rotates around a point C lying on the axis of symmetry ($u-u$ axis) at a distance of

$$u_c = \frac{u_s}{\left(1 - \frac{r_{tu}^2}{r_u^2}\right)} \tag{4.12}$$

as shown in Fig. 4.2. Since the torsional resistance of angle sections is small, u_c will be only slightly greater than u_s, which means that the centre of rotation is close to the shear centre.

4.2.1.3. Critical Load for Columns with Unsymmetric Sections

When the end conditions are identical for torsion and flexure, the critical buckling load for unequal-leg angles is given by the smallest root of the following cubic equation (Timoshenko and Gere, 1961, eqn 5.32):

$$\frac{I_{pc}}{I_{ps}} P_{cr}^3 + \left[\frac{A}{I_{ps}}(P_v u_s^2 + P_u v_s^2) - (P_u + P_v + P_t)\right] P_{cr}^2 \tag{4.13}$$
$$+ (P_u P_v + P_v P_t + P_u P_t)P_{cr} - P_u P_v P_t = 0$$

where (u_s, v_s) are the coordinates of the shear centre with reference to the centroidal principal axes as shown in Fig. 4.3. The smallest root for P_{cr} is less than P_u, P_v and P_t; this indicates that unequal-leg single

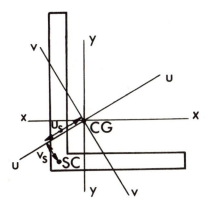

Fig. 4.3. Unequal-leg single angle.

angles always fail in a torsional–flexural mode when subjected to concentric axial load.

4.2.1.4. Local Plate Buckling

For *ideal* single equal-leg angles, there is no distinction between the torsional–flexural buckling mode and the local plate buckling mode. (An *ideal* single equal-leg angle is one which is perfectly straight, and is made of homogeneous, isotropic, linearly elastic material with each leg of angle having exactly the same geometric properties.) However, for single unequal-leg angles and compound angles, the torsional–flexural buckling mode is distinctly different from the local plate buckling mode. Each leg of an ideal equal-leg angle behaves as a plate simply supported on three sides and free on the fourth side; since both legs have equal width, they buckle at the same time and neither leg can provide restraint to the other one. The local buckling stress σ_{cr} can be computed from the following equation (Bleich, 1952, eqn 670):

$$\frac{\sigma_{cr}}{\sqrt{\eta}} = \frac{\pi^2 E}{12(1-\nu^2)} \left(\frac{t}{b}\right)^2 . k \qquad (4.14)$$

in which $\eta = E_t/E$ = ratio of tangent modulus to elastic modulus; and k = plate buckling coefficient, which approaches 0.425 for long equal-leg angles. In the case of unequal-leg angles, the shorter leg exerts a certain restraining effect upon the longer leg, depending on the ratio of the leg widths; if the ratio of widths (of long leg to short leg) is 2 to 3, the plate buckling coefficient for the long leg becomes 0.504. If the ratio of widths is 1 to 2, the plate buckling coefficient for the long leg is 0.568 (Bleich, 1952, p. 342).

4.2.2. Elastic Buckling: Eccentric Axial Load

The basic differential equations of equilibrium of a column, loaded with axial end loads and biaxial eccentricities, are (Timoshenko and Gere, 1961, p. 245)

$$EI_y u^{iv} + Pu'' + P(y_s - e_y)\phi'' = 0 \qquad (4.15)$$

$$EI_x v^{iv} + Pv'' - P(x_s - e_x)\phi'' = 0 \qquad (4.16)$$

$$EC_w \phi^{iv} - \left(GJ - Pe_y\beta_1 - Pe_x\beta_2 - P\frac{I_{ps}}{A}\right)\phi''$$
$$+ P(y_s - e_y)u'' - P(x_s - e_x)v'' = 0 \qquad (4.17)$$

where E = modulus of elasticity; I_x, I_y = moments of inertia of the cross-section about the major and minor centroidal principal axes (x–x

axis and $y-y$ axis, respectively); P = external applied load; x_s, y_s = x- and y-coordinates of the shear centre with reference to the centroidal principal axes; e_x, e_y = x- and y-coordinates of point of application of the eccentric axial load with reference to the centroidal principal axes; u, v = deflection components of the shear centre along the major and minor centroidal principal axes, respectively; ϕ = rotation of the shear centre about the longitudinal axis ($z-z$ axis); $\beta_1 = (1/I_x)(\int_A y^3 \, dA + \int_A x^2 y \, dA) - 2y_s$; and $\beta_2 = (1/I_y)(\int_A x^3 \, dA + \int_A xy^2 \, dA) - 2x_s$.

The above differential equations of equilibrium were formulated on the basis of the following assumptions:

1. The column is initially straight.
2. Effects of the residual stresses are negligible.
3. The geometry of the cross-section of the member does not change during buckling; this assumption implies that the displacement of each point in the cross-section can be specified in terms of the displacement components u, v and ϕ of the shear centre.
4. Shear and axial deformations are insignificant.
5. Deflection components u and v are small in comparison with the length of the member, and ϕ is small in comparison with $\pi/2$.
6. The material is linearly elastic and the stress–strain curve is elastic–perfectly plastic, having a well-defined yield point.

Differential equations of equilibrium for the general case of biaxial eccentricities (eqns 4.15 to 4.17) have been solved by Vlasov (1940), Thürlimann (1953), Dabrowski (1961), Prawel and Lee (1964), Culver (1966), and Peköz and Winter (1969) using different procedures.

4.2.2.1. Critical Load for Columns with Doubly-Symmetric Sections
If the cross-section of the member has two axes of symmetry (e.g. compound angles shown in Fig. 4.1(b)), the shear centre coincides with the centroid. If the coordinates of the point of application of the axial load are e_x and e_y with reference to the centroidal principal axes, the critical load can be computed by solving the cubic equation obtained by expanding the following determinant:

$$\begin{bmatrix} (P_y - P_{cr}) & 0 & P_{cr} \cdot e_y \\ 0 & (P_x - P_{cr}) & -P_{cr} \cdot e_x \\ P_{cr} \cdot e_y & -P_{cr} \cdot e_x & \dfrac{I_{ps}}{A}(P_t - P_{cr}) \end{bmatrix} = 0 \qquad (4.18)$$

The smallest root of this cubic equation is the critical buckling load, caused by combined bending and torsion. If the eccentric load acts along one of the axes of symmetry, say along the y–y axis (i.e. eccentricity about the x–x axis), then $e_x = 0$; whence buckling about the x–x axis occurs independently and the corresponding ciritical load is given by the Euler load P_x (eqn (4.1)). Flexural buckling about the y–y axis and torsional buckling are coupled, and in this case the buckling load is given by the following quadratic equation (Timoshenko and Gere, 1961, eqn 5.77):

$$P_{cr}^2\left(1-\frac{Ae_y^2}{I_{ps}}\right) - P_{cr}(P_y + P_t) + P_y P_t = 0 \qquad (4.19)$$

A study of eqn (4.19) shows that one value of P_{cr} is less than P_y and P_t, corresponding to the torsional–flexural buckling load P_{ty}. The failure load is then the smaller value of either P_x or P_{ty}.

4.2.2.2. Critical Load for Columns with Singly-Symmetric Sections
Assuming that the y–y axis is the axis of symmetry, then for the compound angles shown in Fig. 4.1(a), the critical load is computed by solving the cubic equation obtained by expanding the following determinant:

$$\begin{bmatrix} (P_y - P_{cr}) & 0 & -P_{cr}(y_s - e_y) \\ 0 & (P_x - P_{cr}) & -P_{cr}e_x \\ -P_{cr}(y_s - e_y) & -P_{cr}e_x & \left(P_t\dfrac{I_{ps}}{A} - P_{cr}e_y\beta_1 - P_{cr}\dfrac{I_{ps}}{A}\right) \end{bmatrix} = 0 \qquad (4.20)$$

After expanding the determinant, it is found that the buckling of such columns occurs by combined bending and torsion, with the smallest root of the cubic equation being the critical buckling load. For the special case, when the load acts on the y–y axis of symmetry ($e_x = 0$), eqn (4.20) yields the critical load for buckling about the x–x axis equal to the Euler buckling load P_x. However, flexural buckling about the y–y axis is coupled with torsional buckling and the critical load is given by the following quadratic equation (Timoshenko and Gere, 1961, eqn 5.76):

$$(P_y - P_{cr})\left[P_t\frac{I_{ps}}{A} - P_{cr}\left(e_y\beta_1 + \frac{I_{ps}}{A}\right)\right] - P_{cr}^2(y_s - e_y)^2 = 0 \qquad (4.21)$$

The smaller root of eqn (4.21), i.e. $P_{cr} = P_{ty}$, is less than the Euler buckling load P_y about the y–y axis, and therefore the failure load will be the lesser of either P_x or P_{ty}. For the special case when the line of action of the load passes through the shear centre, $e_y = y_s$, eqn (4.21) reduces to

$$(P_y - P_{cr})\left[P_t \frac{I_{ps}}{A} - P_{cr}\left(e_y \beta_1 + \frac{I_{ps}}{A} \right) \right] = 0 \qquad (4.22)$$

with the two solutions

$$P_{cr} = P_y$$

and

$$P_{cr} = \frac{P_t}{1 + e_y \beta_1 (A/I_{ps})} \qquad (4.22a)$$

Thus when an axial load is applied through the shear centre for a section having one axis of symmetry, the two flexural buckling modes (about the principal axes x–x and y–y) and the torsional buckling mode are uncoupled. The failure load is then the smallest of P_x, P_y or $P_t/[1 + e_y \beta_1 (A/I_{ps})]$.

Note. For the case of equal-leg single angles, the principal axes are u–u and v–v axes and the axis of symmetry is the u–u axis (Fig. 4.2). Therefore, in eqns (4.20) to (4.22a), we must interchange x and y by v and u, respectively.

4.2.2.3. Critical Load for Columns with Unsymmetric Sections

For an unequal-leg angle having no axis of symmetry with x–x and y–y as the centroidal principal axes, the critical load is computed from the cubic equation obtained by expanding the following determinant:

$$\begin{bmatrix} (P_y - P_{cr}) & 0 & -P_{cr}(y_s - e_y) \\ 0 & (P_x - P_{cr}) & P_{cr}(x_s - e_x) \\ -P_{cr}(y_s - e_y) & P_{cr}(x_s - e_x) & \left(P_t \dfrac{I_{ps}}{A} - P_{cr} e_y \beta_1 \right. \\ & & \left. -P_{cr} e_x \beta_2 - P_{cr} \dfrac{I_{ps}}{A} \right) \end{bmatrix} = 0 \qquad (4.23)$$

Such angles fail in the torsional–flexural buckling mode at a load corresponding to the smallest root of eqn (4.23). Even for an unequal-leg angle, the three types of buckling modes become uncoupled if the load passes through the shear centre; thus, substituting $e_x = x_s$ and $e_y = y_s$, the solutions of eqn (4.23) reduce to

$$P_{cr} = P_y$$
$$P_{cr} = P_x \qquad (4.24)$$
$$P_{cr} = \frac{P_t}{1 + e_y \beta_1 A / I_{ps} + e_x \beta_2 A / I_{ps}}$$

The failure load is the smallest of the three buckling loads given by eqn (4.24).

Note. If the principal centroidal axes are denoted by $u - u$ and $v - v$, as shown in Fig. 4.3, x and y in eqns (4.23) and (4.24) are to be replaced by v and u, respectively.

4.2.3. Inelastic Buckling

For stocky and intermediate columns (i.e. for members having small or moderate slenderness ratios), the stress at buckling may exceed the proportional limit of the material, and hence inelastic buckling pertains. In the inelastic range, for flexural buckling, the elastic modulus E is replaced by $E\eta$ (where η is the ratio of the tangent modulus to the elastic modulus and is dependent on the stress level) and the equations developed in the preceding sections can be used. However, for torsional and torsional–flexural buckling, there is no consensus on the value to be used for the shear modulus G in the inelastic range. For the sake of simplicity, Bleich (1952) suggested the use of $G\eta$ for the tangent shear modulus (Bleich, 1952, p. 124). This approach leads to conservative results and also makes it possible to use readily the equations of elastic torsional and torsional–flexural buckling for inelastic buckling, by replacing G with $G\eta$. The same procedure was also followed by Chajes *et al.* (1966).

4.3. INTERACTION CURVES FOR ANGLES UNDER AXIAL LOAD AND BIAXIAL BENDING

Research was carried out by Bez and Hirt (1982) to determine the plastic ultimate resistance of angles subjected to combined axial forces and bending moments and to consider the eventual instability phenomena for such sections. An unsymmetrical $150 \times 100 \times 10$ mm angle section was analyzed. First an elastic analysis was carried out assuming bending moments M_x and M_y only, with no axial force. Figure 4.4 illustrates the stress distributions inside the section for the following three loading cases:

—maximum possible bending moment M_x in the elastic domain, acting alone as shown in Fig. 4.4(a).

—maximum possible bending moment M_y in the elastic domain, acting alone as shown in Fig. 4.4(b).

—M_x and M_y acting together as shown in Fig. 4.4(c).

Two interesting results are evident from these figures:

1. The neutral axis resulting from the horizontal bending (Fig. 4.4(a)) or the vertical bending (Fig. 4.4(b)) is neither horizontal nor vertical. This is due to the fact that the principal axes of inertia of the angle are neither horizontal nor vertical. Therefore, in order to have a horizontal or vertical neutral axis, the section should be subjected simultaneously to M_x and M_y.

2. When the two moments M_x and M_y in Fig. 4.4(a) and (b) are superimposed as shown in Fig. 4.4(c), the resulting maximum stress can be less than the maximum values when M_x and M_y are acting separately. Therefore, the interaction between the two moments M_x and M_y becomes of interest. The interaction curve between M_x and M_y, shown in Fig. 4.5, reveals the fact that after having reached a limit state in bending with M_x acting alone (point A in Fig. 4.5), the section can still resist an additional moment M_y (point B in Fig. 4.5) prior to reaching the elastic limit state.

If in addition to bending moments, an axial force P is applied, then it is possible to determine the interaction curves between M_x, M_y and P for different states of compression or tension. The resulting interaction curves are given in Fig. 4.6(a) for the case of a tensile axial force and in Fig. 4.6(b) for the case of a compressive axial force. It should be noted that the reduction in the carrying capacity due to the presence of axial force is not always proportional to the intensity of the axial force.

4.3.1. Plastic Design

Figure 4.7 illustrates the distribution of internal stresses at the plastic limit state for an angle acted upon by a moment M_x. Similar to the elastic design, it is possible to determine at the plastic limit state the

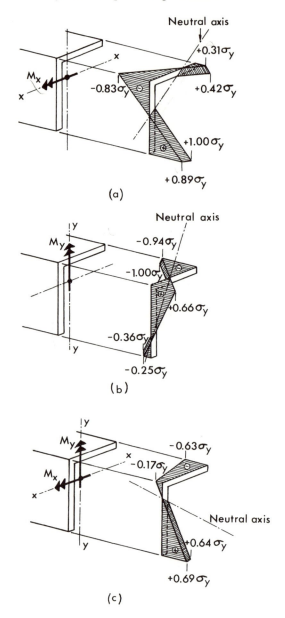

Fig. 4.4. Stress distribution in a $150 \times 100 \times 10$ mm angle subjected to limiting maximum moment: (a) M_x; (b) M_y; (c) M_x and M_y.

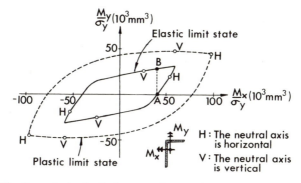

Fig. 4.5. Elastic and plastic limit states interaction curves for M_x and M_y for angle in Fig. 4.4.

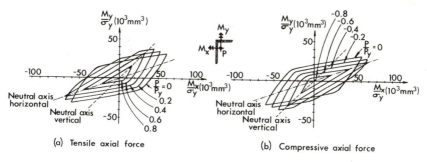

(a) Tensile axial force

(b) Compressive axial force

Fig. 4.6. Elastic limit state interaction curves for M_x, M_y and axial force P in (a) tension, (b) compression, for angle in Fig. 4.4.

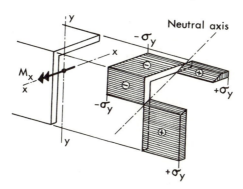

Fig. 4.7. Stress distribution in an angle at the plastic limit state due to moment M_x.

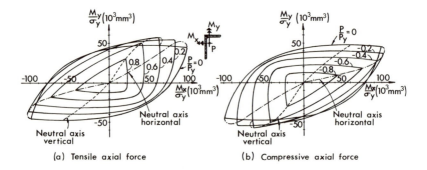

Fig. 4.8. Plastic limit state interaction curves for M_x, M_y and axial force P in (a) tension, (b) compression, for angle in Fig. 4.4.

interaction curves between M_x, M_y and P; these curves are shown in Fig. 4.8(a) and (b). The interaction curve in the plastic limit state for the case $P = 0$ is also shown in Fig. 4.5 for easy comparison of the elastic and plastic interaction curves; this reveals that the two curves have similar slopes and the strength at the plastic limit state can be as much as twice the strength at the elastic limit state for certain cases. But the designer must be aware that the plastic limit state can be reached only if buckling is precluded.

Elastic interaction curves for angles under axial load and biaxial bending have also been derived by Chen and Atsuta (1972, 1974); these will be presented in Chapter 8 as design aids.

4.4. DESIGN OF WELDED OR MULTIPLE BOLTED EQUAL-LEG SINGLE ANGLE WEB COMPRESSION MEMBERS IN TRUSSES

Woolcock and Kitipornchai (1980) developed three-dimensional computer models using a first-order three-dimensional frame analysis program; they recommended a design method based on the methods originally proposed by Trahair *et al.* (1969) and Leigh and Galambos (1972). Basically, the recommended method uses the combined stresses interaction equation of SAA Steel Structures Code (Standards Association of Australia, 1981) for buckling and bending in the plane perpendicular to the truss. Out-of-plane bending moments at the ends of each strut are calculated considering the eccentricity of the connection and the interaction of out-of-plane flexure between adjacent web members.

The following is a summary of the recommended design method:

1. Determine axial forces in the adjoining web members and design such members in tension. Calculate the stress f_{ac} in the web strut under investigation for the trial section assumed.
2. Determine the slenderness ratio L/r_x, where r_x is the radius of gyration of the trial section for the web strut about an axis parallel to the plane of the truss.
3. Determine allowable axial compressive stress σ_a and the Euler buckling stress about the x–x axis, σ_{ex}. σ_a is the allowable axial stress based on the full member's length between intersections as well as on the radius of gyration r_x about the axis parallel to the plane of the truss. These are calculated as

$$\sigma_a = 0 \cdot 60 \left[\frac{\sigma_y + (\mu + 1)\sigma_{ex}}{2} - \sqrt{\left\{ \frac{\sigma_y + (\mu + 1)\sigma_{ex}}{2} \right\}^2 - \sigma_y \sigma_{ex}} \right]$$

(4.25)

where $\mu = 0 \cdot 00003(L/r_x)^2$; and $\sigma_{ex} =$ Euler critical stress $= \pi^2 E/(L/r_x)^2$. Values of σ_a are given in SAA Steel Structures Code (Standards Association of Australia, 1981, Table 6.1.1) and are reproduced herein in Table 4.1.

4. Calculate M_{TZ} and M_{BZ} (Fig. 4.9), the out-of-plane couples about the longitudinal z-axes of the top and bottom chords, respectively. The out-of-plane couple M_{TZ} about the longitudinal axis of the top chord can be expressed as

$$M_{TZ} = -[P_2 e_2 \sin \gamma_{2T} + P_3 e_3 \sin \gamma_{3T}]$$
(4.26)

where P_2 and P_3 are the axial forces in members 2 and 3, taking compression as positive. Members 2 and 3 intersect at the top chord (see Fig. 4.9). Member 2 is the web strut to be designed; e_2 and e_3 are the transverse eccentricities of members 2 and 3 measured in the y-direction from the longitudinal centroidal axis of the chord; and γ_{2T} and γ_{3T} are the angular inclinations between the centroidal axes of the chord and members 2 and 3 measured counterclockwise from the chord z-axis (see Fig. 4.9). These inclinations are always positive. If there are no chord shear forces or external loads applied at the

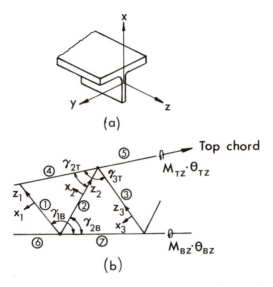

Fig. 4.9. Truss geometry: (a) chord axes; (b) rotation.

joint, then the components of the forces in members 2 and 3 normal to the chord must be equal and opposite, in which case M_{TZ} simplifies to

$$M_{TZ} = -P_2(e_2 - e_3) \sin \gamma_{2T} \qquad (4.27)$$

In other cases where there are more than two web members at a joint or where there are external loads applied to the top chord, the moment M_{TZ} can be determined in a similar manner.

The corresponding expression for the out-of-plane couple M_{BZ} at the bottom chord joint is given by

$$M_{BZ} = P_2 e_2 \sin \gamma_{2B} + P_1 e_1 \sin \gamma_{1B} \qquad (4.28)$$

which in the absence of external loads applied to the bottom chord can be more simply expressed as

$$M_{BZ} = P_2(e_2 - e_1) \sin \gamma_{2B} \qquad (4.29)$$

It should be noted that the eccentricities e_1, e_2 and e_3 have the same sign when the web members are all connected on the same side of the chords (see Fig. 4.10).

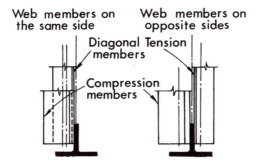

Fig. 4.10. Connection arrangements between web and chord members in a truss.

5. (a) Calculate M_{2T} and M_{2B}, the end moments at the top and bottom of strut 2 about its x-axis, by distributing the out-of-plane couples to the chord and web members framing into the joint, according to

$$M_{2T} = -\frac{\dfrac{I_2}{L_2} \sin \gamma_{2T}}{\sum \dfrac{I_n}{L_n} \sin^2 \gamma_{nT}} \cdot M_{TZ} \qquad (4.30)$$

the summation extending over all the *web* members meeting at the top joint; and

$$M_{2B} = -\frac{\dfrac{I_2}{L_2} \sin \gamma_{2B}}{\sum \dfrac{I_n}{L_n} \sin^2 \gamma_{nB}} \cdot M_{BZ} \qquad (4.31)$$

the summation extending over all the web members meeting at the bottom joint.

(b) Ensure that the magnitudes of M_{2T} and M_{2B} are not less than the minimum moment, $P_2[\bar{y} - (t/2)]$, where P_2 = axial compressive force in member 2, i.e. the member under investigation; $\bar{y}$ = perpendicular distance from the centroid to the contact face of the gusset (see Fig. 4.11); and t = thickness of the angle leg.

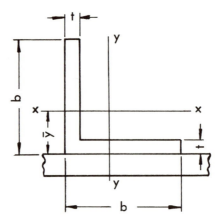

Fig. 4.11. Geometry of angle connection to gusset plate.

6. Calculate the maximum compressive stress f_{bcx} using M_2, the numerically larger of the two moments M_{2T} and M_{2B}, as

$$f_{bcx} = \frac{M_2 \bar{y}}{I_x} \qquad (4.32)$$

If in the unlikely situation that the end moments cause the outstand of the angle to be more highly stressed in compression than the heel of the angle, then

$$f_{bcx} = \frac{M_2(b - \bar{y})}{I_x} \qquad (4.33)$$

where $b =$ width of the angle leg, as shown in Fig. 4.11.

7. Calculate the equivalent uniform moment coefficient C_{mx} from $C_{mx} = 0 \cdot 6 - 0 \cdot 4 M_{min}/M_{max}$. Normally, the member end moments M_{min} and M_{max} will be of opposite sign so that the member will be bent in single curvature and the ratio M_{min}/M_{max} will be negative.

8. Determine the allowable bending stress σ_b from the following:

$$\text{If } \frac{L}{t} < \frac{65\,000}{\sigma_y\,(\text{MPa})},$$

$$\sigma_b = 0 \cdot 66 \sigma_y \qquad (4.34)$$

Otherwise, calculate the elastic buckling stress of an equal-leg angle beam from

$$\sigma_{cr} = \frac{\pi E}{2\sqrt{2 \cdot 6}} \cdot \frac{t}{L} \qquad (4.35)$$

Substituting $E = 200\,000$ MPa,

$$\sigma_{cr} \text{ (in MPa)} = \frac{195\,000}{L/t} \qquad (4.36)$$

If σ_{cr} is equal to or less than σ_y, then

$$\sigma_b = \left[0 \cdot 55 - 0 \cdot 10 \frac{\sigma_{cr}}{\sigma_y} \right] \sigma_{cr} \qquad (4.37)$$

If σ_{cr} is equal to or greater than σ_y,

$$\sigma_b = \left[0 \cdot 95 - 0 \cdot 50 \sqrt{\frac{\sigma_y}{\sigma_{cr}}} \right] \sigma_y \qquad (4.38)$$

9. Substitute the above values into the following combined stress equations and ensure that they are satisfied:

$$\frac{f_{ac}}{\sigma_a} + \frac{C_{mx} f_{bcx}}{\left(1 - \frac{f_{ac}}{0 \cdot 60 \sigma_{ex}} \right) \sigma_b} \leqslant 1 \cdot 0 \qquad (4.39a)$$

$$\frac{f_{ac}}{0 \cdot 6 \sigma_y} + \frac{f_{bcx}}{\sigma_b} \leqslant 1 \cdot 0 \qquad (4.39b)$$

10. Check that the tensile stress in the outstand of the web strut is less than $0 \cdot 66 \sigma_y$ from the following equation:

$$\frac{P_2}{A_2} - \frac{M_2(b - \bar{y})}{I_{x_2}} \leqslant -0 \cdot 66 \sigma_y \qquad (4.40)$$

where the suffix 2 refers to the web strut being designed.

11. Select new member size if the combined stress ratios are either too small or greater than unity, or if the tensile stress in the outstand of the angle is greater than $0 \cdot 66 \sigma_y$.

Based on the above theory, a computer program was developed to check the suitability of a trial section for a web strut and is available from the authors.

4.5. SOLVED EXAMPLES

Example 4.1

For a $150 \times 150 \times 10$ mm equal-leg single angle of effective length 3 m, determine the ultimate concentric axial load.

Solution

From Table 1.1(a): $A = 2900$ mm^2; $I_{min} = I_v = (2 \cdot 58)(10^6)$ mm^4; $r_{min} = r_v = 29 \cdot 8$ mm; $I_{max} = I_u = (10 \cdot 2)(10^6)$ mm^4; $J = (96 \cdot 7)(10^3)$ mm^4; $x_s = y_s = -36 \cdot 2$ mm; $I_{ps} = (20 \cdot 3)(10^6)$ mm^4; $C_w = (169)(10^6)$ mm^6. From Fig. 4.12, $u_s = \sqrt{(x_s^2 + y_s^2)} = 51 \cdot 2$ mm; $r_u^2 = I_u/A = 3517$ mm^2; $r_u = 59 \cdot 3$ mm.

Substituting in eqn (4.6)

$$r_t = \sqrt{\frac{1}{(20 \cdot 3)(10^6)} \left[\frac{(96 \cdot 7)(10^3)(3000)^2}{2\pi^2(1 + 0 \cdot 3)} + (169)(10^6) \right]} = 41 \cdot 0 \text{ mm}$$

Substituting in eqn (4.11)

$$\left(1 - \frac{59 \cdot 3^2}{r_{tu}^2} \right) \left(1 - \frac{41 \cdot 0^2}{r_{tu}^2} \right) - \frac{(2900)(51 \cdot 2)^2}{(20 \cdot 3)(10^6)} = 0$$

This is a quadratic equation in r_{tu}^2. Solving, $r_{tu}^2 = 1359 \cdot 8$, or $r_{tu} = 36 \cdot 9$ mm. From eqn (4.10), the torsional–flexural buckling load is

$$P_{tu} = \frac{(\pi^2)(200\,000)(2900)(1359 \cdot 8)}{(3000)^2} = 864\,900 \text{ N} = 865 \text{ kN}$$

Alternatively, the torsional–flexural buckling load can be computed from eqn (4.8) after computing P_u from eqn (4.2) and P_t from eqn (4.5). From eqn (4.2),

$$P_u = \frac{\pi^2 E I_u}{(KL)^2} = \frac{(\pi^2)(200\,000)(10 \cdot 2)(10^6)}{(3000)^2} = (2 \cdot 237)(10^6) \text{ N}$$

From eqn (4.3),

$$P_t = \frac{2900}{(20 \cdot 3)(10^6)} \left[(77\,000)(96 \cdot 7)(10^3) + \frac{(\pi^2)(200\,000)(169)(10^6)}{(3000)^2} \right]$$

$$= (1 \cdot 069)(10^6) \text{ N}$$

Then from eqn (4.8),

$$P_{tu} = 0 \cdot 8[(2 \cdot 237)(10^6) + (1 \cdot 069)(10^6)$$
$$- \sqrt{[(2 \cdot 237)(10^6) + (1 \cdot 069)(10^6)]^2 - (2 \cdot 5)(2 \cdot 237)(10^6)(1 \cdot 069)(10^6)}]$$
$$= 864\ 100\ \text{N}$$

which is approximately the same as before.

The Euler load for flexural buckling about the minor axis, $v-v$, is

$$\frac{\pi^2 E I_v}{(KL)^2} = \frac{(\pi^2)(200\ 000)(2 \cdot 58)(10^6)}{(3000)^2} = 566\ 000\ \text{N} = 566\ \text{kN}$$

The ultimate concentric axial load is the smaller of the torsional–flexural buckling load about the major axis and the flexural buckling load about the minor axis, i.e. 566 kN. Therefore, the angle will fail by flexural buckling about the minor axis.

Example 4.2

For the angle in Example 4.1, determine the ultimate concentric axial load if the effective length of the column is 2 m, assuming elastic behaviour. If the failure is by torsional–flexural buckling, locate the centre of twist.

Solution

Repeating the steps in Example 4.1 yields the following results: from eqn (4.6), $r_t = 27 \cdot 4$ mm; from eqn (4.11), $r_{tu} = 26 \cdot 2$ mm; from eqn (4.10), $P_{tu} = 985$ kN; from eqn (4.1), $P_v = 1273$ kN. Since the torsional–flexural buckling load is less than the Euler buckling load about the minor axis, the column fails by torsional–flexural buckling, by twisting about point C lying on the $u-u$ axis of symmetry as shown in Fig. 4.12.

The distance between the centroid and the centre of twist, u_c, can be computed from eqn (4.12). With $u_s = 51 \cdot 2$ mm, $r_{tu} = 26 \cdot 2$ mm, and $r_u = 59 \cdot 3$ mm, eqn (4.12) gives

$$u_c = \frac{51 \cdot 2}{\left(1 - \dfrac{26 \cdot 2^2}{59 \cdot 3^2}\right)} = 63 \cdot 7\ \text{mm}$$

Example 4.3

Using Woolcock and Kitipornchai's method, investigate whether a $55 \times 55 \times 8$ mm angle is satisfactory for the member CL of the truss

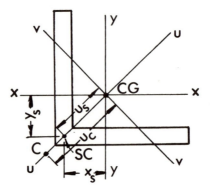

Fig. 4.12. Angle in Example 4.2.

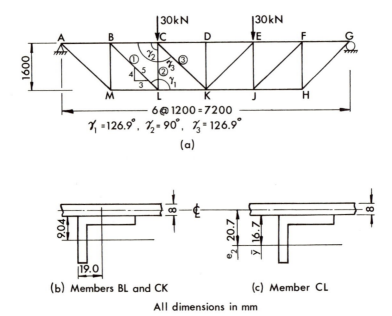

Fig. 4.13. Truss geometry and connection details in Example 4.3.

shown in Fig. 4.13. The adjoining web members BL and CK are $55 \times 35 \times 6$ mm angles with the long leg connected. Assume the loads are applied symmetrically about the truss centre line and lateral restraints are provided at joints A, B, D, F and G. The gusset plates at the top and bottom of strut CL are 8 mm thick and the web members are all on the same side of the gusset. Assume a yield stress of 300 MPa for all members.

Solution
From Table 1.1(b), for the members BL and CK, the moment of inertia about an axis parallel to the plane of the truss $I = (0 \cdot 048)(10^6)$ mm^4 and the transverse eccentricity of the members from the centre line of the chord (see Fig. 4.13(b)) is $9 \cdot 04 + (8/2) = 13 \cdot 04$ mm. Number the web members as shown in Fig. 4.13(a); $e_1 = e_3 = 13 \cdot 04$ mm. Force in web strut $2 = P_2 = 30$ kN (compression is assumed positive). Force in web tie $1 = P_1 = -30/(4/5) = -37 \cdot 5$ kN (tension). Force in web tie $3 = P_3 = 0$. The properties of the trial section for web strut 2 from Table 1.1(a) are $A = 816$ mm^2; $I_x = (0 \cdot 225)(10^6)$ mm^4; $\bar{y} = 16 \cdot 7$ mm (see Fig. 4.13(c)); and

$$r_x = \sqrt{\frac{I_x}{A}} = \sqrt{\frac{(0 \cdot 225)(10^6)}{816}} = 16.6 \text{ mm}$$

The transverse eccentricity of member 2 from the centre line of the chord, e_2, from Fig. 4.13(c) $= 16 \cdot 7 + (8/2) = 20 \cdot 7$ mm. Thus,

1. $f_{ac} = P_2/A_2 = 30\,000/816 = 36 \cdot 8$ MPa.
2. $L = 1600$ mm, then

$$\frac{L}{r_x} = \frac{1600}{16 \cdot 6} = 96$$

3. From Table 4.1, for $L/r_x = 96$ and $\sigma_y = 300$ MPa, $\sigma_a = 92$ MPa, and $\sigma_{ex} = 213$ MPa.
4. Using eqn (4.26), with $P_2 = 30\,000$ N, $e_2 = 20 \cdot 7$ mm, $\sin \gamma_{2T} = \sin 90°$, $P_3 = 0$, $e_3 = 13 \cdot 04$ mm, $\sin \gamma_{3T} = \sin 126 \cdot 9°$, $M_{TZ} = -(30\,000)(20 \cdot 7) = -621\,000$ N.mm. Similarly, using eqn (4.28), with $P_2 = 30\,000$ N, $e_2 = 20 \cdot 7$ mm, $\sin \gamma_{2B} = \sin 90°$, $P_1 = -37\,500$ N, $e_1 = 13 \cdot 04$ mm, $\sin \gamma_{1B} = \sin 126 \cdot 9°$,

$$M_{BZ} = (30\,000)(20 \cdot 7)(\sin 90°) + (-37\,500)(13 \cdot 04)(\sin 126 \cdot 9°)$$
$$= 621\,000 - 391\,000 = 230\,000 \text{ N.mm}$$

Table 4.1

Maximum Permissible Stress, σ_a (MPa) on the Gross Cross-section of a Strut for Concentric Axial Compression for Steels with Various Values of Yield Stress, σ_y (MPa)

σ_y	230		240		250		260		280		300	
KL/r	0	5	0	5	0	5	0	5	0	5	0	5
0	138	138	144	144	150	150	156	156	168	168	180	180
10	138	137	144	143	150	149	156	155	167	167	179	179
20	136	135	142	141	148	147	154	153	166	165	178	176
30	134	132	140	138	146	144	151	150	163	161	175	172
40	130	128	136	133	142	139	147	144	158	155	169	166
50	125	122	130	127	136	132	141	137	151	147	162	156
60	118	114	123	118	128	122	132	127	141	135	150	143
70	109	104	113	107	117	111	121	114	128	120	135	127
80	98	92	101	95	104	98	107	100	113	105	118	109
90	87	81	89	83	91	85	93	87	97	90	101	93
100	76	70	77	72	79	73	81	75	83	77	86	79
110	66	61	67	62	68	63	69	65	72	66	73	68
120	57	53	58	54	59	55	60	56	62	57	63	59
130	50	47	51	47	52	48	52	49	53	50	55	51
140	44	41	45	42	45	42	46	43	47	44	48	45
150	39	37	39	37	40	37	40	38	41	39	42	39
160	34	33	35	33	35	33	36	34	36	34	37	35
170	31	29	31	30	32	30	32	30	32	31	33	31
180	28	26	28	27	28	27	29	27	29	28	30	28
190	25	24	25	24	26	24	26	25	26	25	27	25
200	23	22	23	22	23	22	23	22	24	23	24	23
210	21	20	21	20	21	20	21	20	22	21	22	21
220	19	18	19	18	19	18	19	19	20	19	20	19
230	17	17	17	17	18	17	18	17	18	17	18	18
240	16	15	16	15	16	16	16	16	17	16	17	16
250	15	14	15	14	15	14	15	15	15	15	16	15
260	14	13	14	13	14	13	14	13	14	14	14	14
270	13	12	13	12	13	12	13	13	13	13	13	13
280	12	11	12	11	12	12	12	12	12	12	12	12
290	11	11	11	11	11	11	11	11	11	11	12	11
300	10	10	10	10	10	10	11	10	11	10	11	11

Table 4.1—*contd.*

310		330		340		360		410		480		σ_e	
0	5	0	5	0	5	0	5	0	5	0	5	0	5
186	186	198	198	204	204	216	216	246	246	288	288		78957
185	185	197	197	203	203	215	214	245	244	287	286	19739	8773
184	182	195	194	201	200	213	212	243	241	284	282	4935	3158
180	178	192	189	198	195	209	206	238	235	278	274	2193	1611
175	171	186	182	192	187	203	198	230	224	268	260	1234	975
167	161	177	171	182	175	192	184	216	206	249	235	790	653
155	147	163	154	167	158	175	165	195	181	218	200	548	467
138	129	145	135	148	137	154	142	167	153	181	164	403	351
120	111	125	115	127	117	131	120	139	126	148	133	308	273
103	95	106	97	107	98	110	100	115	105	121	109	244	219
87	80	89	82	90	83	92	85	96	88	100	91	197	179
74	69	76	70	77	71	78	72	81	74	83	77	163	149
64	59	65	60	65	61	66	62	69	63	71	65	137	126
55	51	56	52	56	53	57	53	59	55	61	56	117	108
48	45	49	46	49	46	50	47	51	48	53	49	101	94
42	40	43	40	43	40	44	41	45	42	46	43	88	82
37	35	38	36	38	36	39	36	39	37	40	38	77	73
33	31	34	32	34	32	34	32	35	33	36	34	68	64
30	28	30	29	30	29	31	29	31	30	32	30	61	58
27	26	27	26	27	26	28	26	28	27	29	27	55	52
24	23	25	23	25	24	25	24	25	24	26	25	49	47
22	21	22	21	22	21	23	22	23	22	24	23	45	43
20	19	20	20	21	20	21	20	21	20	22	21	41	39
18	18	19	18	19	18	19	18	19	19	20	19	37	36
17	16	17	17	17	17	17	17	18	17	18	17	34	33
16	15	16	15	16	15	16	15	16	16	17	16	32	30
15	14	15	14	15	14	15	14	15	15	15	15	29	28
13	13	14	13	14	13	14	13	14	14	14	14	27	26
13	12	13	12	13	12	13	12	13	13	13	13	25	24
12	11	12	11	12	11	12	12	12	12	12	12	23	23
11	11	11	11	11	11	11	11	11	11	12	11	22	21

Since there are no external loads applied to the bottom chord nor chord shear forces, and with only two web members, eqn (4.29) becomes applicable. Thus M_{BZ} can be calculated as $(30\,000)(20\cdot7 - 13\cdot04)(\sin 90°) = 230\,000$ N.mm, which is the same as above.

5. (a) From eqn (4.30),

$$M_{2T} = -\frac{\dfrac{I_2}{L_2}\sin\gamma_{2T}}{\dfrac{I_2}{L_2}\sin^2\gamma_{2T} + \dfrac{I_3}{L_3}\sin^2\gamma_{3T}} M_{TZ}$$

Substituting $I_2 = (0\cdot225)(10^6)$ mm^4; $L_2 = 1600$ mm; $\gamma_{2T} = 90°$; $I_3 = (0\cdot048)(10^6)$ mm^4; $L_3 = 2000$ mm; $\gamma_{3T} = 126\cdot90°$; $M_{TZ} = -621\,000$ N.mm, in eqn (4.30) yields $M_{2T} = 560\,000$ N.mm. Similarly, M_{2B} is computed from eqn (4.31) as

$$M_{2B} = -\frac{\dfrac{I_2}{L_2}\sin\gamma_{2B}}{\dfrac{I_1}{L_1}\sin^2\gamma_{1B} + \dfrac{I_2}{L_2}\sin^2\gamma_{2B}} M_{BZ}$$

Substituting $I_2 = (0\cdot225)(10^6)$ mm^4; $L_2 = 1600$ mm; $\gamma_{2B} = 90°$; $I_1 = (0\cdot048)(10^6)$ mm^4; $L_1 = 2000$ mm; $\gamma_{1B} = 126\cdot9°$; $M_{BZ} = 230\,000$ N.mm, yields $M_{2B} = -207\,000$ N.mm.

(b) Minimum moment $= P_2(\bar{y} - (t/2)) = 30\,000(16\cdot7 - (8/2)) = 381\,000$ N.mm, which is greater than the value of $207\,000$ N.mm for M_{2B} calculated above. Therefore, M_{2B} is increased to the minimum value, i.e. $M_{2B} = -381\,000$ N.mm.

6. M_2 is the larger of M_{2T} and M_{2B}; hence $M_2 = 560\,000$ N.mm. From eqn (4.32), calculate the bending stress f_{bcx}. Substituting $M_2 = 560\,000$ N.mm, $\bar{y} = 16\cdot7$ mm, and $I_x = (0\cdot225)(10^6)$ mm^4 in eqn (4.32) yields $f_{bcx} = 41\cdot6$ MPa.

7. The equivalent uniform moment coefficient

$$C_{mx} = 0\cdot6 - 0\cdot4(-381\,000/560\,000) = 0\cdot87$$

8. Check whether L/t is less than $65\,000/\sigma_y$(MPa):

$$\frac{L}{t} = \frac{1600}{8} = 200; \quad \frac{65\,000}{\sigma_y} = \frac{65\,000}{300} = 217. \text{ Hence, } \frac{L}{t} < 217$$

Therefore, from eqn (4.34), $\sigma_b = 0\cdot66\sigma_y = 198$ MPa.

9. (a) Substituting $f_{ac} = 36 \cdot 8$ MPa (step 1); $\sigma_a = 92$ MPa (step 3); $C_{mx} = 0 \cdot 87$ (step 7); $f_{bcx} = 41 \cdot 6$ MPa (step 6); $\sigma_{ex} = 213$ MPa (step 3); $\sigma_b = 198$ MPa (step 8), in eqn (4.39a) yield

$$\frac{36 \cdot 8}{92} + \frac{(0 \cdot 87)(41 \cdot 6)}{\left(1 - \dfrac{36 \cdot 8}{(0 \cdot 6)(213)}\right)198} = 0 \cdot 4 + 0 \cdot 26$$

$$= 0 \cdot 66 < 1 \cdot 0. \text{ Therefore acceptable}$$

(b) Substituting the above values in eqn (4.39b),

$$\frac{36 \cdot 8}{(0 \cdot 6)(300)} + \frac{41 \cdot 6}{198} = 0 \cdot 20 + 0 \cdot 21 = 0 \cdot 41 < 1 \cdot 0. \text{ Acceptable}$$

10. Stress in the outstand is checked by using eqn (4.40). Substituting $P_2 = 30\,000$ N; $A_2 = 816$ mm^2; $M_2 = 560\,000$ N.mm; $b = 55$ mm; $\bar{y} = 16 \cdot 7$ mm; $I_x = (0 \cdot 225)(10^6)$ mm^4 in eqn (4.40),

$$\frac{30\,000}{816} - \frac{(560\,000)(55 - 16 \cdot 7)}{(0 \cdot 225)(10^6)} = -58 \cdot 5 \text{ MPa}$$

$$< -0 \cdot 66\sigma_y. \text{ Therefore acceptable}$$

It is concluded that a $55 \times 55 \times 8$ mm angle is satisfactory for the web strut CL. Since the stress ratios in step 9 are much less than $1 \cdot 0$, a smaller section would be more economical.

Chapter 5

ANGLES IN CONNECTION

5.1. INTRODUCTION

Most beam-to-beam, beam-to-column, and column-to-base plate connections are made by angles which are either riveted, bolted or welded to the structural members which are being joined together. Often, when a connection is made between axially loaded members by means of a gusset plate, short angles, called lug angles (Fig. 5.1), are used to reduce the length of the connection. Beam-to-beam, beam-to-girder and beam-to-column connections can be either shear type (flexible) connections (see Figs. 5.2, 5.6, 5.7 and 5.10) or moment-resistant (rigid) connections. A type of moment-resistant beam-to-column connection in which angles are used is referred to as the 'flexible wind connection' (Fig. 5.14). In this type of connection, angles connecting the beam web to the column flange are sized for shear due to gravity loading whereas angles connecting beam flanges to the column flange are designed to resist the moment due to wind loading.

In this chapter, the discussion is focussed on the factors governing the design of connection angles themselves and not on the fasteners. For the design of fasteners, the reader should consult other references such as American Institute of Steel Construction (1980, 1984), Australian Institute of Steel Construction (1979), Blodgett (1966), Canadian Institute of Steel Construction (1980), and McGuire (1968).

5.2. LUG ANGLES

Lug angles are sometimes used to connect the outstanding legs of axially loaded structural members, such as angles and channels, to gusset plates (Fig. 5.1). Such members are either in tension or in

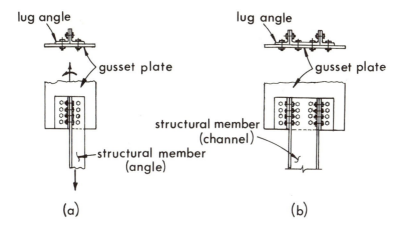

Fig. 5.1. Connections with lug angles.

compression and are generally found in trusses. The following are some of the advantages of providing lug angles:

(a) Reduction in the secondary bending stresses in the axially loaded structural member (angle or channel section);

(b) Reduction of gusset plate dimensions; and

(c) Increase in the stiffness of the connection.

If the end-connections are flexible, the axially loaded member should be strong enough to resist the additional stresses due to the eccentricity of load. (The end-connections themselves are designed for axial force only.) On the other hand, if the end-connections are so stiff that the member has no end rotations, then the member is designed for axial force only. (The end-connections are designed to resist both the axial force and the end moment.)

Lug angles connecting a channel-shaped member shall be disposed symmetrically with respect to the section of the member (Fig. 5.1(b)). They should be capable of transmitting the force in the flanges of the channel section to the gusset plate. Similarly, lug angles connecting an angle section to a gusset plate (Fig. 5.1(a)) must be strong enough to transmit the force in the outstanding leg of the angle section. The detailed requirements for the design of lug angles are given in the specifications of the British Standards Institution (1969*a*), clause 49, and of the Indian Standards Institution (1984), clause 8.1.8.

The beneficial effect of lug angles is taken into account in clause 42 of British Standard 449: Part 2: 1969 (British Standards Institution, 1969a) which states that even for a single angle in tension connected through one leg, the net sectional area of the whole of the angle member can be considered effective. Similar provision exists in clause 4.2.1.1 of the Indian Standard 800-1984 (Indian Standards Institution, 1984).

5.3. WEB FRAMING ANGLES—DOUBLE-ANGLE CONNECTIONS

For many years 'standard double-angle connections' have been most commonly used (Fig. 5.2). The connection angles should not be too thick because the flexibility of the connection is primarily due to the bending and twisting of the angles (Fig. 5.3). Angles of the order of 10 mm thickness will offer very little resistance and will conform to the end slope of the beam. To assure flexibility, the AISC Manual (American Institute of Steel Construction, 1980, p. 4.13) recommends a maximum thickness of $\frac{5}{8}$ in (16 mm). For practical reasons, the minimum thickness of connection angles is taken as 6 mm.

Since the connection has to provide lateral support to the beam being supported, i.e. provide restraint against twisting, the connection

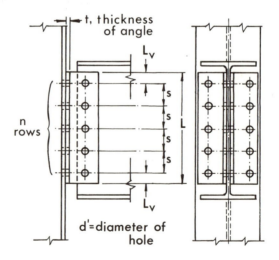

Fig. 5.2. Double-angle connection.

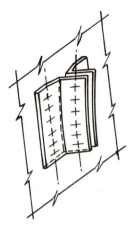

Fig. 5.3. Flexibility of a double-angle connection.

angles must have a certain minimum length, which is generally one-half the clear depth of the web (i.e. one-half the depth of the web between the fillets) of the beam being supported; whereas, the maximum length of connection angles is the depth of the web between the fillets of the beam being supported.

As proved by test data and justified by experience, the conventional practice is to neglect the effect of eccentricity in the design of bolted double angle connections. Referring to Fig. 5.4, the effect of eccentricities e_1 and e_2 is neglected, and the shear is assumed uniformly

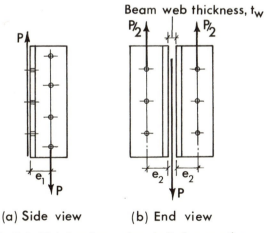

(a) Side view   (b) End view

Fig. 5.4. Web framing angles—bolted connection.

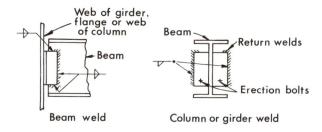

Fig. 5.5. Web framing angles—welded connection.

distributed among the bolts. However, eccentricity has an effect on welded connections (Fig. 5.5) for connection angles up to 310 mm in length (Canadian Institute of Steel Construction, 1980, page 3–54). For longer connection angles, the weld capacity is not reduced by the effect of eccentricity.

Although double-angle connections are designed for shear only, they provide some moment resistance which depends on:

(a) the properties of the members being joined together; (b) the thickness of the connection angles; and (c) the bolt gauge distance (if bolted) or the length of the outstanding leg (if welded). Proper choice of these variables will ensure that the moment-resistance of such connections remains small. For bolted connections, the gauge distance should be as large as possible. For welded connections, the outstanding legs should be large to assist in rotation. Column or girder welds should not be placed near the heel but on the toes of the angles (Fig. 5.5). If fitting bolts are to be used for erection purposes and if these bolts are to be left in place after erection, they should be placed below the mid-depth of the connection angles as shown in Fig. 5.5. The designer should be aware of the inherent rigidity of this connection and should consider the rigidity in cases where it is critical.

The thickness of the connection angles is based on the bearing capacity of bolts, shear on the gross area of the connection angles and shear on the net area of the connection angles. The bearing capacity of one bolt (P_b) on the connection angles depends on the ultimate tensile strength of the material of the connection angle (σ_u), diameter of bolt (d), thickness of the connection angle (t), distance between the centres of bolt holes (s), and distance from the centre of the hole to the edge of the connection angle (L_v) (see Fig. 5.2).

According to the AISC Specification (American Institute of Steel

Construction, 1978), the bearing capacity of bolts on connection angles is the least of the following three values:

Bearing capacity of the bolt based on the projected area of contact (clause 1.5.1.5.3)
$$P_b = 1 \cdot 5\sigma_u dt \tag{5.1}$$

Bearing capacity of the bolt based on the bolt spacing (clause 1.16.4.2)
$$P_b = 0 \cdot 5\sigma_u t\left(s - \frac{d}{2}\right) \tag{5.2}$$

Bearing capacity of the bolt based on the edge/end distance of the connection angles (clause 1.16.5.2)
$$P_b = 0 \cdot 5\sigma_u t L_v \tag{5.3}$$

The connection angles should be thick enough to transfer the beam reaction (P) without exceeding the permissible shear stress. The permissible shear stress on the gross area is taken as $0 \cdot 4\sigma_y$ (American Institute of Steel Construction, 1978, clause 1.5.1.2.1). If 'L' is the length of the connection angles, then for two angles

$$P = 2(L)(t)(0 \cdot 4\sigma_y) = 0 \cdot 8Lt\sigma_y \tag{5.4}$$

The permissible shear stress on the net area is $0 \cdot 3\sigma_u$ (American Institute of Steel Construction, 1978, clause 1.5.1.2.2).

If there are 'n' holes in a vertical line and if P_n is the load carried by 'n' bolts in these holes, and if the diameter of the hole is d', then the

$$\text{net area } A_n = t(L - nd') \tag{5.5}$$
and
$$P_n = (0 \cdot 3\sigma_u)(A_n) = 0 \cdot 3\sigma_u t(L - nd') \tag{5.6}$$

In calculating the net area in shear, the actual diameter of the hole is used. This is different from the case when the failure mode is in tension (viz., diameter of hole $+1 \cdot 5$ or 2 mm allowance for incipient cracking around the hole).

5.4. WEB FRAMING ANGLES—SINGLE-ANGLE CONNECTIONS

For cases where speed of erection is a primary consideration, and for cases where limited access makes the erection of beams with double-angle connections difficult, single-angle connections (Fig. 5.6) are

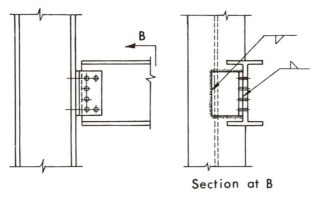

Section at B

Fig. 5.6. Web framing angles—single-angle connection.

preferred to double-angle connections. The following are some of the advantages of beam-to-girder (or beam-to-column) single-angle connections:

(a)   Both material and fabrication costs are reduced because only one angle is required for each connection.
(b)   The connection angles are shop-attached (either bolted or welded) to the girder or column and the beams, which are usually more numerous, are made plain-holed beams, thus reducing the shop work considerably.
(c)   Plain-holed beams can usually be erected more easily than beams with web framing angles.

In these connections, the fasteners (rivets, bolts, or welds) are subjected to stresses due to eccentric loading on the angle. For bolted single-angle connections, it is customary to consider vertical shear and bearing on all bolts, and the effect of eccentricity only for the bolts in the supporting member (girder or column). For bolted double-angle connections, it can be recalled that the practice is to completely ignore the effect of eccentricity for bolts both on the supporting member and on the member being supported. As is the case with welded double-angle connections, eccentricity is considered in the design of welds for welded single-angle connections also.

For bolted single-angle connections, the AISC Manual (American Institute of Steel Construction, 1980, page 4–84) recommends a minimum angle thickness of $\frac{3}{8}$ in (10 mm) for $\frac{3}{4}$ in and $\frac{7}{8}$ in (20 mm and

22 mm) diameter bolts and a minimum thickness of $\frac{1}{2}$ in (13 mm) for 1 in (24 mm) diameter bolts. The thickness of the angle must be sufficient to provide adequate bolt bearing capacity and adequate shear capacity on the gross and net section as for double-angle connections. In addition, it must have sufficient moment capacity at the net section. Using the same notation as in Fig. 5.2

Length of net section $L_n = L - nd'$ (5.7)

Section modulus $S = (\frac{1}{6})(t)(L - nd')^2$ (5.8)

Moment capacity $M = (S)(0 \cdot 6\sigma_y) = 0 \cdot 1\sigma_y t(L - nd')^2$ (5.9)

This capacity should be greater than or equal to the external moment of $P \cdot e$.

To aid in the design of single-angle connections, tables and examples are provided in the AISC Manual (American Institute of Steel Construction, 1980, pages 4–84 and 4–85) and in the CISC Handbook (Canadian Institute of Steel Construction, 1980, pages 3–62 and 3–63).

5.5. UNSTIFFENED SEAT ANGLE CONNECTIONS

Unstiffened seat angle connections (Fig. 5.7) are popular as both beam-to-column flange and beam-to-column web connections, because

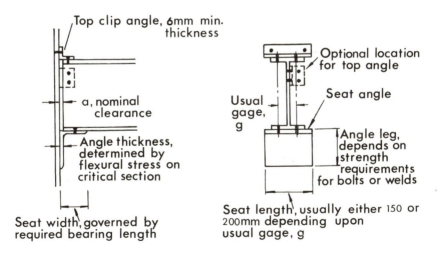

Fig. 5.7. Unstiffened seat angle connection.

of the following advantages:

(a) They permit fabrication of plain-holed (either punched or drilled) beams. (b) They provide the means for supporting the beams during alignment of holes and insertion of bolts during erection. (c) They allow greater length tolerance for the beam than most other connections. (d) They make erection easier and faster.

Such connections are used both in industrial and commercial construction.

The unstiffened angle seat consists of a relatively heavy angle either shop welded or bolted to the column, with the beam bolted or welded to the seat in the field. The seat angle is designed to carry the entire beam reaction. A seat angle connection must be stabilized with a flexible clip angle ($75 \times 75 \times 5$ or $100 \times 100 \times 6$ mm) that is attached either to the top flange of the beam or near the top of the beam web (Fig. 5.7); welds or bolts are used to connect the top clip angle to the beam and the column. However, when welds are used, care must be exercised to ensure that they do not inhibit rotation of the beam; this is accomplished by locating the welds along the toes of the clip angle and not along the sides. Web clip angles are always bolted.

For beams 250 mm deep and smaller, seat angle connections will not be economical (Australian Institute of Steel Construction, 1979, page 4–46) since the clip angle is too large in relation to the beam depth; therefore, other alternative connections (web framing angles—either double angle connections or single angle connections) would generally be found more economical.

Eccentricities produced by the seat angle connections are normally larger than those for double angle web framing connections. These may influence the design of the supporting members, even though all seat angle connections are designed for simple shear only.

The thickness of the seat angle is determined by the bending stress at the critical section of the seat angle, as shown in Fig. 5.8. If the seat angle is bolted to the column and the beam is simply resting on top of the angle without being attached to it either by bolts or welds, the critical section would probably be a–a in Fig. 5.8(a)—the net section through the upper bolt line of the vertical leg. When the beam is bolted to the top of the seat angle as shown in Fig. 5.8(b), the critical section for bending is taken at 10 mm from the face of the vertical leg of the angle. If the seat angle is welded to the column as shown in Fig. 5.8(c), the critical section will be the same as in Fig. 5.8(b), whether the beam is attached to the horizontal leg of the seat angle or not. Of

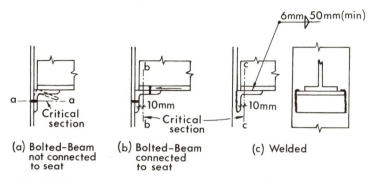

Fig. 5.8. Critical section for bending of an unstiffened seat angle.

course, in practice, the beam will never be left unattached to the seat angle, and therefore the critical section for bending can be assumed to be at 10 mm from the face of the angle both for welded as well as bolted connections. In order to calculate the moment at the critical section, it is necessary to determine the point at which the beam reaction is applied to the seat angle. A conservative approach is to assume the reaction at the centre of the full contact width (Fig. 5.9(a)). Tables in the AISC Manual (American Institute of Steel Construction, 1980, pages 4–38 to 4–43) and CISC Handbook (Canadian Institute of Steel Construction, 1980, pages 3–66 to 3–69) use the less conservative approach of assuming the reaction at the centre of the *required*

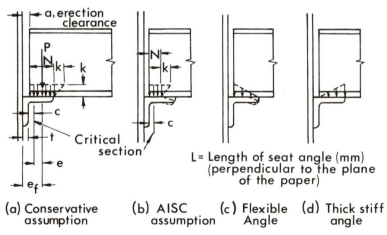

Fig. 5.9. Bearing stress assumptions for unstiffened seat angle connection.

bearing length N (Fig. 5.9(b)) measured from the end of the beam. For flexible seat angle, the bearing stress distribution shown in Fig. 5.9(c) is also rational, while for a stiff seat angle, the actual distribution is closer to that shown in Fig. 5.9(d).

The following are the steps in the design of unstiffened seat angles:

1. Determine the required bearing length, N, from web crippling considerations. As per AISC Specification (American Institute of Steel Construction, 1978, clause 1.10.10.1),

$$N \text{ (mm)} = \frac{P}{0 \cdot 75 \sigma_{yb} t_w} - k \geqslant k \qquad (5.10)$$

where P = beam reaction (newtons); t_w = thickness of web of beam (mm); σ_{yb} = yield stress of material of beam (MPa); k = distance from outer face of flange of beam to web toe of fillet (mm).

2. Determine the moment arm, e (mm). Referring to Fig. 5.9(a),

$$e \text{ (mm)} = \left(a + \frac{N}{2} - t - c \right) \qquad (5.11)$$

where a = erection clearance (13 mm nominal, 20 mm for design); t = thickness of the seat angle (mm); c = distance of the critical section from the face of the seat angle (mm).

3. Calculate the bending moment at the critical section, M.

$$M \text{ (N.mm)} = P \cdot e = P \left(a + \frac{N}{2} - t - c \right) \qquad (5.12)$$

4. Compute the section modulus, S, of the horizontal leg of the seat angle.

$$S \text{ (mm}^3) = \tfrac{1}{6} L t^2 \qquad (5.13)$$

where L = length of the seat angle (mm).

5. Determine the bending stress, σ_b, at the critical section

$$\sigma_b \text{ (MPa)} = \frac{M}{S} = \frac{P \left(a + \dfrac{N}{2} - t - c \right)}{\tfrac{1}{6} L t^2} \qquad (5.14)$$

6. Equate the above bending stress to the permissible bending stress of $0 \cdot 75 \sigma_{ya}$ (solid rectangular section bent about its weak axis) (American Institute of Steel Construction, 1978, clause

1.5.1.4.3) and solve the resulting quadratic equation for the unknown 't'.

$$0{\cdot}75\sigma_{ya} = \sigma_b = \frac{M}{S} = \frac{P\left(a + \frac{N}{2} - t - c\right)}{\frac{1}{6}Lt^2} \tag{5.15}$$

where σ_{ya} = yield stress of the material of the seat angle (MPa).

CISC Handbook (Canadian Institute of Steel Construction, 1980, page 3–67), using limit states design method (Canadian Standards Association, 1978) gives the following expression for the thickness of the seat angle:

$$t \text{ (mm)} = \frac{-\beta + \sqrt{\beta^2 + 4\alpha\gamma}}{2\alpha} \tag{5.16}$$

where

$$\alpha = 0{\cdot}625(0{\cdot}9)^2\sigma_{ya}\sigma_{yb}t_wL \tag{5.17}$$

$$\beta = 2{\cdot}5(0{\cdot}9)t_w\sigma_{yb}P_f \tag{5.18}$$

where P_f is the factored reaction (newtons).

$$\gamma = P_f^2 - \beta\left(\frac{k}{2} - 10\right) \tag{5.19}$$

Required length of bearing $N = \dfrac{2P_f^2}{\beta} - k$ $\qquad$ (5.20)

5.6. STIFFENED SEAT ANGLE CONNECTIONS

For heavy reactions, say in excess of 200 kN, unstiffened seat angles become excessively thick and a stiffened seat angle connection (Fig. 5.10) is more economical. When a stiffened seat is used, owing to the tendency of the beam to rotate, the reaction is concentrated near the part of the seat away from the support (Fig. 5.9(d) and Fig. 5.10(a) and (b)). Thus for welded stiffened seat angle connections, the moment on the welds attaching the stiffened seat angle to the column is greater than for unstiffened seat angles. For bolted connections, it is customary to neglect the eccentricity and design the bolts for simple shear only. In bolted construction, stiffening normally consists of providing two vertical angles with the outstanding leg finished to bear under the horizontal leg of the seat angle as shown in Fig. 5.10. In the AISC Manual

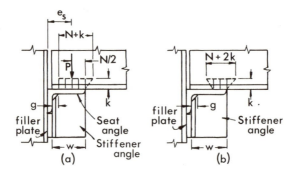

Fig. 5.10. Stiffened seat angle connection.

(American Institute of Steel Construction, 1980, page 4–47), the size of the largest stiffener outstanding leg is 5 in (125 mm), which fixes the maximum outstanding leg of a seat angle at about 6 in (150 mm). Thus, for eccentricities greater than this, the designer should include the effect of eccentricity when designing the bolts. In welded connections, the eccentricity is always considered.

The size of the horizontal leg of the seat angle is obtained from consideration of crippling of the beam web as for unstiffened seat angles. Thus,

$$N \text{ (mm)} = \frac{P}{0 \cdot 75 \sigma_{yb} t_w} - k \geqslant k \qquad (5.10)$$

Assuming the beam reaction P is located at $N/2$ from the *edge* of the seat (Fig. 5.10(a)), the thickness of each of the stiffening angles, t_s, is

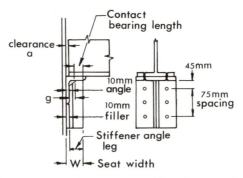

Fig. 5.11. Bearing stress on stiffened seat angle.

determined from the following equation (American Institute of Steel Construction, 1978, clause 1.5.1.5 bearing on contact area):

$$t_s \text{ (mm)} = (0\cdot5) \frac{P}{0\cdot90\sigma_{ys}(w - g)} \qquad (5.21)$$

where σ_{ys} = yield stress of material of the stiffening angles (MPa); w = size of outstanding leg of the stiffening angles (mm); g = amount of the stiffener angle clipped off so as to get close bearing on the seat angle, usually 13 mm ($\frac{1}{2}$ in) (Fig. 5.11). Equation (5.21) assumes no eccentricity of load with respect to the centre of the bearing contact length.

5.7. HANGER CONNECTIONS AND FLEXIBLE WIND CONNECTIONS

A typical hanger connection is shown in Fig. 5.12. In the design of such connections 'prying action' must be considered. To facilitate trial design, tables are provided in the AISC Manual (American Institute of Steel Construction, 1980, page 4–88) and the CISC Handbook (Canadian Institute of Steel Construction, 1980, pages 3–22 and 3–23). In general, prying effects can be minimized by making the dimension 'b' as small as possible and the dimension 'a' as large as possible, Fig. 5.13. For repeated loading, the connecting angles must be made thick enough and stiff enough to virtually eliminate the deformation of the angle legs.

AISC Manual of Steel Construction (American Institute of Steel Construction, 1980, page 4–89) suggests the following design method for determining the thickness of angles in hanger type connections. (The same method is applicable for the design of flexible wind connections (American Institute of Steel Construction, 1984, page 4–17)).

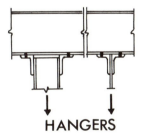

HANGERS

Fig. 5.12. A double angle hanger connection.

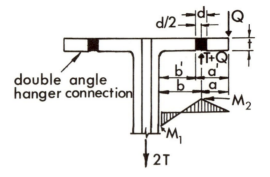

Fig. 5.13. Definition of symbols for design of angles in hanger and flexible wind connections.

Referring to Fig. 5.13,

$$\delta = 1 - d'/p \tag{5.22}$$

$$M = \frac{M_p}{2} = \frac{pt^2\sigma_y}{8} \tag{5.23}$$

$$\alpha = \frac{\dfrac{Tb'}{M} - 1}{\delta} \tag{5.24}$$

$$B_c = T\left[1 + \frac{\delta\alpha}{(1+\delta\alpha)}(b'/a')\right] \tag{5.25}$$

$$\text{Required } t = \left[\frac{8B_c a'b'}{p\sigma_y[a' + \delta\alpha(a' + b')]}\right]^{1/2} \tag{5.26}$$

where T = applied tension per bolt (exclusive of initial tightening); Q = prying force per bolt at design load = $B_c - T$; B = allowable load on bolt; B_c = load per bolt including prying action; M_p = plastic moment; σ_y = yield strength of the flange material; p = length of flange, parallel to leg, contributory to each bolt; t = required thickness of angle leg; M = allowable resisting moment contributed by a flange of length p and thickness t; b = distance from bolt centre line (gage line) to face of angle leg; a = distance from bolt centre line to edge of angle leg but not more than $1\cdot25b$; d = bolt diameter; d' = width of bolt hole in flange parallel to angle leg; $b' = b - d/2$; $a' = a + d/2$; $\alpha = M_2/\delta M_1$ for $0 < \alpha < 1\cdot0$; when $\alpha > 1\cdot0$ use $\alpha = 1\cdot0$; when $\alpha < 0\cdot0$, use $\alpha = 0\cdot0$; δ = ratio of net area (at bolt line) and the gross area (at the face of the angle leg). Prying force is maximum at $\alpha = 1$ and minimum at $\alpha = 0$. When $1\cdot0 > \alpha > 0\cdot0$, both the flange material thickness and the tension capacity of the bolts govern simultaneously.

The bolt pitch should be selected such that 'p' lies between 4 and 5 times the bolt diameter ($4\cdot0d \leqslant p \leqslant 5\cdot0d$) and '$p$' should be kept as small as practicable to reduce any two-way action.

When $\alpha \geqslant 1\cdot0$, connection angles become flexible and the strength of the connection is governed by the strength of the connection angles. Bolts will have excess capacity to resist the applied loads, even after the effect of prying action is included. The limiting strength condition is reached when the angle leg bends in double curvature with plastic hinges at the bolt line and at the face of the angle, i.e. $M_1 = M_2 = M_p$ as shown in Fig. 5.13.

Using Limit States Design method (Canadian Standards Association, 1978), CISC Handbook (Canadian Institute of Steel Construction, 1980, page 3–19) gives the following formula for the thickness of angle when $\alpha \geqslant 1\cdot0$:

$$t = \sqrt{\frac{(T_f 2b)}{(0\cdot9 p\sigma_y)}} = \sqrt{\frac{2\cdot22 T_f b}{p\sigma_y}} \tag{5.27}$$

where T_f is the factored tensile force per bolt and $0\cdot9$ is the performance factor.

When $\alpha \leqslant 0\cdot0$, the angle leg is sufficiently thick and stiff so that there is a substantial reduction in the prying force, i.e. $M_2 \approx 0$ in Fig. 5.13. The capacity of the connection is then governed by the tensile capacity of the bolts. Using Limit States Design method (Canadian Standards Association, 1978), the CISC Handbook gives the following formula for the thickness of angle when $\alpha \leqslant 0\cdot0$:

$$t = \sqrt{\frac{(T_f 4b)}{(0\cdot9 p\sigma_y)}} = \sqrt{\frac{4\cdot44 T_f b}{p\sigma_y}} \tag{5.28}$$

In the Allowable Stress Design method with a factor of safety of $2\cdot0$, formulas (5.27) and (5.28) will be modified as follows: when $\alpha \geqslant 1\cdot0$,

$$t = \sqrt{\left(\frac{4Tb}{p\sigma_y}\right)} \tag{5.29}$$

when $\alpha \leqslant 0\cdot0$,

$$t = \sqrt{\left(\frac{8Tb}{p\sigma_y}\right)} \tag{5.30}$$

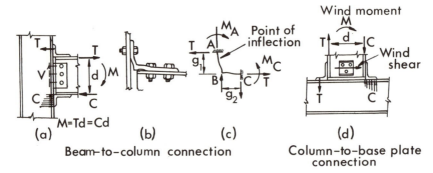

(a)   M=Td=Cd   (b)   (c)   (d)
    Beam-to-column connection   Column-to-base plate
                                            connection

Fig. 5.14. Flexible wind connection.

Flexible wind connections can be either beam-to-column or column-to-base plate connections (Fig. 5.14(a) and (d)). The shear is carried by the web framing angles in the usual manner (see Section 5.2). The wind moment is resisted by the tensile and compressive forces in the flanges of the member being supported (beam in Fig. 5.14(a); column in Fig. 5.14(d)). The tensile force is transferred to the angle by flange bolts with the angle assumed to deform as shown in Fig. 5.14(b). A point of contraflexure is assumed between the bolt gauge line and the top (outer) face of the angle; the thickness of the angle is then determined in a manner identical to that in hanger type connections.

5.8. SOLVED EXAMPLES

Example 5.1 (Web Framing Angles—Double-Angle Connections)
Determine the size of web framing angles for a double angle beam-to-column connection, Fig. 5.15, given the following data: beam reaction, $P = 2 \cdot 0$ MN; beam web thickness, $t_w = 24 \cdot 0$ mm; 22 mm diameter bolts; bolt hole diameter $= 23 \cdot 5$ mm; bolt spacing, $s = 75$ mm; number of bolts in one vertical row, $n = 10$; end distance, $L_v = 40$ mm; length of connection angles $= 40 + 9 \times 75 + 40 = 755$ mm; yield stress of connection angles, $\sigma_y = 250$ MPa; ultimate tensile strength of connection angles, $\sigma_u = 400$ MPa.

Solution

$$\text{Load per bolt, } P_b = \frac{(2 \cdot 0)(10^6)}{20} = 100\ 000 \text{ N}$$

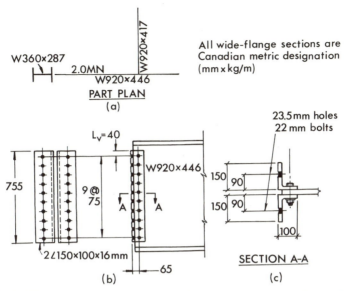

Fig. 5.15. Web framing angles in a double-angle connection in Example 5.1.

't' required from eqn (5.1), with $\sigma_u = 400$ MPa, $d = 22$ mm, and $P_b = 100\,000$ N:

$$t = 7 \cdot 6 \text{ mm} \tag{a}$$

't' required from eqn (5.2), with $s = 75$ mm, $d = 22$ mm, $\sigma_u = 400$ MPa and $P_b = 100\,000$ N:

$$t = 7 \cdot 8 \text{ mm} \tag{b}$$

't' required from eqn (5.3), with $L_v = 40$ mm, $\sigma_u = 400$ MPa and $P_b = 100\,000$ N:

$$t = 12 \cdot 5 \text{ mm} \tag{c}$$

't' required from eqn (5.4), with $P = (2.0)(10^6)$ N, $L = 755$ mm, $\sigma_y = 250$ MPa:

$$t = 13.2 \text{ mm} \tag{d}$$

't' required from eqn (5.6), with $P_n = P/2 = (1 \cdot 0)(10^6)$ N, $\sigma_u = 400$ MPa, $L = 755$ mm, $n = 10$, $d' = 23 \cdot 5$ mm:

$$t = 16 \cdot 0 \text{ mm} \tag{e}$$

Use the largest of the above five values, i.e. 16 mm thick angle. Use 150 × 100 × 16 mm angles 755 mm long. The leg size is based on the clearances required for tightening 22 mm diameter bolts in the field (American Institute of Steel Construction, 1980, Part 4, Table of Assembling Clearances). The double-angle connection is detailed as shown in Fig. 5.15(c).

Example 5.2 (Web Framing Angles—Single-Angle Connections)
Investigate whether the thickness of connection angle shown in Fig. 5.16 is adequate or not, given the following: beam reaction = 70 kN; connection angle: size 90 × 90 × 10 mm; length, $L = 210$ mm; diameter of bolts, $d = 20$ mm; centre-to-centre of bolts, $s = 75$ mm; diameter of holes, $d' = 21·5$ mm; yield stress of material of angle, $\sigma_y = 250$ MPa; permissible bending stress, $0·6\sigma_y = 150$ MPa; ultimate tensile strength of angle material, $\sigma_u = 400$ MPa; gauge distance = 60 mm; end distance, $L_v = 30$ mm; connection angle is shop-bolted to W530 × 92 (mm × kg/m, Canadian metric designation); filler beams, W310 × 39 (mm × kg/m, Canadian metric designation) are plain punched beams; thickness of web = 5·8 mm.

Solution

$$\text{Load per bolt, } P_b = \frac{70\,000}{3} = 23\,333 \text{ N}$$

't' required from eqn (5.1), with $\sigma_u = 400$ MPa, $d = 20$ mm, and $P_b = 23\,333$ N:

$$t = 1·9 \text{ mm} \tag{a}$$

't' required from eqn (5.2), with $s = 75$ mm, $d = 20$ mm, $\sigma_u = 400$ MPa,

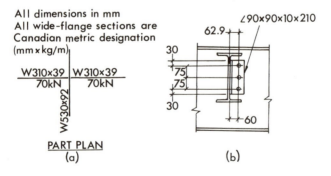

All dimensions in mm
All wide-flange sections are
Canadian metric designation
(mm × kg/m)

W310×39 W310×39
70kN   70kN

W530×92

PART PLAN
(a)

∠90×90×10×210
62.9
30
75
75
30
60

(b)

Fig. 5.16. Web framing angles in a single-angle connection in Example 5.2.

and $P_b = 23\,333$ N:

$$t = 1\cdot8 \text{ mm} \tag{b}$$

't' required from eqn (5.3), with $L_v = 30$ mm, $\sigma_u = 400$ MPa and $P_b = 23\,333$ N:

$$t = 3\cdot9 \text{ mm} \tag{c}$$

't' required from eqn (5.4), with $P = (2)(70\,000)$ N (the formula is applicable for double-angle connection; since the load on one angle is 70 000 N, multiply the load by 2, before substituting in eqn (5.4)), $L = 210$ mm, $\sigma_y = 250$ MPa:

$$t = 3\cdot3 \text{ mm} \tag{d}$$

't' required from eqn (5.6), with $P_n = 70\,000$ N, $\sigma_u = 400$ MPa, $L = 210$ mm, $n = 3$, $d' = 21\cdot5$ mm:

$$t = 4\cdot0 \text{ mm} \tag{e}$$

$$\text{Moment, } M = P \cdot e = (70\,000)\left(60 + \frac{5\cdot8}{2}\right) = (4\cdot403)(10^6) \text{ N.mm}$$

From eqn (5.9), with $M = (4\cdot403)(10^6)$ N.mm, $\sigma_y = 250$ MPa, $L = 210$ mm, $n = 3$, $d' = 21\cdot5$ mm:

$$\text{'}t\text{' required} = 8\cdot3 \text{ mm} \tag{f}$$

The thickness required is the maximum of the 't' required values (a) to (f) above.

Therefore thickness required $= 8\cdot3$ mm < 10 mm provided. The thickness of connection angle is adequate.

Example 5.3 (Unstiffened Seat Angle Connection)
Determine whether a 20 mm thick seat angle is satisfactory or not for the connection shown in Fig. 5.17, given the following: beam reaction, $P = 170$ kN; beam size: W460 × 113 (mm × kg/m, Canadian metric designation); $t_w = 10\cdot8$ mm, $k = 34$ mm, $\sigma_y = 250$ MPa, $\sigma_u = 400$ MPa, flange width $= 280$ mm; the beam is connected to the flange of W310 × 107 column; nominal set back, $a = 10$ mm; design value of $a = 20$ mm, to allow for fabrication and erection length tolerances; yield stress for angle, $\sigma_{ya} = 250$ MPa; yield stress for beam, $\sigma_{yb} = 250$ MPa; permissible bending stress in seat angle $= 0\cdot75\sigma_{ya} = 187\cdot5$ MPa; allowable compressive bearing stress at the web toe of fillet $= 0\cdot75\sigma_{yb} = 187\cdot5$ MPa. Assume the critical section for bending in the horizontal leg of the seat angle is at 10 mm from the face of the angle ($c = 10$ mm).

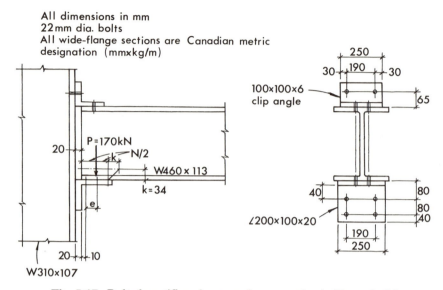

All dimensions in mm
22mm dia. bolts
All wide-flange sections are Canadian metric
designation (mmxkg/m)

Fig. 5.17. Bolted unstiffened seat angle connection in Example 5.3.

Solution

1. Required bearing length, N, from eqn (5.10) with $P = 170\,000$ N, $\sigma_{yb} = 250$ MPa, $t_w = 10\cdot8$ mm, $k = 34$ mm is: $N = 50\cdot0$ mm.

2. Moment arm, e, from eqn (5.11) with $a = 20$ mm, $N = 50\cdot0$ mm, and $c = 10$ mm, is: $e = (35 - t)$ mm.

3. Bending moment at critical section, from eqn (5.12) with $P = 170\,000$ N and $e = (35 - t)$ mm is: $M = (170\,000)(35 - t)$ N.mm.

4. Section modulus of horizontal leg of seat angle, S, from eqn (5.13) with $L = 250$ mm is: $S = 41\cdot67t^2$ mm^3.

5. Bending stress, σ_b, at critical section, from eqn (5.14) is

$$\sigma_b = \frac{(170\,000)(35 - t)}{41\cdot67t^2}\ \text{MPa}$$

6. From eqn (5.15),

$$(0\cdot75)(250) = \frac{(170\,000)(35 - t)}{41\cdot67t^2}$$

giving $t = 18\cdot8$ mm.

20 mm thick seat angle shown in Fig. 5.17 is therefore satisfactory.

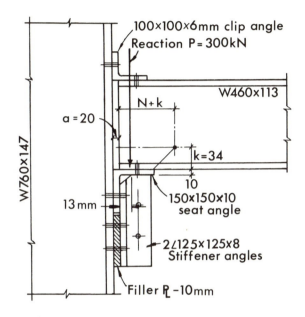

20 mm dia. bolts
All dimensions in mm
All wide-flange sections are Canadian
metric designation (mm×kg/m)

Fig. 5.18. Bolted stiffened seat angle connection in Example 5.4.

Example 5.4 (Stiffened Seat Angle Connection)
Investigate the adequacy of the seat angle and the stiffener angles for the bolted stiffened seat angle connection shown in Fig. 5.18. The properties of the beam are listed in Example 5.3. Assume the yield stress for all materials, σ_{ya}, σ_{yb}, σ_{ys} = 250 MPa.

Solution
Required length of bearing N, from eqn (5.10), with $P = 300\,000$ N, $\sigma_{yb} = 250$ MPa, $t_w = 10\cdot8$ mm, $k = 34$ mm,

$$N = 114\cdot1 \text{ mm}$$

From Fig. 5.18, minimum size of horizontal leg of seat angle = $a + N$ = $134\cdot1$ mm < 150 mm provided; therefore, acceptable. Required thickness of stiffener angle, t_s from eqn (5.21) with $P = 300\,000$ N, $\sigma_{ys} =$

250 MPa, $w = 125$ mm, $g = 13$ mm is

$t_s = 6 \cdot 0$ mm $< 8 \cdot 0$ mm provided; therefore, acceptable

Example 5.5 (Flexible Wind Connection)
Investigate the top flange angle of the flexible wind connection shown in Fig. 5.19. The beam is W410×54 (Canadian metric designation, mm × kg/m), $t_w = 7 \cdot 5$ mm, depth = 403 mm; the flange angles at top and bottom are 150×100×16 mm and 200 mm long; given 20 mm diameter bolts, 21·5 mm diameter holes, and $\sigma_y = 250$ MPa.

Solution
Referring to Fig. 5.14, the flange forces in tension and compression

$$= \frac{M}{\text{depth}} = \frac{(70)(10^6)(\text{wind reduction factor of } 0 \cdot 75)}{403} = 130\,273 \text{ N}$$

The top flange angle is checked for prying action and thickness. The tensile load is shared by the two bolts connecting the vertical leg of the top flange angle to the column flange. Tensile load per bolt,

$$T = 130\,273/2 = 65\,136 \text{ N}$$

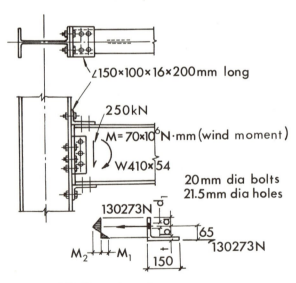

All dimensions in mm

Fig. 5.19. Flexible wind connection in Example 5.5.

Using the notation in section 5.7, $p = 200/2 = 100$ mm; $b = 65 - 16 = 49$ mm; $a = 100 - 65 = 35$ mm $< 1 \cdot 25b$; $b' = b - d/2 = 49 - 20/2 = 39$ mm; $a' = a + d/2 = 35 + 20/2 = 45$ mm; $a' + b' = 45 + 39 = 84$ mm; $d' = 21 \cdot 5$ mm. From eqn (5.22)

$$\delta = 1 - \frac{d'}{p} = 1 - \frac{21 \cdot 5}{100} = 0 \cdot 785$$

From eqn (5.23)

$$M = \frac{M_p}{2} = \frac{pt^2\sigma_y}{8} = \frac{(100)(16)^2(250)}{8} = 800\,000 \text{ N.mm}$$

From eqn (5.24)

$$\alpha = \frac{\left(\frac{Tb'}{M} - 1\right)}{\delta} = \left[\frac{\frac{(65\,136)(39)}{800\,000} - 1}{0 \cdot 785}\right] = 2 \cdot 77$$

When $\alpha > 1 \cdot 0$, use $\alpha = 1 \cdot 0$. From eqn (5.25), with $T = 65\,136$ N, $\delta = 0 \cdot 785$, $\alpha = 1 \cdot 0$, $b' = 39$ mm and $a' = 45$ mm,

$$B_c = 89\,962 \text{ N}$$

From eqn (5.26), with $B_c = 89\,962$ N, $a' = 45$ mm, $b' = 39$ mm, $p = 100$ mm, $\sigma_y = 250$ MPa, $\delta = 0 \cdot 785$, $\alpha = 1 \cdot 0$, the required thickness of angle, $t = 21 \cdot 3$ mm > 16 mm provided; therefore not acceptable. The thickness of the flange angles is not satisfactory. Because of the reversible nature of wind, both top and bottom angles have to be made identical.

The absolute minimum thickness of flange angle can be determined from eqn (5.29)

$$t = \sqrt{\frac{(4)(65\,136)(49)}{(100)(250)}} = 22 \cdot 6 \text{ mm}$$

This will result in maximum prying force on the bolts. The thickness of the flange angle required to make the prying force negligible can be computed from eqn (5.30)

$$t = \sqrt{\frac{(8)(65\,136)(49)}{(100)(250)}} = 32 \cdot 0 \text{ mm}$$

The tensile force in each bolt will remain at 65 136 N for such an arrangement.

Chapter 6

REVIEW OF EXPERIMENTAL AND
ANALYTICAL RESEARCH

6.1. INTRODUCTION

In this chapter, the available literature on the experimental and theoretical investigations on the behaviour of angles is reviewed. Both hot-rolled and cold-formed angles in steel and aluminium are included. Only those theoretical investigations which have not been mentioned in earlier chapters, and which are directly related to the behaviour of angle sections, are presented.

6.2. ANGLES IN TENSION

One of the earliest tests on angles in tension was carried out by Batho (1915). Experiments were carried out on two single-angle members and one double-angle member. In the experiments $3 \times 3 \times \frac{1}{4}$ in angles were used, riveted to end plates of the same width; it was found that the effect of end constraints was insignificant in the case of the single angle. The experiments were repeated with end plates resembling gusset plates used in practice. The effect of lock angles (lug angles) at the ends of the members was also studied. The investigation led to the following conclusions:

1. In single- and double-angle tension members connected at their ends by means of rivets to wide and rigidly held gusset plates, the stiffness of the gusset plate in its own plane has a considerable effect on the distribution of stress in the member, there being in every case a particular stiffness which will give the least maximum stress in the member for a given load. 2. In such members lock angles are of little value, if any, in providing a more equable distribution of stress in the member, or in increasing the effective length of end connections. 3. A

slight change in the line of application of the load to the gusset plates does not materially affect the distribution of stress in the member, except possibly close to the end connections.

However, Young (1935), after a study of previous work (McKibben, 1906, 1907), concluded that an angle connected with a lug angle can be taken as if the net area is fully effective. For single angles connected by one leg, Young suggested that the following factor '*e*' be applied to the net section area:

$$e = 1 \cdot 0 - 0 \cdot 18 \frac{u}{c} \qquad (6.1)$$

in which '*u*' and '*c*' are the lengths of the unconnected (outstanding) and connected legs, respectively.

The conventional practice of connecting angle members to gusset plates consists of distributing the welds along the heel and toe of the angle so that the working strengths of the welds are balanced about the projection of the centre of gravity of the angle on the connected leg. Such a balanced design requires approximately twice as much weld along the heel of the angle compared to that along the toe of the angle and it is often difficult or expensive to provide space for such connections. The primary purpose of the investigation undertaken by Gibson and Wake (1942) was to determine whether it is necessary to adhere to this theoretical balanced design or whether other arrangments of welds are equally effective. The investigation consisted of fifty-four ultimate strength tests of welded connections of angles to flat plates which were designed to fail in the welds. The fifteen different arrangements of welds which were investigated comprise most of the types of joints commonly used for angle connections. The following conclusions, among others, were drawn from the study:

1. The ultimate strengths of the common types of connections which have only one leg of the angle connected show little difference between the balanced and unbalanced connections. 2. The measurements made at working loads and the ultimate strengths of the specimens tested both show that the eccentricity normal to the plane of the welds of the common types of connection for angle tension members has a major effect on the strength. 3. The unbalanced arrangements of the welds are as capable of developing the working stress and ultimate strength of the angles as are balanced connections. 4. The conventional theory that the working strengths of the welds connecting an angle member must be balanced about the projection of the centre of gravity of the

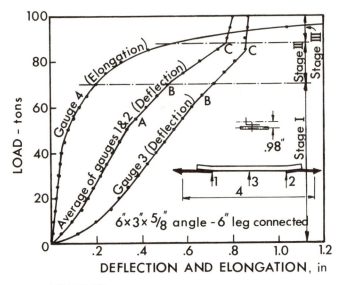

Fig. 6.1. Lateral deflections and elongation of an eccentrically loaded $6 \times 3 \times \frac{5}{8}$ in angle.

angle on the connected leg is therefore not essential to the design of adequate connections for angle tension members.

Nelson (1953) carried out tension tests on eighteen angles at the suggestion of the British Constructional Steelwork Association. All specimens had bolted connections. No significant effect of either the length of the specimen or of the end attachment was noted. The elongation was measured between the end attachments to the testing machine, i.e., it included the connection and the effects of any slip in the bolts. The lateral deflections perpendicular to the plane of the gusset plates were recorded at the centre of the specimens and just inside the connections at each end. Figure 6.1 shows typical results obtained from a $6 \times 3 \times \frac{5}{8}$ in $(152 \times 76 \times 16 \text{ mm})$ angle connected by the long leg. Strains, in the axial direction only, recorded at the critical section of the connected leg, i.e. through the innermost bolt holes,

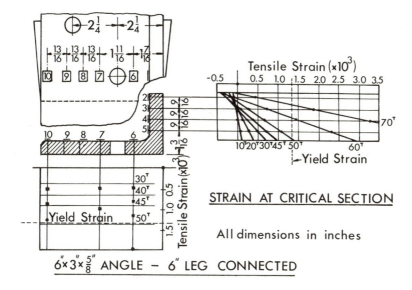

Fig. 6.2. Axial strain values at a critical section of an eccentrically loaded $6 \times 3 \times \frac{5}{8}$ in angle.

were greatly affected by the presence of the bolts and showed wide variations. The outstanding leg was undisturbed and gave a more useful indication of average conditions. Figure 6.2 shows the strain distribution at the critical section of a $6 \times 3 \times \frac{5}{8}$ in ($152 \times 76 \times 16$ mm) angle connected by the long leg.

All angles failed by necking down and tearing at the critical section through the innermost bolt. The permanent deformation of both angle and gusset plate was evident and in some cases the end nuts, which were firmly tightened before the test, were easily removed by hand. Damage to bolts was in general confined to the end bolts and hole elongation was serious only at the innermost hole, i.e. at the critical section. This latter did not imply that the inside bolt was the most heavily loaded but merely that the strain of the specimen was concentrated at the critical section and hence the hole became elongated.

All specimens were single angles so that the load was eccentric in a horizontal plane as well as in a vertical plane. This produced bending in the plane of the gusset as well as the major deflections already mentioned. This secondary deflection of the same $6 \times 3 \times \frac{5}{8}$ in ($152 \times 76 \times 16$ mm) angle mentioned above, is shown in Fig. 6.3 to a

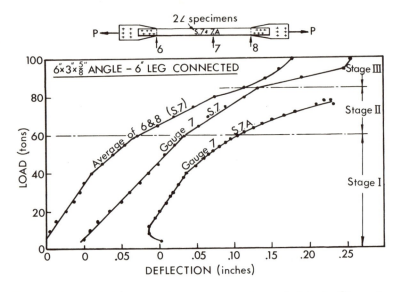

Fig. 6.3. Lateral deflections of two eccentrically loaded $6 \times 3 \times \frac{5}{8}$ in angles.

larger scale than that of Fig. 6.1. The same general characteristics are evident. As a result of this deflection in two perpendicular planes and the restraint offered by the gussets to bending in their own plane, the angle twisted. This was visible to the eye at high loads and is shown in Fig. 6.4 by the deflections measured at the toe and heel of the connected leg of a $6 \times 3 \times \frac{3}{8}$ in ($152 \times 76 \times 9 \cdot 5$ mm) angle.

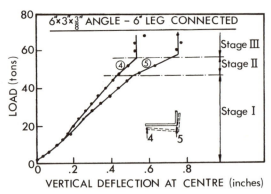

Fig. 6.4. Lateral deflections at centre of an eccentrically loaded $6 \times 3 \times \frac{3}{8}$ in angle.

Chesson and Munse, after an extensive study (Chesson and Munse, 1963, Munse and Chesson, 1963), concluded that angle members in tension connected with lug angles appear to be fully effective when the first stitch rivet is behind the first gusset rivet a distance no greater than one-half the pitch of the gusset rivets.

In 1969 Marsh developed a theoretical expression for the net effective area of an angle connected by one leg and subjected to a tensile force. Values obtained from the theory were compared with some of the available results of tensile tests on aluminium angles; good agreement was observed for angles connected by the longer leg, whereas the prediction was optimistic for the angles connected by the short leg. It was also concluded that lug angles have a negligible influence on the ultimate load.

A total of 721 single angle single-bolted connections were tested by Kennedy and Sinclair (1969) in tension to determine the relationship between end and edge distances, mode of failure and the ultimate load of the connection; the following conclusions were reached:

1. Failure through either the end or edge is a distinct function of end and edge distance and can be predicted. 2. For end type failures the ultimate load can be reasonably predicted by $P = 5t\sigma_y(2\cdot011x + 0\cdot279)/8$ in which $x =$ the end distance in inches and $t =$ the thickness of the angle in inches. 3. For edge type failures the ultimate load can be reasonably predicted by $P = 5t\sigma_y(4\cdot024y - 0\cdot901)/8$ in which $y =$ the edge distance in inches. 4. Failure in bearing occurs at a nominal bearing stress equal to approximately 4·5 times the yield stress. 5. Bearing stresses equal to 2·25 times the yield stress can produce insignificant hole elongation depending upon end and edge distances. However, such bearing stresses cannot be developed with an end distance less than one inch or edge distance less than $\frac{5}{8}$ in. 6. The development of local stresses in the immediate neighborhood of the hole, equal to or greater than the yield stress, is not a reliable indication of approaching failure of the connection.

6.3. ANGLES UNDER TRANSVERSE LOADING

Ashby (1953) carried out tests on a full scale section of corrugated asbestos roofing in order to obtain some information on the adequacy of the recommendations of British Standard 449:1948, para 55 regarding the design of angle purlins for roof slopes below 30°. The test section carried three rows of sheets on four purlins at 4 ft 6 in (1370 mm) centres which were in turn supported on four rakers. The spacing of the rakers was adjustable to 15 ft, 12 ft 6 in or 10 ft (4·57, 3·81 or 3·05 m) centres to suit $4 \times 3 \times \frac{5}{16}$ in, $3\frac{1}{2} \times 2\frac{1}{2} \times \frac{1}{4}$ in and $2\frac{1}{2} \times 2 \times \frac{1}{4}$ in ($102 \times 76 \times 8$ mm, $89 \times 64 \times 6$ mm, $64 \times 51 \times 6$ mm) size of angle purlins, respectively. It was concluded that the basis of design given by British Standard 449:1948 is more rational than the application of structural theory that ignores the stiffening effect of the sheeting.

Thomas, Leigh and Lay (Thomas and Leigh, 1970; Thomas *et al.*, 1973) performed a total of 15 tests on laterally unsupported angles with equal and unequal legs ($3 \times 3 \times \frac{3}{16}$ in, $3\frac{1}{2} \times 2\frac{1}{2} \times \frac{3}{16}$ in, $2\frac{1}{2} \times 2 \times \frac{1}{4}$ in) with L/t ratios ranging from 400 to 1600. The loading condition was a uniform moment over the entire laterally unsupported span, the loading being applied about an axis parallel to an angle leg. From the results of these tests the following conclusions were drawn:

1. The angle of twist (ϕ) causes a reduction in the maximum section stress produced. Therefore, the first order theory (i.e., assuming $\phi = 0$) gives a conservative estimate of this stress, and the expression

$$\sigma_{max} = 1·25 \sigma_a = 1·25 \frac{M_a}{S_a} \qquad (6.1a)$$

where M_a is the applied moment and S_a is the elastic section modulus about the axis of load application, gives conservative results at all stress levels. 2. The angle of twist (ϕ) has a significant influence on the maximum loading plane deflection beyond a deflection of $L/180$; and, second order theory (i.e. small deflection theory taking ϕ into account, but neglecting the product of small quantities) gives a conservative estimate of the deflection above this level. 3. Failure stresses will be unaffected by elastic buckling if the elastic buckling stress is at least three times the material yield stress. 4. Practical angle sections are seen to be governed by stress or deflection limitations rather than by buckling.

Warnick and Walston (1980) presented a linear analysis of lateral stability of beams with the aid of a coordinate system whose orientation remains fixed in space. In place of the moment vector projected on a rotated coordinate system, the beam flexural rigidity is expressed as a function of the angle of rotation of the beam cross-section. This formulation yielded a straightforward interpretation of lateral buckling of the not-so-narrow rectangular cross-section along with a unified approach to problems of transverse loading oblique to the principal axes. A limiting load depending upon the direction of the load was found for cantilevers of angle cross-section transversely loaded parallel to one leg.

6.4. ANGLES SUBJECTED TO AXIAL COMPRESSION

The earliest tests on plain and flanged angles, made of aluminium, were carried out by Wagner and Pretschner (1934) to confirm Wagner's theoretical results about the torsional buckling of open thin-walled sections. Tests on thin angle struts were made by Thomas (1941); and Kollbrunner (1935, 1946) tested more than 500 steel and aluminium equal-leg angles of various cross-sectional dimensions and lengths to check the theoretical results on torsional buckling. Mackey and Williamson (1951, 1953) conducted tests on two steel lattice girders consisting of double-angle chord members and single-angle web members; one of the aims of their investigation was to obtain information about the effect of adjacent members and joints on the actual end restraint of compression members in lattice girders. More recently, Marshall, Nelson and Smith (1963) carried out tests on aluminium alloy equal-leg, unequal-leg and bulb angles; they found that for slenderness ratios greater than 60, failure was primarily due to excessive deformation; angles with smaller slenderness ratios failed by either overstressing or local buckling. No significant difference was observed in the load-carrying capacities of multiple-bolted connections as compared to single-bolted connections; they concluded that unequal-leg angles connected by the short leg were stronger than the angles connected by the long leg. Wakabayashi and Nonaka (1965) studied experimentally the buckling strength of $90 \times 90 \times 7$ mm structural steel angles; various eccentricities and slenderness ratios were included in the test program; test results agreed with the theoretical predictions. Fifty-seven mild steel equal-leg angles of $90 \times 90 \times 7$ mm size were also tested by Yokoo, Wakabayashi and Nonaka (1968); concentric as well as eccentric loading tests (including eccentricity about the weak axis, eccentricity about the strong axis, and eccentricity about both axes) were conducted; both positive and negative eccentricities (Fig. 6.5) were included in the experimental program. Tests on concentrically loaded angles showed that more torsional deformation occurred at the middle region of the member than at the end regions, confirming that the buckling strength of equal-leg single angles is not

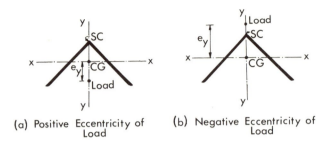

(a) Positive Eccentricity of   (b) Negative Eccentricity of
Load   Load

Fig. 6.5. Definition of positive and negative eccentricities of load.

significantly affected by the boundary conditions for twisting. For all slenderness ratios, angle specimens loaded eccentrically with respect to their weak axis showed predominantly flexural deformations with a considerable reduction in the load-carrying capacity as compared to concentrically loaded specimens. Angle specimens loaded eccentrically with respect to their strong axis showed considerable torsional deformation at early stages of loading; the decrease in the load-carrying capacity was not appreciable for slender angles which failed mainly by bending about the weak axis; on the other hand, the load-carrying capacity of angles with smaller slenderness ratios was considerably reduced (as compared to concentrically loaded angles), due to failure caused by local plate buckling.

Tests were conducted by Ishida (1968) on semi-killed high strength 'SHY' steel angles of size $75 \times 75 \times 6$ mm and $65 \times 65 \times 6$ mm. Both concentric and eccentric loading (eccentricity about the weak axis) tests were carried out. Because of higher residual stresses found in the test specimens, the behaviour of rolled high-strength steel angles was found to be different from that of rolled mild-steel angles; the load-carrying capacity of the former, when concentrically loaded, was generally less than that of mild-steel angles; however, for eccentric loads, the residual stresses did not have any significant effect on the load-carrying capacity.

Marsh (1969) conducted tests on $25 \times 25 \times 2 \cdot 5$ mm and $38 \times 38 \times 2 \cdot 5$ mm aluminium equal-leg single angles; for single-bolt connection, no difference was found between slack and tight bolts. The use of an effective length of $0 \cdot 8L$ for single-bolt connection and $0 \cdot 7L$ for double-bolt connection provided good agreement between the experimental results and the results obtained by the use of the following analytical expression:

$$\sigma_{cr} = 0{\cdot}9\,\pi^2\,\frac{E}{\lambda_e^2} \qquad (6.2)$$

in which

$$\lambda_e = \sqrt{\left(5\,\frac{b}{t}\right)^2 + (K\lambda_{max})^2} \qquad (6.3)$$

with b = leg width measured from the root fillet; t = thickness of leg; K = end-fixity factor, $0{\cdot}8$ for single-bolt connection and $0{\cdot}7$ for double-bolt connection; and, $\lambda_{max} = KL/r_{min}$. It was suggested that eqn (6.2) be used up to $\sigma_{cr} = 0{\cdot}5\sigma_y$ for angles with single-bolt end connections, and up to $\sigma_{cr} = 0{\cdot}67\sigma_y$ for angles with double-bolt end connections. In a report for the Canadian Steel Industries Construction Council, Marsh (1971) correlates simplifications of the classical theory with the results of compression and bending tests on $2\frac{1}{2} \times 2\frac{1}{2} \times \frac{1}{8}$, $2\frac{1}{2} \times 2\frac{1}{2} \times \frac{3}{16}$, $2\frac{1}{2} \times 2 \times \frac{3}{16}$, $2\frac{1}{2} \times 2 \times \frac{1}{4}$, and $2\frac{1}{2} \times 1\frac{1}{2} \times \frac{3}{16}$ in size single angles.

The earliest tests on angles in compression in North America were carried out by the United States Bureau of Standards (1924). After a gap of 24 years, Foehl (1948) reported tests on seven single-angle steel columns. One leg of the ends of these columns was welded to the stems of structural tee sections, thus simulating the arrangement in the web of a long span joist. The main objectives of these tests were to determine the effective slenderness ratios of these columns and to ascertain which leg of an unequal-leg angle should be placed perpendicular to the plane of the truss. It was concluded that the long leg should be placed in this position.

At Washington University theoretical and experimental investigations were carried out on single-angle columns under biaxially eccentric loading (Leigh and Galambos, 1972; Trahair *et al.*, 1969; Usami, 1970; Usami and Galambos, 1971); the test specimens were representative of the web members used in standard long span steel joists and with their ends welded to structural T-sections to simulate the chords of such joists. It was found that the method of loading the T-section end blocks had an effect on the load-carrying capacity of angles; an analytical investigation was carried out by assuming that the column is made of an elastic–perfectly plastic material, and representing the out-of-plane end restraint by an elastic–plastic rotational spring and the in-plane end restraint by an elastic rotational spring; good correlation between theory and experimental results was found. Usami and Fukumoto (1972) studied the behaviour of bracing members of steel bridges; it was found that the effect of residual stresses was not significant, a conclusion which agrees with the earlier finding of Ishida (1968). It was also revealed that the cross-sectional dimensions did not have any marked influence on the non-dimensional column curves, i.e. P_{cr}/P_{yield} versus $(L/r_x)\sqrt{\sigma_y/\pi^2 E}$, where r_x is the radius of gyration about the centroidal axis parallel to the gusset plate. It was recommended that the maximum load of an eccentrically loaded angle bracing member can be taken as 58 percent of the load of a corresponding concentrically loaded member.

Tests were carried out by Kennedy and Murty (1972) on 72 single- and double-angle struts with hinged and fixed end-conditions, under concentric axial loading. The results from the experimental investigation provided verification of the established theoretical solutions for inelastic flexural, torsional–flexural and plate buckling. Klöppel and Ramm (1972) conducted tests on lattice columns to find the effective lengths of leg members. The influence of end connections on the load-carrying capacity of web members was experimentally studied by Lorin and Cuille (1977). They found that increasing the yield strength of the gusset plate did not increase the load-carrying capacity of the web member; however, doubling the thickness of the gusset plate from 10 mm to 20 mm increased the buckling load by approximately 40 percent; the tests showed that if the crossing web members are continuous at their intersection (Fig. 6.6(a)), their capacity is 40 percent more than the capacity of crossing web members which are discontinuous at the intersection (Fig. 6.6(b)). The use of a double-angle compound section instead of a larger single angle, at approximately the same cost, increased the strength by 30 percent. The use of a thicker gusset plate with the compound section increased the load-carrying capacity by 70 percent. In addition, Lorin and Cuille (1977)

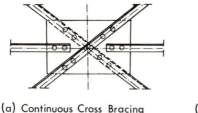

(a) Continuous Cross Bracing   (b) Discontinuous Cross Bracing

Fig. 6.6. Cross bracing in latticed towers.

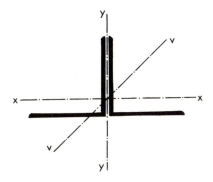

Fig. 6.7. Definition of $x-x$, $y-y$ and $v-v$ axes for a compound angle.

also derived empirical formulae for the strength of single-bolt and two-bolt connections.

Fourteen tests were carried out by Short (1977a) on compound angles to investigate their buckling about the $x-x$ axis (Fig. 6.7); while thirteen tests were performed to investigate buckling of compound angles about the symmetric $y-y$ axis. The effect of varying the gap between the angles was also studied by Short (1977b); it was found that for compound angles having two bolts at each end, the effect of end eccentricity must be considered for buckling about the $x-x$ axis. Slotting of end connection holes took place in a direction transverse to the axial load thus providing very little end-fixity in the plane of the connected legs; it was suggested that for buckling about the symmetric $y-y$ axis, the effect of spacing between the stitch bolts and the effect of gap between the angles should be considered by computing the effective slenderness ratio λ_{eff} as

$$\lambda_{\text{eff}}^2 = A^2 + 0 \cdot 5 B^2 \qquad (6.4)$$

in which A = geometric slenderness ratio based on a gap equal to $\frac{1}{5}$ of the true gap; and B = slenderness ratio of single angle between stitch bolts. Tests were also carried out by Short (1977c) on single angles to study their buckling about the $x-x$ axis (Fig. 6.8) as well as buckling about the weak axis. Results for the weak-axis buckling agreed well with curves recommended by the European Convention for Constructional Steelwork (1978). However, angles which are prevented from failing about their weak axis failed about the $x-x$ axis at considerably less load than the load obtained by using the recommended ECCS curves; this point should be kept in mind when designing transmission

212   *Single and Compound Angle Members*

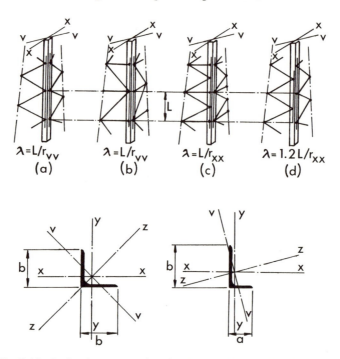

Fig. 6.8. Critical slenderness ratios for leg angles of latticed towers for different bracing arrangements.

towers using single-angle shapes (Short and Morse, 1979). Reasonably good agreement with the experimental results can be expected if the buckling load for buckling about the x–x axis is computed by considering the angle as a beam column with a bending stress equal to 70 percent of the axial stress.

Requirements regarding interconnection of starred angles (Fig. 6.9(a)) vary from code to code: CAN3-S16.1-M78 (Canadian Standards Association, 1978), clause 18.1.3(a); AISC Specification (American Institute of Steel Construction, 1978), clause 1.18.2.4; German Buckling Specifications DIN 4114 (Deutsches Institut für Normung e.V., 1952), clauses 8.22 and 8.36; and BS 449: Part 2: 1969 (British Standards Institution, 1969a), clauses 30, 36 and 37. To study the problem of interconnection, a series of tests were conducted by Temple and Schepers (1980) with the number of interconnectors varying from zero to five. From the study it was found that the interconnection requirements of North American codes are adequate if the buckling

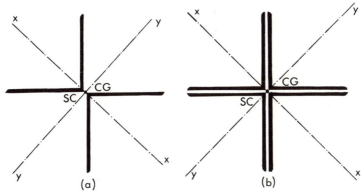

CG is centroid; SC is shear centre; Axes x-x and y-y axes of symmetry

Fig. 6.9. Computed angles—doubly symmetric.

load is calculated as twice the buckling load of one angle buckling about its weak axis, using an effective length factor of 0·6. To utilize the load tables for starred angles given in the *Limit States Design Steel Manual* (Canadian Institute of Steel Construction, 1977), two interconnectors, i.e. at third points, are required.

Some specifications deem that if the eccentricity of load is positive, Fig. 6.5(a), it is more unfavourable than the case of negative eccentricity, Fig. 6.5(b). However, based on analytical study, Chen (1980) concluded that the lateral–torsional buckling load of double-angle sections under load with positive eccentricity is larger than the failure load with a negative eccentricity; these theoretical results were confirmed by tests:

Angle specimens were tested under static and slow dynamic loading by Jain *et al.* (1980) to quantify residual elongation and reduction in maximum compressive strength with number of cycles. It was concluded that the effective slenderness ratio of a member is the most influential parameter on its hysteresis behaviour, and that the total energy dissipation through hysteretic cycles is independent of the direction of loading.

Astaneh-Asl and Goel (1984) investigated the behaviour of double-angle bracing members subjected to in-plane buckling due to severe cyclic load reversals. Eight full-size test specimens made of back-to-back double-angle sections, connected to the end gusset plates by fillet welds or high strength bolts, were tested under large amplitude cyclic loading. Some test specimens, designed by current code procedures, showed failures during early cycles of loading. Based on the observations and analysis of the behaviour of test specimens, new design procedures were proposed to improve the ductility and energy dissipation capacity of double-angle bracing members and their connections to withstand severe cyclic loadings.

El-Tayem and Goel (1984) tested five single-angle x-bracing specimens under quasi-static loading with a view to explore their response and to synthesize a composite hysteresis model. The sizes of the angles included in the investigation were $2\frac{1}{2} \times 2\frac{1}{2} \times \frac{1}{4}$ in, $2\frac{1}{2} \times 2\frac{1}{2} \times \frac{5}{16}$ in, $4 \times 4 \times \frac{1}{4}$ in and $4 \times 4 \times \frac{3}{8}$ in. The slenderness ratios varied from 87·6 to 142·6. The results showed that slenderness ratio, width–thickness ratio and displacement level were the main parameters which affected the overall size of the hysteresis loops. Members of small slenderness ratio dissipated more energy than members of larger slenderness ratio; furthermore, sections of small width–thickness ratio outperformed sections of larger width–thickness ratio.

Tests were also conducted by Wakabayashi *et al.* (1980) on the elastic–plastic behaviour of angle-braced frames under repeated horizontal loading. The test results showed that there is no significant difference between the behaviour of angle braces and those braces with an H-shaped cross-section, notwithstanding the local buckling and significant torsional deformation observed in angle braces. Experimental and analytical investigations were carried out by Massonnet and Plumier (1981) to ascertain the effectiveness of reinforcing the relatively thin leg angles of transmission towers.

A general finite element solution for the stability analysis of biaxially loaded thin-walled beam-columns was recently developed at Lehigh University (Hu *et al.*, 1982; and Lu *et al.*, 1983). It was applied to predict the response of some angle columns which have been tested in previous investigations. The required element stiffness matrix was developed by applying the Principle of Minimum Potential Energy. The total potential energy expression is believed to be the most general ever presented. It is valid for any type of loading and boundary conditions. The effects of initial crookedness, initial twist and residual stress were also included in the derivation. In the elastic range, direct solution of the governing equation was achieved with minimum computational effort. In the inelastic range, however, an iterative procedure based on the Newton-Raphson method was adopted. The solution provided good predictions of the load–deformation relationships and ultimate strength of biaxially loaded columns. From the investigation, it was concluded that the use of cubic functions to represent

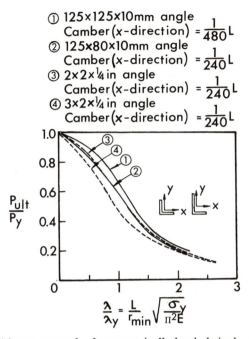

Fig. 6.10. Ultimate strength of concentrically loaded single-angle columns.

the displacements u, v and ϕ is quite satisfactory for both elastic and inelastic stability analyses.

Numerical calculations were carried out on four selected angle columns made with a material of 36 ksi yield stress. The four columns, $125 \times 125 \times 10$ mm, $125 \times 80 \times 10$ mm, $2 \times 2 \times \frac{1}{4}$ in and $3 \times 2 \times \frac{1}{4}$ in, were simply supported in both bending and torsion. Figure 6.10 shows the ultimate strength of the column as a function of the slenderness ratio KL/r_{min}. The camber (crookedness) is assumed to be in the negative direction of the x-axis; for unequal-leg angles this represents the most critical situation. The effect of residual stresses was taken into account in the calculations. The results show that the amount of camber has a significant influence on the strength of the angles when the non-dimensional slenderness ratio

$$\frac{\lambda}{\lambda_y} = \frac{\left(\dfrac{KL}{r_{min}}\right)}{\sqrt{\dfrac{\pi^2 E}{\sigma_y}}}$$

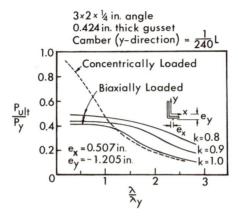

Fig. 6.11. Ultimate strength of single-angle columns loaded through gusset plates, long leg outstanding.

is less than about 1·5; also, the unequal-leg angles are weaker than the equal-leg angles with the same camber.

The strength of an eccentrically loaded angle column (loaded through gusset plates) was also investigated. The shape selected was $3 \times 2 \times \frac{1}{4}$ in with a gusset thickness of 0·424 in. The angle was oriented so that the x-axis was parallel to the gusset. The camber was assumed to be in the positive direction of the y-axis with a maximum value of $L/240$ at mid-height. Again, the direction of the camber was selected to correspond to the most critical situation. The angles were rotationally restrained at the ends in both the x and y directions. The results shown in Fig. 6.11 are for the case where the long leg is the outstanding leg, while those in Fig. 6.12 are for the case where the short leg is the outstanding leg. A comparison of the results shows that the 'long leg outstanding' arrangement is not always the more favourable arrangement. In fact, higher ultimate loads may be obtained with the 'short leg outstanding' arrangement for relatively short members (with $\lambda/\lambda_y < 1·2$ for $K = 0·8$). The results also indicate that end restraint can significantly increase the strength of an eccentrically loaded single-angle column.

A committee (Wood, 1975) undertook a series of tests to establish the performance of crossed diagonals in lattice towers. A total of 153 tests were conducted on crossed diagonals attached with 1, 2 and 3 bolts. The arrangement of the test panel was selected to produce the

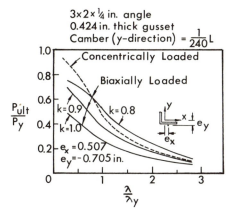

Fig. 6.12. Ultimate strength of single-angle columns loaded through gusset plates, short leg outstanding.

behaviour of the diagonals subjected to buckling loads similar to that which occurs in members of a transmission line tower. The following conclusions were drawn from the tests:

1. The critical buckling stress for slenderness ratios between 120 and 250 for crossed diagonals is higher than the critical load according to Euler theory. 2. The relation of the critical buckling stress to Euler buckling stress, called restraint coefficient, increases slowly with increasing slenderness ratio.

Torsional–flexural buckling of cold-formed thin-walled angles (plain and lipped) both in the elastic and inelastic range under concentric loading was investigated by Chajes, Fang and Winter (Chajes *et al.*, 1966; Chajes and Winter, 1965; Fang, 1966); a simple method of calculating the torsional–flexural buckling load of singly-symmetric sections was presented. Since the buckling load of singly-symmetric sections can occur either in flexural or torsional–flexural mode, curves for determining the critical modes were presented; for single equal-leg angles, it was shown that torsional–flexural buckling occurs when [thickness × effective length/(width of leg)²] < 1·1. Tests on cold-formed angles, as well as other shapes, were carried out to check the accuracy of the analytical procedures developed. The behaviour of singly-symmetric thin-walled open sections under eccentric axial load acting in the plane of symmetry was investigated by Peköz and Celebi (1969). Interaction-type equations were suggested for eccentrically loaded sections, for both positive and negative eccentricities (Fig. 6.5(a) and 6.5(b)). In order to check the behaviour of cold-formed equal-leg angles when used as diagonal members in transmission towers, a series of buckling tests were carried out by Carpena *et al.* (1976). For comparison, tests on hot-rolled sections were also made using the same test setup; the results showed that cold-formed angles had an average buckling strength greater than that of hot-rolled angles. The specifications for the design of cold-formed steel structural members published by the American Iron and Steel Institute (1980) are based mostly on the work mentioned above of Professor Winter and his associates at Cornell University; section 3.7.4 of the specifications states that the strength of singly-symmetric shapes subjected to both axial compression and bending applied out of plane of symmetry must be determined by tests. An exploratory study was conducted recently by Haaijer *et al.* (1981) to investigate the feasibility of using a finite element analysis in lieu of a physical test; only the elastic behaviour was considered so that the results are applicable to relatively slender members.

An experimental investigation was carried out recently at the Technical University of Milan (Wilhoite *et al.*, 1984) in order to study the behaviour and strength of different cold-formed angle sections ($50 \times 50 \times 4$ mm, $80 \times 80 \times 3$ mm plain and $80 \times 80 \times 3$ mm lipped angles). Specimens were loaded either concentrically or eccentrically. Hot-rolled angles ($50 \times 50 \times 4 \cdot 3$ mm) were also tested to make possible a direct comparison. Slenderness ratios varied from 60 to 120. A total of 110 tests under concentric and eccentric load were performed and it was found that the performance and strength of cold-formed angles is comparable to hot-rolled angles.

Tests were performed by Bez and Hirt (1982) on built-up sections consisting of two $150 \times 100 \times 10$ mm angles, 380 mm apart, with the long legs vertical and toes of horizontal legs facing each other as shown in Fig. 6.13. The specimens were subjected to axial compression and transverse bending by the application of axial and transverse forces. A total of seven tests were carried out with axial force varying from 0 to 60% of squash load; two different types of steel (with ultimate tensile strengths 360 MPa and 510 MPa) were used in the investigation. It was observed that:

1. The local buckling failure of the beam is reached before total plastification of the section; however, in the absence of normal load the plastic limit state was reached first. 2. The elastic limit state was

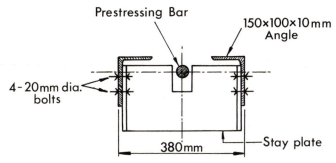

Fig. 6.13. Arrangement of a built-up section under test.

exceeded in all the tests. 3. Steel type did not play an important role. 4. With respect to plastic design, the following reductions in failure loads were observed: 0% for zero axial force; 25% for axial force equal to 20% of squash load; and, 40% for both axial forces equal to 40% and 60% of squash load. 5. Webs of the angles failed by local buckling in those tests for which axial force was present.

Recently Mueller and Erzurumlu (1983) ran a series of tests on $3 \times 3 \times \frac{1}{4}$ in single angle (with L/r ratios ranging from 60 to 200) and $5 \times 3 \times \frac{1}{4}$ in single angle (with L/r ratio of 200) to investigate the overall member performance and to determine if the results were sensitive to any particular parameters. Some preliminary tests were also performed on a full scale indeterminate truss; the purpose of the tests was to observe the load transfer which occurred after a compression member failed. A feasibility study of how an existing linear analysis model could be modified to perform a limit state analysis was also carried out. The test program revealed the following specific observations about the performance of single angles loaded in compression:

1. A brittle failure will occur if the member is short and concentrically loaded in compression. 2. The higher the steel yield stress, the more ductile the failure mode. 3. Short members with an eccentric load, causing buckling about the weak axis, perform as if they were concentrically loaded with a larger L/r ratio. 4. Member performance does not seem to be sensitive to load eccentricity about the strong axis. 5. The parametric study can be useful in determining the amount of unloading which will occur for increased axial deflection beyond the maximum load carrying capacity of the member.

Tests were carried out on eight $45 \times 45 \times 3$ mm and eight $65 \times 65 \times 4$ mm plain cold-formed angles under concentric axial loading

(Madugula *et al.*, 1983). The nominal slenderness ratios of the test specimens varied from 90 to 250. A finite element computer program, which takes into account the effect of the initial out-of-straightness, was developed to predict the failure loads of cold-formed angle sections. In addition to the above, tests were performed on fifteen $65 \times 50 \times 4$ mm (nine specimens with long leg connected and six with long leg outstanding) and nine $55 \times 55 \times 4$ mm eccentrically loaded cold-formed angles (Madugula and Ray, 1984a and 1984c). The test specimens were connected at the ends to the test frame by bolts on one leg and were subjected to eccentric thrust (eccentricity about both principal axes). Three different slenderness ratios (80, 120 and 170) and three different end connections (one-, two- and three-bolt end connections) were used in the test program. The effects of the location of the shear centre and magnitude of the warping constant on the ultimate strength were found to be insignificant.

A short series of tests on hot-rolled angles was carried out in 1979 at the Technical University of Milan (Zavelani, 1984); an extensive study is currently underway at that university (Wilhoite *et al.*, 1984) which includes the behaviour of hot-rolled and cold-formed angles subjected to concentric and eccentric loads. For all the tests, the lengths of the specimens have been chosen so as to obtain effective slenderness ratios of 60, 90 and 120.

An experimental investigation was conducted by Kitipornchai and Lee (1984) on the inelastic buckling of axially loaded, pinned end single- and double-angle struts. A total of 26 single equal- and unequal-leg angle struts and 16 double equal- and unequal-leg angle struts with modified slenderness ratios ranging from 0·57 to 1·07 were tested. Specially designed pinned end supports allowed the end cross-sections to rotate about the major and minor axes but restrained them against twisting about the longitudinal axis. All struts failed in the inelastic range by excessive bending and twisting. It was found that the design rules in the Standards Association of Australia Standard AS 1250 (1981) and American Institute of Steel Construction Specification (1978) are satisfactory. It was recommended that curve 2 of the multiple column curves of the Structural Stability Research Council (Johnston, 1976) be adopted for single- and double-angle struts.

Wagner *et al.* (1984) studied the effect of intermediate supports and end-fixity on the post-buckling performance of steel angles. The series of tests consisted of testing $3 \times 3 \times \frac{1}{4}$ in ($76 \times 76 \times 6\cdot4$ mm), $2 \times 2 \times \frac{1}{8}$ in ($51 \times 51 \times 3\cdot2$ mm), $1\frac{3}{4} \times 1\frac{3}{4} \times \frac{1}{8}$ in ($45 \times 45 \times 3\cdot2$ mm) and $1\frac{1}{2} \times 1\frac{1}{2} \times \frac{1}{8}$ in

($38 \times 38 \times 3 \cdot 2$ mm) angles. Each angle was $210 \cdot 5$ in (5347 mm) long and was supported in the centre by a tension member of the same size. The force in the tension member was also varied. Results of this series of tests revealed that the performance of the compression member in a cross-brace configuration is unaffected by the magnitude of the force in the tension member.

The test series designed to study the effect of the rotational end restraint on the member performance consisted of testing the single angles of $105 \cdot 25$ in (2673 mm) length, of the four series listed earlier. One end was always supported by a ball joint, while the degree of rotational restraint at the other end was varied. It was concluded that the effective member length defines the pre-buckling as well as post-buckling performance of axially loaded angles.

Ojalvo *et al.* (1984) tested twenty-eight single-angle columns braced intermediately in a non-principal direction. Tests were conducted on specimens 50, 140, 150 and 166 in long, each braced at mid-length. Angles utilized in the tests consisted of $2 \times 2 \times \frac{3}{16}$, $3 \times 2 \times \frac{1}{4}$, $3 \times 3 \times \frac{1}{4}$, $4 \times 4 \times \frac{3}{8}$, $5 \times 5 \times \frac{3}{8}$, $6 \times 4 \times \frac{3}{8}$ and $6 \times 4 \times \frac{1}{2}$ in sections. Based on the results of the tests, an empirical method of predicting inelastic column strength was then proposed.

Among the early theoretical researchers, Bijlaard (1940–41, 1947) formulated a rational theory for the stability of angles beyond the elastic limit based upon modern failure theories. A mathematical model governing the inelastic deformational response of restrained beam-columns under biaxial bending and torsion was developed by Vinnakota and Äystö (1974). The effects of residual thermal strains and warping strains were included in the study. The equilibrium equations were formulated with respect to an arbitrary coordinate system of an arbitrary thin-walled open section with no reference made to the shear centre, centroid or principal axes. Such a formulation is very convenient because the shift in the shear centre and the shift and rotation of principal axes of partially plastified sections are taken care of automatically. Since the problem is not amenable to closed-form solution, a finite difference procedure was employed to obtain a numerical solution. The predicted ultimate loads and load–deformation responses show satisfactory agreement with the available test and analytical results. The proposed numerical method could be used as a means of estimating the accuracy of the various design procedures, or whenever a new type of situation not covered by the simplified methods is encountered.

Vinnakota (1984) carried out parametric studies to investigate the influence of asymmetry, residual stress distribution, member geometry, end eccentricity, end restraint, and initial crookedness on the inelastic strength of double-angle beam-columns (connected back to back).

Chuenmei (1984) studied the elastoplastic buckling of single-angle columns using a non-linear, large deformation, finite element analysis with a plate element. The computed results were found to be in agreement with the test results.

The theory of torsional buckling of cruciform sections consisting of four angles was presented by Loomis *et al.* (1980) as part of the study of the failure of Hartford Coliseum. Loomis *et al.* recommended that it would be best for the engineering profession to avoid the use of cruciform sections until there is more reliable information available in the codes for designing such sections.

Smith (1983) examined the elastic and inelastic buckling of cruciform section columns formed from four equal-leg angles, Fig. 6.9(b), and determined the elastic critical loads for flexural, torsional and plate buckling. Two extreme self-equilibrating residual stress distributions were used to determine the effective elastic section properties to evaluate the tangent and reduced modulus buckling loads. It was shown that the American Institute of Steel Construction (1978) equations are not conservative for small to medium slenderness ratios for four angle cruciforms.

Studnicka (1980) used the theory of folded plates to treat the problem of stability of a bar subjected to axial compression. In the parametric studies for cruciform and angle sections, the results for the exact solutions are compared with the solutions obtained for rigid cross-section and with values derived from the local buckling of the cross-section walls. From this study it was found that in the case of long bars, the deformation of the cross-section is negligible; whereas, for short bars, it is of considerable influence, particularly for cross-sections with very slender walls.

6.5. ANGLES IN CONNECTIONS

Tests were carried out by Lyse, Schreiner and Stewart (Lyse and Schreiner, 1935; Lyse and Stewart, 1935) on 29 welded unstiffened seat-angle connections and on three photoelastic models. The investigation was made in order to obtain experimental information from

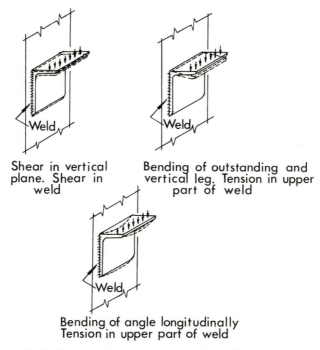

Shear in vertical
plane. Shear in
weld

Bending of outstanding and
vertical leg. Tension in upper
part of weld

Bending of angle longitudinally
Tension in upper part of weld

NOTE: Full lines indicate position of angle under no
load. Broken lines indicate position under load

Fig. 6.14. Behaviour of welded angle seats.

which a rational theory of design of welded seat angles could be
developed. On the basis of the results from this investigation a method
of design of seat angles was recommended. Lyse offered the comment
that 'in general, the failure of this type of connection was gradual and
would cause excessive deflection of the beam rather than a collapse of
the structure'. Lyse viewed the behaviour as occupying three phases
(see Fig. 6.14), viz.,

(i)   owing to the reaction of the load on the angle, a vertical shear
        acts on the weld causing a downward deflection;

(ii)   the outstanding leg bends downward and the vertical leg bends
        away from the column at the heel of the angle. This causes a
        corresponding compressive reaction toward the toe of the
        vertical leg thus inducing an upward frictional force which

offsets part of the vertical load. For a short distance from the ends of the angle, the weld restrains the vertical leg from bending outwards;

(iii)   the angle acts as a short stubby beam, elastically restrained at the ends by the weld. This action causes a greater deflection at the centre than at the ends.

Lyse also commented that

The beam flanges which are supported by the angle bend under the reaction and cause the reaction to be concentrated on an area under the web. The amount of this bending is determined by the relative stiffness of the flange and the outstanding leg. Since the flanges are also fastened to the outstanding leg, the two act more or less as a unit and the state of stress in the outstanding leg is thereby affected.

An experimental and analytical investigation was carried out at the University of British Columbia on web framing angles—single-angle connections, using $4 \times 3 \times \frac{3}{8}$ in angle (Lipson, 1968, 1977; Lipson and Antonio, 1980; Lipson and Haque, 1978). This resulted in a design table given in the CISC Handbook of Steel Construction (Canadian Institute of Steel Construction, 1980, page 3–63).

Finally, Redwood and Eyre (1984) studied the behaviour of a simple beam framing connection consisting of two clip angles $100 \times 100 \times 10$ mm ($4 \times 4 \times \frac{3}{8}$ in approximately). The angles were welded to the beam and bolted to the column and the connection was subjected to a constant shearing force and a reversed cyclic load applied along the axis of the beam. A total of 20 connections was included in the test program. It was found that the connections retained their ductility and exhibited considerable reserve of strength and ductility after 15 cycles of tension–compression loading at load amplitudes considerably in excess of normal factored design loads.

6.6. SCOPE FOR FURTHER RESEARCH

Review of the work done on the buckling of single and computed angle members reveals scope for further research. For example, while the design of angle members in transmission towers is based on empirical formulae derived from full-scale tower tests, analytical work is required to account for: the interaction between plate and torsional–

flexural buckling; interaction between the designed member and its adjoining members; effect of spatial deformation of the tower; and the restraint provided by the end connections. Because of the smaller torsional stiffness and greater yield stress in corners of cold-formed angles versus hot-rolled angles, separate design specifications should be established in North America for cold-formed construction used in transmission towers. The effects of the number of interconnectors in compound angles and gap width between angles connected back to back require further study; and the recent findings, contrary to some specifications, on the increased load-carrying capacity of double angle members with positive load eccentricity should be verified. For partial restraint of compound angle members in transmission towers, the ECCS Manual requires at least three bolts in line while North American practice requires only two bolts in line; this discrepancy in the two design practices should be examined. The buckling of leg members of latticed towers with staggered bracing needs further work since the ECCS Stability Manual gives the critical slenderness ratio as $(1 \cdot 2L/r_x)$ versus the value of (L/r_x) given in the ASCE Manual No. 52. Finally, for the design of an earthquake-resistant bracing system, the load-carrying and energy-absorption capacities of angle members under alternate repeated loading should be assessed. The distribution of residual stresses in hot-rolled and cold-formed angles requires some additional study. Furthermore, more research work is desirable on the behaviour of angles as beams to supplement the limited work which has been carried out in Australia.

Chapter 7

DESIGN PRACTICES

7.1. INTRODUCTION

In this chapter, attention will be focussed on the specifications, design recommendations and design practices prevailing in North America, Europe and Japan. Only those specifications that deal specifically with the analysis/design of angles and which were not discussed in earlier chapters are included here. Specifications relating to hot-rolled steel angles, cold-formed steel angles, as well as aluminium angles, are discussed. Because of their place of origin some specifications are in Imperial units while others are in SI units; some deal with allowable stresses while others give ultimate strength. However, no effort is made herein to change the nomenclature, since it is felt that it would be best to include the specifications with minimal changes.

7.2. NORTH AMERICAN PRACTICE

7.2.1. Hot-Rolled Angles

7.2.1.1. ASCE Manual No. 52 (American Society of Civil Engineers, 1971)

The American Society of Civil Engineers Manual No. 52, entitled *Guide for Design of Steel Transmission Towers* (1971) has been the basis for the design of axially loaded columns of angle shapes in transmission towers. The recommendations in the 'Guide' are not intended to be used when the width-to-thickness ratio, b/t, exceeds 20; the width 'b' is not the outside width of the leg but is the width measured from the root of the fillet. The pertinent requirements of the

226

'Guide' will now be discussed:

(i) The L/r ratio of leg members cannot exceed 150; that of other load-carrying members cannot exceed 200; and that of non-load-carrying bracing members cannot exceed 250. It is to be noted that these slenderness ratios are calculated on the basis of length between panel points without any regard to end-fixity.

(ii) The limiting b/t ratio, $(b/t)_{\text{limit}} = 2500/\sqrt{(\sigma_y)}$, where σ_y is the yield stress of the material in psi. If the b/t ratio does not exceed this value, the member is sufficiently compact to develop its material yield stress at small values of L/r without local buckling. If the b/t ratio exceeds the above limit, values of $\sigma_{y_{\text{eff}}}$, given by eqns (7.1) and (7.2), should be substituted for σ_y in eqns (7.3) and (7.5). Thus, if $(b/t)_{\text{limit}} \leqslant b/t \leqslant 3750/\sqrt{(\sigma_y)}$,

$$\sigma_{y_{\text{eff}}} = \left[1\cdot8 - \frac{0\cdot8b/t}{(b/t)_{\text{limit}}}\right]\sigma_y \tag{7.1}$$

For $b/t > 3750/\sqrt{(\sigma_y)}$

$$\sigma_{y_{\text{eff}}} = \frac{8\,400\,000}{(b/t)^2} \tag{7.2}$$

(iii) For $KL/r \leqslant C_c$, the ultimate maximum stress, σ_{cr} is obtained from

$$\sigma_{cr} = \left[1 - \frac{(KL/r)^2}{2C_c^2}\right]\sigma_y \tag{7.3}$$

When $KL/r > C_c$

$$\sigma_{cr} = \frac{286\,000\,000}{(KL/r)^2} \tag{7.4}$$

in which

$$C_c = \pi\sqrt{\frac{2E}{\sigma_y}} \tag{7.5}$$

The formulae for the ultimate maximum stress are based on the Column Research Council's Column Strength Curve (Johnston, 1976, p. 64) in the inelastic range and Euler's formula in the elastic range.

(iv) The effective length factor K is taken as $1\cdot0$ for leg sections or post members bolted at connections in both faces. For all other compression members, the following adjusted slenderness ratios, KL/r, shall be used:

For members with concentric loading at both ends, and $L/r \leqslant 120$

$$\frac{KL}{r} = \frac{L}{r} \qquad (7.6)$$

For members with concentric loading at one end and normal framing eccentricities at the other end, and $L/r \leqslant 120$

$$\frac{KL}{r} = 30 + 0 \cdot 75 \frac{L}{r} \qquad (7.7)$$

For members with normal framing eccentricities at both ends, and $L/r \leqslant 120$

$$\frac{KL}{r} = 60 + 0 \cdot 50 \frac{L}{r} \qquad (7.8)$$

For members unrestrained against rotation at both ends, and $120 < L/r \leqslant 200$

$$\frac{KL}{r} = \frac{L}{r} \qquad (7.9)$$

For members partially restrained against rotation at one end, and $120 < L/r \leqslant 225$,

$$\frac{KL}{r} = 28 \cdot 6 + \frac{0 \cdot 762L}{r} \qquad (7.10)$$

For members partially restrained against rotation at both ends, and $120 < L/r \leqslant 250$,

$$\frac{KL}{r} = 46 \cdot 2 + \frac{0 \cdot 615L}{r} \qquad (7.11)$$

Furthermore, a single-bolt connection shall not be considered as offering restraint against rotation, whereas a multiple-bolt connection properly detailed to minimize eccentricities shall be considered to offer partial restraint if the connection is made to a sufficiently strong member.

7.2.1.2. AISC-Proposed Load and Resistance Factor Design Specification for Structural Steel Buildings (*American Institute of Steel Construction, 1983*)

In 1978 the American Institute of Steel Construction published a revised allowable stress specification for the design, fabrication and erection of structural steel for buildings; and, in September 1983, they published for trial use a load and resistance factor design specification for buildings.

Angles are classified as non-compact sections if the nominal width-to-thickness ratio (b/t) of legs of single angle struts and legs of double angle struts with separators does not exceed $76/\sqrt{(\sigma_y)}$ where σ_y is the yield stress in ksi. (A non-compact section will permit attainment of yield moment only, but not the plastic moment capacity and with no redistribution of moment.) If the b/t ratio exceeds $76/\sqrt{(\sigma_y)}$ the following reduction factor Q_s shall be applied to the design strength of axially loaded single angles in compression:
when

$$\frac{76}{\sqrt{(\sigma_y)}} < \frac{b}{t} < \frac{155}{\sqrt{(\sigma_y)}}$$

$$Q_s = 1 \cdot 340 - 0 \cdot 00447 \left(\frac{b}{t}\right) \sqrt{(\sigma_y)} \tag{7.12}$$

when

$$\frac{b}{t} \geqslant \frac{155}{\sqrt{(\sigma_y)}}$$

$$Q_s = \frac{15\,500}{\sigma_y \left(\frac{b}{t}\right)^2} \tag{7.13}$$

Similar clauses exist in the allowable stress specification of the American Institute of Steel Construction (1978) as well.

The proposed load and resistance factor design specification has a special clause (clause F1.6) dealing with double-angle beams as follows:

The nominal strength of double-angle beams loaded in the plane of symmetry, and with flange and web slenderness less than $76/\sqrt{(\sigma_y)}$, is determined as follows

$$M_{cr} = \frac{C_b \pi \sqrt{EI_y GJ}}{L_b} [B + \sqrt{1 + B^2}] \leqslant M_y \tag{7.14}$$

where

$$B = \pm 2 \cdot 3 \frac{d}{L_b} \sqrt{\frac{I_y}{J}} \tag{7.15}$$

The plus sign in eqn (7.15) applies when the web is in tension while the minus sign applies when the web is in compression. In eqns (7.14) and

(7.15), M_{cr} = buckling moment (inch-kip); and an equivalent moment factor

$$C_b = 1 \cdot 75 + 1 \cdot 05 \left(\frac{M_1}{M_2}\right) + 0 \cdot 3 \left(\frac{M_1}{M_2}\right)^2 \leqslant 2 \cdot 3 \qquad (7.16)$$

where M_1 is the smaller and M_2 the larger end-moment in the unbraced segment of the beam; M_1/M_2 is positive when the moments cause reverse curvature; E = modulus of elasticity of steel, 29 000 ksi; I_y = moment of inertia about the y-axis; L_b = laterally unbraced length; J = torsion constant, in^4; d = overall depth of member; G = shear modulus, $G/E = 0 \cdot 385$; and M_y = yield moment = (elastic section modulus) × (yield stress).

7.2.1.3. *CSA-S37 Antenna Towers and Antenna Supporting Structures (Canadian Standards Association, 1981)*

This standard applies to both aluminium and steel lattice towers. The effective lengths of leg members of towers are discussed in clauses 6.2.3.1 and 6.2.3.2 as follows:

Where web members on adjacent tower faces connect to a leg member at the same elevation, the length of the leg member shall be the centre-to-centre distance between the web member connections (L_1 on Fig. 7.1). The least radius of gyration of the member shall be used, and K shall be taken as 1.0. Where web members on adjacent tower faces do not connect to a leg member at the same elevation, two conditions shall be considered:

(a) L = centre-to-centre distance of web member connections on a face (L_1 in Fig. 7.2)
r = radius of gyration about an axis parallel to plane of adjacent tower face
$K = 1 \cdot 0$

(b) L = centre-to-centre distance of web member connections on opposite tower faces (L_2 or L_3 in Fig. 7.2)
r = least radius of gyration
$K = 1 \cdot 0$

The leg members are designed as axially loaded compression members. On the other hand, web members are eccentrically loaded single or double angles. For such members, the eccentricity can be ignored, and the strength taken as 80% to 100% of the strength of an axially loaded

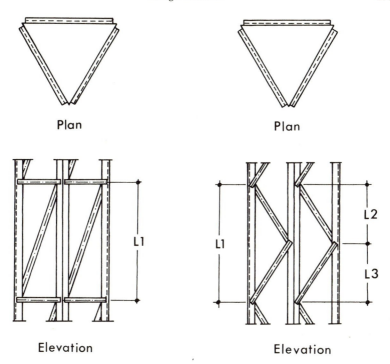

| Plan | Plan |

| Elevation | Elevation |

Fig. 7.1. Web members in a tower structure connected to a leg member at the same elevation.

Fig. 7.2. Web members in a tower structure not connected to a leg member at the same elevation.

member (depending on the slenderness ratio and the number of bolts) as shown in Table 7.1.

In a double web member system, where a compression member connects to a tension member, the length of the compression web member shall be the centre-to-centre distance from the intersection of the two members to the intersection of centroids of members at the end of the compression member (L_1 or L_2 in Fig. 7.3). K shall be 1·0.

7.2.2. Cold-formed Angles

7.2.2.1. American Iron and Steel Institute Specifications (1980)
The American Iron and Steel Institute Specifications for cold-formed members are applicable to cold-formed angles as well as hot-rolled

Table 7.1
Ultimate Strength of Web Members in Latticed Towers

Web members

Description of member	Description of connection	K	Ultimate strength as percentage of ultimate axial compression strength
Single angle	Two or more bolts, $KL/R \geqslant 120$	0·9	100%
Single angle	Two or more bolts, $KL/R < 120$	0·9	80% but in no case less than 100% for $KL/R = 120$
Single angle	Single bolt	1·0	80%
Double angle	Two or more bolts	0·9	100%
Double angle	Single bolt	1·0	100%
Double web member systems:			
Single angle	All connections	1·0	80%
Double angle	All connections	1·0	100%

angles which fail by torsional–flexural buckling. Clause 3.6.1.2 gives the elastic torsional–flexural buckling stress under concentric loading for singly-symmetric angle sections

$$\sigma_{tf} = \frac{1}{2\beta} \left[(\sigma_{ex} + \sigma_t) - \sqrt{(\sigma_{ex} + \sigma_t)^2 - 4\beta\sigma_{ex}\sigma_t} \right]$$

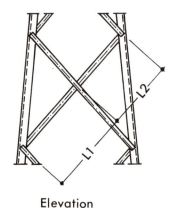

Elevation

Fig. 7.3. Double web member arrangement in a tower structure.

where

σ_{ex} = Euler buckling stress about the centroidal principal axis of symmetry $(x-x$ axis$) = \dfrac{\pi^2 E}{\left(\dfrac{KL}{r_x}\right)^2}$;

σ_t = torsional buckling stress = $\dfrac{1}{A r_{ps}^2} \left[GJ + \dfrac{\pi^2 E C_w}{(KL)^2} \right]$;

$\beta = 1 - \left(\dfrac{x_s}{r_{ps}}\right)^2$;

A = cross-sectional area;

$r_{ps} = \sqrt{r_x^2 + r_y^2 + x_s^2}$

= polar radius of gyration of cross-section about the shear centre;

r_x, r_y = radii of gyration of cross-section about centroidal principal axes;

and E, G, K, L, x_s, J have their usual meaning. We should remind the reader that the principal $x-x$ axis used in AISI specifications corresponds to the $u-u$ axis shown in Fig. 1.4. The values of r_x, r_y and x_s^2 are equal to $\sqrt{I_u/A}$, r_v and $(x_s^2 + y_s^2)$ respectively, obtained from Tables 1.1 to 1.3.

A computer program was developed by the authors to determine the safe loads of axially loaded angle members according to the AISI Specifications. Table 8.2 in Chapter 8 gives the safe loads of cold-formed angle members for slenderness ratios ranging from 20 to 240 and inludes all the angle sections listed in the Cold-formed Steel Design Manual of the American Iron and Steel Institute (1971, 1977).

7.2.2.2. American Design Recommendations for Cold-formed Angles (Wilhoite, 1984)

The recommendations outlined reflect the design and testing experience with angles shown in Fig. 7.4 and are applicable for a minimum thickness of members of $\frac{1}{8}$ in (3 mm) and minimum thickness of gusset plates of $\frac{3}{16}$ in (5 mm). These recommendations follow the ASCE Manual No. 52 (American Society of Civil Engineers, 1971) applicable to hot-rolled sections. The effective slenderness ratios (KL/r values) are calculated using exactly the same equations given in ASCE Manual

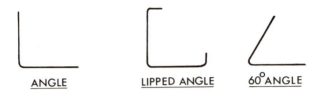

ANGLE   LIPPED ANGLE   60°ANGLE

Fig. 7.4. Some cold-formed sections.

No. 52. The determination of the flat width-to-thickness ratio, w/t, is shown in Fig. 7.5.

(i)   For $KL/r \leq C_c$, the ultimate maximum stress on the gross section of axially loaded compression members is

$$\sigma_a = \left[1 - \frac{1}{2}\left(\frac{KL/r}{C_c}\right)^2 \right]\sigma_y \qquad (7.17)$$

When $KL/r > C_c$,

$$\sigma_a\,(\text{ksi}) = \frac{291\,000}{(KL/r)^2} \qquad (7.18)$$

in which

$$C_c = \pi\sqrt{\frac{2E}{\sigma_y}} \qquad (7.19)$$

σ_y = minimum guaranteed yield stress (ksi); E = modulus of elasticity = 29 500 ksi; KL/r = largest effective slenderness ratio of any unbraced segment of the member, with axes designated as shown in Fig. 7.6.

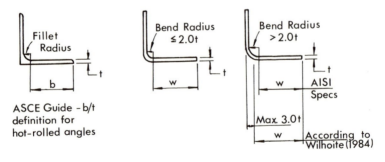

Fillet
Radius

b

ASCE Guide - b/t
definition for
hot-rolled angles

Bend Radius
≤ 2.0t

w

Bend Radius
> 2.0t

w   AISI
Specs

Max. 3.0t

w   According to
Wilhoite (1984)

Fig. 7.5. Determination of w/t ratios.

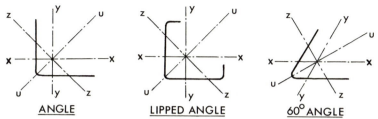

ANGLE   LIPPED ANGLE   60° ANGLE

NOTE: AISI Specs. uses x-x for u-u and y-y for z-z

Fig. 7.6. Designation of principal axes for different angle shapes.

(ii) For equal-leg angles, eqns (7.17), (7.18) and (7.19) apply only if the ratio w/t does not exceed the limiting value given by

$$\left(\frac{w}{t}\right)_{\text{lim}} = \frac{79}{\sqrt{(\sigma_y)}} \qquad (7.20)$$

If w/t exceeds $(w/t)_{\text{lim}}$, then eqns (7.17) and (7.19) must be modified by substituting for σ_y the value of $\sigma_{y_{\text{eff}}}$, given by

$$\sigma_{y_{\text{eff}}} = \left[1 \cdot 659 - \frac{0 \cdot 659 w/t}{(w/t)_{\text{lim}}}\right]\sigma_y \qquad (7.21)$$

for

$$\left(\frac{w}{t}\right)_{\text{lim}} \leqslant \frac{w}{t} \leqslant \frac{144}{\sqrt{(\sigma_y)}}$$

and

$$\sigma_{y_{\text{eff}}} = \frac{9500}{(w/t)^2} \qquad (7.22)$$

for

$$\frac{w}{t} \geqslant \frac{144}{\sqrt{(\sigma_y)}}$$

(iii) For lipped angles, eqns (7.17), (7.18) and (7.19) apply only if the ratio w/t of the leg does not exceed the limiting value given by

$$\left(\frac{w}{t}\right)_{\text{lim}} = \frac{221}{\sqrt{(\sigma_y)}} \qquad (7.23)$$

No provision is made for (w/t) ratios exceeding $221/\sqrt{(\sigma_y)}$.

The edge stiffener, which consists of a single lip bent at right angles to the stiffened element, should be determined as follows:

$$d_{min} = 2 \cdot 8t \sqrt[6]{\left(\frac{w}{t}\right)^2 - \frac{4000}{\sigma_y}} \geqslant 4 \cdot 8t \qquad (7.24)$$

where d_{min} = overall depth of lip; w = width of stiffened leg; and t = thickness of stiffened leg.

Lipped angles must be checked for flexural buckling and torsional–flexural buckling. Torsional–flexural buckling can be checked by using the equivalent radius of gyration r_{tf}, given by

$$\frac{2}{r_{tf}^2} = \frac{1}{r_t^2} + \frac{1}{r_u^2} + \sqrt{\left(\frac{1}{r_t^2} - \frac{1}{r_u^2}\right)^2 + \left(\frac{2u_s}{r_t r_u r_{ps}}\right)^2} \qquad (7.25)$$

in which r_t is the equivalent radius of gyration for torsional buckling, and given by

$$r_t = \sqrt{\frac{C_w + 0 \cdot 04J(KL)^2}{I_{ps}}} \qquad (7.26)$$

where C_w = warping constant; J = St. Venant torsion constant;

$$I_{ps} = \text{polar moment of inertia} = I_u + I_z + Au_s^2 \qquad (7.27)$$

where A = area of member; u_s = distance from centroid to shear centre;

$$r_{ps} = \sqrt{I_{ps}/A} \qquad (7.28)$$

and r_u = radius of gyration of the section referred to the u-axis.

If there are no intermediate supports, the allowable stress is given by eqns (7.17), (7.18) and (7.19), using for KL/r the larger of KL/r_z and KL/r_{tf}. KL/r_u does not apply because torsion and flexure about the u-axis are coupled in torsional–flexural buckling. If there is intermediate support, the lengths L used to determine these two slenderness ratios should be determined in accordance with the nature of the intermediate support, i.e. whether it restrains only flexural buckling, only torsional–flexural buckling, or both. It should be noted that the z–z axis referred to in this section corresponds to the v–v axis shown in Fig. 1.4.

7.2.2.3. CAN3-S136-M84 Cold-Formed Steel Structural Members (Canadian Standards Association, 1984)

The following are the specifications for angle members:

According to clause 6.3.3, the factored tensile resistance of single angles with unstiffened legs connected by fasteners in one leg shall be the lesser of

(a)
$$0{\cdot}75[A - (0{\cdot}7b + md')t]\sigma_u \qquad (7.29)$$

(b)
$$0{\cdot}90A\sigma_y \qquad (7.30)$$

where A = gross cross-sectional area; b = width of outstanding leg of angle; t = thickness; d' = diameter of fastener hole; m = number of holes across the connected leg; σ_u = tensile strength; and, σ_y = yield strength.

According to clause 6.6.3.1, for single or double plain and lipped angles, which may be subject to torsional–flexural buckling, the reduced critical elastic buckling stress σ_p is given by the lesser of the following:

$$\sigma_p = 0{\cdot}833\sigma_{tf} \qquad (7.31)$$

$$\sigma_p = 0{\cdot}833\sigma_e \qquad (7.32)$$

where σ_e = Euler elastic buckling stress

$$= \frac{\pi^2 E}{\left(\dfrac{KL}{r}\right)^2}$$

for buckling about the material axis; or

$$\sigma_e = \frac{\pi^2 E}{\left[\left(\dfrac{KL}{r}\right)^2 + \left(\dfrac{a}{r_1}\right)^2\right]}$$

for buckling of compound angles about the built-up member axis, in which KL/r = overall slenderness ratio of the complete section about the built-up member axis; a/r_1 = slenderness ratio of an individual section between points of connection about an axis parallel to the built-up member axis; a = fastener spacing; r_1 = radius of gyration of the gross cross-sectional area of an individual section in a built-up member; σ_{tf} = torsional–flexural elastic buckling stress =

$[1/(2\beta)]\{\sigma_e + \sigma_t - \sqrt{[(\sigma_e + \sigma_t)^2 - 4\beta\sigma_e\sigma_t]}\}$ in which

$$\sigma_e = \frac{\pi^2 E}{\left(\dfrac{KL}{r}\right)^2}; \qquad \sigma_t = \frac{1}{Ar_{ps}^2}\left[GJ + \frac{\pi^2 EC_w}{(K_t L_t)^2}\right]; \quad \text{and} \quad \beta = 1 - \left(\frac{x_s}{r_{ps}}\right)^2$$

where A = gross cross-sectional area of member; $r_{ps}^2 = r_x^2 + r_y^2 + x_s^2$; r_x, r_y = radii of gyration of gross cross-section about the centroidal principal axes; K_t = effective length factor for torsional buckling; L_t = length of member unsupported against twisting; x_s = distance from shear centre to centroid of section; and, KL/r = effective slenderness ratio associated with bending about the axis of symmetry of the gross cross-section. Here again, we should remind the reader that the principal $x-x$ and $y-y$ axes used in CAN3-S136-M84 specifications correspond to the $u-u$ and $v-v$ axes shown in Fig. 1.4. The values of r_x, r_y and x_s^2 are equal to $\sqrt{I_u/A}$, r_v and $(x_s^2 + y_s^2)$ respectively, obtained from Tables 1.1 to 1.3.

For single-angle sections with unstiffened flanges, the factored compression resistance, C_r, shall be further limited as follows (clause 6.6.3.2):

$$C_r = \frac{(0\cdot75)(0\cdot50)\pi^2 EA}{12(1 - \nu^2)W^2} \tag{7.33}$$

where W = width-to-thickness ratio of unstiffened flange element; and ν = Poisson's ratio.

For cruciform sections which may be subject to torsional buckling and which are not braced against twisting, the reduced critical elastic buckling stress σ_p is the lesser of $0\cdot833\sigma_e$ or $0\cdot833\sigma_t$ (clause 6.6.4).

For double-angle built-up compression members, the reduced initial elastic buckling stress σ_p for buckling about the built-up member axis is given by (clause 6.6.7.1):

$$\sigma_p = 0\cdot833\sigma_e \tag{7.34}$$

where

$$\sigma_e = \frac{\pi^2 E}{\left(\dfrac{KL}{r}\right)^2 + \left(\dfrac{a}{r_1}\right)^2}$$

For single angles loaded at each end through the same leg by bolts or welds, the reduced critical elastic buckling stress σ_p is, according to clause 6.7.4,

$$\sigma_p = 0\cdot833\sigma_e \tag{7.35}$$

where

$$\sigma_e = \frac{\pi^2 E}{\left[\left(\dfrac{KL}{r_v}\right)^2 + \left(\dfrac{5b}{t}\right)^2\right]}$$

in which L = unbraced length of member; r_v = least radius of gyration of the gross cross-sectional area; b = leg width; t = leg thickness; and $K = 0\cdot8$ for connections using a single bolt, $0\cdot7$ for connections using two or more bolts and welds.

The compression resistance (clause 6.6.1.2)

$$C_r = 0\cdot9 A_e \sigma_a \qquad (7.36)$$

where A_e = effective cross-sectional area; σ_a = compression limit stress. If $\sigma_p > \sigma_y/2$, then $\sigma_a = \sigma_y - \sigma_y^2/4\sigma_p$. If $\sigma_p < \sigma_y/2$, then $\sigma_a = \sigma_p$.

7.2.3. Aluminium Angles

The new edition of the Canadian Standard CAN3-S157-M83 entitled 'Strength Design in Aluminum' (Canadian Standards Association, 1983) uses limit states approach. The following are the clauses that deal specifically with single and double angles.

In order to avoid vibration due to wind forces, the width–thickness ratio (w/t) of double angles should be limited to the value given by (clause 1.5.2)

$$\frac{w}{t} < \frac{(1\cdot2)(10^{-5})E}{L\rho g} \approx \frac{30}{L} \qquad (7.37)$$

where t = thickness of the wider leg of the component angles; w = the breadth of the wider leg of the component angles; L = length (m); g = acceleration due to gravity (m/s^2); and ρ = density of aluminium, 2700 kg/m^3.

To avoid local or torsional buckling prior to member buckling in flexure, the following limits are placed (clause 1.5.3):

$$\frac{w}{t} \text{ ratio of single or double angles} < 0\cdot2\lambda \qquad (7.38)$$

$$\text{Spacing of fasteners in double-angle members, } \frac{s}{t} \text{ or } \frac{g}{t} < 0\cdot67\lambda \qquad (7.39)$$

where s, g = longitudinal and transverse spacing of fasteners, respectively; w = element width; t = thickness; and λ = slenderness ratio of the member.

For angles in tension connected by one leg, the effect of eccentricity is taken into account by reducing the effective area in tension as given below (clause 1.7.6):

(a) For single angles where the distance from the heel to the fastener $\leq w/2$,

$$A_e = A_n - \tfrac{2}{3}wt \qquad (7.40)$$

(b) For double angles fixed to one side of the gusset,

$$A_e = A_n - wt \qquad (7.41)$$

(c) For double angles fixed to each side of the gusset where the distance from the heel to the fastener $\leq w/2$,

$$A_e = A_n - \frac{wt}{2} \qquad (7.42)$$

where A_e = effective area; A_n = net area of member; w = width of outstanding leg; and t = thickness of outstanding leg.

Table 7.2
Effective Length Factors (K)

Member		K_x	K_y	K_z(Single angles) 1 bolt	2 bolts
	AB	1	k	$\frac{1+2k}{3}$	
	AB AC	1	1	0.8	0.7
	AB	0.5	0.5	0.45	0.4
	AB	0.5	1	0.5	0.45
	AB	0.5	1.0	0.5	0.45
	AB	0.45	0.5	0.4	0.35

For internal members Axis y-y is parallel to the plane of bracing

* C = compression, T = tension, T = C

The compressive resistance of single angles connected through one leg, not in a continuous chord, is computed using the following value for slenderness (clause 1.7.10):

$$\lambda = \sqrt{\lambda_f^2 + \lambda_t^2} \qquad (7.43)$$

where $\lambda_t = 5w/t$, and $\lambda_f = KL/r_v$; w = width of longer leg; t = thickness of longer leg; KL = effective length, as determined from Table 7.2; and r_v = minimum radius of gyration.

The compressive resistance of double angles buckling about the built-up axis is based on the following slenderness ratio (clause 1.7.11.3):

$$\lambda = \sqrt{(\lambda_{ft}^2 + \lambda_a^2)} \qquad (7.44)$$

where $\lambda_a = a/r$; a = distance between stitch bolts; r = radius of gyration of a single angle about the axis parallel to the built-up axis; $\lambda_{ft} = \sqrt{(\lambda_f^2 + 0 \cdot 7\lambda_t^2)}$; λ_f = overall slenderness KL/r'; KL = effective length; r' = radius of gyration of the complete section about the built-up axis; $\lambda_t = 5w/t$; w = width of longer leg; and t = thickness of longer leg.

If λ_t is greater than λ_f, then the values are interchanged in the expression for λ_{ft}.

7.3. EUROPEAN PRACTICE

7.3.1. Hot-Rolled Angles

7.3.1.1. ECCS Recommendations (*European Convention for Constructional Steelwork, 1978*)

For angles in tension, ECCS recommendations are similar to the specifications found in the SAA Steel Structures Code (Standards Association of Australia, 1981), British Standard BS 449: Part 2: 1969 (British Standards Institution, 1969a) and Indian Standard IS: 800-1984 (Indian Standards Institution, 1984) discussed in Chapter 2.

The ECCS recommendations for angles in compression are applicable for both equal and unequal leg angles with leg width ratio (ratio of width of larger leg to width of smaller leg) between 1 and 2. The maximum ratios of nominal width b to thickness t depend on the type of steel:

for steel Fe 510 (yield stress 355 MPa), maximum b/t ratio = 15;

for steel Fe 430 (yield stress 275 MPa), maximum b/t ratio = 17; and

for steel Fe 360 (yield stress 235 MPa), maximum b/t ratio = 18.

For axially loaded angle members in compression, the buckling stress is directly determined from Tables 7.3(a), (b) and (c) for thickness up to 20 mm and from Tables 7.4(a), (b) and (c) for thickness over 20 mm. For angles in compression loaded through one leg, the effect of eccentricity is taken into account by modifying the slenderness ratio as shown below (R4.1.5.3). For $\lambda/\lambda_y \le 1\cdot41$,

$$\left(\frac{\lambda}{\lambda_y}\right)_{\text{eff}} = 0\cdot60 + 0\cdot57\,\frac{\lambda}{\lambda_y} \qquad (7\cdot45)$$

For $\lambda/\lambda_y \ge 1\cdot41$,

$$\left(\frac{\lambda}{\lambda_y}\right)_{\text{eff}} = \left(\frac{\lambda}{\lambda_y}\right) \qquad (7\cdot46)$$

Table 7.3(a)
Dimensional Buckling Curve B3 for Steel Fe 360 ($t \le 20$ mm)

Limiting stress σ_{cr} MPa

λ	0	1	2	3	4	5	6	7	8	9	λ
0	225·0	225·0	225·0	225·0	225·0	225·0	225·0	225·0	225·0	225·0	0
10	225·0	225·0	225·0	225·0	225·0	225·0	225·0	225·0	225·0	225·0	10
20	224·4	223·6	222·8	222·0	221·2	220·3	219·5	218·7	217·8	216·9	20
30	216·0	215·1	214·2	213·2	212·3	211·3	210·4	209·5	208·5	207·6	30
40	206·6	205·7	204·6	203·9	203·0	202·0	201·1	200·1	199·1	198·1	40
50	197·0	196·0	194·9	193·8	192·7	191·6	190·4	189·2	188·1	186·9	50
60	185·7	184·4	183·2	182·0	180·7	179·4	178·2	176·9	175·6	174·2	60
70	172·9	171·6	170·2	168·9	167·5	166·1	164·7	163·3	161·8	160·4	70
80	159·0	157·5	156·0	154·5	152·9	151·4	149·8	148·3	146·7	145·2	80
90	143·6	142·1	140·6	139·1	137·7	136·2	134·7	133·2	131·7	130·3	90
100	128·8	127·4	126·0	124·5	123·2	121·8	120·4	119·0	117·7	116·3	100
110	115·0	113·6	112·3	111·0	109·7	108·4	107·1	105·9	104·6	103·4	110
120	102·1	100·9	99·7	98·5	97·4	96·2	95·1	94·0	92·9	91·6	120
130	90·7	89·7	88·6	87·6	86·6	85·6	84·6	83·6	82·6	81·7	130
140	80·7	79·8	78·9	77·9	77·1	76·2	75·3	74·5	73·7	72·8	140
150	72·7	71·3	70·5	69·7	68·9	68·2	67·4	66·7	65·9	65·2	150
160	64·5	63·8	63·1	62·3	61·7	61·0	60·3	59·7	58·9	58·5	160
170	57·9	57·3	56·7	56·2	55·6	55·1	54·5	54·0	53·4	52·9	170
180	52·4	51·8	51·3	50·8	50·3	49·8	49·3	48·8	48·4	47·9	180
190	47·4	47·0	46·6	46·1	45·7	45·3	44·9	44·5	44·1	43·7	190
200	43·3	42·9	42·5	42·1	41·7	41·4	41·0	40·7	40·4	40·0	200
210	39·7	39·3	39·0	38·6	38·3	38·0	37·7	37·4	37·0	36·7	210
220	36·4	36·1	35·8	35·4	35·2	34·9	34·6	34·3	34·0	33·7	220
230	33·5	33·2	32·9	32·7	32·4	32·1	31·9	31·7	31·4	31·2	230
240	31·0	30·7	30·5	30·2	30·0	29·8	29·6	29·4	29·2	29·0	240
250	28·8	—	—	—	—	—	—	—	—	—	250

Table 7.3(b)
Dimensional Buckling Curve B3 for Steel Fe 430 ($t \leqslant 20$ mm)

Limiting stress σ_{cr} MPa

λ	0	1	2	3	4	5	6	7	8	9	λ
0	250·0	250·0	250·0	250·0	250·0	250·0	250·0	250·0	250·0	250·0	0
10	250·0	250·0	250·0	250·0	250·0	250·0	250·0	250·0	250·0	249·3	10
20	248·4	247·4	246·5	245·5	244·6	243·6	242·6	241·6	240·5	239·5	20
30	238·4	237·3	236·2	235·1	234·0	232·8	231·7	230·6	229·5	228·5	30
40	227·4	226·3	225·2	224·1	223·0	221·9	220·7	219·5	218·2	217·0	40
50	215·7	214·4	213·1	211·7	210·4	209·0	207·6	206·2	204·7	203·3	50
60	201·5	200·4	198·9	197·4	195·8	194·3	192·8	191·2	189·6	188·0	60
70	186·4	184·8	183·1	181·5	179·8	178·1	176·4	174·7	173·0	171·2	70
80	169·4	167·6	165·7	163·9	162·1	160·3	158·5	156·7	155·0	153·2	80
90	151·5	149·8	148·0	146·3	144·6	142·9	141·2	139·6	137·9	136·3	90
100	134·7	133·1	131·5	129·9	128·3	126·7	125·2	123·7	122·1	120·6	100
110	119·1	117·6	116·2	114·7	113·3	111·8	110·4	109·1	107·7	106·4	110
120	105·0	103·8	102·5	101·2	100·0	98·7	97·5	96·3	95·2	94·0	120
130	92·8	91·7	90·6	89·5	88·4	87·3	86·3	85·2	84·2	83·2	130
140	82·2	81·3	80·3	79·4	78·5	77·6	76·7	75·8	74·9	74·0	140
150	73·2	72·3	71·5	70·6	69·8	69·0	68·2	67·4	66·7	65·8	150
160	65·1	64·5	63·8	63·1	62·5	61·8	61·2	60·5	59·9	59·3	160
170	58·7	58·0	57·4	56·8	56·2	55·6	55·1	54·5	53·9	53·4	170
180	52·8	52·3	51·8	51·3	50·8	50·3	49·9	49·4	48·9	48·5	180
190	48·0	47·5	47·1	46·6	46·2	45·8	45·4	45·0	44·6	44·2	190
200	43·8	43·3	42·9	42·5	42·2	41·8	41·5	41·1	40·7	40·3	200
210	40·0	39·6	39·2	38·9	38·5	38·2	37·9	37·6	37·2	36·9	210
220	36·6	36·3	36·0	35·7	35·4	35·1	34·9	34·6	34·3	34·0	220
230	33·7	33·5	33·2	33·0	32·8	32·6	32·3	32·0	31·7	31·5	230
240	31·2	31·0	30·8	30·6	30·4	30·1	29·9	29·7	29·5	29·3	240
250	29·0	—	—	—	—	—	—	—	—	—	250

Table 7.3(c)
Dimensional Buckling Curve B3 for Steel Fe 510 ($t \leqslant 20$ mm)

Limiting stress σ_{cr} MPa

λ	0	1	2	3	4	5	6	7	8	9	λ
0	340·0	340·0	340·0	340·0	340·0	340·0	340·0	340·0	340·0	340·0	0
10	340·0	340·0	340·0	340·0	340·0	340·0	339·4	338·0	336·5	335·0	10
20	333·5	332·0	330·4	328·8	327·1	325·5	323·7	322·0	320·2	318·4	20
30	316·7	314·9	313·2	311·5	309·8	308·1	306·3	304·6	302·8	301·0	30
40	299·1	297·1	295·1	293·1	291·0	288·9	286·8	284·5	282·4	280·1	40
50	277·8	275·6	273·2	270·9	268·5	266·1	263·6	261·1	258·7	256·1	50
60	253·6	251·0	248·4	245·8	243·1	240·0	237·7	234·9	232·1	229·2	60

Table 7.3(c)—*contd.*

Limiting stress σ_{cr} MPa

λ	0	1	2	3	4	5	6	7	8	9	λ
70	226·3	223·4	220·5	217·7	214·9	212·1	209·3	206·5	203·8	201·0	70
80	198·3	195·6	192·9	190·3	167·7	185·1	182·5	180·0	177·4	174·9	80
90	172·5	170·0	167·6	165·2	162·8	160·4	158·1	155·7	153·5	151·2	90
100	149·0	146·9	144·7	142·7	140·6	138·6	136·6	134·6	132·7	130·3	100
110	129·0	127·1	125·3	123·5	121·8	120·0	118·3	116·7	115·1	113·5	110
120	111·9	110·4	108·9	107·4	106·0	104·5	103·2	101·8	100·9	99·0	120
130	97·7	96·3	95·0	93·7	92·5	91·2	90·0	88·7	87·8	86·7	130
140	85·6	84·6	83·6	82·5	81·5	80·5	79·6	78·6	77·6	76·7	140
150	75·7	74·8	73·9	73·0	72·2	71·3	70·5	69·7	68·9	68·2	150
160	67·4	66·7	65·9	65·2	64·5	63·7	63·0	62·4	61·7	61·1	160
170	60·5	59·9	59·2	58·5	57·9	57·3	56·8	56·2	55·6	55·0	170
180	54·4	53·8	53·2	52·7	52·2	51·6	51·1	50·5	50·1	49·6	180
190	49·1	48·7	48·2	47·8	47·3	46·9	46·4	46·0	45·6	45·2	190
200	44·8	44·5	44·1	43·6	43·2	42·8	42·3	42·0	41·7	41·4	200
210	41·0	40·7	40·3	40·0	39·6	39·3	38·9	38·5	38·3	37·9	210
220	37·6	37·2	36·9	36·6	36·3	36·0	35·7	35·4	35·0	34·7	220
230	34·4	34·1	33·9	33·6	33·3	33·0	32·7	32·4	32·2	31·9	230
240	31·6	31·3	31·1	30·8	30·6	30·3	30·1	29·8	29·6	29·4	240
250	29·1	—	—	—	—	—	—	—	—	—	250

Table 7.4(a)

Dimension Buckling Curve B4 for Steel Fe 360 ($t > 20$ mm)

Limiting stress σ_{cr} MPa

λ	0	1	2	3	4	5	6	7	8	9	λ
0	210·0	210·0	210·0	210·0	210·0	210·0	210·0	210·0	210·0	210·0	0
10	210·0	210·0	210·0	210·0	210·0	210·0	210·0	210·0	210·0	210·0	10
20	209·9	209·2	208·5	207·8	207·0	206·3	205·6	204·8	204·1	203·3	20
30	202·5	201·7	200·9	200·0	199·2	198·3	197·5	196·6	195·7	194·9	30
40	194·0	193·2	192·4	191·5	190·7	189·9	189·0	188·2	187·3	186·4	40
50	185·6	184·6	183·7	182·7	181·7	180·7	179·7	178·7	177·7	176·6	50
60	175·6	174·5	173·4	172·3	171·2	170·1	168·9	167·8	166·6	165·5	60
70	164·3	163·1	161·9	160·7	159·5	158·3	157·0	155·8	154·5	153·3	70
80	152·0	150·7	149·4	148·1	146·8	145·4	144·1	142·7	141·3	139·9	80
90	138·5	137·1	135·7	134·3	132·9	131·6	130·2	128·9	127·5	126·2	90
100	124·9	123·5	122·2	120·9	119·6	118·3	117·0	115·8	114·5	113·2	100
110	112·0	110·8	109·6	108·4	107·1	105·9	104·8	103·6	102·4	101·2	110
120	100·1	98·9	97·8	96·7	95·6	94·5	93·4	92·3	91·2	90·2	120
130	89·2	88·2	87·2	86·2	85·2	84·3	83·3	82·4	81·4	80·5	130
140	79·6	78·7	77·8	77·0	76·1	75·3	74·4	73·6	72·8	72·0	140
150	71·2	70·4	69·7	68·9	68·2	67·4	66·7	66·0	65·3	64·6	150
160	63·9	63·3	62·6	61·9	61·2	60·5	59·9	59·3	58·6	58·0	160

Table 7.4(a)—*contd.*

Limiting stress σ_{cr} MPa

λ	0	1	2	3	4	5	6	7	8	9	λ
170	57·4	56·8	56·2	55·6	54·9	54·5	54·0	53·5	53·0	52·5	170
180	51·9	51·5	51·0	50·5	50·0	49·5	49·0	48·6	48·1	47·6	180
190	47·2	46·7	46·3	45·8	45·4	45·0	44·6	44·1	43·7	43·4	190
200	43·0	42·6	42·2	41·9	41·5	41·1	40·8	40·4	40·1	39·7	200
210	39·4	39·0	38·7	38·4	38·1	37·8	37·5	37·2	36·8	36·5	210
220	36·2	35·9	35·6	35·3	35·0	34·8	34·5	34·2	33·9	33·6	220
230	33·3	33·0	32·8	32·5	32·2	32·0	31·7	31·5	31·2	31·0	230
240	30·8	30·5	30·3	30·1	29·8	29·6	29·4	29·2	29·0	28·8	240
250	28·6	—	—	—	—	—	—	—	—	—	250

Table 7.4(b)
Dimensional Buckling Curve B4 for Steel Fe 430 ($t > 20$ mm)

Limiting stress σ_{cr} MPa

λ	0	1	2	3	4	5	6	7	8	9	λ
0	235·0	235·0	235·0	235·0	235·0	235·0	235·0	235·0	235·0	235·0	0
10	235·0	235·0	235·0	235·0	235·0	235·0	235·0	235·0	235·0	234·8	10
20	234·0	233·1	232·3	231·4	230·5	229·7	228·8	227·9	226·9	226·0	20
30	225·0	224·0	223·0	222·0	221·0	220·0	219·0	218·0	217·0	216·0	30
40	215·0	214·0	213·0	212·0	211·0	210·0	209·0	207·9	206·8	205·7	40
50	204·6	203·4	202·3	201·1	199·9	198·6	197·4	196·1	194·8	193·5	50
60	192·2	190·9	189·6	188·2	186·9	185·5	184·1	182·7	181·3	179·9	60
70	178·4	177·0	175·5	174·0	172·5	171·0	169·5	168·0	166·5	164·9	70
80	163·3	161·7	160·1	158·4	156·7	155·1	153·4	151·8	150·1	148·5	80
90	146·9	145·3	143·7	142·2	140·6	139·0	137·4	135·9	134·3	132·8	90
100	131·3	129·8	128·3	126·8	125·3	123·9	122·4	121·0	119·6	118·1	100
110	116·7	115·3	114·0	112·6	111·2	109·9	108·5	107·2	105·9	104·6	110
120	103·4	102·1	100·9	99·7	98·5	97·3	96·1	95·0	93·9	92·7	120
130	91·6	90·5	89·5	88·4	87·4	86·3	85·3	84·3	83·3	82·3	130
140	81·3	80·4	79·5	78·6	77·7	76·8	75·9	75·1	74·2	73·4	140
150	72·5	71·7	70·9	70·1	69·3	68·6	67·8	67·0	66·2	65·5	150
160	64·7	64·0	63·3	62·6	61·8	61·2	60·7	60·1	59·4	58·8	160
170	58·2	57·6	57·0	56·5	55·9	55·3	54·8	54·2	53·7	53·1	170
180	52·6	52·0	51·5	51·0	50·5	50·0	49·5	49·0	48·6	48·1	180
190	47·7	47·2	46·8	46·4	45·9	45·5	45·1	44·7	44·2	43·8	190
200	43·4	43·1	42·7	42·3	42·0	41·6	41·3	40·9	40·5	40·1	200
210	39·8	39·5	39·1	38·8	38·5	38·1	37·8	37·4	37·1	36·8	210
220	36·5	36·1	35·8	35·5	35·2	35·0	34·7	34·4	34·1	33·8	220
230	33·6	33·3	33·1	32·8	32·6	32·3	32·0	31·8	31·5	31·3	230
240	31·1	30·9	30·7	30·4	30·2	29·9	29·7	29·4	29·2	29·0	240
250	28·9	—	—	—	—	—	—	—	—	—	250

Single and Compound Angle Members

Table 7.4(c)
Dimensional Buckling Curve B4 for Steel Fe 510 ($t > 20$ mm)

Limiting stress σ_{cr} MPa

λ	0	1	2	3	4	5	6	7	8	9	λ
0	320·0	320·0	320·0	320·0	320·0	320·0	320·0	320·0	320·0	320·0	0
10	320·0	320·0	320·0	320·0	320·0	320·0	320·0	318·8	317·5	316·1	10
20	314·7	313·3	311·9	310·5	309·0	307·5	305·9	304·4	302·8	301·1	20
30	299·5	297·9	296·3	294·7	293·2	291·6	290·1	288·5	286·9	285·3	30
40	283·6	281·9	280·1	278·3	276·5	274·6	272·7	270·7	268·7	266·7	40
50	264·7	262·6	260·5	258·4	256·3	254·1	251·9	249·7	247·5	245·2	50
60	242·9	240·6	238·3	235·9	233·6	231·2	228·7	226·3	223·8	221·2	60
70	218·7	216·0	213·4	210·7	208·1	205·5	202·9	200·4	197·8	195·3	70
80	192·8	190·3	187·8	185·3	182·8	180·4	178·0	175·6	173·3	170·9	80
90	168·6	166·3	164·1	161·8	159·6	157·3	155·1	153·0	150·8	148·7	90
100	146·6	144·5	142·4	140·4	138·4	136·5	134·6	132·7	130·8	129·0	100
110	127·2	125·5	123·7	122·0	120·3	118·7	117·0	115·4	113·8	112·3	110
120	110·7	109·2	107·7	106·3	104·9	103·5	102·2	100·8	99·5	98·2	120
130	96·9	95·7	94·4	93·2	91·9	90·7	89·5	88·3	87·2	86·0	130
140	85·0	83·6	82·9	81·9	80·9	79·9	79·0	78·1	77·1	76·2	140
150	75·3	74·4	73·5	72·7	71·8	70·9	70·1	69·3	68·5	67·7	150
160	67·0	66·2	65·5	64·8	64·1	63·4	62·7	62·1	61·4	60·7	160
170	60·0	59·4	58·8	58·2	57·6	57·1	56·5	55·9	55·3	54·7	170
180	54·2	53·6	53·1	52·6	52·0	51·5	51·0	50·4	49·9	49·4	180
190	48·9	48·5	48·0	47·5	47·1	46·6	46·2	45·7	45·3	44·9	190
200	44·5	44·1	43·7	43·3	42·9	42·5	42·2	41·9	41·6	41·2	200
210	40·8	40·4	40·0	39·7	39·4	39·1	38·7	38·4	38·1	37·8	210
220	37·5	37·2	36·8	36·5	36·2	35·9	35·6	35·3	35·0	34·7	220
230	34·4	34·1	33·8	33·5	33·3	33·0	32·7	32·4	32·2	31·9	230
240	31·6	31·4	31·1	30·9	30·6	30·4	30·1	29·8	29·6	29·4	240
250	29·1	—	—	—	—	—	—	—	—	—	250

If the chords provide good end restraints to the web members and if at least two bolts or rivets in line are present at the end connections of the web members, then for $1\cdot41 \le \lambda/\lambda_y \le 3.5$,

$$\left(\frac{\lambda}{\lambda_y}\right)_{eff} = 0\cdot35 + 0\cdot75\frac{\lambda}{\lambda_y} \qquad (7\cdot47)$$

where $\lambda = KL/r =$ slenderness ratio

$$\lambda_y = \pi\sqrt{\frac{E}{\sigma_y}} \qquad (7.48)$$

and $\sigma_y =$ yield stress. For steels with yield stresses not given in the above tables, the values from non-dimensional buckling curve 'b' in Table 7.5(a) can be conveniently used.

7.3.1.2. ECCS Stability Manual (European Convention for Constructional Steelwork, 1976)

The European practice for the design of angle members is found in the Introductory Report of the European Convention for Constructional Steelwork (ECCS), published in connection with the Second International Colloquium on Stability; this Introductory Report is often referred to as the 'Stability Manual'. Sub-chapter 3.1.5 of the Stability Manual deals with single angles for use in structures other than transmission towers, while sub-chapter 9.2 deals specifically with angles in latticed transmission towers. These form the basis for the ECCS European Recommendations for Steel Construction (European Convention for Constructional Steelwork, 1978). Sub-chapter 3.1.5 deals with concentrically as well as with eccentrically loaded angles connected by one leg. To eliminate the problem of torsional–flexural buckling, the width–thickness ratios of legs are limited to the following: $b/t = 15$ for steel Fe 510; $b/t = 17$ for steel Fe 430; and $b/t = 18$ for steel Fe 360. Here b is the nominal width of leg, unlike ASCE Manual No. 52 in which b is taken as the width measured from the root of the fillet.

The ECCS Stability Manual gives five non-dimensional buckling curves designated a_0, a, b, c, d, as shown in Fig. 7.7; this figure also shows calculated buckling load curves obtained by numerical simulation for angles with and without residual stresses. The experimental results of centrally loaded angles agreed well with curve (b) for non-dimensional slenderness ratios

$$\frac{\lambda}{\lambda_y} = \frac{KL/r}{\pi\sqrt{E/\sigma_y}} \tag{7.49}$$

greater than 1; for $\lambda/\lambda_y < 1$, the experimental results were lower than curve (b). Therefore, ECCS 'Stability Manual' recommended that the yield stress be lowered and the dimensional buckling curves B_3 and B_4 be used (Tables 7.3 and 7.4).

For angles in latticed transmission towers, ECCS 'Stability Manual' adopted the non-dimensional a_0 curve in Fig. 7.7 (or Table 7.5(b)) as basic buckling–load curve. Both local and torsional buckling states are taken into account by reducing the yield stress for larger b/t ratios

Table 7.5(a)

σ_{cr}/σ_y Value of Nondimensional Column Curve 'b'

λ/λ_y	0·00	0·01	0·02	0·03	0·04	0·05	0·06	0·07	0·08	0·09
·0	1·000 0	1·000 0	1·000 0	1·000 0	1·000 0	1·000 0	1·000 0	1·000 0	1·000 0	1·000 0
·1	1·000 0	1·000 0	1·000 0	1·000 0	1·000 0	1·000 0	1·000 0	1·000 0	1·000 0	1·000 0
·2	1·000 0	0·996 7	0·993 3	0·989 9	0·986 5	0·983 0	0·979 5	0·976 0	0·972 4	0·968 7
·3	0·965 0	0·961 2	0·957 3	0·953 3	0·949 3	0·945 3	0·941 2	0·937 2	0·933 1	0·929 1
·4	0·925 0	0·921 1	0·917 1	0·913 2	0·909 3	0·905 4	0·901 4	0·897 4	0·893 3	0·889 2
·5	0·885 0	0·880 7	0·876 2	0·871 7	0·867 1	0·862 4	0·857 7	0·852 9	0·848 0	0·843 0
·6	0·838 0	0·832 9	0·827 8	0·822 7	0·817 4	0·812 2	0·806 8	0·801 5	0·796 0	0·790 5
·7	0·785 0	0·779 4	0·773 8	0·768 1	0·762 4	0·756 6	0·750 8	0·744 9	0·739 0	0·733 0
·8	0·727 0	0·721 0	0·714 8	0·708 7	0·702 4	0·696 1	0·689 7	0·683 2	0·676 6	0·670 0
·9	0·663 3	0·656 6	0·650 0	0·643 4	0·636 9	0·630 5	0·624 1	0·617 7	0·611 4	0·605 1
1·0	0·598 7	0·592 4	0·586 1	0·579 9	0·573 7	0·567 6	0·561 5	0·555 4	0·549 5	0·543 5
1·1	0·537 6	0·531 8	0·526 0	0·520 2	0·514 5	0·508 8	0·503 1	0·497 5	0·491 9	0·486 4
1·2	0·480 9	0·475 4	0·470 0	0·464 7	0·459 3	0·454 1	0·448 9	0·443 8	0·438 7	0·433 7
1·3	0·428 8	0·424 0	0·419 2	0·414 5	0·409 8	0·405 2	0·400 7	0·396 2	0·391 8	0·387 4
1·4	0·383 1	0·378 8	0·374 6	0·370 4	0·366 3	0·362 2	0·358 2	0·354 2	0·350 3	0·346 4
1·5	0·342 6	0·338 9	0·335 2	0·331 7	0·328 1	0·324 6	0·321 2	0·317 8	0·314 4	0·311 1
1·6	0·307 8	0·304 6	0·301 4	0·298 2	0·295 0	0·291 9	0·288 8	0·285 7	0·282 6	0·279 6

	0	1	2	3	4	5	6	7	8	9
1·7	0·2766 6	0·2737 7	0·2709 9	0·2681 1	0·2654 4	0·2617 7	0·2601 1	0·2576 6	0·2551 1	0·2526 6
1·8	0·2502 2	0·2478 8	0·2455 5	0·2431 1	0·2408 8	0·2385 5	0·2362 2	0·2340 0	0·2317 7	0·2295 5
1·9	0·2273 3	0·2251 1	0·2230 0	0·2208 8	0·2188 8	0·2167 7	0·2147 7	0·2127 7	0·2108 8	0·2089 9
2·0	0·2070 0	0·2052 2	0·2034 4	0·2016 6	0·1999 9	0·1982 2	0·1965 5	0·1948 8	0·1931 1	0·1914 4
2·1	0·1897 7	0·1880 0	0·1864 4	0·1848 8	0·1833 3	0·1818 8	0·1804 4	0·1790 0	0·1776 6	0·1761 1
2·2	0·1746 6	0·1730 0	0·1715 5	0·1701 1	0·1688 8	0·1675 5	0·1662 2	0·1648 8	0·1635 5	0·1621 1
2·3	0·1607 7	0·1594 4	0·1580 0	0·1567 7	0·1555 5	0·1542 2	0·1530 0	0·1518 8	0·1506 6	0·1494 4
2·4	0·1483 3	0·1471 1	0·1460 0	0·1449 9	0·1438 8	0·1427 7	0·1417 7	0·1407 7	0·1397 7	0·1387 7
2·5	0·1377 7	0·1366 6	0·1356 6	0·1346 6	0·1336 6	0·1327 7	0·1319 9	0·1311 1	0·1303 3	0·1293 3
2·6	0·1283 3	0·1273 3	0·1263 3	0·1253 3	0·1244 4	0·1237 7	0·1230 0	0·1222 2	0·1214 4	0·1206 6
2·7	0·1198 8	0·1190 0	0·1182 2	0·1174 4	0·1166 6	0·1158 8	0·1150 0	0·1142 2	0·1134 4	0·1127 7
2·8	0·1119 9	0·1111 1	0·1104 4	0·1096 6	0·1088 8	0·1081 1	0·1074 4	0·1066 6	0·1059 9	0·1052 2
2·9	0·1045 5	0·1038 8	0·1031 1	0·1024 4	0·1017 7	0·1010 0	0·1003 3	0·0997 7	0·0990 0	0·0983 3
3·0	0·0977 7	0·0971 1	0·0964 4	0·0958 8	0·0951 1	0·0945 5	0·0939 9	0·0932 2	0·0926 6	0·0920 0
3·1	0·0914 4	0·0908 8	0·0902 2	0·0896 6	0·0891 1	0·0885 5	0·0879 9	0·0874 4	0·0868 8	0·0863 3
3·2	0·0857 7	0·0852 2	0·0846 6	0·0841 1	0·0835 5	0·0830 0	0·0825 5	0·0819 9	0·0814 4	0·0809 0
3·3	0·0804 4	0·0799 9	0·0794 4	0·0789 9	0·0784 4	0·0779 9	0·0774 4	0·0769 9	0·0764 4	0·0760 0
3·4	0·0755 5	0·0750 0	0·0746 6	0·0742 2	0·0737 7	0·0733 3	0·0729 9	0·0724 4	0·0720 0	0·0716 6
3·5	0·0712 2	0·0708 8	0·0704 4	0·0700 0	0·0697 7	0·0693 3	0·0689 9	0·0686 6	0·0682 2	0·0679 9
3·6	0·0675 5									

Table 7.5(b)
Non-dimensional Buckling Curve 'a$_0$'
σ_{cr}/σ_y Values of Nondimensional Column Curve 'a$_0$'

λ/λ_y	0·00	0·01	0·02	0·03	0·04	0·05	0·06	0·07	0·08	0·09
·0	1·0000	1·0000	1·0000	1·0000	1·0000	1·0000	1·0000	1·0000	1·0000	1·0000
·1	1·0000	1·0000	1·0000	1·0000	1·0000	1·0000	1·0000	1·0000	1·0000	1·0000
·2	1·0000	0·9983	0·9966	0·9948	0·9930	0·9910	0·9891	0·9872	0·9852	0·9833
·3	0·9813	0·9794	0·9775	0·9756	0·9737	0·9719	0·9700	0·9682	0·9664	0·9645
·4	0·9627	0·9608	0·9590	0·9571	0·9552	0·9533	0·9515	0·9496	0·9477	0·9459
·5	0·9440	0·9421	0·9403	0·9384	0·9366	0·9346	0·9327	0·9308	0·9288	0·9269
·6	0·9249	0·9229	0·9208	0·9188	0·9168	0·9148	0·9129	0·9108	0·9087	0·9065
·7	0·9040	0·9013	0·8982	0·8949	0·8914	0·8876	0·8836	0·8794	0·8751	0·8708
·8	0·8659	0·8610	0·8560	0·8509	0·8456	0·8401	0·8345	0·8267	0·8228	0·8166
·9	0·8103	0·8039	0·7973	0·7905	0·7838	0·7765	0·7692	0·7618	0·7543	0·7467
1·0	0·7390	0·7313	0·7235	0·7157	0·7078	0·6999	0·6920	0·6840	0·6761	0·6681
1·1	0·6601	0·6522	0·6443	0·6364	0·6286	0·6208	0·6131	0·6055	0·5979	0·5904
1·2	0·5831	0·5758	0·5685	0·5614	0·5543	0·5473	0·5404	0·5335	0·5268	0·5202
1·3	0·5136	0·5071	0·5007	0·4944	0·4882	0·4820	0·4760	0·4701	0·4643	0·4586
1·4	0·4529	0·4474	0·4419	0·4366	0·4313	0·4261	0·4209	0·4159	0·4109	0·4060
1·5	0·4011	0·3964	0·3917	0·3871	0·3828	0·3781	0·3737	0·3694	0·3651	0·3610

	0	1	2	3	4	5	6	7	8	9
1·6	0·3569	0·3528	0·3488	0·3449	0·3410	0·3372	0·3335	0·3298	0·3262	0·3226
1·7	0·3191	0·3156	0·3122	0·3089	0·3056	0·3023	0·2991	0·2959	0·2928	0·2898
1·8	0·2868	0·2838	0·2809	0·2780	0·2752	0·2724	0·2696	0·2669	0·2642	0·2618
1·9	0·2590	0·2564	0·2539	0·2514	0·2489	0·2465	0·2441	0·2418	0·2395	0·2372
2·0	0·2349	0·2327	0·2305	0·2284	0·2262	0·2241	0·2220	0·2200	0·2180	0·2160
2·1	0·2140	0·2121	0·2102	0·2083	0·2064	0·2046	0·2028	0·2010	0·1992	0·1974
2·2	0·1957	0·1940	0·1923	0·1907	0·1891	0·1875	0·1859	0·1843	0·1827	0·1812
2·3	0·1797	0·1782	0·1767	0·1753	0·1738	0·1724	0·1710	0·1696	0·1683	0·1669
2·4	0·1656	0·1642	0·1629	0·1616	0·1603	0·1591	0·1578	0·1566	0·1554	0·1542
2·5	0·1530	0·1518	0·1506	0·1495	0·1483	0·1472	0·1461	0·1450	0·1439	0·1428
2·6	0·1417	0·1407	0·1396	0·1386	0·1376	0·1366	0·1356	0·1346	0·1336	0·1326
2·7	0·1317	0·1307	0·1298	0·1289	0·1279	0·1270	0·1261	0·1253	0·1244	0·1235
2·8	0·1227	0·1216	0·1210	0·1201	0·1193	0·1185	0·1177	0·1169	0·1161	0·1153
2·9	0·1145	0·1138	0·1130	0·1123	0·1115	0·1108	0·1100	0·1093	0·1086	0·1079
3·0	0·1072	0·1065	0·1058	0·1051	0·1045	0·1038	0·1031	0·1025	0·1018	0·1012
3·1	0·1005	0·0999	0·0993	0·0987	0·0981	0·0975	0·0969	0·0963	0·0957	0·0951
3·2	0·0945	0·0939	0·0934	0·0928	0·0922	0·0917	0·0911	0·0906	0·0901	0·0895
3·3	0·0890	0·0885	0·0880	0·0874	0·0869	0·0864	0·0859	0·0854	0·0849	0·0844
3·4	0·0839	0·0834	0·0830	0·0825	0·0820	0·0815	0·0811	0·0806	0·0802	0·0797
3·5	0·0793	0·0788	0·0784	0·0779	0·0775	0·0771	0·0767	0·0762	0·0758	0·0754
3·6	0·0750									

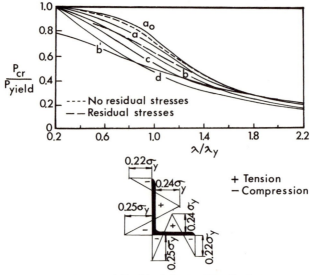

Assumed Residual Stress Distribution
for Numerical Simulation

Fig. 7.7. Non-dimensional buckling curves based on ECCS Recommendations.

according to the following formulas:

Hot-rolled equal-leg angles

$$\left(\frac{b}{t}\right)_{\text{limit}} = 0\cdot567\sqrt{\frac{E}{\sigma_y}} = \frac{260}{\sqrt{(\sigma_y)}} \tag{7.50}$$

where σ_y is the yield stress in MPa.
    For $b/t < (b/t)_{\text{limit}}$,

$$\sigma_{y\text{ effective}} = \sigma_y \tag{7.51}$$

For $(b/t)_{\text{limit}} < b/t < (4/3)(b/t)_{\text{limit}}$,

$$\sigma_{y\text{ effective}} = \sigma_y\left[2 - \frac{(b/t)}{(b/t)_{\text{limit}}}\right] \tag{7.52}$$

For $b/t > (4/3)(b/t)_{\text{limit}}$,

$$\sigma_{y\text{ effective}} = \frac{\pi^2 E}{(5\cdot1 b/t)^2} = \frac{80\,000}{(b/t)^2} \tag{7.53}$$

For legs and chords braced as in Fig. 6.8, the method of computation of slenderness ratios is as shown in the same figure.

Compound angles. In order to take into account the possible additional deformations due to shear, the slenderness ratio λ of a compound angle shown in Fig. 7.8 is computed from

$$\lambda^2 = \lambda_0^2 + \lambda_1^2 \tag{7.54}$$

in which $\lambda_0 =$ slenderness ratio of the compound member, assuming composite action; and $\lambda_1 =$ slenderness ratio of one component angle, C/r_{vv} (see Fig. 7.8 for definition of C, and Fig. 6.8 for definition of the v–v axis). It is good practice to have $\lambda_0 > \lambda_1$ with λ_1 approximately 40 to 50. The design of intermediate connections is based on a shear force of 1 to 1·5% of the total buckling load.

Buckling curves for web members. Because web members are eccentrically loaded, the effect of eccentricity is taken into account by modifying the non-dimensional slenderness ratios. This procedure is the same as that followed in the ASCE Manual No. 52.
For $\lambda/\lambda_y \leqslant \sqrt{2}$:

(a) Eccentricity at one end only: Buckling about axis v–v,

$$\left(\frac{\lambda}{\lambda_y}\right)_{\text{modified}} = 0 \cdot 25 + 0 \cdot 8232 \left(\frac{\lambda}{\lambda_y}\right) \tag{7.55}$$

Buckling about axis x–x or y–y (see Fig. 6.8),

$$\left(\frac{\lambda}{\lambda_y}\right)_{\text{modified}} = 0 \cdot 35 + 0 \cdot 7525 \left(\frac{\lambda}{\lambda_y}\right) \tag{7.56}$$

(b) Eccentricities at both ends: Buckling about axis v–v,

$$\left(\frac{\lambda}{\lambda_y}\right)_{\text{modified}} = 0 \cdot 35 + 0 \cdot 7525 \left(\frac{\lambda}{\lambda_y}\right) \tag{7.56}$$

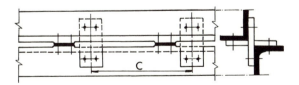

Fig. 7.8. Arrangement of stitch plates and stitch bolts in compound angles.

Buckling about axis $x–x$ or $y–y$,

$$\left(\frac{\lambda}{\lambda_y}\right)_{\text{modified}} = 0\cdot50 + 0\cdot6464\left(\frac{\lambda}{\lambda_y}\right) \tag{7.57}$$

These modified slenderness ratios are based on two or more bolts at each end for single angles and three or more bolts in line at each end for compound angles back to back. If there are only two bolts in line for compound angles back to back, eqns (7.56) and (7.57) are to be modified as follows for buckling about the $x–x$ axis. For eccentricity at one end only,

$$\left(\frac{\lambda}{\lambda_y}\right)_{\text{modified}} = 0\cdot35 + 0\cdot82\left(\frac{\lambda}{\lambda_y}\right) \tag{7.58}$$

For eccentricities at both ends,

$$\left(\frac{\lambda}{\lambda_y}\right)_{\text{modified}} = 0\cdot50 + 0\cdot82\left(\frac{\lambda}{\lambda_y}\right) \tag{7.59}$$

For $\lambda/\lambda_y > \sqrt{2}$, end restraint has a greater effect than eccentricity; this is accounted for by modifying the non-dimensional slenderness ratios as follows:

(a)   Restraint at one end only: Buckling about axis $v–v$, $x–x$ or $y–y$,

$$\left(\frac{\lambda}{\lambda_y}\right)_{\text{modified}} = 0\cdot35 + 0\cdot7525\left(\frac{\lambda}{\lambda_y}\right) \tag{7.56}$$

(b)   Restraint at both ends: Buckling about axis $v–v$, $x–x$ or $y–y$,

$$\left(\frac{\lambda}{\lambda_y}\right)_{\text{modified}} = 0\cdot50 + 0\cdot6464\left(\frac{\lambda}{\lambda_y}\right) \tag{7.57}$$

Nominally unstressed members (*redundants*). In order to reduce the effective length of the main legs and sometimes that of bracings, it is frequently necessary to introduce stabilizing members, or so-called redundants, which are nominally unstressed. In order to satisfactorily design these redundants, it is necessary to introduce a hypothetical force acting transverse to the member being stabilized at the node point of the attachment of the redundant. This force varies with the slenderness ratio of the member being stabilized and is expressed as a percentage of the load in the member. Values of this percentage for

Table 7.6
Design Forces for Redundants

Slenderness ratio of the member being stabilized, λ	Design force for redundants expressed as a percentage of the force in the member being stabilized
0–40	1·02
45	1·15
50	1·28
55	1·42
60	1·52
65	1·60
70	1·65
75	1·70
80	1·75
85	1·80
90	1·85
95	1·92
100	2

various slenderness ratios of the member being stabilized are given in Table 7.6.

This slenderness ratio λ is usually L/r_{min} where L = length between the nodes. This load shall be applied at each node in turn and in the plane of the bracing. The bracing shall also be checked for 2·5% of the load in the member; this load is shared equally between all the node points along the length of the member in a panel, excluding the first and last, all these loads acting together and in the same direction, i.e. at right angles to the leg and in the plane of the bracing. It should be noted that these loads are not additive to existing loads on the towers.

If the main member is eccentrically loaded, the aforementioned stabilizing force may be unsafe, and a more refined value is obtained taking into account the moment due to the eccentricity of the load.

Design of web members

Single lattice without redundants (Fig. 7.9(a)).

$$\text{Design slenderness ratio } \lambda = \frac{L}{r_{min}} \qquad (7.60)$$

Single lattice with redundants (Fig. 7.9(b)). When force is constant

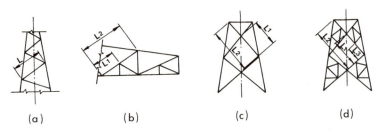

(a)   (b)   (c)   (d)

Fig. 7.9. Relevant lengths of bracing web members in latticed structures.

throughout the length L_2

Design slenderness ratio

$$= \text{greater of } \frac{L_1}{r_{\min}} \text{ and } \frac{L_2}{r_{xx} \text{ or } r_{yy} \text{ (whichever is appropriate)}} \quad (7.61)$$

When secondary loads are introduced at the intermediate support

Design force for $(L_1/r_{\min})$ slenderness ratio
= Force in the bracing over the short length L_1

Design force for $(L_2/[r$ about the plane of the frame]) slenderness ratio
$= \frac{3}{4}$ of the larger $+\frac{1}{4}$ of the smaller force.

Cross-bracing without redundants (Fig. 7.9(c)). If the compressive and tensile forces in the two crossing diagonals are approximately equal, the point of intersection of diagonals can be considered restrained both transverse to and in the plane of the bracing; as such the design slenderness ratio can be taken as

$$\lambda_1 = \frac{L_1}{r_{\min}} \quad (7.62)$$

If the compressive and tensile forces in the two crossing diagonals are not equal, the compression diagonal must be checked as above for the worst compressive load. In addition, it is necessary to carry out a further check as follows: the sum of the load carrying capacities of both bars in compression must be at least equal to the algebraic sum of the forces in the two bars. For the calculation of the load-carrying capacities, the slenderness ratio $\lambda_2 = L_2$/radius of gyration about the rectangular axis parallel to the plane of bracing.

Cross-bracing with redundants (*Fig. 7.9(d)*). Slenderness ratio for buckling over length L_3

$$\lambda_3 = \frac{L_3}{r_{\min}} \tag{7.63}$$

It is also necessary to check buckling over length L_1 on the rectangular axis for buckling transverse to the bracing and then over length L_2 for the algebraic sum of the loads, similar to the situation for cross-bracing without redundants.

Cross-bracing with diagonal corner stays (*Fig. 7.10(a)*). Sometimes a corner stay is introduced to reduce the buckling length transverse to the plane of bracing. In this case five stability checks are required:

1. Stability of bar against maximum load over length L_1 on minimum axis ($\lambda = L_1/r_{\min}$).
2. Stability of bar against maximum load over length L_2 on transverse rectangular axis ($\lambda = L_2/r_{xx}$ or L_2/r_{yy}, whichever is appropriate).
3. Stability of two bars in cross-brace against algebraic sum of loads in cross-brace over length L_3 on transverse axis.
4. Stability of two bars (one in each of the two adjacent faces) against algebraic sum of loads in two bars connected by diagonal corner stay over length L_4 on transverse axis.
5. Stability of four bars (each member of cross-brace in the two adjacent faces) against algebraic sum of loads in all four bars over length L_5 on transverse axis.

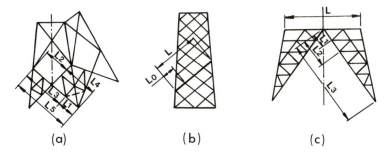

(a)   (b)   (c)

Fig. 7.10. Relevant lengths of bracing web members in latticed structures (a) with diagonal corner stays; (b) with mesh-type bracing; (c) with K-bracing.

Table 7.7
Effective Length Factor (for Buckling Transverse to the Plane of the Bracing)

Ratio of tensile force to compressive force	Effective length factor K
0	0·73
0·2	0·67
0·4	0·62
0·6	0·57
0·8	0·53
1·0	0·50

Multiple lattice (*Fig. 7.10(b)*). For the stability of panel, $r_{xx}/r_{vv} >$ 1·25 (where r_{xx} = radius of gyration about the axis parallel to the plane of the lattice) and $L/r_{xx} < 350$ to 400. Furthermore, the stability of the member must be checked under the applied load for a slenderness ratio $\lambda = L_0/r_{min}$.

K-bracing (*Fig. 7.10(c)*). Since the horizontal member usually has compression in one-half of its length and tension in the other, theoretically the effective length of the horizontal member transverse to the frame varies from $0·5L$ to $0·73L$ depending on the ratio of the tensile force to the compressive force as shown in Table 7.7. The effective radius of gyration is the rectangular one for buckling transverse to the frame. The transverse length is sometimes reduced by providing diagonal corner stays.

Compound members (*Fig. 7.11*). For buckling about the x–x axis, formulae (7.58) and (7.59) or (7.56) and (7.57) are applicable.

For buckling about the y–y axis, there is a secondary effect due to the distance between the stitch bolts and the consequent shear defor-

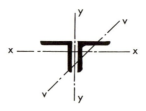

Fig. 7.11. Cross-section of a compound-angle member showing axes.

mation. This effect is taken into account by modifying the slenderness ratio of the full member about the y–y axis, L/r_{yy}, to

$$\lambda^2 = \left(\frac{L}{r_{yy}}\right)^2 + \left(\frac{C}{r_{min}}\right)^2 \qquad (7.64)$$

where $C/(r_{min})$ = slenderness ratio of one component angle about its v–v axis for the length C between the stitch bolts. In order to keep the effect of this interaction to a minimum, it is usual to limit the spacing between the stitch bolts to a maximum value of $C/r_{min} = 90$, or $0{\cdot}75(L/r_{yy})$, whichever is smaller.

For buckling about the y–y axis, the basic buckling curve can be applied since there is no load eccentricity about this axis; however, for very high b/t ratios, a reduction in strength can be produced by the interaction of torsional and flexural buckling. In order to reduce this effect to a minimum, the load has to be applied as near as possible to the 'flange' of the built-up T-section.

7.3.1.3. DIN 4114: German Buckling Specification (1952)

These are allowable stress specifications. The clauses that deal specifically with single and compound angles are discussed below.

Built-up columns, consisting of m individual angles, and having a material axis x–x (Figs 7.12, 7.13(a) and (b)) must be designed against buckling at right angles to this axis as single-member columns (clause 8.211). Therefore

$$\omega_x \frac{P}{A} \le \sigma_{all} \qquad (7.65)$$

where ω_x is a buckling coefficient corresponding to $\lambda_x = (KL/r)_x$, obtained from Table 7.8 for steels 'St 37' and from Table 7.9 for steels

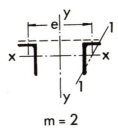

$m = 2$

Fig. 7.12. Arrangement of a compound angle for a built-up column.

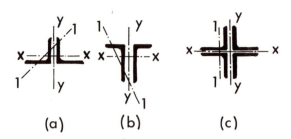

Fig. 7.13. Back-to-back arrangement of angles for built-up columns.

Table 7.8
Buckling Coefficients ω for St 00.12, Commercial Steel for Construction, and St 37.12 (Carbon Steel for Bridges)[a]

λ	0	1	2	3	4	5	6	7	8	9	λ
20	1·04	1·04	1·04	1·05	1·05	1·06	1·06	1·07	1·07	1·08	20
30	1·08	1·09	1·09	1·10	1·10	1·11	1·11	1·12	1·13	1·13	30
40	1·14	1·14	1·15	1·16	1·16	1·17	1·18	1·19	1·19	1·20	40
50	1·21	1·22	1·23	1·23	1·24	1·25	1·26	1·27	1·28	1·29	50
60	1·30	1·31	1·32	1·33	1·34	1·35	1·36	1·37	1·39	1·40	60
70	1·41	1·42	1·44	1·45	1·46	1·48	1·49	1·50	1·52	1·53	70
80	1·55	1·56	1·58	1·59	1·61	1·62	1·64	1·66	1·68	1·69	80
90	1·71	1·73	1·74	1·76	1·78	1·80	1·82	1·84	1·86	1·88	90
100	1·90	1·92	1·94	1·96	1·98	2·00	2·02	2·05	2·07	2·09	100
110	2·11	2·14	2·16	2·18	2·21	2·23	2·27	2·31	2·35	2·39	110
120	2·43	2·47	2·51	2·55	2·60	2·64	2·68	2·72	2·77	2·81	120
130	2·85	2·90	2·94	2·99	3·03	3·08	3·12	3·17	3·22	3·26	130
140	3·31	3·36	3·41	3·45	3·50	3·55	3·60	3·65	3·70	3·75	140
150	3·80	3·85	3·90	3·95	4·00	4·06	4·11	4·16	4·22	4·27	150
160	4·32	4·38	4·43	4·49	4·54	4·60	4·65	4·71	4·77	4·82	160
170	4·88	4·94	5·00	5·05	5·11	5·17	5·23	5·29	5·35	5·41	170
180	5·47	5·53	5·59	5·66	5·72	5·78	5·84	5·91	5·97	6·03	180
190	6·10	6·16	6·23	6·29	6·36	6·42	6·49	6·55	6·62	6·69	190
200	6·75	6·82	6·89	6·96	7·03	7·10	7·17	7·24	7·31	7·38	200
210	7·45	7·52	7·59	7·66	7·73	7·81	7·88	7·95	8·03	8·10	210
220	8·17	8·25	8·32	8·40	8·47	8·55	8·63	8·70	8·78	8·86	220
230	8·93	9·01	9·09	9·17	9·25	9·33	9·41	9·49	9·57	9·65	230
240	9·73	9·81	9·89	9·97	10·05	10·14	10·22	10·30	10·39	10·47	240
250	10·55										

Intermediate values need not be interpolated.
[a] Min. yield point = 24 kg/mm^2 = 34 100 psi.
Min. ultimate tensile strength: 37·0 kg/mm^2 = 52 500 psi.

'St 52'; P = maximum compressive force; A = gross cross-sectional area of column; and σ_{all} = allowable *tensile* stress for the selected type of steel and the particular loading condition.

For buckling at right angles to the axis y–y (Figs 7.12 and 7.13), such columns must be designed as single-member columns with a 'modified' slenderness ratio (clause 8.212).

$$\lambda_{yi} = \sqrt{\lambda_y^2 + \frac{m}{2}\lambda_1^2} \tag{7.66}$$

Thus,

$$\omega_{yi}\frac{P}{A} \leqslant \sigma_{all} \tag{7.67}$$

where ω_{yi} is the buckling coefficient (obtained from Table 7.8 or 7.9) corresponding to the modified slenderness ratio λ_{yi} and m is the number of similarly shaped individual rolled sections or of similarly shaped groups of rolled sections for buckling at right angles to y–y axis as shown in Figs 7.12 and 7.15.

In bridge and crane construction, the l/r ratio for buckling about axis 1–1 (Figs 7.12 and 7.13) must satisfy the following equation

$$\left(\frac{l}{r}\right)_{\text{about axis 1–1}} \leqslant \tfrac{1}{2}\lambda_x \tag{7.68}$$

In building construction (including bridges for conveyor systems) formula (7.68) is modified to

$$\left(\frac{l}{r}\right)_{\text{about axis 1–1}} \leqslant \tfrac{1}{2}\lambda_x\left(4 - 3\frac{\omega_{yi}P}{A\sigma_{all}}\right) \tag{7.69}$$

If a plate filler, continuous between gusset plates, is used in a built-up compression member comprising two angles or pairs of angles (Figs 7.13(b) and (c)), spaced back-to-back a distance equal to or only slightly larger than the thickness of the gusset plates, then λ_y may be used for λ_{yi} in calculating the buckling coefficient ω_{yi} in eqn (7.67) (clause 8.214).

Members comprising two angles placed corner-to-corner (Figs 7.14(a) and (b)) need be investigated for buckling only in the direction at right angles to the material axis x–x (clause 8.22). Again,

$$\omega_x\frac{P}{A} \leqslant \sigma_{all} \tag{7.70}$$

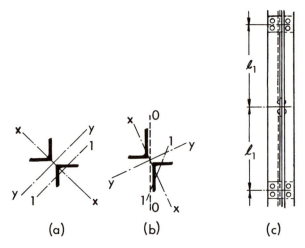

Fig. 7.14. Corner-to-corner arrangement of (a) two equal-leg angles; (b) two unequal-leg angles in (c) a built-up column.

where ω_x is the buckling coefficient corresponding to the slenderness ratio $\lambda_x = (KL/r)_x$ obtained from Table 7.8 or 7.9, whichever is appropriate. To compute the effective length (KL) about the x–x axis, the arithmetical mean of the two effective lengths for buckling in the truss plane and at right angles to it, is used. The ratio (l_1/r_1) for buckling about the axis 1–1 (Figs 7.14(a) and (b)) must not exceed 50. (For definition of l_1 see Fig. 7.14(c)). For members shown in Fig. 7.14(b), r_x may be taken approximately as $r_0/1\cdot15$, where r_0 is the radius of gyration about the axis parallel to the long legs of the angles (clause 8.224).

For built-up members which have a cross-section without a 'material axis' (Figs 7.15(a) through (e)) (clause 8.231),

$$\omega_{yi}\frac{P}{A} \leq \sigma_{all} \tag{7.71}$$

and

$$\omega_{xi}\frac{P}{A} \leq \sigma_{all} \tag{7.72}$$

where the buckling coefficients ω_{yi} and ω_{xi} (taken from Tables 7.8 and 7.9) correspond to the modified slenderness ratios

$$\lambda_{yi} = \sqrt{\lambda_y^2 + \frac{m}{2}\lambda_{1y}^2} \tag{7.73}$$

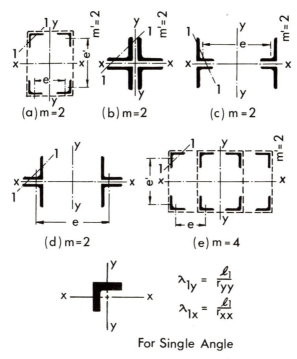

For Single Angle

Fig. 7.15. Various cross-sections of built-up members with no 'material axis.'

and

$$\lambda_{xi} = \sqrt{\lambda_x^2 + \frac{m'}{2}\lambda_{1x}^2} \qquad (7.74)$$

where m' = number of similarly shaped individual rolled sections or of similarly shaped groups of rolled sections for buckling at right angles to x–x axis, as shown in Fig. 7.15.

During buckling at right angles to the axis y–y, the cross-connections parallel to the y–y are not stressed (clause 8.232); therefore the column groups connected by these cross-connections may be considered as 'single' members; for the calculation of λ_{yi} for the cross-sections shown in Fig. 7.15(a) through (d), $m = 2$; and for the cross-section shown in Fig. 7.15(e), $m = 4$. The same consideration holds for buckling at right angles to the x–x axis; therefore, for the calculation of λ_{xi} for all the cross-sections shown in Fig. 7.15, $m' = 2$. For columns of the shapes shown in Figs. 7.15(a) and 7.15(e), the rectangular shape must be maintained by diaphragms.

Table 7.9
Buckling Coefficients ω for St 52 (High-Strength Steel for Bridges)[a]

λ	0	1	2	3	4	5	6	7	8	9	λ
20	1·06	1·06	1·07	1·07	1·08	1·08	1·09	1·09	1·10	1·11	20
30	1·11	1·12	1·12	1·13	1·14	1·15	1·15	1·16	1·17	1·18	30
40	1·19	1·19	1·20	1·21	1·22	1·23	1·24	1·25	1·26	1·27	40
50	1·28	1·30	1·31	1·32	1·33	1·35	1·36	1·37	1·39	1·40	50
60	1·41	1·43	1·44	1·46	1·48	1·49	1·51	1·53	1·54	1·56	60
70	1·58	1·60	1·62	1·64	1·66	1·68	1·70	1·72	1·74	1·77	70
80	1·79	1·81	1·83	1·86	1·88	1·91	1·93	1·95	1·98	2·01	80
90	2·05	2·10	2·14	2·19	2·24	2·29	2·33	2·38	2·43	2·48	90
100	2·53	2·58	2·64	2·69	2·74	2·79	2·85	2·90	2·95	3·01	100
110	3·06	3·12	3·18	3·23	3·29	3·35	3·41	3·47	3·53	3·59	110
120	3·65	3·71	3·77	3·83	3·89	3·96	4·02	4·09	4·15	4·22	120
130	4·28	4·35	4·41	4·48	4·55	4·62	4·69	4·75	4·82	4·89	130
140	4·96	5·04	5·11	5·18	5·25	5·33	5·40	5·47	5·55	5·62	140
150	5·70	5·78	5·85	5·93	6·01	6·09	6·16	6·24	6·32	6·40	150
160	6·48	6·57	6·65	6·73	6·81	6·90	6·98	7·06	7·15	7·23	160
170	7·32	7·41	7·49	7·58	7·67	7·76	7·85	7·94	8·03	8·12	170
180	8·21	8·30	8·39	8·48	8·58	8·67	8·76	8·86	8·95	9·05	180
190	9·14	9·24	9·34	9·44	9·53	9·63	9·73	9·83	9·93	10·03	190
200	10·13	10·23	10·34	10·44	10·54	10·65	10·75	10·85	10·96	11·06	200
210	11·17	11·28	11·38	11·49	11·60	11·71	11·82	11·93	12·04	12·15	210
220	12·26	12·37	12·48	12·60	12·71	12·82	12·94	13·05	13·17	13·28	220
230	13·40	13·52	13·63	13·75	13·87	13·99	14·11	14·23	14·35	14·47	230
240	14·59	14·71	14·83	14·96	15·08	15·20	15·33	15·45	15·58	15·71	240
250	15·83										

Intermediate values need not be interpolated.
[a] Min. yield point = 36 kg/mm² = 51 200 psi.
Min. ultimate tensile strength: 52 kg/mm² = 74 000 psi.

In bridge and crane construction the ratios l_{1y}/r_1 and l_{1x}/r_1 of the individual sections must not exceed 50 (clause 8.233). In building construction (including bridges for conveyor systems) this condition may be written in the following form:

$$\frac{l_{1y}}{r_1} \leqslant 50\left(4 - 3\,\frac{\omega_{yi}P}{A\sigma_{all}}\right) \tag{7.75}$$

and

$$\frac{l_{1x}}{r_1} \leqslant 50\left(4 - 3\,\frac{\omega_{xi}P}{A\sigma_{all}}\right) \tag{7.76}$$

For members with the cross-section shown in Fig. 7.15(b), λ_x and λ_y

may be substituted for λ_{xi} and λ_{yi}, respectively, if the angles are connected not only with the prescribed connection plates, but with rivets on washers, spaced along the member axis at spacings not over $15r_1$ (clause 8.234). By the same reasoning λ_x may be substituted for λ_{xi} for the cross-sections shown in Figs 7.15(c) and (d), if the pairs of adjacent angles are connected with rivets on washers at spacings not over $15r_1$.

Eccentrically loaded angles. If the point of load application lies on one of the two principal axes, the following formula is to be used for cross-sections in which the centre of gravity lies midway between the extreme compressive and tensile fibres ($y_t = y_c$, Fig. 7.16(a)) or for cross-sections in which the centre of gravity lies closer to the extreme tensile fibre ($y_t < y_c$, Fig. 7.16(b)) (clause 10.02):

$$\omega \frac{P}{A} + 0 \cdot 9 \frac{My_c}{I} \leqslant \sigma_{\text{all}} \tag{7.77}$$

For cross-sections in which the centre of gravity lies closer to the extreme compressive fibre ($y_t > y_c$, Fig. 7.16(c)), the following two conditions must be fulfilled:

$$\omega \frac{P}{A} + 0 \cdot 9 \frac{My_c}{I} \leqslant \sigma_{\text{all}} \tag{7.78}$$

and

$$\omega \frac{P}{A} + \frac{300 + 2\lambda}{1000} \frac{My_t}{I} \leqslant \sigma_{\text{all}} \tag{7.79}$$

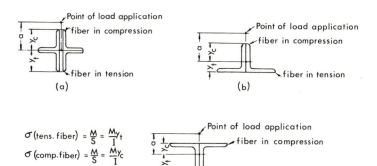

Fig. 7.16. Angle sections subjected to eccentric load.

If the moment varies along the column axis, then the maximum moment is to be used in eqns (7.77) to (7.79) (clause 10.04). When maximum moment occurs at one of the two column ends, and if both ends are restrained from lateral motion in the direction of bending, then the arithmetical mean of the two end moments may be used in these equations; however, the moment may not be less than one-half of the maximum moment (Fig. 7.17); for vertical columns this reduction applies only when the upper end is also prevented from lateral motion, and for frames it applies only when the cross member cannot be displaced in the direction of its axis.

Intentionally centrally loaded horizontal or sloping compression members, subject to moment from their own weight, must also be designed for combined bending and compressive stress (clause 10.05). The approximate value $M = (Wl_H/10)$ may be used for the moment, where W is the dead weight of the member, and l_H is the horizontal projection of the length of the member. If the length l_H is not over 6·00 m, then the influence of the weight may be neglected.

7.3.1.4. *British Standard BS 449: Part 2: 1969 (British Standards Institution, 1969a)*

This is an allowable stress specification. The effective lengths and permissible stresses of angles as struts are as follows (subclause 30c):

(i) For single-angle discontinuous struts connected to gussets or to a section either by riveting or bolting by not less than two rivets or

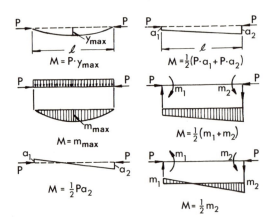

Fig. 7.17. Values of moment M for design.

bolts in line along the angle at each end, or by their equivalent in welding, the eccentricity of the connection with respect to the centroid of the strut may be ignored and the strut designed as an axially-loaded member provided that the calculated average stress does not exceed the allowable stresses given in Table 7.10, in which *KL* is taken as 0·85 times the length of the strut, centre-to-centre of intersections at each end, and *r* is the minimum radius of gyration. Single-angle struts with single-bolted or riveted connections shall be treated similarly, but

Table 7.10(a)

Allowable Stress f_{ac} on Gross Section for Axial Compression

KL/r	f_{ac} (MPa) for grade 43 steel									
	0	*1*	*2*	*3*	*4*	*5*	*6*	*7*	*8*	*9*
0	155	155	154	154	153	153	153	152	152	151
10	151	151	150	150	149	149	148	148	148	147
20	147	146	146	146	145	145	144	144	144	143
30	143	142	142	142	141	141	141	140	140	139
40	139	138	138	137	137	136	136	136	135	134
50	133	133	132	131	130	130	129	128	127	126
60	126	125	124	123	122	121	120	119	118	117
70	115	114	113	112	111	110	108	107	106	105
80	104	102	101	100	99	97	96	95	94	92
90	91	90	89	87	86	85	84	83	81	80
100	79	78	77	76	75	74	73	72	71	70
110	69	68	67	66	65	64	63	62	61	61
120	60	59	58	57	56	56	55	54	53	53
130	52	51	51	50	49	49	48	48	47	46
140	46	45	45	44	43	43	42	42	41	41
150	40	40	39	39	38	38	38	37	37	36
160	36	35	35	35	34	34	33	33	33	32
170	32	32	31	31	31	30	30	30	29	29
180	29	28	28	28	28	27	27	27	26	26
190	26	26	25	25	25	25	24	24	24	24
200	24	23	23	23	23	22	22	22	22	22
210	21	21	21	21	21	20	20	20	20	20
220	20	19	19	19	19	19	19	18	18	18
230	18	18	18	18	17	17	17	17	17	17
240	17	16	16	16	16	16	16	16	16	15
250	15	—	—	—	—	—	—	—	—	—
300	11	—	—	—	—	—	—	—	—	—
350	8	—	—	—	—	—	—	—	—	—

Intermediate values may be obtained by linear interpolation.

Table 7.10(b)
Allowable Stress f_{ac} on Gross Section for Axial Compression

				f_{ac} (MPa) for grade 50 steel						
KL/r	0	1	2	3	4	5	6	7	8	9
0	215	214	214	213	213	212	212	211	211	210
10	210	209	209	208	208	207	207	206	206	205
20	205	204	204	203	203	202	202	201	201	200
30	200	199	199	198	197	197	196	196	195	194
40	193	193	192	191	190	189	188	187	186	185
50	184	183	181	180	179	177	176	174	173	171
60	169	168	166	164	162	160	158	156	154	152
70	150	148	146	144	142	140	138	135	133	131
80	129	127	125	123	121	119	117	115	113	111
90	109	107	106	104	102	100	99	97	95	94
100	92	91	89	88	86	85	84	82	81	80
110	78	77	76	75	74	72	71	70	69	68
120	67	66	65	64	63	62	61	60	60	59
130	58	57	56	55	55	54	53	52	52	51
140	50	50	49	48	48	47	47	46	45	45
150	44	44	43	43	42	42	41	41	40	40
160	39	39	38	38	37	37	36	36	36	35
170	35	34	34	34	33	33	33	32	32	31
180	31	31	30	30	30	30	29	29	29	28
190	28	28	27	27	27	27	26	26	26	26
200	25	25	25	25	24	24	24	24	23	23
210	23	23	23	22	22	22	22	22	21	21
220	21	21	21	20	20	20	20	20	20	19
230	19	19	19	19	19	18	18	18	18	18
240	18	18	17	17	17	17	17	17	17	16
250	16	—	—	—	—	—	—	—	—	—
300	11	—	—	—	—	—	—	—	—	—
350	8	—	—	—	—	—	—	—	—	—

Intermediate values may be obtained by linear interpolation.

Table 7.10(c)
Allowable Stress f_{ac} on Gross Section for Axial Compression

				f_{ac} (MPa) for grade 55 steel						
KL/r	0	1	2	3	4	5	6	7	8	9
0	265	264	264	263	262	262	261	260	260	259
10	258	258	257	256	256	255	254	254	253	252
20	252	251	250	250	249	248	248	247	246	246
30	245	244	244	243	242	241	240	239	239	238
40	236	235	234	233	232	230	229	227	226	224

Table 7.10(c)—*contd.*

KL/r	f_{ac} (MPa) for grade 55 steel									
	0	1	2	3	4	5	6	7	8	9
50	222	220	219	217	214	212	210	208	205	203
60	200	197	195	192	189	186	183	180	178	175
70	172	169	166	163	160	157	154	151	148	146
80	143	140	138	135	133	130	128	125	123	121
90	118	116	114	112	110	108	106	104	102	100
100	99	97	95	93	92	90	89	87	86	84
110	83	82	80	79	78	76	75	74	73	72
120	71	69	68	67	66	65	64	63	62	62
130	61	60	59	58	57	56	56	55	54	53
140	53	52	51	50	50	49	49	48	47	47
150	46	45	45	44	44	43	43	42	42	41
160	41	40	40	39	39	38	38	37	37	37
170	36	36	35	35	34	34	34	33	33	33
180	32	32	32	31	31	31	30	30	30	29
190	29	29	28	28	28	28	27	27	27	27
200	26	26	26	25	25	25	25	25	24	24
210	24	24	23	23	23	23	23	22	22	22
220	22	22	21	21	21	21	21	20	20	20
230	20	20	20	19	19	19	19	19	19	18
240	18	18	18	18	18	18	17	17	17	17
250	17	—	—	—	—	—	—	—	—	—
300	12	—	—	—	—	—	—	—	—	—
350	9	—	—	—	—	—	—	—	—	—

Intermediate values may be obtained by linear interpolation.

the calculated stress shall not exceed 80 percent of the values given in Table 7.10, and the full length centre-to-centre of intersections shall be taken as *KL*. In no case, however, shall the ratio of slenderness for such single-angle struts exceed 180.

(ii) For double-angle discontinuous struts, back-to-back connected to both sides of a gusset or section by not less than two bolts or rivets in line along the angles at each end, or by the equivalent in welding, the load may be regarded as applied axially. The effective length *KL* shall be taken as between 0·7 and 0·85 times the distance between intersections, depending on the degree of restraint, and the calculated average stress shall not exceed the values obtained from Table 7.10 for the ratio of slenderness based on the minimum radius of gyration about a rectangular axis of the strut.

(iii)   Double-angle discontinuous struts back-to-back, connected to one side of a gusset or section by one or more bolts or rivets in each angle, or by the equivalent in welding, shall be designed as for single angles in accordance with (i) above.

Note. For values of KL/r less than 30 the value of f_{ac} shall not exceed that obtained from linear interpolation between the value of f_{ac} for $KL/r = 30$ as found above, and a value of f_{ac} for $KL/r = 0$ from Tables 7.10. Tables 7.10 are based on eqn (4.25) given in Chapter 4.

Compression members composed of two components back-to-back (*clause 37*). Compression members composed of two angles back-to-back in contact or separated by a small distance shall be connected together by riveting, bolting or welding so that the maximum ratio of slenderness KL/r of each member between the connections is not greater than 40 or greater than 0·6 times the most unfavourable ratio of slenderness of the strut as a whole, whichever is the less.

In no case shall the ends of the strut be connected together with less than two rivets or bolts or their equivalent in welding, and there shall be not less than two additional connections spaced equidistant in the length of the strut. Where the members are separated back-to-back the rivets or bolts through these connections shall pass through solid washers or packings, and where the legs of the connected angles are 125 mm wide or over, not less than two rivets or bolts shall be used in each connection, one on the line of each gauge mark.

Where these connections are made by welding, solid packings shall be used to effect the jointing unless the members are sufficiently close together to permit welding, and the members shall be connected by welding along both pairs of edges of the main components.

The rivets, bolts or welds in these connections shall be sufficient to carry the shear forces and moments (if any) specified for battened struts, and in no case shall the rivets or bolts be less than 16 mm diameter for members up to and including 10 mm thick; 20 mm diameter for members up to and including 16 mm thick; and 22 mm diameter for members over 16 mm thick. Compression members connected by such riveting, bolting or welding shall not be subjected to transverse loading in a plane perpendicular to the washer-riveted, bolted or welded surfaces.

Lug angles (*clause 49*). In the case of angle members the lug angles and their connection to the gusset or other supporting member shall be capable of developing a strength not less than 20 percent in excess of the force in the outstanding leg of the angle, and the attachment of the lug angle to the angle member shall be capable of developing 40 percent in excess of that force. In no case shall fewer than two bolts or rivets be used for attaching the lug angle to the gusset or other supporting member. Where lug angles are used to connect an angle member the whole area of the member shall be taken as effective.

Angle purlins of grade 43 steel for roof slopes not exceeding 30° pitch (*clause 45*). The leg or the depth of the purlin taken approximately in the plane of action of the maximum load or maximum component of the load shall be not less than $L/45$; the other leg or width of the purlin shall be not less than $L/60$, and the numerical value of the section modulus of the purlin in centimetre units shall be not less than $(WL/1.8) \times 10^{-3}$ where L is the centre-to-centre distance in millimetres of the steel principals or other support of the purlins and W is the total distributed load, in kN, on the purlin arising from dead load and snow, but excluding wind, both assumed as acting normal to the roof.

7.3.1.5. East European Practice (*American Institute of Steel Construction, 1982*)

For triangulated structures consisting of angle members, the slenderness ratios of compression elements are calculated as follows.

German Democratic Republic and Czechoslovakian specifications. If compression prevails

$$\lambda = 0 \cdot 8 L / r_{min} \tag{7.80}$$

If bending prevails

$$\lambda = 0 \cdot 7 L / r_{min} \tag{7.81}$$

Soviet specification

$$\lambda = \bar{\mu} L / r_x \tag{7.82}$$

where $\bar{\mu}$ is given in Fig. 7.18, in which l and l_d correspond to lengths L of vertical member and diagonal member respectively, and J and J_d correspond to the moments of inertia of vertical member and diagonal member respectively.

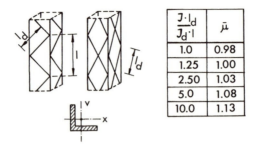

$\dfrac{J \cdot l_d}{J_d \cdot l}$	$\bar{\mu}$
1.0	0.98
1.25	1.00
2.50	1.03
5.0	1.08
10.0	1.13

Fig. 7.18. Values of coefficient $\bar{\mu}$.

7.3.2. Cold-Formed Angles

7.3.2.1. *ECCS Stability Manual (European Convention for Constructional Steelwork, 1976)*

Due to the lack of heel, cold-formed angles are torsionally less stiff than hot-rolled angles. On the other hand, cold working produces strain hardening and increases the yield stress at the corners. These two influences lead to smaller buckling loads for cold-formed angles at low slenderness and b/t ratios. This is reflected in the following specifications:

Equal-leg cold-formed angles

$$\left(\frac{b}{t}\right)_{limit} = 0 \cdot 503 \sqrt{\frac{E}{\sigma_y}} = \frac{231}{\sqrt{\sigma_y}} \tag{7.83}$$

where σ_y is the yield stress in MPa.

For $(b/t) < (b/t)_{limit}$,

$$\sigma_{y\,effective} = \sigma_y \tag{7.84}$$

For $(b/t)_{limit} < b/t < \frac{3}{2}(b/t)_{limit}$,

$$\sigma_{y\,effective} = \sigma_y\left[\frac{5}{3} - \frac{2}{3}\frac{(b/t)}{(b/t)_{limit}}\right] \tag{7.85}$$

For $b/t > \frac{3}{2}(b/t)_{limit}$,

$$\sigma_{y\,effective} = \frac{\pi^2 E}{(5 \cdot 1 b/t)^2} = \frac{80\,000}{(b/t)^2} \tag{7.86}$$

7.3.2.2. *Addendum No. 1 (1975) to BS 449: Part 2: 1969 (British Standards Institution, 1975)*

The specifications for cold-formed angles are included in the Addendum No. 1 to BS 449 issued in 1975. For axially loaded cold-formed angles, the permissible stresses are computed as follows:

The permissible stress on the gross area of an axially loaded strut shall not exceed the lesser of $0 \cdot 59\sigma_y$ and f_{ac} obtained from Table 7.11, in which $\sigma_y =$ yield stress and $\alpha KL/r$ is the factored slenderness ratio where KL is the effective length; r is the appropriate radius of gyration; α is a factor taking into account the torsional–flexural instability (Tables 7.12 and 7.13); and C_{Lm} is the weighted mean stress factor for the cross-section, determined from:

(a) For steel where σ_y is 250 MPa, the value of the stress factor C_L for each constituent flat plate component is obtained from Table 7.14, in which b/t is the width-to-thickness ratio. The weighted mean stress factor is then compounded from the C_L values by the formula

$$C_{Lm} = \frac{\sum C_L bt}{\sum bt} \tag{7.87}$$

(b) For steel where σ_y is greater than 250 MPa the procedure in (a) is followed except that in entering Table 7.14 to obtain C_L the value of b/t shall be modified by multiplying it by $\sqrt{(\sigma_y/250)}$; and that the values of C_L so obtained shall be then multiplied by $\sigma_y/250$ before they are used in the formula for C_{Lm}.

The values in Table 7.11 are derived from eqn (4.25), in which σ_y is taken as $250C_{Lm}$.

7.3.3. Aluminium Angles

The design of aluminium angles is dealt with in the British Standard Code of Practice BS CP 118: 1969 (British Standards Institution, 1969b), which is an allowable stress specification. Single-bay ties of single and double angles may be designed as axially loaded members, and the variation in stress in the outstanding leg or legs ignored, provided that the effective area is obtained by deducting part of the area of the outstanding leg as shown in Table 7.15. For end bays of multiple-bay angles, the effective area must be calculated in the same way as for single-bay ties. For intermediate bays of multiple-bay

Table 7.11

Permissible Axial Compressive Stress f_{ac} (MPa) in Struts

| | | | | | | | | C_{Lm} | | | | | | | | |
$\alpha(KL/r)$	0·25	0·30	0·35	0·40	0·45	0·50	0·55	0·60	0·65	0·70	0·75	0·80	0·85	0·90	0·95	1·00
0	37·1	44·5	51·8	59·2	66·5	73·9	81·3	88·6	96·0	103	111	118	125	133	140	148
10	36·7	44·0	51·3	58·6	66·0	73·3	80·6	88·0	95·3	103	110	117	125	132	139	147
20	36·3	43·6	50·8	58·1	65·4	72·6	79·9	87·2	94·4	102	109	116	124	131	138	145
30	35·8	42·9	50·1	57·2	64·3	71·5	78·6	85·8	92·9	100	107	114	121	129	136	143
40	35·0	42·0	49·0	55·9	62·9	69·8	76·8	83·7	90·6	97·5	104	111	118	125	132	139
50	34·0	40·8	47·5	54·2	60·9	67·6	74·3	80·9	87·5	94·1	101	107	114	120	127	133
60	32·8	39·3	45·7	52·1	58·5	64·8	71·0	77·3	83·4	89·6	95·6	102	108	114	119	125
70	31·4	37·6	43·6	49·6	55·5	61·4	67·1	72·8	78·4	83·9	89·2	94·5	99·7	105	110	115
80	29·9	35·6	41·2	46·7	52·1	57·4	62·6	67·6	72·4	77·2	81·7	86·1	90·4	94·5	98·4	102
90	28·2	33·5	38·6	43·6	48·4	53·1	57·5	61·8	65·9	69·8	73·6	77·1	80·4	83·6	86·6	89·4
100	26·5	31·3	35·9	40·3	44·5	48·5	52·3	55·9	59·3	62·4	65·4	68·2	70·7	73·1	75·3	77·4
110	24·7	29·0	33·1	37·0	40·6	44·0	47·2	50·1	52·9	55·4	57·7	59·9	61·8	63·7	65·3	66·9
120	22·9	26·8	30·4	33·7	36·9	39·7	42·3	44·8	47·0	49·0	50·8	52·5	54·1	55·5	56·8	58·0
130	21·2	24·6	27·8	30·7	33·3	35·7	37·9	39·9	41·7	43·4	44·8	46·2	47·4	48·5	49·6	50·5
140	19·6	22·6	25·4	27·9	30·1	32·2	34·0	35·6	37·1	38·5	39·7	40·8	41·8	42·7	43·5	44·2
150	18·0	20·7	23·1	25·3	27·2	29·0	30·5	31·9	33·1	34·2	35·2	36·2	37·0	37·7	38·4	39·0
160	16·6	19·0	21·1	23·0	24·7	26·1	27·5	28·6	29·7	30·6	31·5	32·2	32·9	33·5	34·1	34·6
170	15·3	17·4	19·3	20·9	22·4	23·7	24·8	25·8	26·7	27·5	28·2	28·9	29·4	30·0	30·5	30·9
180	14·1	16·0	17·7	19·1	20·4	21·5	22·5	23·3	24·1	24·8	25·4	26·0	26·5	26·9	27·4	27·7
190	13·0	14·7	16·2	17·5	18·6	19·5	20·4	21·2	21·8	22·4	23·0	23·5	23·9	24·3	24·7	25·0
200	12·0	13·6	14·9	16·0	17·0	17·9	18·6	19·3	19·9	20·4	20·9	21·3	21·7	22·1	22·4	22·7
210	11·2	12·5	13·6	14·7	15·6	16·4	17·0	17·6	18·2	18·6	19·1	19·4	19·8	20·1	20·4	20·6
220	10·3	11·6	12·6	13·6	14·3	15·0	15·6	16·2	16·6	17·1	17·4	17·8	18·1	18·4	18·6	18·9
230	9·6	10·7	11·7	12·5	13·2	13·9	14·4	14·9	15·3	15·7	16·0	16·3	16·6	16·9	17·1	17·3
240	8·9	10·0	10·9	11·6	12·2	12·8	13·3	13·7	14·1	14·5	14·8	15·0	15·3	15·5	15·7	15·9
250	8·3	9·3	10·1	10·8	11·4	11·9	12·3	12·7	13·1	13·4	13·7	13·9	14·1	14·3	14·5	14·7

Table 7.11—*contd.*

C_{Lm}

$\alpha(KL/r)$	1·05	1·10	1·15	1·20	1·25	1·30	1·35	1·40	1·45	1·50	1·55	1·60	1·65	1·70	1·75	1·80
0	155	162	170	177	184	192	199	206	214	221	228	236	243	250	258	265
10	154	161	169	176	183	191	198	205	213	220	227	235	242	249	257	264
20	153	160	167	174	182	189	196	203	211	218	225	232	240	247	254	261
30	150	157	164	171	178	185	192	200	207	214	221	228	235	242	249	256
40	146	153	159	166	173	180	187	193	200	207	213	220	226	234	240	247
50	140	146	152	158	165	171	177	183	189	195	201	207	213	219	225	230
60	131	136	142	147	153	157	163	168	173	178	183	187	192	196	200	204
70	119	124	128	132	137	141	144	148	152	155	158	161	164	167	170	172
80	106	109	112	116	118	121	124	126	129	131	133	135	137	138	140	142
90	92·0	94·5	96·8	98·9	101	103	105	106	108	109	111	112	113	114	115	116
100	79·3	81·1	82·7	84·3	85·7	87·0	88·2	89·4	90·5	91·4	92·4	93·2	94·1	94·8	95·5	96·2
110	68·3	69·6	70·8	72·0	73·0	74·0	74·9	75·7	76·5	77·2	77·9	78·5	79·1	79·7	80·2	80·7
120	59·1	60·1	61·0	61·8	62·6	63·4	64·0	64·7	65·3	65·8	66·3	66·8	67·3	67·7	68·1	68·5
130	51·4	52·1	52·9	53·5	54·2	54·7	55·3	55·8	56·2	56·7	57·1	57·5	57·8	58·1	58·5	58·8
140	44·9	45·6	46·2	46·7	47·2	47·7	48·1	48·5	48·9	49·2	49·6	49·9	50·2	50·4	50·7	50·9
150	39·6	40·1	40·6	41·0	41·5	41·8	42·2	42·5	42·8	43·1	43·4	43·7	43·9	44·1	44·4	44·6
160	35·1	35·5	36·0	36·3	36·7	37·0	37·3	37·6	37·8	38·1	38·3	38·5	38·7	38·9	39·1	39·3
170	31·3	31·7	32·0	32·4	32·7	32·9	33·2	33·4	33·7	33·9	34·1	34·2	34·4	34·6	34·7	34·9
180	28·1	28·4	28·7	29·0	29·2	29·5	29·7	29·9	30·1	30·3	30·5	30·6	30·8	30·9	31·1	31·2
190	25·3	25·6	25·9	26·1	26·3	26·5	26·7	26·9	27·1	27·3	27·4	27·5	27·7	27·8	27·9	28·0
200	22·9	23·2	23·4	23·6	23·8	24·0	24·2	24·4	24·5	24·6	24·8	24·9	25·0	25·1	25·2	25·3
210	20·9	21·1	21·3	21·5	21·7	21·8	22·0	22·1	22·3	22·4	22·5	22·6	22·7	22·8	22·9	23·0
220	19·1	19·3	19·5	19·6	19·8	19·9	20·1	20·2	20·3	20·4	20·5	20·6	20·7	20·8	20·9	21·0
230	17·5	17·7	17·8	18·0	18·1	18·3	18·4	18·5	18·6	18·7	18·8	18·9	19·0	19·1	19·1	19·2
240	16·1	16·3	16·4	16·6	16·7	16·8	16·9	17·0	17·1	17·2	17·3	17·4	17·5	17·5	17·6	17·7
250	14·9	15·0	15·2	15·3	15·4	15·5	15·6	15·7	15·8	15·9	16·0	16·0	16·1	16·2	16·2	16·3

Note: Values apply to all steels, but shall not exceed $0.59\sigma_y$.

Table 7.12
Values of α for Angle Section Struts

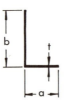

$(KL/r)(t/a)$	$\dfrac{b}{a} = 1$	$\dfrac{b}{a} = 1\cdot5$	$\dfrac{b}{a} = 2\cdot0$
4	1·29	—	—
5	1·04	—	—
6	1·00	1·27	—
7	1·00	1·17	—
8	1·00	1·11	1·31
9	1·00	1·08	1·24
10	1·00	1·06	1·19
11	1·00	1·05	1·15
12	1·00	1·04	1·11
13	1·00	1·03	1·09
14	1·00	1·02	1·08
15	1·00	1·01	1·07

angles, the effective area is the gross sectional area minus the deductions for holes.

7.3.3.1. Axially Loaded Struts

With struts, the main requirement is resistance to column buckling (i.e. overall flexural buckling), for which the permissible average stress on the gross area is obtained from the appropriate graph in Fig. 7.19 at $\lambda = l/r$, where l is the effective length estimated from Table 7.16 and r is the appropriate radius of gyration. One further requirement is resistance to torsional buckling.

7.3.3.2. Eccentrically Loaded Struts—Single-bay Struts *(clause 4.3.2)*

For single-bay struts consisting of a single angle connected by one leg only, the average stress must not exceed 0·4 times the permissible stress for an axially loaded strut. Struts consisting of two angles, connected to both sides of end gussets, may be taken as axially loaded provided that they are properly connected at intervals. The permissible

Table 7.13
Values of α for Effectively Connected Double-Angle Section
Struts

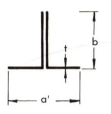

$(KL/r)(t/a')$	b/a'					
	0·25	*0·33*	*0·5*	*0·75*	*1·00*	*1·33*
2	1·04	1·10	1·39	—	—	—
3	1·00	1·00	1·00	1·30	—	—
4	1·00	1·00	1·00	1·16	1·34	—
5	1·00	1·00	1·00	1·10	1·20	—
6	1·00	1·00	1·00	1·06	1·13	1·30
7	1·00	1·00	1·00	1·05	1·09	1·20
8	1·00	1·00	1·00	1·04	1·06	1·15
9	1·00	1·00	1·00	1·03	1·05	1·12
10	1·00	1·00	1·00	1·02	1·04	1·09
11	1·00	1·00	1·00	1·01	1·03	1·08
12	1·00	1·00	1·00	1·00	1·02	1·07
13	1·00	1·00	1·00	1·00	1·01	1·06
14	1·00	1·00	1·00	1·00	1·00	1·05
15	1·00	1·00	1·00	1·00	1·00	1·04

stress for a strut in torsional buckling corresponds to a permissible
stress of an axially loaded strut with a slenderness ratio λ_t calculated as
shown in Table 7.17. In checking for torsional buckling, the eccentricity of connection may be ignored. Torsional buckling will not be
critical if λ_t is less than $l/r_{\min}$.

For a strut whose section has two axes of symmetry, or has point
symmetry, failure is by pure torsional buckling and the permissible
stress is obtained at $\lambda = \lambda_t$, where

$$\lambda_t = \sqrt{\dfrac{I_p}{0\cdot038J + \dfrac{H}{l^2}}} \tag{7.88}$$

Table 7.14

Stress Factor C_L for Plate Components in Compression

Unstiffened components		Stiffened components					
b/t	C_L	b/t	C_L	b/t	C_L	b/t	C_L
1	1·000	1	1·000	51	0·809	105	0·375
2	1·000	2	1·000	52	0·793	110	0·360
3	1·000	3	1·000	53	0·778	115	0·346
4	1·000	4	1·000	54	0·762	120	0·333
5	1·000	5	1·000	55	0·747	125	0·322
6	1·000	6	1·000	56	0·731	130	0·312
7	0·999	7	1·000	57	0·717	135	0·304
8	0·997	8	1·000	58	0·703	140	0·296
9	0·995	9	1·000	59	0·688	145	0·288
10	0·991	10	1·000	60	0·675	150	0·281
11	0·986	11	1·000	61	0·661	155	0·275
12	0·977	12	1·000	62	0·648	160	0·269
13	0·962	13	1·000	63	0·636	165	0·263
14	0·939	14	1·000	64	0·625	170	0·258
15	0·906	15	1·000	65	0·614	175	0·253
16	0·864	16	1·000	66	0·603	180	0·248
17	0·818	17	1·000	67	0·593	185	0·244
18	0·771	18	1·000	68	0·583	190	0·240
19	0·726	19	1·000	69	0·574	195	0·236
20	0·684	20	1·000	70	0·564	200	0·231
21	0·646	21	0·999	71	0·555	205	0·227
22	0·612	22	0·999	72	0·546	210	0·224
23	0·581	23	0·998	73	0·538	215	0·220
24	0·553	24	0·998	74	0·530	220	0·216
25	0·529	25	0·997	75	0·522	225	0·213
26	0·508	26	0·996	76	0·514	230	0·210
27	0·489	27	0·995	77	0·507	235	0·207
28	0·470	28	0·994	78	0·500	240	0·204
29	0·454	29	0·992	79	0·494	245	0·201
30	0·438	30	0·990	80	0·487	250	0·199
		31	0·989	81	0·481	255	0·196
		32	0·987	82	0·475	260	0·194
		33	0·984	83	0·469	265	0·191
		34	0·982	84	0·464	270	0·188
		35	0·978	85	0·458	275	0·186
		36	0·974	86	0·453	280	0·184
		37	0·970	87	0·448		
		38	0·964	88	0·442		
		39	0·958	89	0·437		
		40	0·951	90	0·432		
		41	0·943	91	0·428		
		42	0·934	92	0·423		
		43	0·924	93	0·419		
		44	0·912	94	0·415		
		45	0·900	95	0·411		
		46	0·885	96	0·406		
		47	0·871	97	0·402		
		48	0·856	98	0·399		
		49	0·840	99	0·395		
		50	0·825	100	0·392		

Note: Values given apply when σ_y is 250 MPa.

Table 7.15
Outstanding-leg Deductions for Single-bay Ties

Deduction per outstanding leg

Alloy	*Single angle connected through one leg*	*Two angles back-to-back connected to both sides of gusset*
H30 } H9	0·6A	0·2A
N8	0·4A	nil

Note: A is the gross area of the outstanding leg that lies clear of the connected leg, but disregarding any fillet; e.g. for a $4 \times 4 \times \frac{1}{2}$ in angle, $A = 1·75$ in^2, and for a $100 \times 100 \times 10$ mm angle, $A = 900$ mm^2.

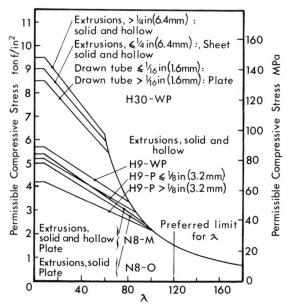

NOTE 1. For clarity, the small differences in properties of H30-WP sheet and thin tube, H30-WP plate and thick tube, and N8-O extrusions and plate, have been ignored.
NOTE 2. For column buckling, $\lambda = \ell/r$
NOTE 3. For torsional buckling, $\lambda = \lambda_t$

Fig. 7.19. Permissible compressive stress in struts.

Table 7.16
Effective Lengths of Struts

End conditions	Effective length of strut
Effectively held in position and restrained in direction at both ends	$0 \cdot 7L$
Effectively held in position at both ends and restrained in direction at one end	$0 \cdot 85L$
Effectively held in position at both ends but not restrained in direction	L
Effectively held in position and restrained in direction at one end, and partially restrained in direction but not held in position at the other end	$1 \cdot 5L$
Effectively held in position and restrained in direction at one end, but not held in position or restrained at other end	$2 \cdot 0L$

Note: L is the length of strut between points of lateral support.

I_p is the polar second moment of area about the shear centre; J is the torsion factor; H is the warping factor; and l is the effective length (clause G.2).

The effective length l depends on the warping restraints at the ends; for a strut completely restrained against warping l is $0 \cdot 5L$, while for one with no warping restraint l is L, where L is the length between lateral supports. Practical struts fall between these two extremes. Column buckling about either axis of symmetry is independent of torsional buckling and should be checked separately.

For a strut having only one axis of symmetry, the permissible stress is obtained as above at $\lambda = k\lambda_t$ or kl/r, whichever is greater, where k is the interaction coefficient given in Fig. 7.20; λ_t is the slenderness ratio for pure torsional buckling as calculated from eqn (7.88) and l/r is the slenderness ratio for ordinary column buckling in the plane normal to the axis of symmetry (i.e. about axis x–x or axis u–u). Column buckling in the plane of the axis of symmetry may take place independently of torsional buckling and should be checked separately (clause G.3).

The torsional stiffness of a thin-walled open section can be much improved by the addition of fillets or bulbs, the contribution to J of

Table 7.17
Values of λ_t for Struts

Section	Limits	Value of λ_t
	$\dfrac{R}{t} \leqslant 3$	$\dfrac{5 \cdot 2a}{t} - 1 \cdot 3\left(\dfrac{R}{t}\right)^2$
Equal circular bulbs	$\dfrac{R}{t} \leqslant 3$ $\dfrac{d}{t} \leqslant 2 \cdot 5$	$\dfrac{5 \cdot 2a}{t} - 1 \cdot 3\left(\dfrac{R}{t}\right)^2 - 2\left(\dfrac{d}{t} - 1\right)^3$ $+ 1 \cdot 5\left(\dfrac{d}{t} - 1\right)\left(\dfrac{R}{t}\right)$
Axis vv	$\dfrac{R}{t} \leqslant 3$ $1 < \dfrac{a}{b} < 2$	$\sqrt{\lambda_0^2 + \lambda_v^2 \sqrt{\dfrac{a}{b}} - 1}$ where $\lambda_0 = 2 \cdot 6\left(\dfrac{a+b}{t}\right) - 1 \cdot 3\left(\dfrac{R}{t}\right)^2$ and $\lambda_v = \dfrac{l}{r_v}$
Equal circular bulbs Axis vv	$\dfrac{R}{t} \leqslant 3$ $1 < \dfrac{a}{b} < 2$ $\dfrac{d}{t} \leqslant 2 \cdot 5$	$\sqrt{\lambda_0^2 + \lambda_v^2 \sqrt{\dfrac{a}{b}} - 1}$ where $\lambda_0 = 2 \cdot 6\left(\dfrac{a+b}{t}\right) - 1 \cdot 3\left(\dfrac{R}{t}\right)^2$ $- 2\left(\dfrac{d}{t} - 1\right)^3 + 1 \cdot 5\left(\dfrac{d}{t} - 1\right)\left(\dfrac{R}{t}\right)$ and $\lambda_v = \dfrac{l}{r_v}$
	$\dfrac{R}{t} \leqslant 3$ $0 \cdot 5 < \dfrac{a}{b} < 2$	$\sqrt{\lambda_0^2 + \lambda_y^2 \left(\dfrac{a}{2b}\right)}$ where $\lambda_0 = 1 \cdot 9\left(\dfrac{a+2b}{t}\right) - 1 \cdot 3\left(\dfrac{R}{t}\right)^2$ and $\lambda_y = \dfrac{l}{r_y}$

Table 7.17—*contd.*

Section	Limits	Value of λ_t
Equal circular bulbs	$\dfrac{R}{t} \leqslant 3$	$\sqrt{\lambda_0^2 + \lambda_y^2\left(\dfrac{a}{2b}\right)}$
	$0{\cdot}5 < \dfrac{a}{b} < 2$	where $\lambda_0 = 1{\cdot}9\left(\dfrac{a+2b}{t}\right) - 1{\cdot}3\left(\dfrac{R}{t}\right)^2$
	$\dfrac{d}{t} \leqslant 2{\cdot}5$	$-2\left(\dfrac{d}{t}-1\right)^3 + 1{\cdot}5\left(\dfrac{d}{t}-1\right)\left(\dfrac{R}{t}\right)$
		and $\lambda_y = \dfrac{l}{r_y}$

Note: l is the effective length; r_v is the radius of gyration about the axis v–v (i.e. the minimum value of r); and, r_y is the radius of gyration about the axis y–y.

such local thickenings commonly exceeding that of the basic thin rectangles. The J-contribution of such elements is given by (clause F.2):

$$J = [(p + qN)t]^4 \qquad (7.89)$$

where J = torsion constant, t is the general thickness of the parts, N is

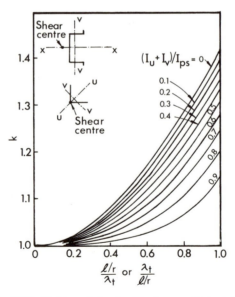

Fig. 7.20. Values of the interaction coefficient k.

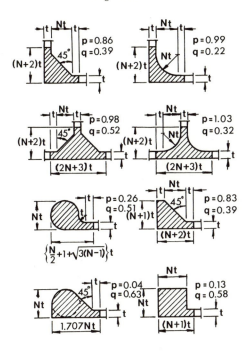

Fig. 7.21. Constants for torsion factor for certain fillets and bulbs.

the fillet or bulb dimension and p and q are empirical constants (see Fig. 7.21). The factor J for a complete cross-section is obtained by adding the fillet and bulb contributions to those of the remaining thin-walled parts, the extent of the fillet or bulb regions being as shaded in Fig. 7.21.

7.4. JAPANESE PRACTICE

Referring to Fig. 7.22 showing built-up compression members for buckling about the open web axis, i.e. the y–y axis, the effective slenderness ratio, λ_{ye}, according to Japanese practice (Architectural Institute of Japan, 1960), is given by (Article 20):

$$\lambda_{ye} = \sqrt{\lambda_{yy}^2 + \lambda_1^2} \qquad (7.90)$$

where λ_{yy} = slenderness ratio of the whole built-up member about the

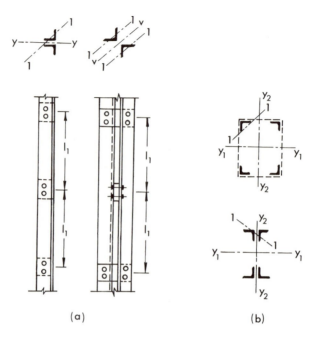

Fig. 7.22. Built-up member with (a) spacer; (b) open webs.

y–y axis; λ_1 = slenderness ratio of segment when the segment buckles independently about its minor principal axis of inertia (axis 1–1 in Fig. 7.22 with buckling length = l_1). λ_1 should not exceed 50. If $\lambda_1 \leqslant 20$, λ_{ye} can be taken as equal to λ_{yy}.

For compression members in trusses, the buckling length of leg (chord) members is found from Tables 7.18 and 7.19 (Article 21). In case of buckling in the plane of the structure, the buckling length is the distance between the panel points. When the ends of the member are connected by 2 or more rivets, the buckling length is the distance between the centres of gravity of the connecting rivets, Fig. 7.23(a). For buckling perpendicular to the plane of the structure, the buckling length for web members is the distance between the panel points (Fig. 7.23b), while that for leg (chord) members of a truss is the distance between the lateral bracing points.

When unequal compressive forces act on the halves of a member which is restrained against translation at both ends, the effective length

Table 7.18
Effective Length of Compressed Vertical Leg Members of Trusses

Shapes of trusses					
Buckling length	⌐L	KL=0.8L	KL=0.7L	KL=L	KL=L
	⊥	KL=0.9L	KL=0.85L	KL=L	KL=L
	$-\text{IL}_y^x$	$KL_x=KL_y=L$	$KL_x=L$ $KL_y=0.5L$	$KL_x=KL_y=L$	$KL_x=KL_y=L$
	$-\text{I}_y^x$	$KL_x=KL_y=L$	$KL_x=L$ $KL_y=0.5L$	$KL_x=KL_y=L$	$KL_x=KL_y=L$

Table 7.19
Effective Length of Compressed Inclined Leg Members of Trusses

Shape of trusses					
Buckling length	⌐L	KL=0.7L	KL=0.6L	KL=L	KL=L
	⊿L	KL=0.85L	KL=0.8L	KL=L	KL=L
	IL_y^x	$KL_x=KL_y=L$	$KL_x=L$ $KL_y=0.5L$	$KL_x=KL_y=L$	$KL_x=KL_y=L$
	II_y^x	$KL_x=KL_y=L$	$KL_x=L$ $KL_y=0.5L$	$KL_x=KL_y=L$	$KL_x=KL_y=L$

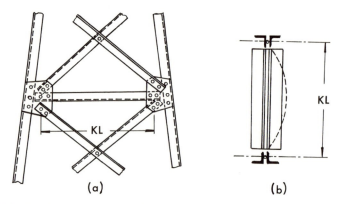

Fig. 7.23. Buckling of compression members (a) in the plane of the structure; (b) perpendicular to the plane of the structure.

is obtained from the following formula, based on the larger compressive force:

$$KL = L\left(0{\cdot}75 + 0{\cdot}25\frac{P_2}{P_1}\right) \qquad (7.91)$$

where L = length of the member (see Fig. 7.24); P_1 = larger compressive force; and, P_2 = smaller compressive force.

The above equation can also be applied when P_2 is a tensile force and $|P_2| < |P_1|$. In this case a negative sign shall be used for P_2. The buckling length of cross-braced web members is given in Fig. 7.25.

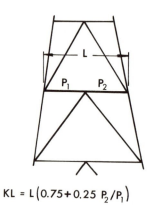

$$KL = L\left(0.75 + 0.25\ P_2/P_1\right)$$

Fig. 7.24. Effective length of member having two unequal compressive forces.

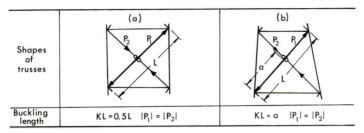

Shapes of trusses	(a)	(b)
Buckling length	KL = 0.5L $|P_1| = |P_2|$	KL = a $|P_1| = |P_2|$

Fig. 7.25. Effective length of cross-braced web members.

The Architectural Institute of Japan (1979) also provides the following specifications: Width-to-thickness ratio limits of single-angle struts and multiple-angle struts with separators are given as (chapter 8.1(1)(a)):

$$\frac{b}{t} \leqslant \frac{20}{\sqrt{F}}$$

where F is the yield stress in t/cm².

Where web members of trusses are composed of single angles and have one of their legs connected to chord members or gusset plates, their effective length shall be taken as the distance between panel points (chapter 11.4(2)). Such web members may be designed as centrally compressed members, the slenderness ratio being computed by the use of the smallest radius of gyration. Where the end connections of webs is accomplished by only one bolt, the allowable compressive stress for such webs shall be reduced by 50%.

When angles are placed only on one side of the gusset plates, design shall take into consideration eccentricity resulting from such connections. In ordinary cases, however, design computation for tension may be based on a reduced section equal to a net section less one-half the area of a projecting flange (chapter 12.3).

7.5. RESIDUAL STRESSES

Residual stress has an insignificant effect on the maximum strength of either straight or initially crooked slender angle columns with strengths determined by the Euler Column formula. On the other hand, it does have some influence on the deflection of such columns. For slender columns made of high strength steels, greater lateral deflection can be tolerated before yielding or instability occurs.

Variations in the shape of the residual stress pattern cause much smaller differences in strength for initially-curved angle columns than for initially-straight columns; a typical pattern, assumed by the ECCS Stability Manual (1976), is shown in Fig. 7.7. In the case of welding of heavy angles, the residual stress distribution is influenced by the welding procedures adopted. The assumption of constant residual stress distribution through the thickness will lead to critical loads and max-imum column strengths which are only slightly less than those derived on the basis of variation in the residual stress distribution through the thickness. Because of the improved straightness and redistribution of residual stress, the strength of a cold-straightened angle column is, in general, greater than that of the corresponding as-rolled angle column.

The column strength curve proposed by the Column Research Council (Johnston, 1976) took into account the effect of residual stress in determining the strength of a concentrically loaded column. There is a large variation in the maximum strength of steel columns depending on the residual stress distribution. However, the uncertainties in deter-mining the column strength are reduced by defining subgroups, each of which is represented by a single average curve. Research basic to the evaluation of 'multiple column curves' resulted in the adoption of column-strength curves 1, 2 and 3 by the Structural Stability Research Council (Johnston, 1976) and column-strength curves a_0, a, b, c and d, shown in Fig. 7.7, by the European Convention for Constructional Steelwork (1976). Canadian Standard S16.1-M78 (Canadian Standards Association, 1978) considers Column Curve 2 as the basic curve for determining the factored compressive resistances of hot-rolled sec-tions. In terms of the non-dimensional slenderness ratio

$$\frac{\lambda}{\lambda_y} = \frac{KL/r}{\pi\sqrt{E/\sigma_y}}$$

the following set of equations provides closefitting approximation to the derived column strength curve:

Column Curve 2

a)   For $0 \leqslant \dfrac{\lambda}{\lambda_y} \leqslant 0 \cdot 15$, $\sigma_{cr} = \sigma_y$

b)   For $0 \cdot 15 \leqslant \dfrac{\lambda}{\lambda_y} \leqslant 1 \cdot 0$,

$$\sigma_{cr} = \sigma_y \left[1 \cdot 035 - 0 \cdot 202 \frac{\lambda}{\lambda_y} - 0 \cdot 222 \left(\frac{\lambda}{\lambda_y} \right)^2 \right] \qquad (7 \cdot 92)$$

c) For $1 \cdot 0 \leqslant \dfrac{\lambda}{\lambda_y} \leqslant 2 \cdot 0$,

$$\sigma_{cr} = \sigma_y \left[-0 \cdot 111 + 0 \cdot 636 \left(\frac{\lambda_y}{\lambda} \right) + 0 \cdot 087 \left(\frac{\lambda_y}{\lambda} \right)^2 \right]$$

d) For $2 \cdot 0 \leqslant \dfrac{\lambda}{\lambda_y} \leqslant 3 \cdot 6$, $\qquad \sigma_{cr} = \sigma_y \left[0 \cdot 009 + 0 \cdot 877 \left(\frac{\lambda_y}{\lambda} \right)^2 \right]$

e) For $\dfrac{\lambda}{\lambda_y} \geqslant 3 \cdot 6$, $\qquad \sigma_{cr} = \sigma_y \left(\dfrac{\lambda_y}{\lambda} \right)^2$ (= Euler curve)

7.6. SOME OBSERVATIONS ON THE VARIOUS CODES OF PRACTICE

The Canadian Standard Specifications CAN 3-S161-M78 are limit states design specifications; they have performance factors built into them. In contrast, the American Iron and Steel Institute (1980), American Institute of Steel Construction (1978), Architectural Institute of Japan (1960, 1979), and German (DIN 4114, 1952) specifications are based on allowable stress. Design Standard for Steel Structures (Architectural Institute of Japan, 1979), Standard for Structural Calculation of Steel Tower Structures (Architectural Institute of Japan, 1960), ECCS Stability Manual (1976), German Specifications (DIN 4114, 1952), Canadian Specifications for Aluminium Structures (Canadian Standards Association, 1983) specify increasing the slenderness ratio of a compound angle member when buckling about the non-material axis is considered. Refer to the definition of σ_e in eqn (7.32); and eqns (7.54), (7.64), (7.66), (7.73), (7.74), (7.90). This increase is dependent on the spacing of the connecting fasteners. No such increase is specified in the American, Australian, British or in the Canadian Standards for hot-rolled and cold-formed steel structures (Canadian Standards Association 1978, 1981, 1984).

If the compressive force acting on the member is not constant throughout the length due to joint details (see Fig. 7.24), then according to the German and Japanese specifications, the effective length of the member is computed on the basis of the relative magnitudes of the larger and smaller compressive forces (refer to eqn (7.91)). However, no such requirements are specified in the other standards.

The slenderness ratios of eccentrically loaded single-angle members are modified in the ASCE Manual No. 52, the ECCS Stability Manual (1976), and in the ECCS Recommendations (1978) to make use of the formulas applicable to concentrically loaded angles. This is to simplify the design of such members. Canadian Standard S37-M1981, AIJ Standard for Steel Structures (1979), British Standard Specifications BS 449 : 1969, and German Specifications (DIN 4114, 1952) ignore the eccentricity in the design of eccentrically loaded single-angle members in compression, and limit the strength of such angles to a certain percentage of the strength of corresponding concentric axially loaded angles. However, similar design simplifications are not allowed in other specifications. Australian Standard AS 1250-1981 and Specifications of the American Institute of Steel Construction (1978) specifically mention that eccentricity cannot be ignored and that such members shall be designed as members under biaxial bending. Since single angles are mostly used as web members in latticed towers which are highly statically indeterminate, taking the eccentricity into account increases considerably the computational effort. Therefore, it seems reasonable and judicious to simplify the design as suggested by the ASCE Manual No. 52 and the ECCS Recommendations.

7.7. SOLVED EXAMPLES

Example 7.1
Given a $150 \times 150 \times 10$ mm size hot-rolled angle with one leg connected by three bolts at each end. Compute the ultimate strength according to (a) ASCE Manual No. 52; (b) ECCS Recommendations; and (c) CSA S37-M1981.

Length of member = 5000 mm (196.85 in); cross-sectional area = 2900 mm² (4·495 in²); minimum radius of gyration = 29·8 mm (1·173 in); and yield stress = 300 MPa (43 511 psi). Assume a fillet radius of 13 mm.

Solution

(a) *ASCE Manual No. 52.*

$$\frac{b}{t} \text{ ratio} = \frac{150 - 10 - 13}{10} = 12·7$$

$$\left(\frac{b}{t}\right)_{\text{limit}} = \frac{2500}{\sqrt{\sigma_y}} = \frac{2500}{\sqrt{43\,511}} = 12 \cdot 0$$

$$\therefore \quad \left(\frac{b}{t}\right) > \left(\frac{b}{t}\right)_{\text{limit}}$$

From eqn (7.1),

$$\sigma_{y_{\text{eff}}} = \left[1 \cdot 8 - \frac{(0 \cdot 8)(12 \cdot 7)}{12 \cdot 0}\right] \times 43\,511 = 41\,480 \text{ psi}$$

From eqn (7.5),

$$C_c = \pi \sqrt{\frac{(2)(29\,000\,000)}{41\,480}} = 117 \cdot 5$$

$$\frac{L}{r_{\min}} = \frac{196 \cdot 85}{1 \cdot 173} = 167 \cdot 8$$

The member is partially restrained against rotation at both ends. Therefore, from eqn (7.11),

$$\frac{KL}{r} = 46 \cdot 2 + (0 \cdot 615)(167 \cdot 8) = 149 \cdot 4 > C_c$$

From eqn (7.4),

$$\sigma_{cr} = \frac{286\,000\,000}{(149 \cdot 4)^2} = 12\,812 \text{ psi}$$

Failure load $= (12\,812)(4 \cdot 495) = 57\,590 \text{ lb } (256 \cdot 2 \text{ kN})$

(b) *ECCS Recommendations.* From eqn (7.48),

$$\lambda_y = \pi \sqrt{\frac{E}{\sigma_y}}$$

$$= \pi \sqrt{\frac{210\,000}{300}} = 83 \cdot 12$$

From (a),

$$\lambda = \frac{L}{r_{\min}} = 167 \cdot 8$$

$$\frac{\lambda}{\lambda_y} = \frac{167 \cdot 8}{83 \cdot 12} = 2 \cdot 019$$

$1 \cdot 41 \leqslant \lambda/\lambda_y \leqslant 3 \cdot 5$. Assuming the chords provide good end-restraint to the web member, from eqn (7.47),

$$\left(\frac{\lambda}{\lambda_y}\right)_{\text{eff}} = 0 \cdot 35 + 0 \cdot 75(2 \cdot 109) = 1 \cdot 864$$

From the non-dimensional buckling curve 'b' (Table 7.5(a)), for $\lambda/\lambda_y = 1 \cdot 864$, $\sigma_{cr}/\sigma_y = 0 \cdot 2353$. Therefore

$$\sigma_{cr} = (0 \cdot 2353)(300) = 70 \cdot 59 \text{ MPa}$$

$$\text{Failure load} = (70 \cdot 59)(2900) = 204\ 711 \text{ N} = 204 \cdot 7 \text{ kN}$$

This is less than $256 \cdot 2$ kN obtained in (a).

(c) *CSA S37-M1981.*

$$\frac{L}{r_{\text{min}}} = 167 \cdot 8, \text{ as in (a) above.}$$

From Table 7.1, for a single angle connected by two or more bolts, effective length factor $K = 0 \cdot 9$. Thus

$$\lambda = \frac{KL}{r_{\text{min}}} = (0 \cdot 9)(167 \cdot 8) = 151$$

$$\frac{\lambda}{\lambda_y} = \frac{151}{\pi\sqrt{\dfrac{E}{\sigma_y}}} = \frac{151}{\pi\sqrt{\dfrac{200\ 000}{300}}} = 1 \cdot 862$$

From eqn (7.92),

$$\sigma_{cr} = 300\left(-0 \cdot 111 + \frac{0 \cdot 636}{1 \cdot 862} + \frac{0 \cdot 087}{1 \cdot 862^2}\right)$$

$$= 76 \cdot 7 \text{ MPa}$$

Hence, the compressive resistance (unfactored) $= (2900)(76 \cdot 7)$

$$= 222\ 430 \text{ N}$$

$$= 222 \cdot 4 \text{ kN}$$

Example 7.2

Determine the torsional–flexural buckling stress of a $150 \times 150 \times 10$ mm hot-rolled angle using AISI Specifications.

Length $= 5000$ mm; $E = 200$ GPa; $G = 78$ GPa.

Solution

In AISI Specifications, x–x axis is taken as the principal axis of symmetry. Since we are using Table 1.1(a), we will substitute u for x in the equations given in Section 7.2.2.1. Thus, from Table 1.1(a), $u_s = \sqrt{(x_s^2 + y_s^2)} = \sqrt{(36 \cdot 2^2 + 36 \cdot 2^2)} = 51 \cdot 19 \, \text{mm}$, $I_u = (10 \cdot 2)(10^6) \, \text{mm}^4$, $A = 2900 \, \text{mm}^2$,

$$r_u = \sqrt{\frac{(10 \cdot 2)(10^6)}{2900}} = 59 \cdot 31 \, \text{mm}$$

$$r_{ps} = \sqrt{\frac{I_{ps}}{A}} = \sqrt{\frac{(20 \cdot 3)(10^6)}{2900}} = 83 \cdot 67 \, \text{mm}$$

$$J = (96 \cdot 7)(10^3) \, \text{mm}^4, \qquad C_w = (169)(10^6) \, \text{mm}^6$$

KL/r_u about the axis of symmetry (assuming $K = 1$) = $(1 \cdot 0)(5000)/59 \cdot 31 = 84 \cdot 3$. From Section 7.2.2.1,

$$\sigma_{tf} = \frac{1}{2\beta} [(\sigma_{eu} + \sigma_t) - \sqrt{(\sigma_{eu} + \sigma_t)^2 - 4\beta\sigma_{eu}\sigma_t}]$$

$$\sigma_{eu} = \frac{\pi^2 E}{\left(\dfrac{KL}{r_u}\right)^2} = \frac{(\pi^2)(200\,000)}{(84 \cdot 3)^2} = 277 \cdot 7 \, \text{MPa.}$$

$$\sigma_t = \frac{1}{A r_{ps}^2} \left[GJ + \frac{\pi^2 E C_w}{(KL)^2} \right]$$

$$= \frac{1}{(2900)(83 \cdot 67)^2} \left[(78\,000)(96\,700) + \frac{(\pi^2)(200\,000)(169 \times 10^6)}{(1 \times 5000)^2} \right]$$

$$= 372 \cdot 2 \, \text{MPa.}$$

$$\beta = 1 - \left(\frac{u_s}{r_{ps}}\right)^2 = 1 - \left(\frac{51 \cdot 19}{83 \cdot 67}\right)^2 = 0 \cdot 6257$$

Substituting these values in the equation the torsional–flexural buckling stress

$$\sigma_{tf} = \frac{1}{(2)(0 \cdot 6257)} [(277 \cdot 7 + 372 \cdot 2)$$

$$- \sqrt{(277 \cdot 7 + 372 \cdot 2)^2 - (4)(0 \cdot 6257)(277 \cdot 7)(372 \cdot 2)}]$$

$$= 196 \, \text{MPa.}$$

Chapter 8

DESIGN AIDS

8.1. INTRODUCTION

In this chapter, the design aids available for the design of angle sections, which were not mentioned in earlier chapters, are discussed. Some of these aids are in the form of design tables, while others are in the form of graphs, interaction equations and computer programs. The analysis and design of tension members is relatively easy. For the analysis/design of angle beams, safe load tables in Imperial and SI units were given in Chapter 3 for the most common hot-rolled angle sections. For the design of connections, design tables are available in handbooks such as the AISC Manual (American Institute of Steel Construction, 1980) and the CISC Handbook (Canadian Institute of Steel Construction, 1980). In addition, American Institute of Steel Construction (1982) has design tables for predesigned framing angle connections to reduce time and cost.

The design of angle members subjected to either axial or eccentric compression is relatively more time-consuming; this chapter deals with the aids available for the design of such members. One such aid is shown in Fig. 8.1 which gives the approximate values of radii of gyration for single and compound angles of conventional proportions.

8.2. DESIGN AIDS GIVEN IN AISI COLD-FORMED STEEL DESIGN MANUAL (AMERICAN IRON AND STEEL INSTITUTE, 1971, 1977)

8.2.1. Linear Method for Computing the Properties of Cold-formed Angles

Computation of the properties of cold-formed angles is considerably simplified by using a linear method. In this method, the material of the

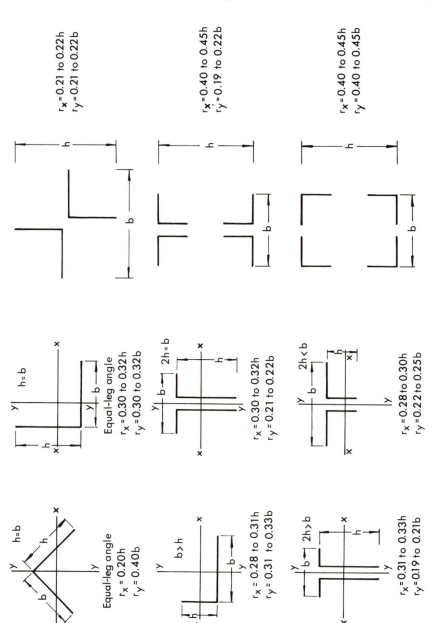

Fig. 8.1. Radii of gyration for some single and compound angles.

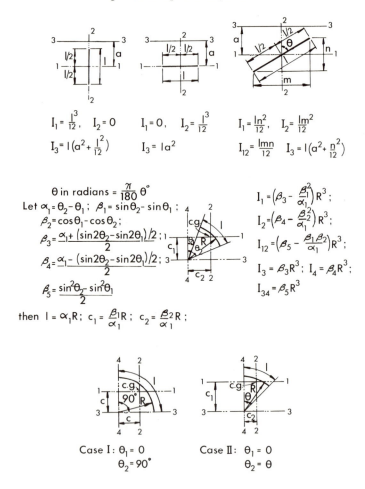

Fig. 8.2. Geometric properties of some line elements.

section is assumed concentrated along the centreline of the angle and the area elements are replaced by line elements (straight line elements and circular arch elements). The lengths, moments of inertia, and the location of the centroid of such elements are given in Fig. 8.2. After completing the linear computations, the values are multiplied by the thickness 't' of the angle section to obtain the area, moment of inertia, etc. of the angle section, e.g

Area of angle section = (Total centreline length) × (Thickness)
and

Moment of inertia of angle section about centroidal axis =
(Total moment of inertia of the line elements about the
centroidal axis) × (Thickness)

8.2.2. Axially Compressed Equal-leg Angles

Such angles can fail either by flexural or by torsional–flexural buckling.
To determine the mode of failure, reference is made to Fig. 8.3. If the
effective length KL of the angle member is greater than the critical
length L_{cr} given in Fig. 8.3, the member fails by flexural buckling.
When $KL < L_{cr}$, the member fails by torsional–flexural buckling. If it is
predicted that failure is by torsional–flexural buckling, the allowable

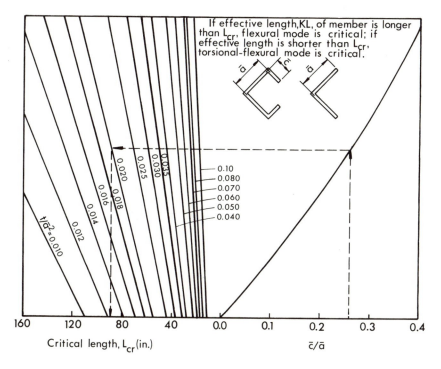

Fig. 8.3. Buckling mode for equal-leg angles with or without lips.

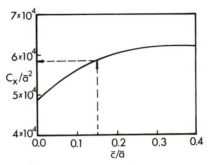

Fig. 8.4. $c_x/\bar{a}^2$ for equal-leg angles with or without lips.

average axial stress σ_a is calculated in *inch-kip units* as follows:

(a) Determine the ratio $\bar{c}/\bar{a}$ for the angle section ($\bar{c}$ and $\bar{a}$ are shown in Fig. 8.3).

(b) Obtain $c_x/\bar{a}^2$ from Fig. 8.4.

(c) Calculate the Euler buckling stress for buckling about the symmetric x–x axis, σ_{ex}, from

$$\sigma_{ex} = \left(\frac{c_x}{\bar{a}^2}\right)\left(\frac{\bar{a}}{KL}\right)^2 \tag{8.1}$$

(d) Obtain $\sigma_{t0}(\bar{a}/t)^2$ from Fig. 8.5, and $c_T/\bar{a}^2$ from Fig. 8.6.

(e) Calculate the torsional buckling stress σ_t from the following expression:

$$\sigma_t = \sigma_{t0}\left(\frac{\bar{a}}{t}\right)^2\left(\frac{t}{\bar{a}}\right)^2 + \left(\frac{c_T}{\bar{a}^2}\right)\left(\frac{\bar{a}}{KL}\right)^2 \tag{8.2}$$

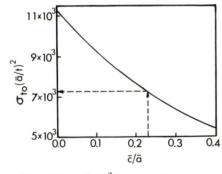

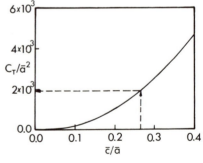

Fig. 8.5. $\sigma_{t0}(\bar{a}/t)^2$ for equal-leg angles with or without lips.

Fig. 8.6. $c_T/\bar{a}^2$ for equal-leg angles with or without lips.

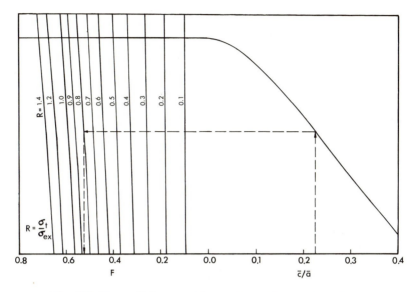

Fig. 8.7. Factor F for equal-leg angles with or without lips.

(f) Determine R

$$R = \frac{\sigma_t}{\sigma_{ex}} \qquad (8.3)$$

(g) From Fig. 8.7, obtain the factor F.

(h) Torsional–flexural buckling stress for axially compressed equal-leg angle, σ_{tf} is given by

$$\sigma_{tf} = (F)(\sigma_{ex}) \qquad (8.4)$$

(i) The allowable average axial stress $\sigma_a (= P/A)$ is given by the following expressions:

If $\sigma_{tf} > 0 \cdot 5\sigma_y$,

$$\sigma_a = 0 \cdot 522\sigma_y - \frac{\sigma_y^2}{7 \cdot 67\sigma_{tf}} \qquad (8.5)$$

If $\sigma_{tf} \leqslant 0 \cdot 5\sigma_y$, then

$$\sigma_a = 0 \cdot 522\sigma_{tf} \qquad (8.6)$$

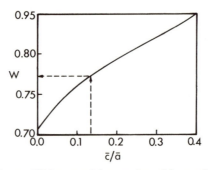

Fig. 8.8. Factor W for equal-leg angles with or without lips.

8.23. Torsional–Flexural Buckling Stress of Eccentrically Compressed Equal-leg Angles

Here it is assumed that bending is in the plane of symmetry and that the load is on the side of the centroid away from the shear centre, i.e. positive eccentricity. Hence

(a) Compute σ_{tf} following the steps specified in section 8.2.2 above.

(b) Obtain the factor W from Fig. 8.8 and use $R = \sigma_t/\sigma_{ex}$ to obtain the factor G_1 from Fig. 8.9.

(c) Compute M_T from

$$M_T = A\sigma_{ex}\bar{a}WG_1 \qquad (8.7)$$

in which $M_T =$ elastic critical moment causing tension on the shear centre side of the centroid, kip-in; and $A =$ area of the cross-section.

(d) Calculate σ_e, the Euler buckling stress for buckling about the axis of bending

$$\sigma_e = \frac{\pi^2 E}{\left(\dfrac{KL_b}{r_b}\right)^2} \qquad (8.8)$$

where $KL_b =$ effective length in plane of bending; and $r_b =$ radius of gyration about the axis of bending.

(e) Calculate the buckling stress parameters ϕ_1 and ϕ_2 from

$$\phi_1 = (\sigma_{tf})(\sigma_e) \qquad (8.9)$$

$$\phi_2 = (\sigma_{tf} + \sigma_e) + \frac{C_{TF}eA}{M_T}\phi_1 \qquad (8.10)$$

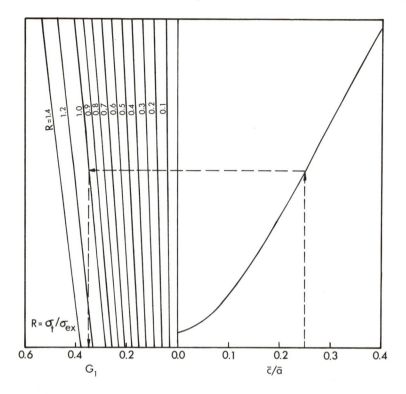

Fig. 8.9. Factor G_1 for equal-leg angles with or without lips.

where e = eccentricity of applied load with respect to the centroid; and C_{TF} = a coefficient whose value is taken as follows: For compression members in frames subjected to joint translation (side sway), $C_{TF} = 0 \cdot 85$. For restrained compression members in frames braced against joint translation, $C_{TF} = 0 \cdot 6 - 0 \cdot 4(M_1/M_2)$ where M_1/M_2 is the ratio of the smaller to the larger moment at the ends of that portion of the member, unbraced in the plane of bending under consideration. M_1/M_2 is positive when the member is bent in double curvature and negative when bent in single curvature.

(f)   Calculate the torsional–flexural buckling stress, σ_{tf}, as

$$\sigma_{tf} = \tfrac{1}{2}\lfloor \phi_2 - \sqrt{\phi_2^2 - 4\phi_1} \rfloor \qquad (8.11)$$

(g)   Calculate the allowable average axial stress σ_a as follows:

If $\sigma_{tf} > 0.5\sigma_y$,

$$\sigma_a = 0.522\sigma_y - \frac{\sigma_y^2}{7.67\sigma_{tf}} \tag{8.12}$$

If $\sigma_{tf} \leq 0.5\sigma_y$,

$$\sigma_a = 0.522\sigma_{tf} \tag{8.13}$$

In eqns (8.5), (8.6), (8.12) and (8.13), it is assumed that the entire section is effective. Otherwise, the term 'σ_y' should be replaced by '$Q\sigma_y$' where Q is a factor specified in clause 3.6.1.1 of AISI specification (American Iron and Steel Institute, 1980).

8.3. INTERACTION CURVES OF CHEN AND ATSUTA

A simple method to obtain interaction relationships of general sections composed of rectangular elements which meet each other at right angles was presented by Chen and Atsuta (1972, 1974). The method is applicable to unequal angles, equal angles, compound angles, etc. Typical interaction curves are shown in Figs 8.10 and 8.11. These are

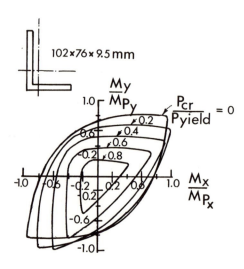

Fig. 8.10. Interaction curves of a single-angle section.

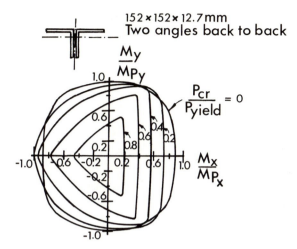

Fig. 8.11. Interaction curves of a double-angle section.

based on the following equations:

$$\frac{P_{cr}}{P_{yield}} = 1 - 2 \sum A_i/A$$

$$\frac{M_x}{M_{px}} = 2 \sum Q_{xi}/Z_x \tag{8.14}$$

and

$$\frac{M_y}{M_{py}} = -2 \sum Q_{yi}/Z_y$$

in which A_i = area of ith element above the neutral axis; A = area of the entire cross-section; Q_{xi}, Q_{yi} = static moments of area above the neutral axis of the ith element; Z_x, Z_y = plastic section moduli; P_{cr} = axial force; P_{yield} = axial force at yielding; and M_{px}, M_{py} = plastic moments about the x and y axes. The formulation and the method are found to be extremely powerful and efficient for computer programming. Figure 8.10 shows the interaction curve of a $102 \times 76 \times 9.5$ mm angle section. The largest oval loop represents the interaction curve without any axial force, i.e. $P_{cr}/P_{yield} = 0$; as the axial force increases, the loop becomes smaller. Since the section has no axis of symmetry, the interaction curves also have no symmetry. Figure 8.11 shows the interaction curves for a compound angle section consisting of two

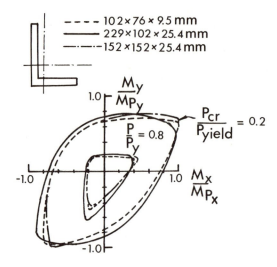

Fig. 8.12. Comparison of interaction curves for various single-angle sections.

equal angles $152 \times 152 \times 12 \cdot 7$ mm connected back to back; here the interaction curves have one axis of symmetry. In order to investigate the effect of cross-section sizes on the interaction curves, two extreme size angle sections $229 \times 102 \times 25 \cdot 4$ mm and $152 \times 152 \times 25 \cdot 4$ mm were investigated; their interaction curves are shown in Fig. 8.12. These curves were found to be close to the interaction curves for the $102 \times 76 \times 9 \cdot 5$ mm angle section. Variations of the interaction curves

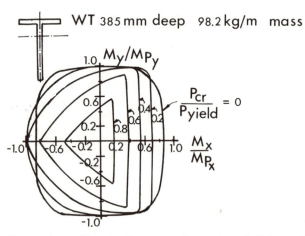

Fig. 8.13. Comparison of interaction curves for various double-angle sections.

due to different thicknesses of the same shape were also investigated and were found to have an insignificant effect. Based on these results, Chen and Atsuta (1974) recommended that Fig. 8.10 be taken to represent the interaction curve for all single angles. The same procedure was followed for compound angles and similar conclusions were arrived at; as a result, Chen and Atsuta (1974) recommended that Fig. 8.11 be taken to represent the interaction curves for all compound angles consisting of two angles connected back to back. As expected, the interaction curves for a T-section shown in Fig. 8.13 are almost identical to the interaction curves for a double-angle section shown in Fig. 8.11. It should be noted that these interaction equations and curves apply only to stocky members which cannot fail by buckling.

8.4. DESIGN TABLES AND GRAPHS IN HANDBOOKS

The following are some of the design tables available:

1. *Handbook of Steel Construction* published by the Canadian Institute of Steel Construction, (1980) gives factored axial compressive resistances for double-angle struts on pages 4–122 to 4–141; these are based on clause 13.3 of CAN3-S16.1-M78 of the Canadian Standards Association (1978).

2. *Manual of Steel Construction* published by the American Institute of Steel Construction (1980) gives the allowable concentric loads on double-angle columns on pages 3–49 to 3–75; these are based on Section 1.5.1.3 of the Specifications of the American Institute of Steel Construction (1978).

It is important to note that the safe load tables for double-angle struts given in the CISC *Handbook of Steel Construction* and the AISC *Manual of Steel Construction* assume that the two component angles of a double-angle strut work together as a single unit. If the actual behaviour of the double-angle strut is different from the above (due to deficiencies in the number of intermediate fasteners), then the tables give values which are unsafe. It is for this reason that the European Recommendations (European Convention for Constructional Steelwork, 1978) specify that the safe loads of compound angles be based on the slenderness ratio of not only the compound angle itself but also on the slenderness ratio of each of the component angles between the stitch bolts (refer to eqn (7.54)).

3. *Handbook of Structural Stability* edited by the Column Research Committee of Japan (1971) has several tables and graphs to aid the

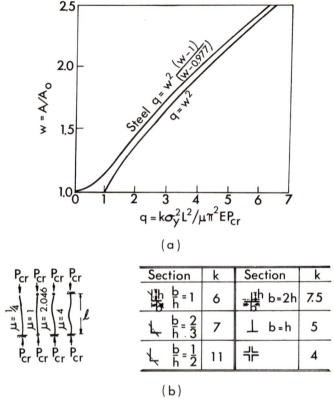

(a)

(b)

Fig. 8.14. Design of concentrically loaded single and compound angles and T-sections for flexural buckling.

designer in routine design calculations, two of which are shown in Figs 8.14 and 8.15. Figure 8.14 is used to determine the required cross-sectional area, A, of concentrically loaded single and compound angles and T-sections which fail by flexural buckling due to a critical load P_{cr}. The table in Fig. 8.14 gives the approximate value of section number k ($k = A^2/I$, where A is the area of the cross-section and I is the moment of inertia) for the chosen cross-section; the influence of the wall thickness has been ignored in the tabulated k values which correspond to average values of commonly used width–thickness ratios. The coefficient μ is associated with end restraint and is obtained from Fig. 8.14(b). The term q can then be computed and the corresponding w for steel columns is obtained from the upper curve in Fig.

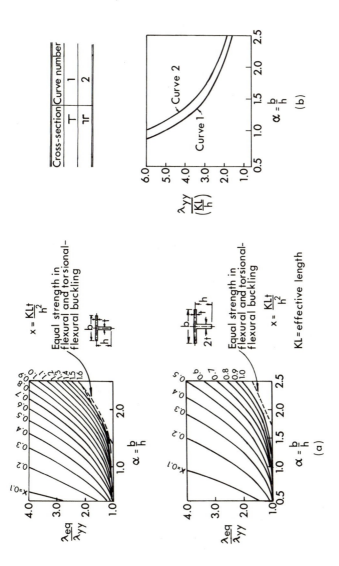

Fig. 8.15. Design of concentrically loaded double angles and T-sections for torsional–flexural buckling.

8.14(a). (The lower curve, viz., the square parabola $q = w^2$ gives values of w required when the column buckles in the elastic range according to the Euler formula.) The required cross-sectional area of the column is then $A = (w)(A_0) = (w)(P_{cr}/\sigma_y)$.

Figure 8.15 is used to compute the torsional–flexural buckling loads, P_{cr}, of double angle sections (connected back-to-back) and T-sections of known cross-sectional geometry. From Fig. 8.15(a), $\lambda_{eq}/\lambda_{yy}$ is obtained from the dimensions and end-conditions of the member; λ_{eq} is computed after finding the value of λ_{yy} from Fig. 8.15(b) (λ_{yy} is the slenderness ratio with respect to the symmetric y–y axis). The torsional–flexural buckling load is then calculated as $P_{cr} = \pi^2 EA/\lambda_{eq}^2$.

8.5. COMPUTER PROGRAMS AND LOAD TABLES

Several computer programs were developed for the calculation of load-carrying capacities of angles in compression as shown below. These computer programs are available from the authors.

1. Safe loads of axially loaded angles, and of angles connected by one leg according to *Specification for the Design, Fabrication and Erection of Structural Steel for Buildings*, American Institute of Steel Construction (1978).
2. Ultimate loads of angles according to the *Guide for Design of Steel Transmission Towers*, Manual No. 52 of the American Society of Civil Engineers (1971).
3. Safe loads of axially loaded cold-formed angles according to the *Specification for the Design of Cold-formed Steel Structural Members*, American Iron and Steel Institute (1980).
4. Buckling loads of axially and eccentrically loaded angles according to the *European Recommendations for Steel Construction*, European Convention for Constructional Steelwork (1978).
5. Buckling loads of cold-formed angle members connected by one leg (under biaxial bending) according to the classical theory of torsional–flexural buckling discussed in Chapter 4.

The safe load tables according to AISC Specification (1978) and AISI Specification (1980) are given in Tables 8.1 and 8.2. Buckling loads of some selected cold-formed angle sections (listed in Table 1.3) connected by one leg are given in Table 8.3.

Table 8.1(a)

Permissible Axial Loads (kips) for Hot-Rolled Equal-Leg Single Angles, According to AISC[a] Specifications ($\sigma_y = 36$ ksi)

KL/r_{min}	$8 \times 8 \times 1\frac{1}{8}$	$8 \times 8 \times 1$	$8 \times 8 \times \frac{7}{8}$	$8 \times 8 \times \frac{3}{4}$	$8 \times 8 \times \frac{5}{8}$	$8 \times 8 \times \frac{1}{2}$	$6 \times 6 \times 1$	$6 \times 6 \times \frac{7}{8}$
20	344	309	272	235	197	146	227	200
30	333	299	263	227	191	141	219	194
40	320	288	253	219	184	136	211	187
50	306	275	242	209	176	131	202	179
60	291	261	230	199	167	125	192	170
70	274	246	217	187	157	118	181	160
80	256	230	203	175	147	111	169	149
90	237	213	188	162	136	104	156	138
100	217	195	171	148	125	95·6	143	126
110	195	175	154	133	112	87·1	128	114
120	172	154	136	117	98·8	78·0	113	100
130	148	133	117	101	84·9	68·4	97·2	86·0
140	127	114	101	86·9	73·2	59·0	83·8	74·1
150	111	99·6	87·6	75·7	63·8	51·4	73·0	64·6
160	97·4	87·5	77·0	66·5	56·1	45·2	64·2	56·8
170	86·3	77·5	68·2	58·9	49·7	40·0	56·8	50·3
180	77·0	69·1	60·8	52·5	44·3	35·7	50·7	44·8
190	69·1	62·0	54·6	47·2	39·8	32·1	45·5	40·2
200	62·3	56·0	49·3	42·6	35·9	28·9	41·1	36·3
210	56·5	50·8	44·7	38·6	32·5	26·2	37·2	32·9
220	51·5	46·3	40·7	35·2	29·7	23·9	33·9	30·0
230	47·1	42·3	37·3	32·2	27·1	21·9	31·1	27·5
240	43·3	38·9	34·2	29·6	24·9	20·1	28·5	25·2

[a] American Institute of Steel Construction (1978).

Table 8.1(a)—*contd.*

KL/r_{min}	$6\times6\times\frac{3}{4}$	$6\times6\times\frac{5}{8}$	$6\times6\times\frac{1}{2}$	$6\times6\times\frac{3}{8}$	$5\times5\times\frac{7}{8}$	$5\times5\times\frac{3}{4}$	$5\times5\times\frac{1}{2}$	$5\times5\times\frac{3}{8}$
20	174	146	118	82·0	164	143	97·8	73·1
30	168	142	115	79·6	159	138	94·7	70·8
40	162	136	110	76·8	153	133	91·2	68·2
50	155	130	106	73·7	146	127	87·2	65·2
60	147	124	100	70·3	139	121	82·8	62·0
70	139	117	94·5	66·6	131	114	78·0	58·5
80	130	109	88·3	62·6	123	107	72·9	54·7
90	120	101	81·7	58·3	113	98·6	67·5	50·7
100	110	92·3	74·6	53·8	104	90·1	61·6	46·4
110	98·5	83·0	67·1	49·0	93·1	81·0	55·4	41·9
120	86·8	73·1	59·1	43·9	82·1	71·4	48·8	37·0
130	74·6	62·8	50·8	38·5	70·5	61·3	42·0	31·9
140	64·3	54·2	43·8	33·2	60·8	52·9	36·2	27·5
150	56·0	47·2	38·2	28·9	53·0	46·1	31·5	24·0
160	49·2	41·5	33·5	25·4	46·5	40·5	27·7	21·1
170	43·6	36·7	29·7	22·5	41·2	35·9	24·5	18·7
180	38·9	32·8	26·5	20·1	36·8	32·0	21·9	16·6
190	34·9	29·4	23·8	18·0	33·0	28·7	19·6	14·9
200	31·5	26·5	21·5	16·3	29·8	25·9	17·7	13·5
210	28·6	24·1	19·5	14·8	27·0	23·5	16·1	12·2
220	26·0	21·9	17·7	13·5	24·6	21·4	14·7	11·1
230	23·8	20·1	16·2	12·3	22·5	19·6	13·4	10·2
240	21·9	18·4	14·9	11·3	20·7	18·0	12·3	9·36

KL/r_{min}	$5 \times 5 \times \frac{5}{16}$	$4 \times 4 \times \frac{3}{4}$	$4 \times 4 \times \frac{5}{8}$	$4 \times 4 \times \frac{1}{2}$	$4 \times 4 \times \frac{3}{8}$	$4 \times 4 \times \frac{5}{16}$	$4 \times 4 \times \frac{1}{4}$	$3\frac{1}{2} \times 3\frac{1}{2} \times \frac{3}{8}$
20	57·0	112	95·0	77·2	58·9	49·3	36·5	51·1
30	55·3	108	91·9	74·8	57·0	47·7	35·4	49·5
40	53·4	104	88·5	72·0	54·9	45·9	34·2	47·6
50	51·2	99·8	84·6	68·8	52·5	43·9	32·8	45·5
60	48·8	94·8	80·4	65·4	49·8	41·7	31·3	43·2
70	46·3	89·4	75·7	61·6	47·0	39·3	29·6	40·7
80	43·5	83·5	70·8	57·6	43·9	36·8	27·8	38·1
90	40·5	77·3	65·5	53·3	40·6	34·0	26·0	35·2
100	37·4	70·6	59·8	48·7	37·1	31·1	23·9	32·2
110	34·0	63·5	53·8	43·8	33·4	28·0	21·8	28·9
120	30·5	55·9	47·4	38·6	29·4	24·7	19·5	25·5
130	26·7	48·1	40·7	33·1	25·3	21·2	17·1	21·9
140	23·1	41·4	35·1	28·6	21·8	18·3	14·8	18·9
150	20·1	36·1	30·6	24·9	19·0	15·9	12·9	16·5
160	17·7	31·7	26·9	21·9	16·7	14·0	11·3	14·5
170	15·7	28·1	23·8	19·4	14·8	12·4	10·0	12·8
180	14·0	25·1	21·2	17·3	13·2	11·1	8·94	11·4
190	12·5	22·5	19·1	15·5	11·8	9·93	8·03	10·3
200	11·3	20·3	17·2	14·0	10·7	8·96	7·24	9·26
210	10·3	18·4	15·6	12·7	9·68	8·13	6·57	8·40
220	9·35	16·8	14·2	11·6	8·82	7·40	5·99	7·65
230	8·55	15·4	13·0	10·6	8·07	6·77	5·48	7·00
240	7·86	14·1	12·0	9·72	7·41	6·22	5·03	6·43

[a] American Institute of Steel Construction (1978).

Table 8.1(a)—*contd.*

KL/r_{min}	$3\frac{1}{2}\times3\frac{1}{2}\times\frac{5}{16}$	$3\frac{1}{2}\times3\frac{1}{2}\times\frac{1}{4}$	$3\times3\times\frac{1}{2}$	$3\times3\times\frac{3}{8}$	$3\times3\times\frac{5}{16}$	$3\times3\times\frac{1}{4}$	$3\times3\times\frac{3}{16}$	$2\frac{1}{2}\times2\frac{1}{2}\times\frac{3}{8}$
20	43·1	33·6	56·6	43·5	36·7	29·7	20·5	35·6
30	41·7	32·6	54·8	42·1	35·5	28·7	19·9	34·5
40	40·1	31·4	52·8	40·5	34·2	27·6	19·2	33·2
50	38·4	30·0	50·5	38·7	32·7	26·4	18·4	31·7
60	36·4	28·6	47·9	36·8	31·0	25·1	17·6	30·2
70	34·3	27·0	45·2	34·7	29·2	23·7	16·6	28·4
80	32·1	25·3	42·2	32·4	27·3	22·1	15·6	26·6
90	29·7	23·5	39·1	30·0	25·3	20·5	14·6	24·6
100	27·1	21·5	35·7	27·4	23·1	18·7	13·5	22·5
110	24·4	19·5	32·1	24·6	20·8	16·8	12·2	20·2
120	21·5	17·3	28·3	21·7	18·3	14·8	11·0	17·8
130	18·5	14·9	24·3	18·6	15·7	12·7	9·62	15·3
140	15·9	12·9	21·0	16·1	13·6	11·0	8·30	13·2
150	13·9	11·2	18·3	14·0	11·8	9·56	7·23	11·5
160	12·2	9·86	16·0	12·3	10·4	8·40	6·36	10·1
170	10·8	8·73	14·2	10·9	9·20	7·44	5·63	8·94
180	9·63	7·79	12·7	9·72	8·20	6·64	5·02	7·97
190	8·65	6·99	11·4	8·73	7·36	5·96	4·51	7·16
200	7·80	6·31	10·3	7·88	6·65	5·38	4·07	6·46
210	7·08	5·72	9·31	7·14	6·03	4·88	3·69	5·86
220	6·45	5·21	8·48	6·51	5·49	4·44	3·36	5·34
230	5·90	4·77	7·76	5·96	5·02	4·06	3·08	4·88
240	5·42	4·38	7·13	5·47	4·61	3·73	2·83	4·49

KL/r_{min}	$2\frac{1}{2}\times2\frac{1}{2}\times\frac{5}{16}$	$2\frac{1}{2}\times2\frac{1}{2}\times\frac{1}{4}$	$2\frac{1}{2}\times2\frac{1}{2}\times\frac{3}{16}$	$2\times2\times\frac{3}{8}$	$2\times2\times\frac{5}{16}$	$2\times2\times\frac{1}{4}$	$2\times2\times\frac{3}{16}$	$2\times2\times\frac{1}{8}$
20	30·1	24·5	18·3	28·0	23·7	19·3	14·7	9·11
30	29·1	23·7	17·7	27·1	22·9	18·7	14·3	8·83
40	28·0	22·8	17·0	26·1	22·1	18·0	13·7	8·52
50	26·8	21·8	16·3	25·0	21·1	17·2	13·1	8·18
60	25·4	20·7	15·5	23·7	20·0	16·3	12·5	7·80
70	24·0	19·6	14·6	22·3	18·9	15·4	11·7	7·39
80	22·4	18·3	13·7	20·9	17·7	14·4	11·0	6·95
90	20·7	16·9	12·7	19·3	16·3	13·3	10·2	6·47
100	18·9	15·4	11·6	17·6	14·9	12·2	9·28	5·97
110	17·0	13·9	10·5	15·9	13·4	10·9	8·35	5·44
120	15·0	12·2	9·25	14·0	11·8	9·64	7·35	4·87
130	12·9	10·5	7·97	12·0	10·2	8·29	6·32	4·27
140	11·1	9·07	6·87	10·4	8·76	7·15	5·45	3·69
150	9·69	7·90	5·99	9·03	7·63	6·23	4·75	3·21
160	8·52	6·94	5·26	7·93	6·71	5·47	4·17	2·82
170	7·54	6·15	4·66	7·03	5·94	4·85	3·69	2·50
180	6·73	5·48	4·16	6·27	5·30	4·32	3·30	2·23
190	6·04	4·92	3·73	5·63	4·76	3·88	2·96	2·00
200	5·45	4·44	3·37	5·08	4·29	3·50	2·67	1·81
210	4·94	4·03	3·05	4·61	3·89	3·18	2·42	1·64
220	4·50	3·67	2·78	4·20	3·55	2·89	2·21	1·49
230	4·12	3·36	2·55	3·84	3·25	2·65	2·02	1·37
240	3·79	3·09	2·34	3·53	2·98	2·43	1·85	1·25

[a] American Institute of Steel Construction (1978).

Table 8.1(b)

Permissible Loads (kips) for Hot-Rolled Equal-Leg Single Angles Connected by One Leg According to AISC[a] Specifications ($\sigma_y = 36$ ksi)

KL/r_{min}	$8\times8\times1\frac{1}{8}$ $g_{(in)}^{b}=4\frac{1}{2}$	$8\times8\times1$ $4\frac{1}{2}$	$8\times8\times\frac{7}{8}$ $4\frac{1}{2}$	$8\times8\times\frac{3}{4}$ $4\frac{1}{2}$	$8\times8\times\frac{5}{8}$ $4\frac{1}{2}$	$8\times8\times\frac{1}{2}$ $4\frac{1}{2}$	$6\times6\times1$ $3\frac{1}{2}$	$6\times6\times\frac{7}{8}$ $3\frac{1}{2}$
20	132	117	102	87·3	71·1	51·9	82·1	72·1
30	131	117	101	86·8	70·0	51·1	81·6	71·6
40	130	116	101	86·1	68·6	50·2	80·9	71·1
50	129	115	99·7	85·3	67·0	49·1	80·1	70·4
60	127	113	98·6	84·3	65·1	47·8	79·2	69·6
70	125	112	97·4	83·3	63·1	46·4	78·2	68·7
80	124	110	96·0	82·2	60·8	44·8	77·1	67·8
90	122	109	94·7	81·0	58·3	43·1	76·0	66·8
100	120	107	93·3	79·9	55·5	41·2	74·8	65·9
110	112	102	91·3	78·8	52·4	39·1	71·1	64·1
120	104	94·2	84·0	73·4	48·9	36·8	65·7	59·2
130	93·9	85·3	76·0	66·3	44·9	34·2	59·7	53·7
140	84·9	77·1	68·6	59·8	41·2	31·5	54·2	48·7
150	77·1	69·9	62·2	54·2	37·9	29·0	49·3	44·2
160	70·2	63·6	56·5	49·2	34·9	26·8	45·0	40·3
170	64·1	58·0	51·6	44·8	32·2	24·7	41·2	36·9
180	58·7	53·1	47·2	41·0	29·7	22·9	37·8	33·8
190	53·9	48·8	43·3	37·6	27·6	21·3	34·8	31·1
200	49·4	44·9	39·8	34·6	25·6	19·8	32·1	28·6
210	45·3	41·5	36·8	31·9	23·8	18·4	29·7	26·5
220	41·7	38·4	34·0	29·5	22·2	17·2	27·5	24·5
230	38·5	35·6	31·5	27·4	20·7	16·1	25·5	22·8
240	35·6	32·9	29·3	25·4	19·3	15·0	23·6	21·2

KL/r_{min}	$6 \times 6 \times \frac{3}{4}$ $g = 3\frac{1}{2}$	$6 \times 6 \times \frac{5}{8}$ $3\frac{1}{2}$	$6 \times 6 \times \frac{1}{2}$ $3\frac{1}{2}$	$6 \times 6 \times \frac{3}{8}$ $3\frac{1}{2}$	$5 \times 5 \times \frac{7}{8}$ 3	$5 \times 5 \times \frac{3}{4}$ 3	$5 \times 5 \times \frac{1}{2}$ 3	$5 \times 5 \times \frac{3}{8}$ 3
20	62·1	50·6	40·2	27·4	57·3	48·8	32·1	23·6
30	61·8	49·8	39·5	27·0	56·9	48·5	31·6	23·2
40	61·3	48·9	38·8	26·5	56·5	48·2	31·0	22·8
50	60·7	47·8	37·9	25·9	56·0	47·7	30·3	22·2
60	60·1	46·5	36·8	25·3	55·3	47·2	29·5	21·6
70	59·3	45·0	35·7	24·5	54·6	46·6	28·6	20·9
80	58·5	43·4	34·4	23·7	53·9	46·0	27·5	20·2
90	57·7	41·7	32·9	22·8	53·1	45·4	26·4	19·4
100	56·9	39·7	31·3	21·8	52·3	44·7	25·2	18·4
110	56·2	37·5	29·6	20·7	50·6	44·1	23·8	17·4
120	52·3	35·1	27·6	19·5	46·8	41·5	22·2	16·3
130	47·4	32·3	25·4	18·1	42·6	37·8	20·5	15·1
140	42·9	29·7	23·4	16·7	38·7	34·3	18·9	13·9
150	38·9	27·3	21·5	15·4	35·3	31·2	17·4	12·8
160	35·5	25·2	19·8	14·3	32·2	28·4	16·1	11·8
170	32·4	23·3	18·3	13·2	29·5	26·0	14·8	11·0
180	29·7	21·5	17·0	12·2	27·1	23·9	13·8	10·2
190	27·3	20·0	15·7	11·4	25·0	22·0	12·8	9·43
200	25·1	18·6	14·6	10·6	23·0	20·3	11·9	8·78
210	23·2	17·3	13·6	9·88	21·3	18·7	11·1	8·18
220	21·5	16·1	12·7	9·23	19·8	17·4	10·3	7·64
230	19·9	15·1	11·9	8·64	18·4	16·1	9·65	7·15
240	18·5	14·1	11·1	8·09	17·1	15·0	9·04	6·70

[a] American Institute of Steel Construction (1978).
[b] Distance from the *heel* of angle to centre of *bolt* group.

Table 8.1(b)—*contd.*

KL/r_{min}	$5 \times 5 \times \frac{5}{16}$ $g = 3$	$4 \times 4 \times \frac{3}{4}$ $2\frac{1}{2}$	$4 \times 4 \times \frac{5}{8}$ $2\frac{1}{2}$	$4 \times 4 \times \frac{1}{2}$ $2\frac{1}{2}$	$4 \times 4 \times \frac{3}{8}$ $2\frac{1}{2}$	$4 \times 4 \times \frac{5}{16}$ $2\frac{1}{2}$	$4 \times 4 \times \frac{1}{4}$ $2\frac{1}{2}$	$3\frac{1}{2} \times 3\frac{1}{2} \times \frac{3}{8}$ $2\frac{1}{4}$
20	18·2	36·4	30·2	24·0	18·0	14·9	10·8	15·0
30	17·9	36·2	29·7	23·7	17·8	14·7	10·7	14·8
40	17·6	36·0	29·2	23·2	17·4	14·4	10·5	14·5
50	17·2	35·6	28·6	22·7	17·0	14·1	10·3	14·2
60	16·8	35·3	27·8	22·1	16·6	13·7	10·0	13·8
70	16·3	34·8	27·0	21·4	16·0	13·3	9·72	13·4
80	15·7	34·4	26·1	20·7	15·5	12·8	9·40	12·9
90	15·1	33·9	25·1	19·9	14·8	12·3	9·04	12·4
100	14·5	33·4	24·0	18·9	14·1	11·7	8·65	11·8
110	13·7	33·0	22·7	17·9	13·4	11·1	8·22	11·2
120	13·0	31·0	21·3	16·8	12·5	10·4	7·76	10·5
130	12·1	28·3	19·7	15·5	11·6	9·58	7·25	9·73
140	11·2	25·8	18·2	14·3	10·7	8·84	6·72	8·99
150	10·3	23·5	16·8	13·2	9·86	8·17	6·22	8·32
160	9·55	21·5	15·5	12·2	9·13	7·56	5·78	7·71
170	8·86	19·7	14·4	11·3	8·46	7·01	5·37	7·15
180	8·23	18·2	13·4	10·5	7·85	6·51	5·00	6·65
190	7·65	16·7	12·4	9·79	7·30	6·05	4·66	6·19
200	7·13	15·5	11·6	9·12	6·80	5·64	4·35	5·77
210	6·66	14·3	10·8	8·51	6·34	5·26	4·07	5·39
220	6·23	13·3	10·1	7·95	5·93	4·92	3·81	5·04
230	5·83	12·4	9·44	7·44	5·55	4·61	3·57	4·72
240	5·47	11·5	8·85	6·98	5·21	4·32	3·36	4·43

KL/r_{min}	$3\frac{1}{2}\times3\frac{1}{2}\times\frac{5}{16}$ $g=2\frac{1}{4}$	$3\frac{1}{2}\times3\frac{1}{2}\times\frac{1}{4}$ $2\frac{1}{4}$	$3\times3\times\frac{1}{2}$ $1\frac{3}{4}$	$3\times3\times\frac{3}{8}$ $1\frac{3}{4}$	$3\times3\times\frac{5}{16}$ $1\frac{3}{4}$	$3\times3\times\frac{1}{4}$ $1\frac{3}{4}$	$3\times3\times\frac{3}{16}$ $1\frac{3}{4}$	$2\frac{1}{2}\times2\frac{1}{2}\times\frac{3}{8}$ $1\frac{3}{8}$
20	12·5	9·65	20·6	15·4	12·6	10·0	6·85	14·3
30	12·3	9·51	20·5	15·4	12·5	9·89	6·75	14·2
40	12·1	9·34	20·3	15·2	12·2	9·69	6·63	14·1
50	11·8	9·13	20·1	15·1	11·9	9·47	6·48	13·9
60	11·5	8·89	19·9	14·9	11·6	9·21	6·32	13·8
70	11·2	8·62	19·6	14·8	11·3	8·92	6·13	13·6
80	10·8	8·32	19·3	14·6	10·9	8·59	5·92	13·4
90	10·3	7·99	19·1	14·4	10·4	8·23	5·69	13·2
100	9·84	7·63	18·8	14·2	9·92	7·84	5·44	12·5
110	9·32	7·24	17·8	14·0	9·38	7·40	5·16	11·6
120	8·73	6·80	16·4	13·1	8·77	6·91	4·86	10·7
130	8·09	6·32	14·9	11·8	8·08	6·37	4·53	9·73
140	7·47	5·85	13·5	10·7	7·42	5·85	4·17	8·76
150	6·92	5·42	12·3	9·72	6·83	5·39	3·85	7·84
160	6·41	5·03	11·3	8·85	6·30	4·97	3·56	7·06
170	5·95	4·68	10·3	8·09	5·82	4·59	3·30	6·38
180	5·53	4·35	9·45	7·41	5·39	4·25	3·06	5·80
190	5·15	4·05	8·69	6·81	5·00	3·94	2·84	5·29
200	4·80	3·78	8·02	6·27	4·64	3·66	2·65	4·85
210	4·48	3·54	7·42	5·79	4·32	3·41	2·47	4·46
220	4·20	3·31	6·87	5·36	4·03	3·18	2·31	4·11
230	3·93	3·11	6·35	4·98	3·77	2·97	2·16	3·81
240	3·69	2·92	5·88	4·63	3·53	2·78	2·02	3·53

[a] American Institute of Steel Construction (1978).
[b] Distance from the *heel* of angle to centre of bolt group.

Table 8.1(b)—*contd.*

KL/r_{min}	$2\frac{1}{2} \times 2\frac{1}{2} \times \frac{5}{16}$ $g = 1\frac{3}{8}$	$2\frac{1}{2} \times 2\frac{1}{2} \times \frac{1}{4}$ $1\frac{3}{8}$	$2\frac{1}{2} \times 2\frac{1}{2} \times \frac{3}{16}$ $1\frac{3}{8}$	$2 \times 2 \times \frac{3}{8}$ $1\frac{1}{8}$	$2 \times 2 \times \frac{5}{16}$ $1\frac{1}{8}$	$2 \times 2 \times \frac{1}{4}$ $1\frac{1}{8}$	$2 \times 2 \times \frac{3}{16}$ $1\frac{1}{8}$	$2 \times 2 \times \frac{1}{8}$ $1\frac{1}{8}$
20	11·9	9·48	6·94	10·9	9·13	7·33	5·45	3·23
30	11·8	9·43	6·90	10·8	9·07	7·28	5·42	3·19
40	11·7	9·35	6·85	10·7	9·00	7·23	5·38	3·13
50	11·6	9·26	6·78	10·6	8·91	7·16	5·32	3·06
60	11·5	9·16	6·71	10·5	8·80	7·07	5·27	2·98
70	11·3	9·04	6·63	10·4	8·68	6·98	5·20	2·89
80	11·2	8·91	6·54	10·2	8·56	6·89	5·13	2·79
90	11·0	8·78	6·45	9·89	8·43	6·79	5·06	2·68
100	10·8	8·66	6·36	9·34	8·15	6·69	4·99	2·56
110	10·1	8·35	6·28	8·74	7·62	6·39	4·92	2·43
120	9·25	7·68	5·90	8·08	7·03	5·89	4·60	2·29
130	8·37	6·94	5·33	7·31	6·38	5·33	4·16	2·13
140	7·56	6·26	4·81	6·52	5·78	4·82	3·75	1·96
150	6·85	5·66	4·34	5·86	5·25	4·37	3·40	1·81
160	6·23	5·14	3·94	5·29	4·78	3·98	3·08	1·67
170	5·68	4·69	3·59	4·80	4·34	3·63	2·81	1·54
180	5·18	4·29	3·28	4·37	3·94	3·32	2·57	1·43
190	4·71	3·93	3·01	4·00	3·59	3·05	2·36	1·32
200	4·30	3·61	2·76	3·67	3·29	2·81	2·17	1·23
210	3·95	3·33	2·55	3·38	3·02	2·59	2·00	1·15
220	3·63	3·08	2·35	3·12	2·78	2·40	1·85	1·07
230	3·36	2·86	2·18	2·89	2·57	2·23	1·72	1·00
240	3·11	2·66	2·03	2·69	2·39	2·06	1·59	0·936

[a] American Institute of Steel Construction (1978).
[b] Distance from the *heel* of angle to centre of bolt group.

Table 8.1(c)

Permissible Loads (kips) for Hot-Rolled Unequal-Leg Single Angles Connected by Long Leg According to AISC[a] Specifications ($\sigma_y = 36$ ksi)

KL/r_{min}	$8 \times 6 \times 1$ $g_{(in)} = 4\frac{1}{2}$	$8 \times 6 \times \frac{3}{4}$ $4\frac{1}{2}$	$8 \times 6 \times \frac{1}{2}$ $4\frac{1}{2}$	$8 \times 4 \times 1$ $4\frac{1}{2}$	$8 \times 4 \times \frac{3}{4}$ $4\frac{1}{2}$	$8 \times 4 \times \frac{1}{2}$ $4\frac{1}{2}$	$7 \times 4 \times \frac{3}{4}$ 4	$7 \times 4 \times \frac{1}{2}$ 4
20	118	88·8	53·8	111	89·0	55·2	75·5	49·5
30	117	88·3	53·5	109	88·8	55·1	75·3	49·3
40	117	87·7	53·2	105	86·8	54·9	75·0	49·1
50	116	86·9	52·7	100	84·5	54·7	73·5	48·8
60	114	86·0	52·3	94·3	81·9	54·2	71·3	48·5
70	113	85·0	51·7	88·3	77·5	52·3	68·7	48·1
80	108	84·0	51·1	82·0	71·6	50·3	65·4	46·1
90	103	81·2	50·5	75·7	65·7	48·0	60·0	43·9
100	95·4	76·5	49·9	69·4	59·8	43·8	54·7	41·5
110	86·2	71·3	47·4	63·3	54·2	39·7	49·5	37·5
120	77·4	64·5	43·9	57·4	48·7	35·8	44·5	33·6
130	69·0	57·1	40·1	51·6	43·5	32·0	39·7	29·8
140	61·6	50·8	36·2	46·5	39·0	28·5	35·6	26·5
150	55·4	45·4	32·7	42·1	35·1	25·6	32·0	23·7
160	50·0	40·8	29·3	38·2	31·7	23·0	29·0	21·4
170	45·4	36·9	26·4	34·9	28·8	20·8	26·3	19·3
180	41·4	33·5	24·0	32·0	26·3	19·0	24·0	17·6
190	37·9	30·6	21·8	29·4	24·1	17·3	22·0	16·0
200	34·8	28·0	19·9	27·1	22·1	15·9	20·2	14·7
210	32·0	25·8	18·3	25·1	20·4	14·6	18·6	13·5
220	29·6	23·7	16·8	23·2	18·9	13·5	17·2	12·5
230	27·4	22·0	15·5	21·6	17·5	12·5	16·0	11·5
240	25·5	20·4	14·4	20·2	16·3	11·6	14·9	10·7

[a] American Institute of Steel Construction (1978).
[b] Distance from the *heel* of the angle to centre of bolt group.

Table 8.1(c)—*contd.*

KL/r_{min}	$7 \times 4 \times \frac{3}{8}$ $g=4$	$6 \times 4 \times \frac{3}{4}$ $3\frac{1}{2}$	$6 \times 4 \times \frac{5}{8}$ $3\frac{1}{2}$	$6 \times 4 \times \frac{1}{2}$ $3\frac{1}{2}$	$6 \times 4 \times \frac{3}{8}$ $3\frac{1}{2}$	$6 \times 3\frac{1}{2} \times \frac{3}{8}$ $3\frac{1}{2}$	$6 \times 3\frac{1}{2} \times \frac{5}{16}$ $3\frac{1}{2}$	$5 \times 3\frac{1}{2} \times \frac{3}{4}$ 3
20	32·2	62·2	52·2	42·0	28·6	28·9	21·6	48·8
30	32·1	61·9	52·0	41·8	28·5	28·8	21·6	48·6
40	31·9	61·6	51·7	41·6	28·3	28·7	21·5	48·3
50	31·8	61·1	51·3	41·3	28·1	28·5	21·4	47·9
60	31·6	60·6	50·9	40·9	27·9	28·4	21·3	47·5
70	31·4	58·7	50·4	40·5	27·7	28·2	21·1	46·4
80	31·2	56·3	49·1	40·1	27·4	28·0	21·0	44·5
90	30·7	53·7	46·7	38·8	27·1	27·2	20·8	42·5
100	29·2	50·0	44·1	36·6	26·8	25·8	20·4	40·3
110	27·6	45·3	40·9	34·2	25·2	24·3	19·3	37·1
120	25·8	40·7	36·6	31·4	23·4	22·5	18·1	33·4
130	23·2	36·3	32·5	27·8	21·4	20·2	16·8	29·8
140	20·7	32·4	29·0	24·7	19·3	17·9	15·3	26·7
150	18·5	29·2	26·0	22·0	17·4	16·0	13·6	24·0
160	16·6	26·4	23·4	19·8	15·6	14·4	12·2	21·7
170	15·0	24·0	21·2	17·9	14·1	13·0	11·0	19·8
180	13·6	21·8	19·3	16·2	12·8	11·8	10·0	18·0
190	12·4	20·0	17·6	14·8	11·6	10·7	9·10	16·5
200	11·3	18·4	16·1	13·6	10·6	9·81	8·33	15·2
210	10·4	16·9	14·9	12·5	9·74	9·01	7·64	14·0
220	9·61	15·7	13·7	11·5	8·97	8·30	7·04	13·0
230	8·89	14·5	12·7	10·6	8·28	7·67	6·51	12·0
240	8·24	13·5	11·8	9·84	7·67	7·11	6·03	11·2

KL/r_{min}	$5 \times 3\frac{1}{2} \times \frac{1}{2}$ $g = 3$	$5 \times 3\frac{1}{2} \times \frac{3}{8}$ 3	$5 \times 3\frac{1}{2} \times \frac{5}{16}$ 3	$5 \times 3 \times \frac{1}{2}$ 3	$5 \times 3 \times \frac{3}{8}$ 3	$5 \times 3 \times \frac{5}{16}$ 3	$5 \times 3 \times \frac{1}{4}$ 3	$4 \times 3\frac{1}{2} \times \frac{1}{2}$ $2\frac{1}{2}$
20	33·2	24·4	18·8	33·2	24·5	18·9	13·4	24·5
30	33·1	24·3	18·7	33·1	24·4	18·9	13·3	24·4
40	32·9	24·1	18·6	32·9	24·3	18·8	13·3	24·2
50	32·6	23·9	18·5	32·7	24·2	18·7	13·2	24·0
60	32·3	23·7	18·4	32·5	24·0	18·6	13·1	23·7
70	32·0	23·5	18·2	32·3	23·8	18·5	13·1	23·5
80	31·7	23·3	18·0	31·0	23·6	18·3	13·0	23·2
90	31·3	23·0	17·8	29·5	23·0	18·2	12·9	22·8
100	29·5	22·8	17·6	27·9	21·8	17·7	12·8	22·5
110	27·6	21·4	17·4	26·1	20·4	16·6	12·6	22·3
120	25·4	19·7	16·2	23·4	18·8	15·4	11·8	21·0
130	23·0	17·9	14·8	20·8	17·0	14·1	11·0	19·1
140	20·8	16·1	13·4	18·5	15·1	12·8	10·1	17·3
150	18·6	14·6	12·1	16·6	13·5	11·6	9·14	15·8
160	16·7	13·3	11·0	15·0	12·1	10·4	8·32	14·4
170	15·1	12·1	10·1	13·5	10·9	9·34	7·59	13·2
180	13·7	11·0	9·21	12·3	9·90	8·47	6·95	12·1
190	12·5	10·0	8·45	11·3	9·02	7·71	6·32	11·1
200	11·4	9·14	7·77	10·3	8·25	7·04	5·78	10·2
210	10·5	8·38	7·16	9·50	7·58	6·46	5·30	9·47
220	9·67	7·71	6·58	8·77	6·98	5·95	4·87	8·78
230	8·94	7·11	6·07	8·12	6·45	5·49	4·50	8·16
240	8·29	6·58	5·62	7·54	5·98	5·09	4·16	7·60

[a] American Institute of Steel Construction (1978).
[b] Distance from the *heel* of the angle to centre of bolt group.

Table 8.1(c)—*contd.*

KL/r_{min}	$4 \times 3\frac{1}{2} \times \frac{3}{8}$ $g = 2\frac{1}{2}$	$4 \times 3\frac{1}{2} \times \frac{5}{16}$ $2\frac{1}{2}$	$4 \times 3\frac{1}{2} \times \frac{1}{4}$ $2\frac{1}{2}$	$4 \times 3 \times \frac{1}{2}$ $2\frac{1}{2}$	$4 \times 3 \times \frac{3}{8}$ $2\frac{1}{2}$	$4 \times 3 \times \frac{5}{16}$ $2\frac{1}{2}$	$4 \times 3 \times \frac{1}{4}$ $2\frac{1}{2}$	$3\frac{1}{2} \times 3 \times \frac{3}{8}$ $2\frac{1}{4}$
20	18·1	15·0	10·9	24·6	18·4	15·4	11·2	15·1
30	17·8	14·8	10·8	24·5	18·4	15·3	11·2	14·9
40	17·5	14·5	10·6	24·4	18·2	15·2	11·1	14·7
50	17·1	14·2	10·4	24·2	18·1	15·1	11·0	14·4
60	16·7	13·8	10·1	24·0	17·9	14·9	10·9	14·0
70	16·2	13·4	9·84	23·7	17·7	14·8	10·8	13·6
80	15·7	12·9	9·53	23·4	17·5	14·6	10·7	13·2
90	15·1	12·4	9·18	23·2	17·3	14·4	10·6	12·7
100	14·4	11·9	8·79	22·5	17·1	14·3	10·5	12·1
110	13·6	11·2	8·37	21·1	16·7	14·1	10·4	11·5
120	12·8	10·5	7·90	19·5	15·4	13·2	10·3	10·8
130	11·8	9·71	7·38	17·8	14·0	12·0	9·53	9·96
140	10·9	8·95	6·82	16·1	12·7	10·8	8·63	9·19
150	10·0	8·26	6·31	14·7	11·5	9·81	7·84	8·49
160	9·26	7·63	5·85	13·4	10·5	8·92	7·14	7·86
170	8·57	7·07	5·43	12·3	9·56	8·14	6·52	7·28
180	7·95	6·55	5·04	11·2	8·76	7·45	5·97	6·76
190	7·38	6·09	4·69	10·2	8·05	6·84	5·48	6·28
200	6·87	5·66	4·37	9·37	7·41	6·30	5·05	5·85
210	6·40	5·28	4·08	8·60	6·84	5·81	4·67	5·46
220	5·97	4·93	3·82	7·93	6·34	5·38	4·32	5·10
230	5·59	4·61	3·58	7·33	5·88	4·99	4·01	4·77
240	5·23	4·32	3·35	6·79	5·47	4·64	3·73	4·47

KL/r_{min}	$3\frac{1}{2} \times 3 \times \frac{5}{16}$ $g = 2\frac{1}{4}$	$3\frac{1}{2} \times 3 \times \frac{1}{4}$ $2\frac{1}{4}$	$3\frac{1}{2} \times 2\frac{1}{2} \times \frac{3}{8}$ $2\frac{1}{4}$	$3\frac{1}{2} \times 2\frac{1}{2} \times \frac{5}{16}$ $2\frac{1}{4}$	$3\frac{1}{2} \times 2\frac{1}{2} \times \frac{1}{4}$ $2\frac{1}{4}$	$3 \times 2\frac{1}{2} \times \frac{3}{8}$ $1\frac{3}{4}$	$3 \times 2\frac{1}{2} \times \frac{1}{4}$ $1\frac{3}{4}$	$3 \times 2 \times \frac{3}{8}$ $1\frac{3}{4}$
20	12·6	9·72	15·5	12·9	9·87	15·6	10·3	15·5
30	12·4	9·59	15·4	12·9	9·83	15·5	10·3	15·5
40	12·2	9·42	15·3	12·8	9·77	15·4	10·2	15·4
50	12·0	9·22	15·2	12·7	9·71	15·2	10·1	15·3
60	11·7	8·99	15·1	12·6	9·63	15·0	9·99	15·2
70	11·3	8·73	14·9	12·5	9·54	14·9	9·87	14·7
80	10·9	8·45	14·8	12·3	9·44	14·7	9·74	14·1
90	10·5	8·12	14·6	12·2	9·34	14·5	9·61	13·4
100	10·0	7·77	14·4	12·1	9·24	13·9	9·48	12·5
110	9·52	7·38	13·8	11·9	9·15	13·0	9·21	11·3
120	8·92	6·94	12·7	11·0	8·89	12·0	8·47	10·2
130	8·25	6·44	11·6	9·95	8·09	10·8	7·66	9·06
140	7·61	5·95	10·5	9·02	7·33	9·80	6·91	8·10
150	7·03	5·50	9·56	8·19	6·66	8·85	6·25	7·28
160	6·50	5·09	8·72	7·47	6·06	7·95	5·68	6·58
170	6·02	4·72	7·98	6·82	5·54	7·19	5·17	5·98
180	5·59	4·38	7·32	6·25	5·08	6·52	4·73	5·45
190	5·19	4·08	6·73	5·75	4·66	5·95	4·34	4·99
200	4·84	3·80	6·21	5·30	4·30	5·45	3·99	4·59
210	4·51	3·55	5·74	4·89	3·97	5·01	3·68	4·23
220	4·21	3·32	5·32	4·53	3·68	4·62	3·40	3·91
230	3·94	3·10	4·93	4·21	3·41	4·27	3·14	3·62
240	3·69	2·91	4·57	3·91	3·17	3·96	2·90	3·37

[a] American Institute of Steel Construction (1978)
[b] Distance from the *heel* of the angle to centre of bolt group.

Table 8.1(c)—*contd.*

KL/r_{min}	$3 \times 2 \times \frac{5}{16}$ $g = 1\frac{3}{4}$	$3 \times 2 \times \frac{1}{4}$ $1\frac{3}{4}$	$3 \times 2 \times \frac{3}{16}$ $1\frac{1}{4}$	$2\frac{1}{2} \times 2 \times \frac{3}{8}$ $1\frac{3}{8}$	$2\frac{1}{2} \times 2 \times \frac{5}{16}$ $1\frac{3}{8}$	$2\frac{1}{2} \times 2 \times \frac{1}{4}$ $1\frac{1}{8}$	$2\frac{1}{2} \times 2 \times \frac{3}{16}$ $1\frac{3}{8}$
20	13·1	10·5	7·13	14·3	12·0	9·64	7·07
30	13·1	10·4	7·11	14·2	11·9	9·58	7·03
40	13·0	10·4	7·07	14·1	11·8	9·51	6·98
50	12·9	10·3	7·02	14·0	11·7	9·42	6·92
60	12·8	10·2	6·97	13·7	11·6	9·31	6·84
70	12·7	10·1	6·91	13·2	11·4	9·20	6·76
80	12·3	10·0	6·84	12·6	11·0	9·07	6·67
90	11·7	9·73	6·77	11·6	10·4	8·67	6·58
100	11·0	9·17	6·69	10·6	9·60	8·16	6·31
110	10·1	8·56	6·29	9·61	8·68	7·53	5·88
120	9·08	7·87	5·84	8·66	7·79	6·73	5·41
130	8·07	6·98	5·34	7·75	6·94	5·97	4·86
140	7·19	6·19	4·82	6·95	6·20	5·31	4·31
150	6·45	5·53	4·36	6·27	5·58	4·76	3·84
160	5·81	4·97	3·91	5·68	5·04	4·28	3·45
170	5·26	4·49	3·53	5·17	4·57	3·88	3·11
180	4·79	4·08	3·19	4·72	4·17	3·52	2·82
190	4·37	3·71	2·91	4·33	3·81	3·22	2·57
200	4·01	3·40	2·66	3·99	3·50	2·95	2·35
210	3·69	3·12	2·44	3·68	3·23	2·71	2·16
220	3·41	2·88	2·24	3·41	2·98	2·50	1·99
230	3·16	2·66	2·07	3·16	2·76	2·32	1·83
240	2·93	2·47	1·92	2·94	2·57	2·15	1·70

[a] American Institute of Steel Construction (1978).
[b] Distance from the *heel* of the angle to centre of bolt group.

Table 8.1(d)

Permissible Loads (kips) for Hot-Rolled Unequal-Leg Single Angles Connected by Short Leg According to AISC[a] Specifications ($\sigma_y = 36$ ksi)

KL/r_{min}	$8 \times 6 \times 1$ $g_{(in)}{}^{b} = 3\frac{1}{2}$	$8 \times 6 \times \frac{3}{4}$ $3\frac{1}{2}$	$8 \times 6 \times \frac{1}{2}$ $3\frac{1}{2}$	$8 \times 4 \times 1$ $2\frac{1}{2}$	$8 \times 4 \times \frac{3}{4}$ $2\frac{1}{2}$	$8 \times 4 \times \frac{1}{2}$ $2\frac{1}{2}$	$7 \times 4 \times \frac{3}{4}$ $2\frac{1}{2}$	$7 \times 4 \times \frac{1}{2}$ $2\frac{1}{2}$
20	78·1	57·9	34·7	45·8	33·8	20·3	33·9	21·5
30	76·9	57·0	34·2	45·2	33·4	20·0	33·4	21·3
40	75·5	55·9	33·6	44·5	32·8	19·7	32·8	20·9
50	73·7	54·6	32·9	43·6	32·2	19·4	32·2	20·5
60	71·7	53·1	32·0	42·6	31·4	18·9	31·4	20·0
70	69·5	51·4	31·1	41·4	30·5	18·5	30·5	19·4
80	66·9	49·5	30·0	40·1	29·6	17·9	29·5	18·8
90	64·1	47·4	28·8	38·6	28·5	17·3	28·3	18·1
100	61·1	45·1	27·6	37·0	27·3	16·7	27·1	17·4
110	57·7	42·6	26·2	35·3	26·0	16·0	25·8	16·6
120	54·0	39·9	24·7	33·4	24·7	15·3	24·4	15·7
130	50·0	36·9	23·1	31·3	23·1	14·4	22·8	14·7
140	46·2	34·1	21·5	29·3	21·7	13·6	21·3	13·8
150	42·7	31·6	19·9	27·4	20·3	12·8	19·9	12·9
160	39·6	29·3	18·6	25·7	19·0	12·0	18·6	12·1
170	36·7	27·2	17·3	24·1	17·9	11·3	17·4	11·3
180	34·1	25·3	16·1	22·6	16·8	10·7	16·3	10·6
190	31·7	23·5	15·0	21·2	15·8	10·0	15·3	10·0
200	29·6	22·0	14·1	19·9	14·8	9·48	14·4	9·40
210	27·6	20·5	13·2	18·8	14·0	8·95	13·5	8·85
220	25·8	19·2	12·4	17·7	13·2	8·46	12·7	8·34
230	24·2	18·0	11·6	16·7	12·5	8·01	12·0	7·87
240	22·7	16·9	10·9	15·8	11·8	7·59	11·3	7·44

[a] American Institute of Steel Construction (1978).
[b] Distance from the *heel* of the angle to the centre of the bolt group.

Table 8.1(d)—*contd.*

KL/r_{min}	$7 \times 4 \times \frac{3}{8}$ $g = 2\frac{1}{2}$	$6 \times 4 \times \frac{3}{4}$ $2\frac{1}{2}$	$6 \times 4 \times \frac{5}{8}$ $2\frac{1}{2}$	$6 \times 4 \times \frac{1}{2}$ $2\frac{1}{2}$	$6 \times 4 \times \frac{3}{8}$ $2\frac{1}{2}$	$6 \times 3\frac{1}{2} \times \frac{3}{8}$ $2\frac{1}{4}$	$6 \times 3\frac{1}{2} \times \frac{5}{16}$ $2\frac{1}{4}$	$5 \times 3\frac{1}{2} \times \frac{1}{4}$ $2\frac{1}{4}$
20	14·0	34·2	28·3	22·5	15·3	12·7	9·57	28·7
30	13·8	33·7	27·9	22·2	15·1	12·6	9·46	28·3
40	13·6	33·1	27·4	21·8	14·9	12·4	9·33	27·8
50	13·4	32·4	26·8	21·3	14·6	12·2	9·17	27·2
60	13·1	31·6	26·1	20·8	14·2	11·9	8·98	26·5
70	12·8	30·6	25·3	20·1	13·8	11·6	8·77	25·7
80	12·4	29·6	24·4	19·4	13·4	11·2	8·53	24·9
90	12·0	28·4	23·5	18·7	12·9	10·8	8·27	23·9
100	11·6	27·2	22·4	17·8	12·4	10·4	7·99	22·9
110	11·1	25·8	21·3	16·9	11·8	9·99	7·68	21·7
120	10·6	24·3	20·0	15·9	11·2	9·51	7·36	20·5
130	10·1	22·6	18·7	14·9	10·5	8·99	7·00	19·1
140	9·53	21·0	17·4	13·9	9·85	8·44	6·62	17·7
150	8·96	19·6	16·2	12·9	9·21	7·92	6·23	16·5
160	8·42	18·3	15·1	12·0	8·62	7·44	5·87	15·4
170	7·93	17·0	14·1	11·2	8·07	6·99	5·54	14·4
180	7·47	15·9	13·2	10·5	7·57	6·58	5·22	13·4
190	7·04	14·9	12·3	9·85	7·10	6·19	4·93	12·6
200	6·64	13·9	11·6	9·23	6·67	5·84	4·65	11·8
210	6·27	13·1	10·8	8·67	6·28	5·51	4·40	11·0
220	5·93	12·3	10·2	8·15	5·91	5·20	4·16	10·4
230	5·61	11·5	9·59	7·67	5·57	4·92	3·94	9·75
240	5·31	10·9	9·04	7·23	5·26	4·65	3·74	9·18

KL/r_{min}	$5 \times 3\frac{1}{2} \times \frac{1}{2}$ $g = 2\frac{1}{4}$	$5 \times 3\frac{1}{2} \times \frac{3}{8}$ $2\frac{1}{4}$	$5 \times 3\frac{1}{2} \times \frac{5}{16}$ $2\frac{1}{4}$	$5 \times 3 \times \frac{1}{2}$ $1\frac{3}{4}$	$5 \times 3 \times \frac{3}{8}$ $1\frac{3}{4}$	$5 \times 3 \times \frac{5}{16}$ $1\frac{3}{4}$	$5 \times 3 \times \frac{1}{4}$ $1\frac{3}{4}$	$4 \times 3\frac{1}{2} \times \frac{1}{2}$ $2\frac{1}{4}$
20	18·9	13·9	10·7	19·0	13·8	10·6	7·48	19·7
30	18·7	13·7	10·6	18·7	13·6	10·5	7·39	19·4
40	18·4	13·5	10·4	18·4	13·4	10·3	7·28	19·0
50	18·0	13·2	10·2	18·0	13·1	10·1	7·14	18·6
60	17·5	12·8	9·95	17·5	12·7	9·86	6·99	18·1
70	17·0	12·5	9·68	17·0	12·4	9·58	6·81	17·6
80	16·4	12·0	9·37	16·4	11·9	9·26	6·62	17·0
90	15·8	11·6	9·04	15·7	11·4	8·92	6·40	16·3
100	15·1	11·1	8·68	15·0	10·9	8·55	6·17	15·5
110	14·3	10·5	8·29	14·2	10·4	8·15	5·92	14·7
120	13·5	9·95	7·87	13·3	9·77	7·72	5·65	13·8
130	12·6	9·30	7·41	12·4	9·11	7·26	5·36	12·8
140	11·7	8·67	6·93	11·5	8·48	6·77	5·05	11·9
150	10·9	8·09	6·48	10·7	7·89	6·32	4·73	11·0
160	10·2	7·56	6·07	9·98	7·35	5·90	4·44	10·2
170	9·52	7·07	5·68	9·30	6·86	5·52	4·16	9·51
180	8·90	6·61	5·33	8·68	6·41	5·17	3·91	8·85
190	8·34	6·20	5·00	8·11	6·00	4·84	3·68	8·26
200	7·81	5·82	4·70	7·59	5·62	4·54	3·46	7·71
210	7·34	5·46	4·43	7·11	5·27	4·27	3·26	7·21
220	6·90	5·14	4·17	6·68	4·95	4·02	3·07	6·76
230	6·49	4·84	3·93	6·27	4·66	3·78	2·90	6·34
240	6·12	4·57	3·72	5·91	4·39	3·57	2·74	5·96

[a] American Institute of Steel Construction (1978).
[b] Distance from the *heel* of the angle to the centre of the bolt group.

Table 8.1(d)—*contd.*

KL/r_{min}	$4 \times 3\frac{1}{2} \times \frac{3}{8}$ $g = 2\frac{1}{4}$	$4 \times 3\frac{1}{2} \times \frac{5}{16}$ $2\frac{1}{4}$	$4 \times 3\frac{1}{2} \times \frac{1}{4}$ $2\frac{1}{4}$	$4 \times 3 \times \frac{1}{2}$ $1\frac{3}{4}$	$4 \times 3 \times \frac{3}{8}$ $1\frac{3}{4}$	$4 \times 3 \times \frac{5}{16}$ $1\frac{3}{4}$	$4 \times 3 \times \frac{1}{4}$ $1\frac{3}{4}$	$3\frac{1}{2} \times 3 \times \frac{3}{8}$ $1\frac{3}{4}$
20	14·6	12·1	8·83	19·6	14·5	12·0	8·71	14·9
30	14·4	12·0	8·71	19·3	14·3	11·8	8·59	14·7
40	14·2	11·7	8·56	18·9	14·0	11·6	8·44	14·4
50	13·8	11·5	8·38	18·5	13·7	11·3	8·25	14·0
60	13·5	11·2	8·17	18·0	13·3	11·0	8·04	13·7
70	13·0	10·8	7·93	17·4	12·9	10·6	7·80	13·2
80	12·6	10·4	7·67	16·8	12·4	10·2	7·53	12·7
90	12·1	10·0	7·39	16·1	11·9	9·78	7·24	12·2
100	11·5	9·54	7·08	15·3	11·3	9·31	6·92	11·6
110	10·9	9·04	6·74	14·5	10·7	8·80	6·58	11·0
120	10·2	8·49	6·38	13·5	9·98	8·24	6·21	10·2
130	9·52	7·89	5·98	12·5	9·24	7·64	5·81	9·45
140	8·82	7·31	5·56	11·6	8·54	7·06	5·39	8·71
150	8·19	6·79	5·18	10·7	7·90	6·54	5·01	8·03
160	7·60	6·31	4·83	9·91	7·32	6·06	4·66	7·42
170	7·07	5·87	4·50	9·19	6·80	5·63	4·33	6·87
180	6·59	5·47	4·21	8·54	6·32	5·24	4·04	6·37
190	6·15	5·11	3·93	7·95	5·88	4·88	3·77	5·92
200	5·75	4·78	3·69	7·41	5·49	4·55	3·53	5·51
210	5·38	4·47	3·46	6·92	5·13	4·26	3·30	5·14
220	5·04	4·19	3·25	6·47	4·80	3·99	3·10	4·80
230	4·73	3·94	3·05	6·06	4·50	3·74	2·91	4·49
240	4·45	3·70	2·88	5·69	4·23	3·51	2·74	4·21

KL/r_{min}	$3\frac{1}{2}\times 3\times \frac{5}{16}$ $g=1\frac{3}{4}$	$3\frac{1}{2}\times 3\times \frac{1}{4}$ $1\frac{3}{4}$	$3\frac{1}{2}\times 2\frac{1}{2}\times \frac{3}{8}$ $1\frac{3}{8}$	$3\frac{1}{2}\times 2\frac{1}{2}\times \frac{5}{16}$ $1\frac{3}{8}$	$3\frac{1}{2}\times 2\frac{1}{2}\times \frac{1}{4}$ $1\frac{3}{8}$	$3\times 2\frac{1}{2}\times \frac{3}{8}$ $1\frac{3}{8}$	$3\times 2\frac{1}{2}\times \frac{1}{4}$ $1\frac{3}{8}$	$3\times 2\times \frac{3}{8}$ $1\frac{1}{8}$
20	12·3	9·44	13·5	11·1	8·50	13·9	9·08	10·3
30	12·1	9·30	13·3	11·0	8·37	13·7	8·93	10·2
40	11·9	9·12	13·0	10·7	8·21	13·4	8·75	9·97
50	11·6	8·91	12·7	10·5	8·02	13·1	8·54	9·74
60	11·3	8·66	12·3	10·2	7·79	12·8	8·30	9·47
70	10·9	8·39	11·9	9·85	7·54	12·4	8·02	9·17
80	10·5	8·08	11·5	9·47	7·26	11·9	7·72	8·84
90	10·1	7·75	11·0	9·06	6·96	11·4	7·38	8·47
100	9·57	7·38	10·5	8·61	6·62	10·9	7·01	8·06
110	9·03	6·98	9·86	8·13	6·26	10·3	6·61	7·62
120	8·44	6·55	9·21	7·59	5·87	9·58	6·16	7·13
130	7·79	6·07	8·50	7·01	5·44	8·81	5·67	6·60
140	7·18	5·60	7·83	6·46	5·02	8·09	5·21	6·09
150	6·63	5·18	7·22	5·96	4·64	7·44	4·79	5·64
160	6·13	4·79	6·67	5·51	4·30	6·85	4·41	5·22
170	5·67	4·44	6·18	5·10	3·99	6·33	4·08	4·84
180	5·26	4·13	5·73	4·74	3·70	5·85	3·77	4·50
190	4·89	3·84	5·32	4·40	3·45	5·42	3·50	4·18
200	4·55	3·58	4·95	4·10	3·21	5·03	3·25	3·90
210	4·25	3·34	4·62	3·82	3·00	4·68	3·02	3·64
220	3·97	3·12	4·31	3·57	2·81	4·36	2·82	3·41
230	3·71	2·93	4·04	3·34	2·63	4·07	2·64	3·19
240	3·48	2·75	3·78	3·14	2·47	3·81	2·47	3·00

[a] American Institute of Steel Construction (1978).
[b] Distance from the *heel* of the angle to the centre of the bolt group.

Table 8.1(d)—contd.

KL/r_{min}	$3 \times 2 \times \frac{5}{16}$ $g = 1\frac{1}{8}$	$3 \times 2 \times \frac{1}{4}$ $1\frac{1}{8}$	$3 \times 2 \times \frac{3}{16}$ $1\frac{1}{8}$	$2\frac{1}{2} \times 2 \times \frac{3}{8}$ $1\frac{1}{8}$	$2\frac{1}{2} \times 2 \times \frac{5}{16}$ $1\frac{1}{8}$	$2\frac{1}{2} \times 2 \times \frac{1}{4}$ $1\frac{1}{8}$	$2\frac{1}{2} \times 2 \times \frac{3}{16}$ $1\frac{1}{8}$
20	8·53	6·75	4·57	10·6	8·81	6·98	5·08
30	8·40	6·65	4·50	10·5	8·67	6·87	5·00
40	8·24	6·52	4·42	10·3	8·50	6·73	4·90
50	8·05	6·37	4·32	10·1	8·31	6·57	4·79
60	7·82	6·19	4·21	9·79	8·08	6·39	4·65
70	7·57	5·99	4·09	9·49	7·82	6·18	4·50
80	7·29	5·77	3·95	9·15	7·53	5·95	4·33
90	6·98	5·52	3·79	8·78	7·22	5·69	4·15
100	6·65	5·25	3·63	8·36	6·87	5·41	3·94
110	6·28	4·96	3·45	7·90	6·48	5·10	3·72
120	5·88	4·65	3·25	7·39	6·06	4·77	3·48
130	5·44	4·31	3·04	6·81	5·58	4·39	3·22
140	5·03	3·98	2·83	6·26	5·14	4·04	2·96
150	4·65	3·69	2·62	5·77	4·73	3·73	2·74
160	4·31	3·42	2·44	5·33	4·37	3·44	2·53
170	4·00	3·18	2·27	4·92	4·04	3·18	2·34
180	3·72	2·96	2·12	4·56	3·74	2·95	2·17
190	3·46	2·75	1·98	4·23	3·47	2·74	2·02
200	3·23	2·57	1·85	3·93	3·23	2·55	1·88
210	3·02	2·40	1·74	3·66	3·01	2·37	1·75
220	2·82	2·25	1·63	3·42	2·81	2·22	1·64
230	2·65	2·11	1·53	3·19	2·62	2·07	1·53
240	2·48	1·98	1·44	2·99	2·46	1·94	1·44

[a] American Institute of Steel Construction (1978).
[b] Distance from the *heel* of the angle to the centre of the bolt group.

Table 8.2

Permissible Axial Loads (kips) for Cold-Formed Equal-Leg Single Angles According to AISI[a] Specifications ($\sigma_y = 36$ ksi)

KL/r_{min}	$4\times4\times0.135$ $R^b = \frac{3}{16}$	$3\times3\times0.135$ $\frac{3}{16}$	$3\times3\times0.105$ $\frac{3}{16}$	$2\frac{1}{2}\times2\frac{1}{2}\times0.135$ $\frac{3}{16}$	$2\frac{1}{2}\times2\frac{1}{2}\times0.105$ $\frac{3}{16}$	$2\times2\times0.135$ $\frac{3}{16}$	$2\times2\times0.105$ $\frac{3}{16}$	$2\times2\times0.075$ $\frac{3}{32}$	$2\times2\times0.060$ $\frac{3}{32}$
20	6·65	8·06	4·26	8·16	4·83	7·76	4·98	2·29	1·16
30	6·64	8·05	4·25	8·15	4·82	7·75	4·98	2·29	1·16
40	6·63	8·04	4·24	8·14	4·81	7·73	4·97	2·28	1·16
50	6·62	8·02	4·24	8·12	4·80	7·71	4·96	2·28	1·16
60	6·60	8·00	4·23	8·09	4·79	7·69	4·94	2·27	1·16
70	6·59	7·97	4·21	8·06	4·77	7·66	4·93	2·26	1·15
80	6·57	7·93	4·20	8·02	4·75	7·35	4·90	2·25	1·15
90	6·54	7·89	4·18	7·98	4·73	6·90	4·88	2·24	1·15
100	6·52	7·84	4·16	7·58	4·70	6·40	4·69	2·23	1·14
110	6·49	7·79	4·14	7·01	4·67	5·84	4·34	2·22	1·14
120	6·45	7·32	4·12	6·38	4·63	5·23	3·95	2·20	1·14
130	6·41	6·68	4·09	5·71	4·26	4·56	3·54	2·19	1·13
140	6·37	5·98	4·06	4·98	3·84	3·93	3·09	2·11	1·13
150	6·32	5·25	3·90	4·33	3·40	3·42	2·69	1·92	1·12
160	5·94	4·61	3·56	3·81	2·99	3·01	2·36	1·72	1·11
170	5·44	4·08	3·20	3·37	2·64	2·66	2·09	1·53	1·10
180	4·91	3·64	2·85	3·01	2·36	2·38	1·87	1·36	1·04
190	4·41	3·27	2·56	2·70	2·12	2·13	1·68	1·22	0·966
200	3·98	2·95	2·31	2·44	1·91	1·93	1·51	1·10	0·885
210	3·61	2·68	2·09	2·21	1·73	1·75	1·37	0·999	0·803
220	3·29	2·44	1·91	2·01	1·58	1·59	1·25	0·911	0·732
230	3·01	2·23	1·75	1·84	1·44	1·46	1·14	0·833	0·670
240	2·76	2·05	1·60	1·69	1·33	1·34	1·05	0·765	0·615

[a] American Iron and Steel Institute (1980).
[b] Inside bend radius (in).

Table 8.3
Ultimate Compressive Strength of Pin-ended Cold-Formed Angles Connected by One Leg

Ultimate compressive strength (kN)

Slenderness ratio	45 × 45 × 3 × 6				55 × 35 × 5 × 15 (long leg connected)			
	g = 15	g = 20	g = 25	g = 30	g = 25	g = 30	g = 35	g = 40
20	28·8	38·4	28·7	20·6	42·3	53·5	51·0	37·6
30	28·2	37·5	28·7	20·4	41·4	52·2	51·4	37·6
40	27·3	36·2	28·6	20·2	40·1	50·4	52·0	37·5
50	26·3	34·7	28·5	20·0	38·5	48·2	52·9	37·4
60	25·1	32·9	28·4	19·6	36·8	45·6	54·6	37·3
70	23·8	30·9	28·4	19·2	34·8	42·6	54·5	37·1
80	22·4	28·8	28·5	18·8	32·4	38·9	49·1	37·0
90	21·0	26·7	29·0	18·3	29·9	35·4	44·1	36·9
100	19·6	24·6	32·5	17·7	27·5	32·3	39·7	36·9
110	18·3	22·6	29·2	17·0	25·4	29·5	35·8	37·1
120	17·0	20·7	26·1	16·3	23·4	27·0	32·3	42·1
130	15·7	18·9	23·4	15·5	21·6	24·7	29·2	37·4
140	14·6	17·3	21·0	14·6	19·9	22·7	26·5	33·2
150	13·5	15·8	18·9	13·8	18·5	20·8	24·1	29·7
160	12·5	14·4	17·0	12·9	17·1	19·2	22·0	26·6
170	11·6	13·2	15·4	12·1	15·9	17·7	20·2	24·0
180	10·8	12·1	14·0	11·3	14·8	16·4	18·5	21·7
190	9·99	11·1	12·7	10·5	13·8	15·2	17·0	30·6
200	9·29	10·3	11·6	9·81	12·9	14·1	15·7	30·3
210	8·65	9·49	10·6	9·14	12·0	13·1	14·5	30·0
220	8·06	8·79	17·2	8·52	11·2	12·2	13·4	29·6
230	7·52	8·16	16·8	7·95	10·5	11·4	12·5	29·1
240	7·03	7·59	16·4	7·43	9·90	10·7	11·6	28·6

Ultimate compressive strength (kN)
$55 \times 55 \times 4 \times 8$

Slenderness ratio	g = 15	g = 20	g = 25	g = 30	g = 35	g = 40
20	39·9	49·0	62·0	49·0	36·5	29·1
30	39·1	47·9	60·6	49·0	36·2	28·8
40	38·0	46·4	58·7	48·9	35·9	28·5
50	36·7	44·6	56·3	48·9	35·5	28·1
60	35·2	42·6	53·5	49·0	35·0	27·6
70	33·5	40·3	50·4	49·4	34·4	27·0
80	31·8	38·0	47·0	50·4	33·7	26·3
90	30·0	35·5	43·6	56·2	32·8	25·5
100	28·2	33·1	40·2	51·3	31·9	24·7
110	26·4	30·7	36·9	46·4	30·8	23·7
120	24·7	28·5	33·8	41·5	29·6	22·8
130	23·0	26·3	30·9	37·2	28·2	21·7
140	21·5	24·4	28·2	33·3	26·6	20·7
150	20·0	22·5	25·8	30·0	25·0	19·6
160	18·7	20·8	23·5	27·1	23·3	18·5
170	17·4	19·3	21·5	24·5	21·6	17·5
180	16·2	17·8	19·7	22·2	20·0	16·5
190	15·1	16·5	18·1	20·3	18·5	15·5
200	14·1	15·3	16·7	18·5	17·1	14·5
210	13·2	14·2	15·4	17·0	15·9	13·6
220	12·4	13·3	14·3	15·6	14·7	12·8
230	11·6	12·4	13·3	14·4	13·6	12·0
240	10·9	11·5	12·3	13·3	12·7	11·3

Note: 1. The size of angle is expressed as: Width of Long Leg (mm) × Width of Short Leg (mm) × Thickness (mm) × Inside Bend Radius (mm).
2. g = gauge distance (mm).

Table 8.3—*contd.*

Ultimate compressive strength (kN)

$65 \times 65 \times 4 \times 8$

Slenderness ratio	g = 15	g = 20	g = 25	g = 30	g = 35	g = 40	g = 45	g = 50
20	45·6	53·6	64·7	79·9	58·6	45·4	37·1	31·2
30	44·7	52·5	63·2	77·9	58·6	45·1	36·8	30·9
40	43·5	50·9	61·1	75·1	58·5	44·8	36·5	30·6
50	42·0	49·0	58·6	71·7	58·5	44·3	36·0	30·1
60	40·3	46·8	55·6	67·8	58·7	43·7	35·3	29·5
70	38·5	44·4	52·5	63·4	59·3	42·9	34·6	28·9
80	36·5	41·9	49·1	58·9	61·3	42·1	33·7	28·1
90	34·5	39·4	45·7	54·3	65·3	41·1	32·7	27·3
100	32·5	36·8	42·4	49·8	59·4	39·9	31·6	26·4
110	30·5	34·3	39·2	45·6	53·4	38·6	30·3	25·4
120	28·6	31·9	36·1	41·6	48·0	37·0	29·0	24·4
130	26·7	29·6	33·3	37·9	43·2	35·2	27·6	23·4
140	24·9	27·5	30·6	34·5	38·9	33·2	26·2	22·3
150	23·3	25·5	28·2	31·4	35·2	30·9	24·7	21·2
160	21·7	23·7	26·0	28·7	31·8	28·6	23·3	20·1
170	20·3	22·0	24·0	26·2	28·9	26·4	21·9	19·0
180	18·9	20·4	22·1	24·0	26·3	24·4	20·5	18·0
190	17·7	19·0	20·5	22·0	24·0	22·5	19·2	17·0
200	16·6	17·7	18·9	20·3	21·9	20·7	17·9	16·0
210	15·5	16·5	17·6	18·7	20·1	19·1	16·8	15·1
220	14·5	15·4	16·3	17·3	18·5	17·7	15·7	14·2
230	13·6	14·4	15·2	16·1	17·1	16·4	14·7	13·4
240	12·8	13·5	14·1	14·9	15·8	15·2	13·8	12·6

Ultimate compressive strength (kN)
$55 \times 35 \times 3 \times 6$ (long leg connected)

Slenderness ratio	g = 15	g = 20	g = 25	g = 30	g = 35	g = 40
20	24·5	30·0	38·3	39·4	28·1	22·0
30	24·0	29·2	36·9	40·6	28·1	21·9
40	23·3	28·1	35·0	42·5	28·2	21·8
50	22·4	26·9	32·8	38·4	28·4	21·6
60	21·5	25·5	30·6	34·6	28·9	21·5
70	20·5	24·0	28·4	31·2	31·9	21·2
80	19·4	22·5	26·0	28·2	29·2	20·9
90	18·3	21·0	23·5	25·5	26·7	20·5
100	17·2	19·5	21·3	23·1	24·4	19·9
110	16·1	17·8	19·4	20·9	22·2	19·2
120	15·0	16·3	17·6	19·0	20·3	22·4
130	13·8	14·9	16·1	17·3	18·5	17·1
140	12·7	13·7	14·7	15·8	16·9	20·9
150	11·8	12·6	13·5	14·5	15·4	14·7
160	10·9	11·6	12·4	13·3	14·1	13·6
170	10·1	10·7	11·4	12·2	13·0	19·6
180	9·38	9·96	10·6	11·2	11·9	11·6
190	8·74	9·25	9·80	10·4	11·0	10·7
200	8·15	8·61	9·09	9·61	10·2	9·92
210	7·62	8·02	8·45	8·91	9·40	9·20
220	7·14	7·49	7·88	8·28	8·71	17·6
230	6·69	7·01	7·35	7·71	8·09	17·2
240	6·29	6·57	6·88	7·20	7·54	16·8

Note: 1. The size of angle is expressed as: Width of Long Leg (mm) × Width of Short Leg (mm) × Thickness (mm) × Inside Bend Radius (mm).

2. g = gauge distance (mm).

Table 8.3—*contd.*

	Ultimate compressive strength (kN) 65 × 65 × 5 × 15					
Slenderness ratio	g = 25	g = 30	g = 35	g = 40	g = 45	g = 50
20	70·6	85·2	77·8	58·3	46·8	38·7
30	69·1	83·6	78·0	58·0	46·4	38·4
40	67·1	81·1	78·5	57·7	46·0	38·0
50	64·5	78·1	79·4	57·2	45·4	37·4
60	61·6	74·4	81·0	56·6	44·7	36·7
70	58·4	70·3	84·9	55·9	43·8	35·9
80	55·0	65·8	81·1	55·0	42·9	35·0
90	51·5	61·2	75·3	54·1	41·7	34·0
100	48·0	56·5	69·1	53·0	40·3	32·9
110	44·5	52·0	62·9	51·6	38·7	31·7
120	41·3	47·7	56·6	50·0	37·1	30·5
130	38·2	43·7	50·8	48·1	35·3	29·2
140	35·3	39·7	45·8	45·5	33·5	27·8
150	32·6	36·2	41·3	42·4	31·6	26·4
160	30·0	33·1	37·4	38·9	29·7	25·1
170	27·6	30·3	34·0	35·5	27·8	23·7
180	25·5	27·9	30·9	32·3	26·0	22·4
190	23·6	25·6	28·3	29·5	24·3	21·1
200	21·9	23·7	25·9	45·8	22·7	19·9
210	20·4	21·9	23·8	44·4	21·2	18·8
220	19·0	20·3	21·9	43·1	19·8	17·7
230	17·7	18·8	20·3	41·7	18·5	16·6
240	16·5	17·5	18·8	40·5	17·3	15·7

Ultimate compressive strength (kN)
65 × 50 × 4 × 8 (long leg connected)

Slenderness ratio	g = 15	g = 20	g = 25	g = 30	g = 35	g = 40	g = 45	g = 50
20	38·4	45·0	54·0	66·7	61·7	46·6	37·5	31·3
30	37·7	44·0	52·5	64·6	62·3	46·5	37·4	31·1
40	36·7	42·6	50·6	61·7	63·4	46·5	37·1	30·8
50	35·4	41·0	48·4	58·3	65·9	46·4	36·8	30·4
60	34·0	39·1	45·8	54·6	65·2	46·4	36·4	29·9
70	32·5	37·1	43·1	50·8	59·8	46·6	35·9	29·4
80	30·9	35·0	40·3	46·9	54·0	47·2	35·3	28·7
90	29·2	32·9	37·5	43·1	48·4	53·4	34·7	28·0
100	27·5	30·8	34·7	39·4	43·6	48·2	33·9	27·1
110	25·9	28·7	32·1	35·6	39·3	43·5	32·8	26·2
120	24·2	26·7	29·6	32·3	35·5	39·2	31·5	25·1
130	22·7	24·9	27·0	29·4	32·2	35·4	29·9	24·0
140	21·2	23·0	24·8	26·8	29·2	32·1	28·1	22·8
150	19·8	21·2	22·7	24·5	26·6	29·1	26·2	21·5
160	18·4	19·6	20·9	22·5	24·3	26·4	24·3	20·3
170	17·1	18·1	19·3	20·6	22·2	24·1	22·4	19·1
180	15·9	16·8	17·8	19·0	20·4	22·0	20·7	17·9
190	14·8	15·6	16·5	17·6	18·7	20·1	19·1	16·7
200	13·8	14·6	15·4	16·3	17·3	18·5	17·7	15·6
210	12·9	13·6	14·3	15·1	16·0	17·0	16·3	14·6
220	12·1	12·7	13·3	14·0	14·8	15·7	15·1	13·7
230	11·4	11·9	12·4	13·0	13·7	14·5	14·1	12·8
240	10·7	11·1	11·6	12·2	12·8	13·5	13·1	12·0

Note: 1. The size of angle is expressed as: Width of Long Leg (mm) × Width of Short Leg (mm) × Thickness (mm) × Inside Bend Radius (mm).

2. g = gauge distance (mm).

Table 8.3—*contd.*

Ultimate compressive strength (kN)

Slenderness ratio	65 × 50 × 5 × 15 (long leg connected)						55 × 35 × 3 × 6 (long leg out)	
	g = 25	g = 30	g = 35	g = 40	g = 45	g = 50	g = 15	g = 20
20	57·1	69·1	84·1	60·9	47·6	39·0	35·9	20·3
30	55·9	67·4	82·3	61·0	47·5	38·7	35·6	20·2
40	54·1	65·1	79·5	61·2	47·2	38·4	35·2	19·9
50	52·0	62·2	75·9	61·5	46·9	37·9	34·7	19·6
60	49·6	58·9	71·6	62·0	46·5	37·4	34·0	19·2
70	46·9	55·4	66·9	63·1	46·0	36·7	33·2	18·8
80	44·2	51·7	61·9	66·0	45·4	35·9	32·1	18·2
90	41·4	48·0	56·0	67·5	44·7	35·0	30·7	17·7
100	38·7	43·8	50·4	60·2	43·9	34·0	29·0	17·0
110	35·6	39·9	45·6	53·8	43·0	32·9	27·0	16·3
120	32·7	36·4	41·2	48·2	41·8	31·6	24·9	15·6
130	30·1	33·3	37·4	43·3	40·3	30·2	22·7	14·8
140	27·7	30·5	34·0	39·0	38·0	28·7	20·6	14·0
150	25·6	28·0	31·0	35·3	35·3	27·2	18·7	13·2
160	23·6	25·7	28·4	31·9	32·5	25·6	16·9	12·4
170	21·9	23·7	26·0	29·0	29·8	24·1	15·4	11·6
180	20·3	21·9	23·9	26·5	27·3	22·6	14·0	10·8
190	18·9	20·3	22·0	24·2	25·0	21·1	12·7	10·1
200	17·6	18·8	20·3	22·2	22·9	19·7	11·6	9·46
210	16·4	17·5	18·8	20·4	21·0	18·4	10·6	8·84
220	15·3	16·3	17·4	18·8	37·5	17·2	9·78	8·27
230	14·3	15·2	16·2	17·4	36·5	16·0	9·01	7·73
240	13·5	14·2	15·1	16·2	35·6	15·0	8·32	7·24

Ultimate compressive strength (kN)

Slenderness ratio	65 × 50 × 4 × 8 (long leg out)					65 × 50 × 5 × 15 (long leg out)		
	g = 15	g = 20	g = 25	g = 30	g = 35	g = 25	g = 30	g = 35
20	45·2	57·3	51·0	36·1	28·0	69·5	46·7	35·2
30	44·4	56·4	50·9	35·8	27·7	69·8	46·4	34·9
40	43·3	55·2	50·8	35·4	27·4	70·4	46·0	34·5
50	41·9	53·5	50·6	34·9	26·9	70·9	45·5	34·0
60	40·3	51·5	50·4	34·3	26·4	69·6	44·8	33·4
70	38·5	49·2	50·3	33·5	25·8	67·8	44·0	32·7
80	36·6	46·6	50·3	32·6	25·0	65·4	43·1	31·8
90	34·5	43·8	50·8	31·6	24·2	62·3	42·0	30·8
100	32·5	40·8	52·8	30·5	23·4	58·6	40·7	29·7
110	30·4	37·9	53·5	29·3	22·5	54·3	39·3	28·6
120	28·4	34·9	48·6	28·0	21·5	49·8	37·7	27·4
130	26·4	32·1	43·5	26·7	20·6	45·3	35·9	26·1
140	24·6	29·5	38·9	25·2	19·6	41·1	33·9	24·8
150	22·8	27·1	34·7	23·6	18·6	37·2	31·9	23·5
160	21·2	24·8	31·0	22·1	17·6	33·8	29·7	22·3
170	19·7	22·8	27·8	20·7	16·7	30·6	27·5	21·0
180	18·3	21·0	25·1	19·3	15·7	27·9	25·5	19·8
190	17·0	19·3	22·7	18·0	14·9	25·4	23·6	18·7
200	15·8	17·8	20·6	16·8	14·0	23·3	21·8	17·6
210	14·8	16·5	18·8	15·6	13·2	21·3	20·2	16·5
220	13·8	15·2	17·2	14·6	12·5	19·6	18·7	15·6
230	12·9	14·1	15·8	13·6	11·7	18·1	17·4	14·6
240	12·0	13·1	14·6	12·7	11·1	16·7	16·1	13·8

Note: 1. The size of angle is expressed as: Width of Long Leg (mm) × Width of Short Leg (mm) × Thickness (mm) × Inside Bend Radius (mm).

2. g = gauge distance (mm).

Table 8.3—*contd.*

Ultimate compressive strength (kN)

Slenderness ratio	55 × 55 × 3 × 6						55 × 35 × 4 × 8 (long leg connected)				55 × 35 × 4 × 8 (long leg out)	
	g = 15	g = 20	g = 25	g = 30	g = 35	g = 40	g = 20	g = 25	g = 30	g = 35	g = 15	g = 20
20	32·5	40·4	51·0	35·7	27·1	21·7	35·1	44·1	51·4	37·6	42·6	27·8
30	31·9	39·4	50·4	35·6	26·9	21·5	34·3	42·8	51·3	37·5	42·4	27·5
40	30·9	38·0	48·3	35·6	26·6	21·3	33·2	41·2	51·1	37·5	41·9	27·2
50	29·8	36·4	45·9	35·5	26·3	20·9	31·9	39·2	49·7	37·5	41·1	26·9
60	28·5	34·6	43·1	35·5	25·9	20·5	30·5	37·0	46·2	37·5	40·2	26·4
70	27·1	32·6	40·2	35·5	25·4	20·1	28·9	34·7	42·3	37·4	39·0	25·8
80	25·6	30·5	37·2	35·5	24·8	19·5	27·2	32·3	37·9	37·3	37·5	25·2
90	24·1	28·5	34·3	35·5	24·1	18·9	25·5	29·6	34·1	37·2	35·8	24·4
100	22·6	26·4	31·4	35·4	21·0	18·3	23·9	26·9	30·7	35·8	33·7	23·2
110	21·1	24·4	28·7	33·0	17·0	17·6	21·9	24·5	27·8	32·1	31·5	19·2
120	19·6	22·6	26·2	29·9	14·1	16·8	20·1	22·4	25·2	28·9	29·2	16·1
130	18·3	20·8	23·9	27·1	12·0	16·0	18·5	20·4	22·9	26·0	26·9	13·7
140	17·0	19·2	21·8	24·5	10·3	15·2	17·1	18·7	20·8	23·5	24·6	11·8
150	15·8	17·7	19·9	22·2	8·82	14·4	15·8	17·2	19·0	21·3	22·5	10·3
160	14·7	16·3	18·1	20·2	7·71	13·6	14·6	15·9	17·4	19·4	20·5	9·07
170	13·7	15·1	16·6	18·4	6·81	12·8	13·5	14·6	16·0	17·7	18·7	8·03
180	12·7	13·9	15·2	16·7	6·05	12·1	12·6	13·5	14·7	16·2	17·1	7·16
190	11·9	12·9	14·0	15·3	5·43	11·4	11·7	12·5	13·6	14·8	15·7	6·43
200	11·1	11·9	12·9	14·0	4·90	10·7	10·9	11·6	12·5	13·7	14·4	5·80
210	10·3	11·1	11·9	12·9	4·44	10·0	10·2	10·8	11·6	12·6	13·3	5·26
220	9·65	10·3	11·0	11·8	4·05	9·43	9·51	10·1	10·8	11·6	12·2	4·80
230	9·03	9·61	10·2	10·9	3·70	8·86	8·91	9·44	10·1	10·8	11·3	4·39
240	8·47	8·96	9·50	10·1	3·40	8·34	8·36	8·84	9·38	10·0	10·5	4·03

Note: 1. The size of angle is expressed as: Width of Long Leg (mm) × Width of Short Leg (mm) × Thickness (mm) × Inside Bend Radius (mm).

2. g = gauge distance (mm).

REFERENCES

ALGOMA STEEL CO. LTD (1978). *Guide to steel standards and specifications.* Toronto, Ontario, Canada, pp. 1B–18 and 1B–19.

AMERICAN ASSOCIATION OF STATE HIGHWAY AND TRANSPORTATION OFFICIALS (1983). *Standard specifications for highway bridges.* Thirteenth Edition, Washington, DC, USA.

AMERICAN INSTITUTE OF STEEL CONSTRUCTION (1984). *Engineering for steel construction.* First Edition, Chicago, Illinois, USA.

AMERICAN INSTITUTE OF STEEL CONSTRUCTION (1980). *Manual of steel construction.* Eighth Edition, Chicago, Illinois, USA.

AMERICAN INSTITUTE OF STEEL CONSTRUCTION (1982). Predesigned bolted framing angle connections. *Engineering Journal,* **19** (1), First Quarter, 1–11.

AMERICAN INSTITUTE OF STEEL CONSTRUCTION (1978). *Specification for the design, fabrication and erection of structural steel for buildings.* Chicago, Illinois, USA.

AMERICAN INSTITUTE OF STEEL CONSTRUCTION (1983). *Proposed load and resistance factor design specification for structural steel buildings.* Chicago, Illinois, USA.

AMERICAN INSTITUTE OF STEEL CONSTRUCTION (1982). *Stability of metal structures: A world view.* Chicago, Illinois, USA.

AMERICAN IRON AND STEEL INSTITUTE (1971). *Cold-formed steel design manual, Part III, supplementary information.* Washington, DC, USA.

AMERICAN IRON AND STEEL INSTITUTE (1977). *Cold-formed steel design manual, Part V, charts and tables.* Washington, DC, USA.

AMERICAN IRON AND STEEL INSTITUTE (1980). *Specification for the design of cold-formed steel structural members.* Washington, DC, USA.

AMERICAN SOCIETY OF CIVIL ENGINEERS (1971). *Guide for design of steel transmission towers,* Manual No. 52. New York, NY, USA.

ARCHITECTURAL INSTITUTE OF JAPAN (1979). *Design standard for steel structures.* Tokyo, Japan.

ARCHITECTURAL INSTITUTE OF JAPAN (1960). *Standard for structural calculation of steel tower structures.* Tokyo, Japan.

ASHBY, R. J. (1953). *Report on an experimental investigation of mild steel angles as purlins under corrugated roofing.* Publication No. 7, British Constructional Steelwork Association, Westminster, UK, pp. 4–7.

ASTANEH-ASL, A., and GOEL, S. C. (1984). Cyclic in-plane buckling of double angle bracing. *Journal of Structural Engineering, ASCE,* **110** (9), 2036–2055.

AUSTRALIAN INSTITUTE OF STEEL CONSTRUCTION (1979). *Steel structures manual—Part 4. Connections.* Standards Association of Australia, North Sydney, NSW, Australia.

BATHO, C. (1915). The effect of the end connections on the distribution of stress in certain tension members. *Journal of the Franklin Institute,* Philadelphia, Pennsylvania, USA, **180** (2), August, 129–172.

BEZ, R., and HIRT, M. A. (1982). Dimensionnemen plasique et phénomènes d'instabilité de cornières métalliques. *Construction Métallique,* No. 1, 33–39.

BIJLAARD, P. P. (1940–41). *Theory of the plastic stability of thin plates.* International Association for Bridge and Structural Engineering, Publications, Sixth volume, pp. 45–69.

BIJLAARD, P. P. (1947). *Some contributions to the theory of elastic and plastic stability.* International Association for Bridge and Structural Engineering, Publications, Eighth volume, pp. 17–80.

BLEICH, F., and BLEICH, H. (1936). *Bending, torsion and buckling of bars composed of thin walls.* Preliminary Publication, 2nd Congress International Association for Bridge and Structural Engineering, English Edition, Berlin, p. 871.

BLEICH, F. (1952). *Buckling strength of metal structures.* McGraw-Hill Book Company, Inc., New York, NY, USA.

BLODGETT, O. W. (1966). *Design of welded structures.* The James F. Lincoln Arc Welding Foundation, Cleveland, Ohio, USA.

BRITISH STANDARDS INSTITUTION (1972). *Hot-rolled structural steel sections—equal and unequal angles,* BS 4848: Part 4, London, UK.

BRITISH STANDARDS INSTITUTION (1969a). *Specification for the use of structural steel in building,* BS 449: Part 2, metric units, London, U.K.

BRITISH STANDARDS INSTITUTION (1975). *Specification for the use of cold-formed steel sections in building,* Addendum No. 1 (April 1975) to BS 449: Part 2, London, UK.

BRITISH STANDARDS INSTITUTION (1969b). *The structural use of aluminium,* BS CP 118, London, UK.

CANADIAN INSTITUTE OF STEEL CONSTRUCTION (1977). *Limit states design steel manual.* First Edition, Willowdale, Ontario, Canada.

CANADIAN INSTITUTE OF STEEL CONSTRUCTION (1980). *Handbook of steel construction.* Third Edition, Willowdale, Ontario, Canada.

CANADIAN STANDARDS ASSOCIATION (1981). *Antenna towers and antenna supporting structures,* CSA-S37-M1981. Rexdale, Ontario, Canada.

CANADIAN STANDARDS ASSOCIATION (1984). *Cold-formed steel structural members,* CAN3-S136-M84. Rexdale, Ontario, Canada.

CANADIAN STANDARDS ASSOCIATION (1978). *Steel structures for buildings—limit states design,* CAN3-S16.1-M78. Rexdale, Ontario, Canada.

CANADIAN STANDARDS ASSOCIATION (1983). *Strength design in aluminum,* CAN3-S157-M83. Rexdale, Ontario, Canada.

CARPENA, A., CAUZILLO, B. A., and NICOLINI, P. (1976). Modern technical and constructional solutions for the new Italian power lines. *International Conference on Large High Voltage Electric Systems (CIGRE),* Paris, Paper No. 22–13.

CHAJES, A., and WINTER, G. (1965). Torsional–flexural buckling of thin-walled members. *Journal of the Structural Division, ASCE,* **91** (ST4), August, 103–124.

CHAJES, A., FANG, P. J., and WINTER, G. (1966). *Torsional–flexural buckling, elastic and inelastic, of cold-formed thin-walled columns.* Research Bulletin 66-1, Department of Structural Engineering, School of Civil Engineering, Cornell University, Ithaca, NY, USA.

CHEN, S-F. (1980). Lateral torsional buckling of T-section steel beam columns. *Structural Stability Research Council Annual Technical Session in New York City,* NY, USA.

CHEN, W. F., and ATSUTA, T. (1972). Interaction equations for biaxially loaded sections. *Journal of the Structural Division, ASCE,* **98** (ST5), 1035–52.

CHEN, W. F., and ATSUTA, T. (1974). Interaction curves for steel sections under axial load and biaxial bending. Canadian Society for Civil Engineering, *Engineering Journal,* **57** (3/4), March/April, 49–56.

CHESSON, E., Jr., and MUNSE, W. H. (1963). Riveted and bolted joints: Truss-type tensile connections. *Journal of the Structural Division, ASCE,* **89** (ST1), Feb., 67–106.

CHUENMEI, G. (1984). Elastoplastic buckling of single angle columns. *Journal of Structural Engineering, ASCE,* **110** (6), 1391–1395.

COLUMN RESEARCH COMMITTEE OF JAPAN, Editor (1971). *Handbook of structural stability.* Corona Publishing Company Limited, Tokyo, Japan.

CONSTRUCTIONAL STEEL RESEARCH AND DEVELOPMENT ORGANIZATION (1972). *Steel designers' manual.* A Halstead Press Book, John Wiley & Sons, New York.

CULVER, C. G. (1966). Exact solution of the biaxial bending equations. *Journal of the Structural Division, ASCE,* **92** (ST2), 63–83.

DABROWSKI, R. (1961). Dünnwandige Stäbe unter zwerachsig aussermittigem Druck, *Der Stahlbau,* December.

DIN (DEUTSCHES INSTITUT FÜR NORMUNG E.V.) (GERMAN INSTITUTE FOR STANDARDIZATION) (1952). *Stabilitätsfälle (Knickung, Kippung, Beulung),* DIN 4114. English translation (1957) by T. V. Galambos and J. Jones, Column Research Council (now Structural Stability Research Council), Fritz Engineering Laboratory, Lehigh University, Bethlehem, Pennsylvania, USA.

EL-DARWISH, I. A., and JOHNSTON, B. G. (1965). Torsion of structural shapes. *Journal of the Structural Division, ASCE,* **91** (ST1), 203–227.

EL-TAYEM, A., and GOEL, S. C. (1984). Cyclic behavior of angle X-bracing. Paper presented at the *ASCE Annual Convention and Structures Congress III,* Oct., San Francisco, California, USA.

EULER, L. (1759). *Sur la force de colonnes.* Mémoires de l'Académie de Berlin.

EUROPEAN CONVENTION FOR CONSTRUCTIONAL STEELWORK (ECCS) (1978). *European recommendations for steel construction.* Second Edition, Brussels, Belgium.

EUROPEAN CONVENTION FOR CONSTRUCTIONAL STEELWORK (ECCS) (1976). *Second international colloquium on stability introductory report* (Stability Manual). Second Edition Sub-chapter 3.1.5 Angles (pp. 98–103), and Sub-chapter 9.2 Angles in Lattice Transmission Towers.

FANG, P. J. (1966). *Inelastic torsional–flexural buckling and post-buckling*

344   Single and Compound Angle Members

behavior of centrally loaded columns with thin-walled open sections. Ph.D. dissertation, Cornell University, Ithaca, NY, USA.

FOEHL, P. J. (1948). Direct method for designing single angle struts in welded trusses. Design Book for Welding, Lincoln Electric Company, November.

GIBSON, G. J., and WAKE, B. T. (1942). An investigation of welded connections for angle tension members. The Welding Journal, The Journal of the American Welding Society, New York, NY, Welding Research Supplement, 21 (1), January, pp. 44-s-49-s.

GOODIER, J. N. (1941). The buckling of compressed bars by torsion and flexure. Cornell University Engineering Expt. Sta. Bull. No. 27.

GOODIER, J. N. (1942). Flexural–torsional buckling of bars of open section. Cornell University Engineering Expt. Sta. Bull. No. 28.·

HAAIJER, G., CARSKADDAN, P. S., and GRUBB, M. A. (1981). Eccentric load test of angle column simulated with MSC/NASTRAN finite element program. Annual Meeting of Structural Stability Research Council, Chicago, Illinois, USA, April.

HU, X. R., SHEN, Z. Y., and LU, L. W. (1982). Inelastic stability analysis of biaxially loaded beam columns by the finite element methods. Proceedings of the International Conference on Finite Element Methods, Shanghai, China, Vol. 2, pp. 52–57.

INDIAN STANDARDS INSTITUTION (1984). Code of practice for general steel construction, IS: 800-1984. New Delhi, India.

ISHIDA, A. (1968). Experimental study on column carrying capacity of 'SHY steel' angles. Yawata Technical Report No. 265, December, pp. 8564–8582 and pp. 8761–8763, Yawata Iron and Steel Co., Ltd, Tekko Building, Tokyo, Japan.

JAIN, A. K., GOEL, S. C., and HANSON, R. D. (1980). Hysteretic cycles of axially loaded steel members, Journal of the Structural Division, ASCE, 106 (ST8), August, 1777–1795.

JOHNSON, L. J. (1906). An analysis of general flexure in a straight bar of uniform cross-section. Transactions, American Society of Civil Engineers, 56, 169–196.

JOHNSTON, B. G., Editor (1976). Guide to stability design criteria for metal structures. John Wiley & Sons, New York, NY, USA.

KAPPUS, R. (1937). Drillknicken zentrisch gedrückter Stäbe mit offenem Profil im elastischen Bereich, Luftfahrtforschung, 14 (9), 444–457, Translated in NACA Tech. Mem. 851, March 1938.

KENNEDY, J. B., and MURTY, M. K. S. (1972). Buckling of steel angle and tee struts. Journal of the Structural Division, ASCE, 98 (ST11), November, 2507–2522.

KENNEDY, J. B., and SINCLAIR, G. R. (1969). Ultimate capacity of single bolted angle connections. Journal of the Structural Division, ASCE, 95 (ST8), August 1969, 1645–1660.

KITIPORNCHAI, S., and LEE, H. W. (1984). Inelastic experiments on angles and tee struts. Research Report No. CE54, Department of Civil Engineering, University of Queensland, St. Lucia, Q4067, Australia.

KLÖPPEL, K., and RAMM, W. (1972). Zur Stabilitätsuntersuchung von mehrteiligen Gitterstäben. Der Stahlbau, No. 1, 14–21.

KOLLBRUNNER, C. F. (1935). Das Ausbeulen des auf Druck Beanspruchten Freistehenden Winkels. *Mitteilungen,* **4,** Institut für Baustatik, Eidgenössische Technische Hochschule, Zurich.

KOLLBRUNNER, C. F. (1946). Das Ausbeulen der auf einseitigen, gleich-mässig verteilten Druck beanspruchten Platten im elastischen und plastischen Bereich. *Mitteilungen,* **17,** Institut für Baustatik, Eidgenössische Technische Hochschule, Zurich.

LEIGH, J. M., and GALAMBOS, T. V. (1972). *The design of compression webs in longspan steel joists.* Research Report No. 21, Department of Civil and Environmental Engineering, Washington University, St Louis, Missouri, USA.

LEIGH, J. M., and LAY, M. G. (1969). The design of laterally unsupported angles. *B.H.P. Technical Bulletin,* **13** (3), 24–29. Melbourne, Australia.

LEIGH, J. M., and LAY, M. G. (1970a). *Laterally unsupported angles with equal and unequal legs.* B.H.P. Melbourne Research Laboratory Report MRL 22/2, Melbourne, Australia.

LEIGH, J. M., and LAY, M. G. (1970b). *Safe load tables for laterally unsupported angles.* B.H.P. Melbourne Research Laboratory Report MRL 22/3, Melbourne, Australia.

LEIGH, J. M., THOMAS, B. F., and LAY, M. G. (1984). Safe load for laterally unsupported angles. *Engineering Journal,* American Institute of Steel Construction, **21** (1), 35–48.

LIPSON, S. L. (1968). Single-angle and single-plate beam framing connections. *Proceedings, Canadian Structural Engineering Conference,* Toronto, Ontario, Canada, pp. 141–162.

LIPSON, S. L. (1977). Single-angle welded-bolted connections. *Journal of the Structural Division, ASCE,* **103** (ST3) March, 559–571.

LIPSON, S. L., and ANTONIO, M. E. (1980). Single-angle welded-bolted beam connections. *Canadian Journal of Civil Engineering,* **7** (2), June, 315–324.

LIPSON, S. L., and HAQUE, M. I. (1978). Elasto–plastic analysis of single-angle bolted-welded connections using the finite element method. *Computers and Structures,* **9,** 533–545.

LOOMIS, R. S., LOOMIS, R. H., LOOMIS, R. W., and LOOMIS, R. W. (1980). Torsional buckling study of Hartford coliseum. *Journal of the Structural Division, ASCE,* **106** (ST1), January, 211–231.

LORIN, M., and CUILLE, J. P. (1977). An experimental study of the influence of the connections of the transmission tower web-members on their buckling resistance. *Second International Colloquium on Stability, Preliminary Report,* Liège, Belgium, pp. 447–456.

LU, L. W., SHEN, Z. Y., and HU, X. R. (1983). Inelastic instability research at Lehigh University. *The Michael R. Horne International Conference on Instability and Plastic Collapse of Steel Structures,* The University of Manchester, England.

LUNDQUIST, E. E., and FLIGG, C. M. (1937). *A theory for primary failure of straight centrally loaded columns.* NACA Tech. Rept. 582.

LYSE, I., and SCHREINER, N. G. (1935). An investigation of welded seat angle connections. American Welding Society, *The Welding Journal,* **14** (2), February, *Supplement,* 1–15.

LYSE, I., and STEWART, D. M. (1935). A photoelastic study of bending in welded seat angle connections. American Welding Society, *The Welding Journal*, **14** (2), February, *Supplement*, 16–20.

MACKEY, S., and WILLIAMSON, N. W. (1951). *Experimental investigation of a 33 ft. span lattice girder.* International Association for Bridge and Structural Engineering, Publications, Zurich, Switzerland, Vol. 11, pp. 303–324.

MACKEY, S., and WILLIAMSON, N. W. (1953). *Report on experimental investigation of two mild steel lattice girders.* Publication No. 7, British Constructional Steelwork Association, London, pp. 19–36.

MADUGULA, M. K. S., PRABHU, T. S., and TEMPLE, M. C. (1983). Ultimate strength of concentrically loaded cold-formed angles. *Canadian Journal of Civil Engineering*, **10** (1), 60–68.

MADUGULA, M. K. S., and RAY, S. K. (1984a). Ultimate strength of eccentrically loaded cold-formed angles. *Canadian Journal of Civil Engineering*, **11** (2), 225–233.

MADUGULA, M. K. S., and RAY, S. K. (1984b). Cross-sectional properties of cold-formed angles. *Canadian Journal of Civil Engineering*, **11** (3), 649–655.

MADUGULA, M. K. S., and RAY, S. K. (1984c). Biaxial bending of cold-formed angle members. *Canadian Journal of Civil Engineering*, **11** (4), 933–42.

MARSH, C. (1969). Single angle members in tension and compression. *Journal of the Structural Division, ASCE*, **95** (ST5), May, 1043–1049.

MARSH, C. (1971). *Buckling of single angles as beams/columns.* Canadian Steel Industries Construction Council, Project No. 712, (unpublished).

MARSHALL, W. T., NELSON, H. M., and SMITH, I. A. (1963). Experiments on single-angle aluminium alloy struts. *Symposium on Aluminium in Structural Engineering*, London, England, June, Paper No. 3.

MASSONNET, CH. and PLUMIER, A. (1981). *Essais de Flambement sur Cornières de Pylones*, effectués à la demande de L'UNERG. March, Liège, Belgium.

MASSEY, C. (1964). The rotation capacity of I-beams. *British Welding Journal*, **18** (8), Aug, 377–385.

MCGUIRE, W. (1968). *Steel structures.* Prentice-Hall, Inc., Englewood Cliffs, New Jersey, USA.

MCKIBBEN, F. P. (1906). Tension tests of steel angles. *Proceedings of the American Society for Testing and Materials*, Vol. 6, pp. 267–274.

MCKIBBEN, F. P. (1907). Tension tests of steel angles with various types of end connections. *Proceedings of the American Society for Testing and Materials*, Vol. 7, pp. 287–295.

MUELLER, W. H., and ERZURUMLU, H. (1983). *Limit state behavior of steel angle columns.* Research Report of Civil–Structural Engineering, Division of Engineering and Applied Science, Portland State University, USA.

MUNSE, W. H., and CHESSON, E., Jr (1963). Riveted and bolted joints: Net section design. *Journal of the Structural Division, ASCE*, **89** (ST1), February, 107–126.

NELSON, H. M. (1953). *Angles in tension.* British Constructional Steelwork Association, Publication No. 7, UK, pp. 8–18.

OJALVO, M., GARNER, S. J., and SAKIMOTO, T. (1984). Angle struts braced in a non-principal axis direction. *ASCE Annual Convention and Structures Congress III*, Oct., San Francisco, California, USA.

OSTENFELD, A. (1931). Politecknisk Laereanstalts Laboratorium for Bygningsstatik. Meddelelse No. 5, Kopenhagen.

PEKÖZ, T. B., and CELEBI, N. (1969). *Torsional flexural buckling of thin-walled sections under eccentric load.* Research Bulletin No. 69-1, Department of Structural Engineering, School of Civil Engineering, Cornell University, Ithaca, NY, USA, September.

PEKÖZ, T. B., and WINTER, G. (1969). Torsional–flexural buckling of thin-walled sections under eccentric load. *Journal of the Structural Division, ASCE*, **95** (ST5), 941–963.

PRAWEL, S. P., Jr., and LEE, G. C. (1964). Biaxial flexure of columns by analog computers. *Journal of the Engineering Mechanics Division, ASCE*, **90** (EM1), 83–111.

REDWOOD, R. G., and EYRE, D. G. (1984). Clip angle connections subjected to cyclic loads. *Journal of Structural Engineering, ASCE*, **110** (1), 162–166.

SHORT, J. (1977*a*). The buckling of compound members consisting of two angles stitch-bolted together. *Second International Colloquium on Stability of Steel Structures*, Liège, April, Preliminary Report, pp. 137–142.

SHORT, J. (1977*b*). The buckling of compound angles with varying gap between angles. *Second International Colloquium on Stability of Steel Structures*, Liège, April, Final Report, pp. 75–77.

SHORT, J. (1977*c*). The buckling of single angles about the XX and VV axes. *Second International Colloquium on Stability of Steel Structures*, Liège, April, Final Report, pp. 271–272.

SHORT, J., and MORSE, J. (1979). The variation between predicted and actual performance of transmission towers under test conditions. *IEE Conference on Progress in Cables and Overhead Lines for 220 kV and Above*, pp. 125–130.

SMITH, E. A. (1983). Buckling of four equal-leg angle cruciform columns. *Journal of Structural Engineering, ASCE*, **109** (2), 439–450.

STANDARDS ASSOCIATION OF AUSTRALIA (1979). *Dimensions of hot-rolled structural steel sections.* AS 1131-1979, North Sydney, NSW, Australia.

STANDARDS ASSOCIATION OF AUSTRALIA (1981). *SAA steel structures code* AS 1250-1981, North Sydney, NSW, Australia.

STUDNICKA, J. (1980). Local and total stability of compression bars (in Slovak). *Stavebnicky Casopis*, Bratislava, Czechoslovakia, **28** (8), 587–598.

TEMPLE, M. C., and SCHEPERS, J. A. (1980). The interconnection of starred angle compression members. *Proceedings, Annual Conference of Canadian Society for Civil Engineering*, May, Winnipeg, Manitoba, Canada, pp. S/22:1–8.

THOMAS, E. W. (1941). Torsional instability of thin angle section struts. *Structural Engineer*, **19** (5), May, 73–82.

THOMAS, B. F., and LEIGH, J. M. (1970). *The behaviour of laterally unsupported angles.* The Broken Hill Proprietary Company Limited, Research Laboratories Report No. MRL 22/4, Melbourne, Australia.

THOMAS, B. F., LEIGH, J. M., and LAY, M. G. (1973). The behaviour of laterally unsupported angles. *Civil Engineering Transactions*, The Institution of Engineers, Australia, pp. 103–110.

THÜRLIMANN, B. (1953). *Deformations of and stresses in initially twisted and eccentrically loaded columns of thin-walled open cross section*. Brown University. Report No. E797, Providence, RI, USA.

TIMOSHENKO, S. P. (1945). Theory of bending, torsion and buckling of thin-walled members of open cross-section. *Journal of the Franklin Inst.*, Philadelphia, Pa, USA, **239** (3), 201–219; **239** (4), 249–268; **239** (5), 343–361.

TIMOSHENKO, S. P., and GERE, J. M. (1961). *Theory of elastic stability*. Second Edition, McGraw-Hill Book Company, New York, NY, USA.

TRAHAIR, N. S., USAMI, T., and GALAMBOS, T. V. (1969). *Eccentrically loaded single angle columns*. Structural Division Research Report No. 11, Civil and Environmental Engineering Department, School of Engineering and Applied Science, Washington University, St Louis, Missouri, USA, also Supplemental Research Report No. 11a by Galambos, January 1970.

UNITED STATES BUREAU OF STANDARDS (1924). *Results of some compression tests of structural steel angles*. Technologic Papers of the Bureau of Standards, No. 218, Government Printing Office, Washington, DC.

USAMI, T. (1970). *Restrained single-angle columns under biaxial bending*. Research Report No. 14, Structural Division, Civil and Environmental Engineering Department, School of Engineering and Applied Science, Washington University, St Louis, Missouri, USA.

USAMI, T., and FUKUMOTO, Y. (1972). Compressive strength and design of bracing members with angle or tee section. *Proceedings of the Japan Society of Civil Engineers*, **201,** May, 43–50 (in Japanese). Abstract (in English) in the *Transactions of the Japan Society of Civil Engineers*, **4,** 28–29.

USAMI, T., and GALAMBOS, T. V. (1971). *Eccentrically loaded single angle columns*. International Association for Bridge and Structural Engineering, Publications, Zurich, Switzerland, Vol. 31-II, pp. 153–184.

VINNAKOTA, S. (1984). Strength of initially crooked double-angle and T-section steel columns. *ASCE Annual Convention and Structures Congress III*, Oct. 1–5, San Francisco, California, USA.

VINNAKOTA, S., and ÄYSTÖ, P. (1974). Inelastic spatial stability of restrained beam-columns. *Journal of the Structural Division, ASCE*, **100** (ST11), November, 2235–2254.

VLASOV, V. Z. (1940). *Thin-walled elastic beams*. Moscow. Translated from Russian by the Israel Program for Scientific Translations, 1961.

WAGNER, A. L., MUELLER, W. H., RADHAKRISHNAN, P., and PURASINGHE, R. (1984). Post-buckling behaviour of single angle struts. *ASCE Annual Convention and Structures Congress III*, Oct. 1–5, San Francisco, California, USA.

WAGNER, H. (1929). *Verdrehung und Knickung von offenen Profilen*. 25th Anniversary Publication, Technische Hochschule Danzig, 1904–1929. Translated in NACA Tech. Memorandum No. 807, October 1936.

WAGNER, H., and PRETSCHNER, W. (1934). Verdrehung und Knickung von offenen Profilen. *Luftfahrtforschung*, **11** (6), December 5, 174–180. Translated in NACA Tech. Memorandum No. 784, January 1936.

WAKABAYASHI, M., NAKAMURA, T., and YOSHIDA, N. (1980). Experimental studies on the elastic–plastic behaviour of braced frames under repeated horizontal loading: Part 2. Experiments of braces composed of steel circular tubes, angle-shapes, flat bars or round bars. *Bulletin of the Disaster Prevention Research Institute*, Kyoto University, Japan, **29**, Part 3, No. 264, March, 99–127.

WAKABAYASHI, M., and NONAKA, T. (1965). On the buckling strength of angles in transmission towers. *Bulletin of the Disaster Prevention Research Institute*, Kyoto University, Japan, **15**, Part 2, No. 91, November, 1–18.

WARNICK, W. L., and WALSTON, W. H., Jr. (1980). Secondary deflections and lateral stability of beams. *Journal of the Engineering Mechanics Division, ASCE*, **106** (EM6), December, 1307–1325.

WILHOITE, G. M. (1984). Design recommendations for cold-formed angles. *American Society of Civil Engineers Spring Convention*, May, Atlanta, Georgia, USA.

WILHOITE, G. M., ZANDONINI, R., and ZAVELANI, A. (1984). Behaviour and strength of angles in compression: An experimental investigation. *ASCE Annual Convention and Structure Congress III*, Oct., San Francisco, California, USA.

WOOD, A. B. (Chairman, Working Group 08 'Towers' of Study Committee No. 22 of International Conference on Large High Voltage Electric Systems (CIGRE), Paris) (1975). Buckling tests on crossed diagonals in lattice towers. *Electra*, January, 89–99.

WOOLCOCK, S. T., and KITIPORNCHAI, S. (1980). The design of single angle struts. *Steel Construction*, Journal of the Australian Institute of Steel Construction, **14** (4), 2–23.

YOKOO, Y., WAKABAYASHI, M., and NONAKA, T. (1968). *An experimental study on buckling of angles.* Yawata Technical Report No. 265, December, pp. 8543–8563 and pp. 8759–8760, Yawata Iron & Steel Co., Ltd, Tekko Building, Tokyo, Japan.

YOUNG, C. R. (1935). *Elementary structural problems in steel and timber.* John Wiley & Sons, Inc., New York, NY, Second Edition.

ZAVELANI, A. (1984). Design recommendations for cold-formed sections. *American Society of Civil Engineers Spring Convention*, May, Atlanta, Georgia, USA.

INDEX

351

DATE DUE

DATE DUE